C000157395

Edwardian Requiem

Edwardian Requiem

A Life of Sir Edward Grey

ooooo

Michael Waterhouse

Biteback Publishing

First published in Great Britain in 2013 by
Biteback Publishing Ltd
Westminster Tower
3 Albert Embankment
London SE1 7SP
Copyright © Michael Waterhouse 2013

Michael Waterhouse has asserted his right under the Copyright, Designs and Patents Act
1988 to be identified as the author of this work.

All rights reserved. No part of this publication may be reproduced, stored in a retrieval
system or transmitted, in any form or by any means, without the publisher's prior
permission in writing.

This book is sold subject to the condition that it shall not, by way of trade or otherwise, be
lent, resold, hired out or otherwise circulated without the publisher's prior consent in any
form of binding or cover other than that in which it is published and without a similar
condition, including this condition, being imposed on the subsequent purchaser.

Every reasonable effort has been made to trace copyright holders of material reproduced
in this book, but if any have been inadvertently overlooked the publishers would be glad
to hear from them.

'A Fallodon Memory' © Siegfried Sassoon by kind permission of the Estate of
George Sassoon.

ISBN 978-1-84954-443-6

10 9 8 7 6 5 4 3 2 1

A CIP catalogue record for this book is available from the British Library.

Set in Baskerville and Snell Roundhand

Printed and bound in Great Britain by
CPI Group (UK) Ltd, Croydon CR0 4YY

A Fallodon Memory

by Siegfried Sassoon

One afternoon I watched him as he stood
In the twilight of his wood.
Among the firs he'd planted, forty years away,
Tall, and quite still, and almost blind,
World patience in his face, stood Edward Grey;
Not listening,
For it was at the end of summer, when no birds sing:
Only the bough's faint dirge accompanied his mind
Absorbed in some Wordsworthian slow self-communing.

In lichen-coloured homespun clothes he seemed
So merged with stem and branch and twinkling leaves
That almost I expected, looking away, to find
When glancing there again, that I had daylight dreamed
His figure, as when some trick of sun and shadow deceives.

But there he was, haunting heart-known ancestral ground;
Near to all Nature; and in that nearness somehow strange;
Whose native humour, human-simple yet profound,
And strength of spirit no calamity could change.
To whom, designed for countrified contentments, came
Honours unsought and unrewarding foreign fame:
And, at the last, that darkened world wherein he moved
In memoried deprivation of life once learnt and loved.

In memory of my great-grandmother, Consuelo Vanderbilt Balsan, who as an eighteen-year-old American heiress, having reluctantly married the 9th Duke of Marlborough, became a much-loved and respected hostess at the apex of Edwardian high society. Her elegant beauty, great taste, charm, intelligence and kindness shine out from this delightful portrait by Paul César Helleu.

Contents

PROLOGUE

3 August 1914

At around 2.45 p.m. on that Monday afternoon, a tall, clean-shaven, good-looking man walked down the steps of the Foreign Office, turned onto the baking pavements of a crowded Whitehall and made his way briskly to the House of Commons. Some said his deeply etched features and strong aquiline nose gave the impression of a large bird of prey at the despatch box. The Foreign Secretary would need all the fortitude of a raptor to deliver his hour-long statement on the European crisis in fifteen minutes' time. It would prove to be the defining moment of his life and represent one of the most dramatic occasions in the long history of parliamentary debate. He had to prepare a divided Cabinet and Parliament for war with Germany.

Sir Edward Grey was fifty-two years old and had been Liberal Foreign Secretary for nine years; he was close to breaking records for longevity in office. The stress of work over one of the most turbulent decades in British history, and more particularly the European crisis of the previous few weeks, had taken its toll. He looked pale and drawn and the bags under his eyes suggested long sleepless nights. He was slowly going blind in the service of his country.

High up on the façade of the Foreign Office, early swallows were gathering for their long journey to South Africa and in the process were refuelling over the insect-rich waters of St James's Park. Grey cast his mind back to his duck ponds at Fallodon and wondered whether a green sandpiper had dropped in on its way south, always the first sign of the autumn migration. His thoughts then turned to his late wife, Dorothy, who although dreading the prospect of public life, had given him so much support during his early days in office. He had resigned himself to live in a sexless marriage for twenty years yet he had still loved Dorothy as deeply as Pamela, the other great love of his life, who would eventually become his second wife and was rumoured by some to have been his mistress for many years.

Grey was something of an enigma. He was full of contradictions. Deep in his heart he was a country-loving fisherman and ornithologist who preferred reading Wordsworth to giving speeches in his constituency and answering questions on foreign policy in the House. Yet he had been in Parliament for nearly thirty years and reluctantly became Foreign Secretary of a country that presided over the greatest empire the world had seen since Roman times. This peace-loving statesman who had rarely left his shores for foreign climes was now about to ask his country to go to war, because the German legions were violating the sovereignty of the Low Countries on their long march to Paris. If this wasn't enough, by birth he was a member of the ruling classes yet he felt no guilt for enthusiastically supporting the Parliament Act which had removed the power of veto from the House of Lords.

As he crossed into Parliament Square, Grey felt strangely calm. He had done all in his power over the past weeks and years to keep the peace. If Parliament now decided to abandon the French in their hour of need, he would resign and retire to the rural life he loved. His speech was not as highly polished as he would have liked; there just was not time to learn it by heart – a technique at which his colleague Winston Churchill was most proficient – but he was confident of his facts and he was convinced that British national interests necessitated fighting for an independent France. Grey had been forced to prepare his notes late on Sunday night. There had been Cabinet meetings throughout Sunday and another on Monday morning, so he did not return to his room at the Foreign Office until two o'clock.

❦

The House was overflowing with members sitting in rows of chairs placed four abreast in the Gangway. The Press Gallery, the Peers' Gallery and the Diplomatic Gallery were packed with expectant faces. Even so, as the Foreign Secretary rose to speak, one could hear a pin drop. His simple, unemotional, serious style of speaking was tailor-made for the occasion. These characteristics, together with his charismatic good looks, meant that Grey held the floor of the House like few others. In grave, dignified and precise terms, he informed the House that Germany was now at war with Russia and that, because of France's treaty with Russia, she was also being dragged into the conflict.

Grey was determined not to stoke up the emotions of the House by accusations of blame over who started the war. He wanted his audience to approach the crisis in a rational fashion, 'from the point of view of British interests, British honour and British obligations, free from all passion as to why peace has not been preserved'. There was no better man for the task. He would later write in his autobiography,

At first it was in my mind to read to the House the German Chancellor's bid for our neutrality, and the reply made to it; but this was deliberately discarded. To read that would stir indignation and the House ought to come to its decisions on grounds of weight, not passion. We were not going into war because Bethmann-Hollweg had made a dishonourable proposal to us. We should not be influenced by that decision. When the decision was made, then the communication with Bethmann-Hollweg should be published and it would no doubt strengthen the feeling; this ought to be later, after the decision, not before it. I was myself stirred with resentment and indignation at what seemed to me Germany's crime in precipitating the war, and all I knew of Prussian militarism was hateful; but these must not be motives of our going into the war.

❦

The Foreign Secretary began his speech by relating the history of the Entente Cordiale. He told the Commons that the country was not legally committed to defend France, as evidenced by the exchange of letters following the naval conversations of 1912. He assured the House that Britain was not bound by any secret treaties that might restrict her freedom to act independently; France was obligated to Russia by treaty, but Britain did not even know the terms of the alliance. He took his audience through the developing friendship with France. He outlined the joint military conversations whereby a plan was drawn up for Britain to send an Expeditionary Force to France in the event of an unprovoked attack on France by Germany; then the Algeciras and the Agadir crises where German diplomatic aggression was countered by Anglo-French defiance.

He moved on to the naval arrangement with France under which Britain had moved her modern battleships into the North Sea, countering the increasing German threat, whereas the French had concentrated their forces in the Mediterranean, leaving their Channel and Atlantic shores undefended. He told the House, 'If the German fleet came down the Channel and bombarded and battered the undefended coasts of France, we could not stand aside and see this going on practically within sight of our eyes, with our arms folded, looking on dispassionately, doing nothing.' The Foreign Secretary was not given to passion, but as he spoke the words 'doing nothing' his clenched fist crashed down on the despatch box and the House burst into cheers. He left them in little doubt that in his personal opinion there was a moral obligation to support the French: 'How far that friendship entails obligation – it has been a friendship between the nations and ratified by the nations – how far that entails an obligation, let every man look into his own heart, and his own feelings, and construe the extent of the obligation for himself.'

He then covered questions of national interest and the neutrality of Belgium. He informed his audience how British interests would be adversely affected both by the fall of France and if Continental Europe were to be dominated by a single power. If Britain stood aside, he warned the House, 'We would sacrifice our respect and good name and reputation before the world and should not escape the most serious and grave economic circumstances.' The final part of his speech was devoted to Britain's commitments to Belgium under the Treaty of 1839, whereby the young country's sovereignty was guaranteed by the great powers. Here he was on safer ground, as public opinion, together with radical opinion in Cabinet, had recently swung massively towards Grey with the German ultimatum to invade Belgium. Grey was from the school of 'old diplomacy'. He was a man of honour and the House knew it. He had been on his feet for an hour and a quarter before he sat down. The Prime Minister's wife, Margot Asquith, wrote that the House broke into 'a hurricane of applause'.

The speech had a remarkable impact on its audience. Asquith wrote to his lover, Venetia Stanley, that evening:'Grey made a most remarkable speech – about an hour long – for the most part almost conversational in tone and with some of his usual ragged ends; but extraordinarily well reasoned and tactful and really cogent – so much so that our extreme peace-lovers were for the moment reduced to silence.'

A discerning intellect in the shape of Lord Hugh Cecil wrote to a friend,

Grey's speech was very wonderful – I think in the circumstances one may say the greatest speech delivered in our time or for a very long period, taking the importance of the occasion, the necessity of persuading many doubtful persons, the extraordinary success which it had in that direction, its great dignity, warm emotion and perfect taste ... I could deliver a lecture on the merits of the speech – its admirable arrangement, its perfect taste, and the extraordinary dexterity with which it dealt with the weak spot in his argument. This was the nature of our obligation to France under the Entente. With wonderful skill he did not argue the point, but he changed to a note of appeal to the individual conscience, thereby disarming criticism in the one matter where he was weak, without any departure real or apparent from perfect sincerity. All these substantial merits set off by his wonderful manner go to make his speech the greatest example of the art of persuasion that I have ever listened to.

People liked Grey; they trusted his judgement. Time and time again observers refer to his honesty and sincerity. These were qualities that reassured waverers, won gritty diplomatic victories and gave him the ear of the House of Commons. Arthur Murray, Grey's Parliamentary Private Secretary, wrote in his retirement:

> The House of Commons is not only a very human assembly, but it is an excellent judge of character. Grey never sought popularity; had shunned self-advertisement and had never at any time endeavoured to build up a political following. He was just himself – and because he was himself; because the House knew from long experience that there was no guile or trickery in him and felt that he had done all that was possible to avoid hostilities; because it admired his sense of justice and had faith in his judgement, it listened to the simple phrases in which he told his story and pointed the path of duty and honour and handed him its trust.

At the Foreign Office, the Permanent Under-Secretary Sir Arthur Nicolson sat waiting in his room in 'an agony of suspense'. A little after 5 p.m., a private secretary rushed in to inform him that Grey had received a tumultuous reception in the Commons. He had been backed by the whole House with the exception of the Labour Party leader, Ramsay MacDonald. An hour later an exhausted Foreign Secretary returned to the Foreign Office. On being congratulated by Nicolson, Grey remained silent. He merely slammed his fists down on the table and cried, 'I hate war, I hate war.'

Grey worked late at his desk that evening. As dusk drew near he was joined in his room by his good friend J. A. Spender, the editor of the *Westminster Gazette*. They were standing at a window overlooking St James's Park. In the street below the lamplighter was busy with his daily task. One can imagine the silence, broken only by the sharp metallic cry of a coot or the whinnying of a dabchick coming from the lake across Horse Guards Parade. He then uttered the words that would bring him immortality: 'The lamps are going out all over Europe. We shall not see them lit again in our lifetime.'

Early Life

Tragedy visited Edward Grey early in life. His father, Colonel George Grey, after serving in the Crimea and India with the Rifle Brigade, became equerry to the Prince of Wales. Edward was only twelve years old and away at prep school when the Colonel unexpectedly died of pneumonia at Sandringham aged thirty-nine. Thereafter, Edward's mother, Harriet Pearson, daughter of an army officer descended from a long line of Shropshire clergymen, brought up her six children at Fallodon Hall near Alnwick in Northumberland, under the protective wing of her father-in-law, Sir George Grey. Edward learnt about duty and responsibility at a tender age. Many years later, one of his sisters recalled,

> After father's death Edward looked on himself as my mother's chief protector. I well remember when he returned with her to Fallodon from Sandringham his collecting us younger children together and telling us that she was to be our first consideration, that we must be very quiet and thoughtful and do everything we possibly could to help her and be a comfort to her.

Edward Grey's Whiggish tendencies were in his genes. His most celebrated ancestor was Charles, second Earl Grey, who, as Prime Minister in 1832, introduced the Reform Bill. But it was Sir George Grey, Earl Grey's nephew and Edward's grandfather, who had the most influence on his upbringing in rural Northumberland. Edward Grey's first biographer, G. M. Trevelyan, describes Sir George as 'a fine example of one of those liberal-minded lay Evangelicals who did so much to found the greatness of nineteenth-century England', and 'a country gentleman, neither rich nor fashionable, devoted to nature and rural pursuits, popular with his neighbours of all ranks of life, wholly without ambition but constrained by a sense of duty to enter the wider sphere of national public life'. He could have been referring to his grandson.

Sir George was a member of the House of Commons for forty years, an immensely experienced Home Secretary, holding office three times under Russell and Palmerston, and an expert on parliamentary procedure. A devout Christian, he kept the interests of the poor close to his heart, introducing a Private Member's Bill for the erection of public baths and wash-houses in towns. He became a national hero in 1848 when the British Establishment watched in horror as revolution swept through the capitals of Europe. In London, the Chartists staged a massive rally on Kennington Common and delivered a petition to Parliament, calling for a wider franchise and generally a more democratic society. Sir George's calm, sensitive handling of the situation allayed people's fears and saved the country from social upheaval.

In 1845, Sir George, at the age of forty-six, inherited the Fallodon estate from an unmarried uncle. He gave up the safe seat of Davenport to put down roots in Northumberland. At the general election in 1847 he managed to win the constituency of North Northumberland, long regarded a Percy, Duke of Northumberland family fiefdom, a feat that was later repeated by his grandson Edward. In the 1852 election, the will of the Tory landowners prevailed in rural Northumberland. Sir George lost his seat and was denounced in the process as an associate of Richard Cobden, the Radical businessman who campaigned for the repeal of the Corn Laws and championed the rights of working people. At a by-election in 1853, Sir George was returned for Morpeth, which he served for the balance of his parliamentary career. After a further Reform Bill in 1867, the miners, now forming a majority of the electorate, put up their own candidate, Thomas Burt, who won the seat in 1874. He was unopposed, as Sir George, who had represented the miners' interests for many years, decided to retire from public life to farm at Fallodon, which was located a few miles from the family seat of the Earls Grey at Howick.

The Grey family line stretched back to the Conquest in the guise of the then newly arrived Norman family of Croy. The family changed their name to Grey and were sent up to guard the Scottish Marches. Here they occupied three castles along the Tweed before acquiring Chillingham and Howick in the thirteenth century. The Greys had soldiering in their blood, commanding armies in the crusades and in the great European battles of the thirteenth century. The family received an earldom in 1419 for taking Le Havre in Normandy, adopting the title of the Earls of Tankerville and incorporating the unusual scaling ladder into the family crest – evidence of a long and proud military heritage. The Tankerville Greys of Chillingham soon died out and it wasn't until the eighteenth century that a new earldom was bestowed on the Howick branch. Charles, the first Earl Grey, had fought at Minden in 1759 with Robert Clive, the British officer who secured India and its associated wealth for the British crown, and Grey then became famous in the American War of Independence. He had earned the nickname of 'No-Flint Grey' by giving the order that his men should execute a night attack with no flints in their muskets, relying only on the bayonet.

Edward Grey's love of the countryside was nurtured during a happy childhood at Fallodon. His grandfather's influence was yet again predominant, Grey writing in an unpublished autobiography:

> My grandparents were very sensible to natural beauty and I have a vivid recollection of his tall figure and her short one, going round the path that went through the trees in front of the house, with gaps that gave a view as far as the moor at the top of Chillingham Park.

They would make a point of doing this at the time of sunset on a clear, fine evening.

Fallodon is sandwiched between the Cheviot Hills and the wild, romantic Northumbrian coast, enshrined by Lindisfarne, the Farne Islands and the great castles of Bamburgh and Dunstanburgh. The small estate offered Grey the opportunity at an early age to indulge his passion for country sports. He writes in his autobiography,

> I never cared much for riding, being naturally a bad rider who was never on good terms with a horse, but I had a passion for fishing and shooting. The fishing at home and the shooting did not amount to much, but there were small burns and one little river, the Aln, within reach. There were a few partridges and pheasants, and the seashore, and these provided the occupation for my holidays, even if the results of my efforts were small. So my holidays were very happy times.

Grey's childhood was sunny enough, yet having to assume the mantle of responsibility at so young an age, it must also have been a relatively lonely one. One can only guess that his early years lacked the relaxed rough-and-tumble and distraction of constant company characteristic of most normal households. He would find himself repeatedly turning to his inner resources to get him through the dull and lonely times. By the time he went away to boarding school this skill would have been highly developed. He would have had more experience than most in organising his own life and that of others. Little wonder Grey became a respected prefect at school and, with angling being a solitary sport, such an accomplished fly fisherman. From early childhood it was second nature for him to compartmentalise his life, which throughout his career would make it easy for him to suddenly turn to fishing and nature, thereby relieving the boredom and pressure of political life. Early self-reliance made Grey very much his own man. Besides giving him an independent nature it also encouraged personal characteristics such as stubbornness and inflexibility which would manifest themselves at a later date by way of resignation threats when in Cabinet.

Grey honed his skills as a fly fisherman at his public school, Winchester College; however, he acquired his passion for angling some years earlier, as a child in Northumberland. In the north country burns 'which run in narrow stony channels between overgrown banks', he would fish stealthily for wild brown trout with a worm and a short line. It was on the Fallodon estate that he learnt the importance of patience and of coping with the disappointment of failure. In *Fly Fishing* he writes,

> There was one burn that I knew intimately from its source to the sea. Much of the upper part was wooded, and it was stony and shallow, till within two miles of its mouth. Here there was for a child another world. There were no trees, the bottom of the burn was of mud and sand and the channel was full of rustling reeds with open pools at some depth at intervals. These pools had a fascination for me, there was something about them which kept me excited with expectation of great events, as I lay behind the reeds, peering through them and watching the line intently. The result of much waiting was generally an eel, or a small flat fish up from the sea; or now and then a small trout, but never for many years one of those monsters which I was sure must inhabit such mysterious pools.

Sure enough, one day Grey caught a three-pound sea trout. He was hooked for life.

There were five defining moments in Grey's early life. In chronological order, they began with his arrival at Winchester College in September 1876 and ended with the acquisition of a lease on the Itchen Cottage in 1890. In between there were equally important events: rustication from Balliol College, Oxford; marriage to Dorothy Widdrington and his entry into politics in November

1885. At Winchester Grey was considered clever but, preferring outdoor activities, he failed to achieve much academic success. He did, however, admit to owing a debt of gratitude to his form master, Dr Fearon, who was responsible 'for the first awakenings of my intellect'. Aside from preparing its students for Oxford entry, Winchester's real gift to Grey lay in nurturing a love for dry-fly fishing, where, on the clear chalk streams of Hampshire, a floating fly is used to hook a fish, as opposed to the sinking fly normally preferred in the fast-running waters of the north. At school he played cricket, fives and racquets. When at Oxford, he took up real tennis, moving on to be British amateur champion at Queen's and Lord's. His special passion, however, was for dry-fly fishing on the river Itchen – perhaps not surprising for someone with a self-contained and independent nature. He would spend the happiest days of his life at the cottage in Itchen Abbas and mature into one of the most accomplished fly-fishermen of his generation, as witnessed by his best-selling book *Fly Fishing*.

It is perhaps interesting that Grey attended Winchester as opposed to another of the top public schools such as Eton or Harrow. The latter two would draw on the offspring of the aristocracy or the landed gentry, while Winchester's constituency tended to be more middle class, attracting boys whose parents had a background in the Church or Civil Service. However, Winchester always topped the academic charts and Grey was one of the brightest pupils of his year. Grey's life at Winchester is best described by Herbert Fisher, Warden of New College, Oxford, who contributed to Grey's obituary in an edition of *The Wykehamist*.

I came as a new man to Du Boulay's in September 1878. Edward Grey was head of the house, and on the strength of previous acquaintanceship my father, much to my consternation, for it seemed a most audacious thing for any parent to do, caught hold of a small boy and sent him into 'toy room' to fetch Grey out into the road. A most brilliant and vivid impression he made upon my immature mind. I can see him now standing bare-headed as he talked to my father with the charming unaffected ease which his friends know so well and I remember how handsome and all alive he looked. As our parents had been friends, he took me under his protection, made me his fag and was as great a friend to me as one of his eminence in the House and School could be expected to be.

Grey was a 'jig' [clever]. Of that we juniors were convinced. Though we believed he did no work, we knew that from time to time he tossed off a copy of Greek and Latin verses which was marked alpha in Senior Division Sixth Book and we were ready to believe that if he had a mind to do it he could sweep the board of school prizes. As with work, so with games, he went his own way. The belief among the juniors in Du Boulay's was that Grey could have got into Lord's as easy as look at you – but there it was, he couldn't be bothered. To us it seemed mysterious, that a man with such a genius for ball games, a man without a scrap of practice could knock up sixty in a House match by most effective though unconventional methods should have so little wish to excel in the game of all others which brought renown.

But Grey was not like that. He went his own way and thought his own thoughts. His heart was not in School games, much as he enjoyed them, or in building up for himself a School reputation for athletics. His heart was in fishing. So on 'half-rems' he would go off by himself to throw his fly on a stream of water in the upper Itchen, nearly always returning with a well-filled basket, some of the contents of which would be judiciously distributed amongst the Dons. 'Why Grey, I take it that even a trout can sometimes rise', observed Doidge Morshead, himself an angler often propitiated by the spoils of these expeditions, on one occasion when Grey came up to books unusually tardy.

He seemed rather solitary. We knew that his father and mother were dead [the latter inaccurate] but that there was a distinguished old grandfather living far away in Northumberland to whom every Sunday he wrote a long letter. Another fact about Grey was a matter of comment among us. It was whispered that he read English poetry for pleasure, and I think also, though here memory may play a trick, that we already knew that his favourite was Wordsworth.

There was something in him which made him stand out from other prefects, a self-sufficiency and aloofness, a certain gravity mingled with his boyish high spirits and rich laughter. His tastes seemed to be fully formed, his mind to be constituted not in opinions but in convictions. The vanities in dress, then much affected, made no appeal to him. So far as I can recollect he showed no interest in politics and never talked in debating societies. All these grave preoccupations came later, when, having gone down from Balliol, he was living at home in Northumberland and there came under the influence of Mandell Creighton; but our Housemaster always predicted a great political future for him and we juniors were certainly of the opinion that Grey could do something big if he wanted.

Not surprisingly, it took Grey time to develop his expertise with a dry fly at Winchester. This is demonstrated by his fishing records. Any fish below three-quarters of a pound had to be returned to the river; in 1877, he caught one trout, in 1878, thirteen, in 1879, thirty-two and in 1880, seventy-six. He writes in *Fly Fishing*,

> Many things are taught at public schools, but Winchester is probably the only school at which the most scientific and highly developed form of angling can be learnt. The art was not taught at Winchester in my time but there were opportunities for learning it which a few of us did not neglect.

School lessons ended at midday. Every day in the spring and early summer, Grey would tear off to the water meadows in his quest for a rising trout. He was only spared an hour before lunch, but luckily this coincided with the best hour of the rise in the day.

In the autumn of 1880, Grey went up to Oxford to read Classics at Balliol. In January 1884, he was sent down for idleness. Before he departed he managed to persuade his tutor to let him change to Law, and after a short period of cramming at home in Northumberland he returned to Oxford that summer to take a third in jurisprudence, commonly known as a 'gentleman's degree'. Midway through his Oxford career, his grandfather died and the young undergraduate had to assume the responsibilities of running the estate and heading the family. This would have weighed heavily on his conscience and might well have explained his lack of academic success. There was, however, one compensation. Grey was a natural athlete with an eye for a ball and Oxford, unlike Winchester, boasted a real-tennis court. In 1883 he achieved a Blue, became Oxford champion and beat his Cambridge opponent in the varsity match by three sets to love.

As at Winchester, Grey spent more time enjoying himself at Balliol than buried in his books. In his book, *Life, Journalism and Politics*, Liberal journalist J. A. Spender tells a story about the antics of a high-spirited group of undergraduates led by Edward Grey:

> The rest of the University encouraged the notion that Balliol men were 'smugs' [swots], but this was not my experience. The College was large and lively; it had all kinds in it and quite its due proportion of 'young barbarians'. In my first term, I shared a double set of rooms in the small front quad with a youth who is now a well-known peer and we had only one 'oak' or outer door between us. This 'oak' was the subject of incessant assaults by my neighbour's friends and he and I were constantly on the defensive. One night we sat for two hours in a vain attempt to keep the invaders out. They finally brought red-hot pokers and pierced holes which fatally weakened the fabric of the 'oak' and then in a rush through landed on top of us. They left me alone, but carried off my partner and did to him the sort of things that undergraduates do to their most intimate friends.

There was an unexpected silver lining to Grey's 'rustication' from Oxford. In the new year of 1884, when living back in the north, he started to build a wildfowl collection. The breeding of ducks in the garden at Fallodon would become a lifelong passion and was documented in the *Fallodon Green Book*. This journal, covering duck-breeding success from 1886 to 1905, covers some 150 pages in Grey's own handwriting. By May 1885 he had already collected seventeen different species of wildfowl. The following year, Grey established another pond in the garden, planting it out with shrubs for nesting cover and surrounding the whole area with a 'fox-proof fence'. He writes:

> When I was sent down from Oxford I lived the months of February and March entirely alone, but I was never dull. I bought my first five pairs of waterfowl, which afterwards became a great interest in life, and I remember finding it extraordinary the opinion of one of my Oxford friends that I should have been bored at home, when on the contrary I had not been conscious of one dull moment. This fact was the first thing that gave me some idea that I was different from other people in this respect.

During his time at Oxford, Grey came under the influence of two remarkable individuals. In their own ways they both left their mark on this headstrong undergraduate, turning him into a serious young man with a strong sense of responsibility and public duty. Benjamin Jowett was Master of Balliol at this time and was renowned as an influential tutor and administrative reformer. A theologian and classical scholar, he became one of the great public figures of Victorian England. A well-known Balliol rhyme about him runs: 'Here come I, my name is Jowett / All there is to know, I know it / I am Master of this College / What I don't know isn't knowledge!' He held court at the Master's Lodge and surrounded himself with leading politicians, lawyers and scientists. He took an immense amount of trouble with any of his undergraduates that he considered to have potential, and laid much store in formulating their future careers. Grey's contemporaries included Lord Curzon and Cosmo Lang, later Archbishop of Canterbury. Frank Pember, a future Warden of All Souls, would become a lifelong friend, as would Louis Mallet, later Grey's private secretary at the Foreign

Office. Jowett loved 'a name' and obviously saw in Edward Grey the potential to carry on his family's tradition of public service. It was Jowett who cleared the path for Grey's return to take his finals, imploring him to work studiously while at Fallodon. J. A. Spender also spotted Grey's hidden talent, writing: 'Grey describes himself as having taken his Oxford career lightly, but before he went down he had somehow got the reputation of being a man who could do anything he liked, if he chose to take the trouble.'

Perhaps the real turning-point in Grey's life came in the summer of 1881, his first long vacation at Oxford, when he became a pupil of Mandell Creighton, then vicar of the neighbouring parish of Embleton and a close friend of his grandfather, Sir George Grey. Creighton was a charismatic churchman of striking presence. He was tall with piercing blue eyes and a full beard. He was confiding and courteous along with the wicked sense of humour which so endeared him to his students. A generation older than Edward Grey, he was a 'self-made man', having been born above his father's furniture shop in Carlisle. He won scholarships to both Durham Grammar School and Merton College, Oxford where he was awarded a fellowship in addition to becoming President of the Oxford Union. He went on to write a celebrated history of the Papacy, becoming Dixie Professor of Ecclesiastical History at Cambridge, and he capped a highly successful career by being appointed Bishop of London.

At Sir George's request Creighton agreed to tutor Edward for his Oxford exams. So it was at the Embleton vicarage with its imposing thirteenth-century peel tower that Edward Grey was forced to read his set books for Classical Moderations. Here he learnt the meaning of concentration and developed an interest in politics, economics, literature and poetry. While walking in the vicarage garden with the great man, his intellect began to stir and he eagerly embraced the radical Liberalism of his mentor. But Creighton's influence did not cease here. The year 1885 would prove to be a most significant one in Grey's life. He would be selected as Liberal candidate for Berwick-on-Tweed in the summer and marry Dorothy Widdrington in the autumn. Creighton would encourage him in both these endeavours.

Grey's interest in politics was aroused during his undergraduate days by Creighton, who, like Jowett, encouraged a sense of public duty. Grey later wrote,

> I do not remember taking any interest in public events till the news of the murder of Lord Frederick Cavendish in Dublin in 1882. I was then an undergraduate at Balliol and I joined in the clamour for martial law. This I repeated to my grandfather who met it with the critical comment, 'Martial law is the suspension of all law.'

On coming down from Oxford in the summer of 1884, Grey made his first move into the real world of politics. He asked his great-uncle, Lord Northbrook, who was First Lord of the Admiralty in Gladstone's administration, to find him some work experience. As a result, in July, at the tender age of twenty-two, he began public life as a private secretary to Sir Evelyn Baring, moving on in October to work for the Chancellor of the Exchequer, H. C. E. Childers. At the same time, while in Northumberland, he began to take an interest in local politics, where he was rapidly to acquire a reputation for his contentious radical views, as witnessed by a special interest in land reform and an extension of the voting franchise. Grey writes,

> In 1884 Gladstone's Government proposed an extension of the franchise to counties on similar terms on which a Conservative Government had given it to the boroughs in 1867. The House of Lords rejected the proposal; there was great indignation in the counties and a franchise demonstration was arranged at Alnwick, the county town near Fallodon.

Grey saw the rejection of the Bill as an affront to the working people he had been brought up with in rural Northumberland and, when asked, willingly accepted the invitation to chair the Alnwick meeting. It was his first attempt at a public speech and it turned out such a success that a movement was initiated to put him forward as the local Liberal candidate for Berwick in the following year's general election. Creighton coached Grey in the art of public speaking, encouraging him, in the process, to stand for election. The Grey family name was as celebrated as that of Percy in north Northumberland and because of the wider franchise he would stand a good chance of winning the seat for the first time since his grandfather took it nearly forty years earlier. On 22 January 1885, Creighton wrote to Grey, 'It will be a great thing to fight Percy in Berwick and will cover you with glory.' Meanwhile Grey continued to devour his books, reading, according to Trevelyan, Virgil, Tennyson, Wordsworth, Mill's *Principles of Political Economy*, Milton, More's *Utopia*, George Eliot's *Scenes of Clerical Life*, Henry George's *Progress and Poverty*, and Seeley's *Expansion of England*. He was duly selected in the summer and set off on a round of speech making in the local villages. The local electors obviously liked the cut of his jib. At the general election in November, Grey defeated Earl Percy with a majority of over 1,400 votes and was to hold the Berwick division for thirty years.

On 20 October 1885, in the middle of the election campaign, Grey married Dorothy Widdrington, which provided Creighton with further satisfaction. The Widdringtons lived at Newton, some sixteen miles south of Fallodon, and were close friends of the Creightons. Although the Widdringtons were by tradition moderate Conservatives, Dorothy had also come under the influence of Mandell Creighton, who decided to promote a union between the young pair. Grey had first met Dorothy when out hunting with the Percy foxhounds in the winter of 1884–5. The courtship then continued amongst London's high society, an environment which proved anathema to both parties. In many ways Dorothy was the

perfect partner for Grey. He was deeply in love with her and shared many of her interests. She would take over from Creighton in nurturing Grey's enthusiasms, most importantly turning him into an accomplished ornithologist. They gradually forsook the hunting field for rod and line, often fishing with the Buxtons on the river Spean in Scotland. Mildred Buxton wrote of Dorothy,

> She always fished with Edward, generally taking out her book and reading at odd moments, but preferring as a rule to watch him when she was not fishing. She was very strong and remained as erect and graceful as ever while wading in deep water and casting the heavy salmon line, even at the end of a long day.

No one is perfect and Dorothy was not an exception. Grey would have liked to have started a family, but Dorothy had an aversion both to the physical side of marriage and to children. Mrs Belloc Lowndes, sister of the 'man of letters' and Liberal MP Hilaire Belloc, writes of the Greys in her book *A Passing World*,

> It was known that their marriage was what is called in France 'un mariage blanc'. The knowledge must have come from Lady Grey, for Grey was deeply reserved. It gave rise to an impression, perhaps natural under the circumstances, that Grey was not what in the Middle Ages was called 'a full man'. This however was not the case. It was, nevertheless, true that when the honeymoon was over, Dorothy Grey told her husband she had discovered in herself a strong aversion to the physical side of marriage. As a result of this admission, Grey agreed that henceforth they should live as brother and sister. This was plainly stated as a fact in a report sent to the German Government by their Ambassador in London just before the outbreak of war in 1914.

Dorothy and Edward's courtship was brief. They met around Christmas and were engaged in July. Shortly afterwards Edward Grey was thrown into a general election campaign and perhaps for political expedience the marriage was brought forward three months to October. They would have had little time together and it is unlikely that Dorothy would have plucked up the courage to admit to her future husband she didn't enjoy the prospect of sex. The very fact that the honeymoon was spent at Fallodon, a shared home with the Dowager Lady Grey and her four additional children, must have been most inhibiting for the young couple.

Dorothy's biographer suggests Grey was a virgin at this time of his marriage. She further implies that Grey may have been relieved at his wife's suggestion that they live a happy, chaste existence as brother and sister in much the same way as their beloved poet William Wordsworth did with his sister, also a Dorothy. This is surely unlikely. Grey was fit, good looking and healthy and, as Mrs Belloc Lowndes reminds us, herself a most reliable society gossip, he was no homosexual. Bearing in mind the frisky company he kept at Oxford, there is every chance he lost his virginity while at university. After all, a generation before, Queen Victoria was convinced that the Prince of Wales nearly caused his father's death through Albert's worry over his son's activities with prostitutes as an undergraduate at Oxford.

Presumably Grey had only discovered his wife's frigidity after they were married; being so in love, it would have come as a huge disappointment. Their relationship, bonded by so many common interests, must have been immensely strong to function without sex. It is, however, worth remembering that many marriages amongst the upper classes at the time were for convenience. Sex could and would be found elsewhere, so one must assume he quickly came to terms with his predicament. Within weeks of his marriage Grey was to find himself yet again coping with bachelor life in London, as Dorothy preferred to remain in the country. As a good-looking young Member of Parliament he must have been in great demand with society hostesses. Surely it would only be a matter of time before he took a mistress? This might explain how he was able to sustain such a quirky marriage for over twenty years. In the process, because he was so reserved, he managed to cover his tracks surprisingly well for a public figure.

Grey had an exciting political career before him and he would need the skills of a political hostess to further his prospects. Dorothy certainly did not see herself filling this role. Although tall, beautiful and charismatic, she was a solitary woman who, according to Louise Creighton, 'was somewhat cold in manner with a kind of shy aloofness which kept others at a distance' – so much so, it seems, that her biographer and distant relation Cecilia Chance refers to her as 'an ice maiden'. She disliked society and rarely attended political parties and court balls, preferring to spirit herself away into the countryside where she could read quietly and commune with nature.

Dorothy was adored by her small group of close friends but to an outsider, particularly a 'townie', she could appear arrogant, self-absorbed and abrupt. She was highly intelligent and chose her few friends carefully. She was almost certainly an intellectual snob. Her demigods of the political world were Lord Rosebery and Richard Haldane, two of the most brilliant minds at Westminster. Rosebery would scale dizzy heights in his political career, proving a most effective Foreign Secretary before disappointing as a short-term Prime Minister. He never really fulfilled his true potential, whereas Haldane was an immensely successful Minister for War who was responsible for finally pushing through Britain's much-needed army reforms. Outside politics, she related to bright people with similar interests, whether it was the countryside or literature; men such as W. H. Hudson, the celebrated nature writer, or Henry Newbolt, the poet and Liberal MP. Lady Monkswell in *A Victorian Diarist* wrote, 'She is a very handsome, delightful and clever woman but could anybody be more "madly with blessedness at strife"?' In her native Northumberland where she felt at home and secure, it was a different story, although her biographer thought she lacked the common touch and was 'too stiff and shy to play the Lady Bountiful'. Even so, Dorothy worked tirelessly for her husband's constituency association, increasing the membership and forming new ward committees. Through her friendship with Ella Pease of Alnmouth she became involved in Poor Law work and set up a new committee around Fallodon for boarding out workhouse children.

In 1887 the Greys spent three winter months on holiday in India. This journey was no doubt instigated by Dorothy, Louise Creighton informing the reader in her appreciation of Dorothy Grey that she 'had dreams of foreign travel'. Money was always tight in the Grey household and this had precluded an earlier visit to the Far East. The celebrated Liberal war leader, David Lloyd George, unfairly mocks Grey in his *War Memoirs* for his lack of overseas travel:

> He was the most insular of our statesmen and knew less of foreigners through contact with them than any Minister in the Government. He rarely, if ever, went abroad. Northumberland was good enough for him, and if he could not get there and needed a change, there was his fishing cottage in Hampshire … He had no real understanding of foreigners – I am not at all sure that for this purpose he would not include Scotland, Ireland and Wales as foreign parts.

Grey relished his trip to India and although he kept muttering to Dorothy of the 'Sun, Moon and Taj', it was the Himalayas that moved him most of all. Perhaps they should have capitalised on the success of their Indian venture and undertaken more foreign travel, particularly as they were to have no family, but as Louise Creighton relates, 'The claims of politics made long journeys impossible for the Greys and a love of fishing and of the English countryside became too strong to allow a taste for foreign travel to grow up … As the years went on, they grew increasingly sure of what they wanted.' It was during their Indian progress that the Greys met the Neville Lytteltons, who would become friends for life. Neville was commissioned into the Rifle Brigade and served as Military Secretary to the Governor of Bombay from 1885 to 1890. He had a very successful army career which would culminate in his appointment as the first Chief of General Staff in 1904. When back in London, his wife, Katherine Stuart-Wortley, struck up a close friendship with Dorothy when in 1892 they became neighbours in Pimlico. Grey, who knew next to nothing about military matters, would find Neville an excellent sounding board in the years to come.

❦

In 1885, Grey was elected as the youngest Member of the House of Commons. He writes in *Twenty-Five Years* of his first years in Parliament: 'Of the first six years spent in the House of Commons little need be said.' This is not entirely true as it was during these early days in Westminster that Grey cemented close political allegiances with a group of talented 'radical thinkers' in the Liberal Party who would in due course become known as the Liberal Imperialists. In 1886, Gladstone advocated a policy of Home Rule for Ireland and split the Liberal Party down the middle. The Liberal Unionists were set against a policy of Home Rule, and powerful figures such as Joseph Chamberlain, the Marquis of Hartington and George Goschen (who famously replaced Lord Randolph Churchill as Chancellor of the Exchequer) left the government and allied themselves with the Conservatives. Grey was an ardent admirer of Gladstone's intellect and convinced himself that a more enlightened system of governing Ireland was badly needed. He was finally converted to the Home Rule banner by John Morley's articles in the *Pall Mall Gazette*. Morley, an intellectual heavyweight, was editor of the *Pall Mall Gazette* and, as a passionate Home Ruler, would be appointed Irish Secretary in Gladstone's final administration. Grey was not called to make his maiden speech on the second reading of the Home Rule Bill on 8 June. The government was defeated by 343 votes to 313 and Gladstone dissolved the six-month-old Parliament.

In the resulting general election the Liberals were defeated, but Grey held on to his seat with a reduced majority against a Liberal Unionist candidate. He finally managed to make his maiden speech on 8 February 1887, when he attacked the government's policy of continued coercion in Ireland and went on to outline the Liberal principles of Home Rule. Over the next two years Grey showed little interest in foreign affairs, yet he was to demonstrate an independently minded radical streak when it came to domestic issues, which the House, and Lloyd George in particular, would come to respect in the years ahead. In 1888 he spoke against the party line and voted in favour of Irish land purchase with the objective of turning tenants into owners. The following year he spoke in favour of payment for Members of Parliament, with the miners' representatives at the forefront of his mind. Throughout his long career, Grey would always fight for the interests of the less privileged.

Grey's early years in the House, characterised by a period of opposition from 1886 to 1892, were the most formative of his political career. It was at this time that a small group of Liberal MPs came together – notably Edward Grey, Richard Haldane, Henry Asquith, Ronald Munro Ferguson and Arthur Acland – who would lay the foundations of the so-called Liberal Imperialist group. They represented an élite band of intellectual Whigs who were concerned at the lack of progressive thought in the Liberal Party. Although the name has connotations of 'right-wing' politics with a penchant for foreign affairs, the Liberal Imperialists were in fact moderate politicians who advocated policies of the centre. During the 1880s the group was almost exclusively interested in domestic politics, at times promoting some quite radical legislation under the influence of Sidney Webb and the Fabians. In 1891, for example, Haldane sponsored the Local Authorities Bill, which gave councils powers for the compulsory purchase of land. It wasn't until the Liberals gained office in 1892 that the Liberal Imperialists began showing an interest in foreign affairs. They saw themselves as a national party with patriotism as an essential part of their creed, hence they supported the Conservative Party on Kitchener's Sudan expedition and the Boer War. The group looked to Lord Rosebery for political leadership and John Morley for intellectual guidance. Haldane was their 'mover and shaker', while Sir William Harcourt and Henry Labouchère proved thorns in their flesh.

Grey's closest parliamentary colleagues at this time were two barristers of formidable intellect, Richard Haldane and Henry Asquith. Haldane was a member of an ancient landed Scottish family but was not wealthy. After attending Edinburgh University he studied philosophy at Gottingen and Dresden, becoming a disciple of everything German – which ironically, in 1915, would

lead to his grossly unfair dismissal from office. At the age of twenty-
one, Haldane decided to study law, and was called to the Bar at
Lincoln's Inn in 1879. He was blessed with both a powerful intellect
and an ability to work all hours, and in the following year he set up
his own practice. Although it was a struggle at the outset, within
four years his income was £1,100 a year, rising to £20,000 in 1905.
In 1885 he entered the House of Commons as Liberal member for
East Lothian. He quickly caught the eye of Liberal leaders such as
Morley and Rosebery. Here was a man who would inject the fresh
ideas into moderate liberalism for which the young 'Imperialists'
so yearned. Haldane did indeed become an energetic coordinator
of policy and as a result was all too often viewed as an unpopular
intriguer, which would place him at a disadvantage with both the
Liberal leadership and the opposition parties.

Haldane soon became friends with Edward and Dorothy Grey.
They both admired his intellectual abilities, Dorothy having a
particular empathy for Haldane. He was shy, awkward, and in his
own words had 'no attractive presence', which combined to detract
from his speaking abilities and give him a tendency to mumble. Like
Dorothy, he was a solitary person who disliked London society and
was uneasy with the opposite sex. Although he once fell in love,
he was deeply hurt by the subsequent termination of the engagement. Thereafter he lived alone with an unmarried sister, writing
every day to his elderly mother who lived in Perthshire. For his part,
Haldane admired the Greys' simplicity of character and outlook,
writing to his mother after a visit to Fallodon, 'He is the same as
ever – they have a good life here – at a very high level and with no
pretence of any kind.'

Asquith was an altogether different character. Unlike Grey and
Haldane, he originated from a modest family who lived in the
textile community of Batley, West Yorkshire. Leaving his family
behind at the age of twelve, Asquith had to board with friends in
London in order to attend a more suitable school to further his
career path. The pain of separation proved worthwhile, as he won
a scholarship to Balliol at seventeen. Success followed success for

Asquith, with the brilliant, driven undergraduate achieving a First
Class Honours in Classics and becoming President of the Oxford
Union. He left Oxford after taking his finals to read for the Bar,
supplementing his paltry earnings through political journalism. At
a dinner in 1881 at Lincoln's Inn, he met Haldane, and four years
later became a Member of Parliament representing East Fife, a seat
he would hold for over thirty years. A short time later he persuaded
his friend Haldane to join him in the House of Commons. Asquith
had married a childhood sweetheart, Helen Melland, at a young
age and in 1891, having given birth to five children, she died of
typhoid while on holiday in Scotland. Soon afterwards the ambitious young parliamentarian began seeing the rich socialite Margot
Tennant. Unlike his late wife and future close colleague Edward
Grey, Asquith had a liking for society and country house weekends.
Having been appointed Home Secretary in Gladstone's fourth
ministry, he married Margot at St George's, Hanover Square,
in May 1894. His financial security and place in society were
now assured.

Asquith, like Haldane, could master any brief, but unlike his
friend he had the advantage of being a fine orator. Above all he was
a consummate politician who was always careful not to associate
himself too closely with any one grouping. In short, he was a leader
in the making. Once Prime Minister, he would become a most effective and decisive chairman in Cabinet. He was a man of few words
who, not surprisingly for an experienced barrister, would home in
on an issue and ask searching questions. He had the difficult task
of keeping his Cabinet together and always sought consensus. He
trusted Grey implicitly and gave him a free hand in conducting
foreign policy, but at the same time sensibly kept close to Lloyd
George, who led the Radical wing of the party. If Asquith had a
weakness, it was for the 'good life'. He adored society, women, wine
and good food. After his marriage to Margot his relationship with
Haldane cooled, the latter disliking what he regarded as Asquith's
more 'frivolous' lifestyle. Interestingly, the same would happen to
Haldane's relationship with Grey when the then Foreign Secretary

took up with Margot's sister-in-law, Pamela Tennant, another powerful Liberal hostess. Haldane, the now confirmed bachelor, disapproved of his friends taking their eyes off the political ball.

Two less heavyweight members of 'the Imperialist group' were Sydney Buxton and Ronald Munro Ferguson, both of whom became close personal friends of Grey, united by a love of fishing and the countryside. Munro Ferguson was a Scottish laird who between 1886 and 1892 became Rosebery's private secretary. Buxton was from a distinguished Quaker family, lived in Sussex and became Governor-General of South Africa in 1914, having held Cabinet jobs as Postmaster-General and President of the Board of Trade. Arthur Acland was the final influential member of the group. He provided some 'grey hair' and was the man who would finally persuade Grey to accept office in December 1905. He was an expert on education and social issues but was forced to retire from politics in 1898 on the grounds of ill health. The group initially sought out the enigmatic Rosebery as their leader, but were soon to be disillusioned by his lack of interest and unreliability. As Prime Minister he had rapidly lost all enthusiasm for running the government. In the last year of his premiership he became increasingly tired as he suffered from insomnia due to the continual dissension in his Cabinet, and took to opium as a result. Policy details were discussed over dinner at meetings of the Articles Club, a dining club set up by a group of young, ambitious and intellectual Liberal MPs led by Asquith who met weekly at the National Liberal Club.

Liberal Imperialism had two main watchwords: 'clean slate' and 'efficiency'. The 'clean slate' advocated a new pragmatic approach to politics, for example a break from the old Gladstonian policy of Home Rule for Ireland. Turning the slogans into policy accepted unanimously by the group proved next to impossible. Grey was initially an enthusiastic Home Ruler, then at a later date accepted Haldane's 'step-by-step' policy, while Rosebery became an evangelistic Unionist and split from the group. The Imperialists also believed that a businesslike 'efficiency' along German lines should be injected into all aspects of domestic policy, such as education,

housing, social reform and army reform. With education policy, this
necessitated a greater degree of state control and the suspension of
individual rights in the face of national needs. The creation of a
single county council authority for education placed the Imperialists
at loggerheads with the important Liberal nonconformist vote, who
were determined to retain their voluntary schools.

By 1890 Grey had become a key member of this élite parliamentary grouping, although a real interest in Imperialism had
to wait until 1892, when he gained a tutelage under Rosebery
as Parliamentary Under-Secretary at the Foreign Office. H. C.
Matthew in his book *The Liberal Imperialists* writes,

> Its aim was to obtain influence by reserved, often secret, political
> activity – not to storm the leadership from without from a regional
> base, as Chamberlain had done, and Lloyd George was to do.
> Imperialism had played little part in establishing these relationships.
> It was, if anything, a divisive factor. Haldane, for example, voted
> against funds for the 1887 Jubilee.

When the Greys were first married, they lived at Hereford Square
in Kensington. In 1890 Grey decided to build his own fishing
cottage ('The Cottage') on the river Itchen near Winchester. It was
to prove one of the most inspired decisions of his life. The land
was acquired from his cousin Lord Northbrook, and the fishing
leased from the Rolls family who lived at nearby Avington Park.
The Greys spent the first year of their married life staying at the
Plough Inn in Itchen Abbas. Then for several years afterwards they
rented a fishing cottage belonging to Lord Northbrook. However,
the happiest days of Dorothy's life were spent at The Cottage,
where the simple existence it offered was exactly what Dorothy
needed. She had been a lover of birds and the countryside since
her childhood at Newton. The Cottage provided for her every
need: peace, solitude, breathtaking scenery, invigorating walks and

abundant wildlife. It should not be forgotten that it also enabled her to escape from what she saw as the horrors of London society. She adored the water meadows in the valley facing The Cottage, spending much of the early summer months alone on the Itchen, reading and enjoying the myriad of birds. For Grey, The Cottage began as a base camp for his fishing, but in time it also became a welcome weekend refuge from the stresses of office. It was in this lush valley that he received his education on birdlife from Dorothy and honed his skills in deciphering the songs of the summer warblers. Here, they lived in relative solitude, eschewing all weekend house parties and any local society. Their only human contact was with the river keeper and the Drover sisters, who undertook the housekeeping.

A favoured few, such as Mrs Creighton and Grey's brother Charlie, were allowed to stay at The Cottage when the Greys went north in late summer. W. H. Hudson, perhaps Britain's most accomplished natural history writer, became a great friend of the Greys, and occasionally lodged at The Cottage during one of his celebrated progresses across southern England. He describes one such visit in June 1900:

> They had told me about their cottage which serves them all the best purposes of a lodge in the vast wilderness. Fortunately in this case 'the boundless contiguity of shade' of the woods is some little distance away, on the other side of the evergreen Itchen valley, which, narrowing at this spot, is not much more than a couple of hundred yards wide. A long field's length away from the cottage is the little ancient, rustic, tree-hidden village. The cottage, too, is pretty well hidden by the trees and has the reed and sedge and grass green valley and swift river before it, and behind and on each side green fields and old untrimmed hedges with a few oak trees growing both in the hedgerows and the fields. There is also an ancient avenue of limes which leads nowhere and whose origin is forgotten. The ground under the trees is overgrown with long grass and nettles and burdock; nobody comes or goes by it, it is only used by the cattle, the white and roan and strawberry shorthorns that graze in the fields and stand in

the shade of the limes on very hot days. Nor is there any way or path
to the cottage; but one must come and go over the green fields, wet or
dry. The avenue ends just at the point where the gently sloping chalk
down touches the level valley, and the half-hidden, low-roofed cottage
stands just there, with the shadow of the last two lime trees falling on
it at one side. It was an ideal spot for a nature-lover and an angler to
pitch his tent upon. Here a small plot of ground, including the end of
the lime-tree avenue, was marked out, a hedge of sweetbriar planted
round it, the cottage erected and a green lawn made before it on the
river side, and beds of roses planted at the back.

Mrs Creighton captures the charm of The Cottage in her *Memoir
of Dorothy Grey*:

> The Cottage itself was simple enough, 'a tin cottage' as Dorothy
> always called it, with its roof painted red, its walls covered with
> trellis, so that it is buried in creepers, honeysuckle, roses, clematis,
> amongst which many birds, blackbirds, thrushes, chaffinches, robins,
> and wagtails built their nests. It was meant only to serve as a neces-
> sary shelter, for all real life was spent out of doors, but like everything
> that Dorothy touched, it has a dainty charm of its own. The little
> sitting room with its great window opening down to the ground, has
> its walls hung with blue linen and there is a bit of soft blue carpet on
> the floor. The comfortable chairs and sofa are covered with blue and
> white chintz and on the wall are two long rows of books.

With a few exceptions, the Greys followed the same routine year
after year. Christmas and New Year would be spent at Fallodon.
They would then open up The Cottage in March – for the Greys,
spring arrived with the chiffchaff – and close it again at the end
of July. For the balance of the year, their country life was based
at Fallodon, interspersed with regular visits to Scotland to fish for
salmon. Sadly, the late spring of 1892 brought an abrupt change to
their rural idyll at The Cottage.

Junior Office

In the spring of 1892 the Greys' cottage life was disrupted by politics and would not be the same again for three long years. At the general election in July, the Liberals and Irish Nationalists held a combined majority of forty seats. Grey retained his seat with a reduced majority and Gladstone became Prime Minister for a fourth time. The widely popular yet ever moody Lord Rosebery reluctantly accepted the Foreign Office. Rosebery's exasperated colleagues simply couldn't survive without him. He had great charisma, was a brilliant public speaker and demonstrated a remarkable ability to connect with the general public. Set against these formidable qualities, he was mercurial, oversensitive and disdainful of hard work. Notwithstanding these defects, the new Foreign Secretary remained to Grey a shining light in an otherwise dull political world.

Rosebery was a true aristocrat, born of immense ability and privilege. He was a man of vast wealth and great houses such as Dalmeny in Scotland, Mentmore in Buckinghamshire and the Durdans near Epsom. He was a 'man of letters', a prolific historical biographer and became perhaps the most celebrated ever chairman of the London County Council. While an undergraduate at Oxford, he once boasted that he would marry an heiress, win the Derby and become Prime Minister. Not only did he marry a Rothschild and win the Derby three times but he was also a highly successful Foreign Secretary in addition to becoming Prime Minister for eighteen months. He was to prove a sagacious statesman who would famously coin the phrase 'the Empire is a

Commonwealth of Nations', and over Christmas 1901 he called for negotiations with the Boers at 'a wayside inn', which paved the path for peace in South Africa. When offered the post of Parliamentary Under-Secretary by such a luminary, it was not surprising that Grey accepted. But like his mentor, Grey entered office without any great enthusiasm. The Greys hated city life and dreaded the prospect of losing precious time spent in the countryside of Northumberland and Hampshire. He writes in *Twenty-Five Years*, 'I realised that the ties of office must intensify the exile, I entered it without any elation; indeed with depression. It would be untrue to imply that the new position brought no interest or excitement; it brought both, but without cancelling the drawback.'

It is worth considering why Gladstone offered Grey such a prestigious job in his new ministry. The Prime Minister would of course have appreciated Grey's support for his Irish policy, but the young member for Berwick-upon-Tweed also had presence and a name. Gladstone was a good friend and colleague of Sir George Grey and felt at ease with intelligent, promising parliamentarians of blue-blooded Whig stock. There is, however, every chance that Rosebery had asked for Grey. Grey had allied himself to the exciting new Liberal Imperialist wing of the party and Rosebery as its leader also had an eye for a good-looking backbencher with an attractive personality who hailed from his own elitist background. Grey played little part in policy making, but with Rosebery in the Lords, to the young minister passed the not inconsiderable task of having to convey government policy in the Commons. Explaining the role of Parliamentary Under-Secretary, Grey writes in his autobiography,

> his business was to make himself thoroughly acquainted with all that was done in the Office, to get up carefully any particular point on which information was sought by Members of the House of Commons, to make statements on foreign affairs that should be in entire accordance with the policy of the Cabinet, and to defend and explain that policy without giving offence to foreign countries.

Grey was excited about the prospect of working for Rosebery at the Foreign Office but if the truth be told he probably would have preferred a junior ministerial position in the Local Government Board where he could pursue some of his more radical policy interests.

In 1892, the young up-and-coming minister joined Haldane as a member of the 'Co-Efficients' dining club, a sort of fashionable brains trust, made up of leading radical intellectuals such as the celebrated Fabian Sidney Webb, Bertrand Russell and H. G. Wells. Beatrice Webb rather unfairly wrote in her diary that Grey lacked any original ideas 'beyond foreign and colonial policy', which is strange as that same year Grey produced a paper on land reform. He had joined the Committee on Land Reform, chaired by Gladstone, in 1887, and was elected a Vice-President two years later. Other committee members included Augustine Birrell and Sidney Webb. Grey was acutely aware of the needs and insecurities of the rural community and, as with his crusade to extend the rural franchise, he was determined to press for reform. He wrote of the aims of land reform in his paper, 'Rural Land':

> In rural districts the effect of the land system on the happiness and welfare of the people is immense; the number of holders, the size of the holdings, the distribution of them, the sort of tenure, all these things have a preponderating influence on the well-being, both moral and material, of all who live in the country. The distribution and use of land should be adapted to its situation and quality and to the character and resources of the people. We want to secure that this shall be so in every county district and every parish and hitherto little or nothing has been done to secure it.

As a first step towards land reform he was eager that district and parish councils be established with powers of compulsory purchase

to acquire land for schools, libraries, recreation grounds and allotments. While being a passionate supporter of the Allotment Act of
1885, he wanted a new Bill introduced that would substitute agricultural values for amenity values and grant some degree of fixed
tenure for tenants. He envisaged a complete system of allotments
as becoming 'an antidote for the restlessness or depression which
is so often characteristic of village life'. He was also keen that local
authorities should follow the example of the Irish Land Purchase
Bill and extend their operations into the acquisition of small farms
from 50 to 200 acres. These would then be tenanted to farmers
who would otherwise have been unable to acquire such holdings,
providing employment for the local rural population.

    Grey had radical ideas on domestic policy but his views on foreign
affairs were much closer to the Conservatives than to his own party
and consequently he felt it important to support imperial expansion
when and where it suited British interests. Within weeks of taking
office a serious policy split opened up in Cabinet that would provide
an early test of Grey's skills on the floor of the Commons. At the time
the 'Scramble for Africa' was at its peak and Britain found herself
constantly rubbing up against the French. The problem dated back
to 1875, when Disraeli acquired a shareholding in the Suez Canal
from the Khedive of Egypt, as the Canal, originally built by the
French, offered Britain a much shorter route to India. Egypt was a
vassal state of the decaying Ottoman Empire and in 1882 a local
rebellion against the Khedive caused Britain and France to intervene.
After the insurgents had been routed the French sailed away. Having
acquired a financial interest in the Canal, the British saw their chance
to protect this vital strategic asset from falling into hostile hands and
stayed. Thus, Egypt became a Protectorate of the Crown.

    The British East Africa Company, responsible for the administra-
tion of Uganda, had run into financial difficulties and threatened
to evacuate the country by December 1892. The Prime Minister,
Harcourt and a large majority of the Cabinet favoured withdrawal. They rightly believed that such additions to the Empire
would stretch Britain both militarily and financially. Rosebery was

adamant that Uganda should remain a British protectorate. He was also determined to send out a message to the other European powers that the new Liberal government would not be a 'soft touch' when it came to imperial matters. Rosebery was a passionate Imperialist but he was also a far-sighted statesman who could see the bigger picture. He was worried that evacuation would leave a vacuum which would be filled by the French. Once in possession of the headwaters of the Nile, the French would be in a position to threaten Egypt, and Egypt was the gateway to India. Grey was to take a similar stance over the revolt in the Sudan a few years later. What is more, the Fashoda Incident in 1898, when a detachment of British troops unexpectedly bumped into a small party of French explorers on the upper reaches of the Nile, proved how dangerous withdrawal might have been. Of the younger 'Imperialists', only Henry Fowler joined Grey with support for the Foreign Secretary. Asquith and Haldane attached themselves to the 'enemy camp'.

At the time of the Uganda crisis there were two groups in the Cabinet with differing views on imperial policy. Rosebery was an out-and-out 'expansionist', believing Britain would need more space in the future for its burgeoning population, whereas the Radicals like Harcourt and Morley were 'consolidators'. The latter were concerned that the cost of maintaining a larger Empire would kill domestic social reform, which was the beating heart of Liberalism. Grey was solidly behind his chief, having a justifiable concern over competitive expansion from France and Germany. The Germans, in particular, were desperate for a colonial empire of their own to match their recently acquired industrial might. Yet there was a touch of hypocrisy about Grey. In January 1895 he wrote about the Europeans to Herbert Paul:

No nation was moved by any aspiration except the sort of malevolent and bastard enthusiasm, which exists in France and Germany, for large slices of Africa, for which they will eventually derive no other satisfaction than of having kept other people out and for that they will have to pay heavily.

Grey always believed in the superior character of the Anglo-Saxon peoples – witnessed, he thought, by Britain and America's indignation over the Turkish atrocities in Armenia, as compared with continental Europe's apathy. The split in Cabinet was chronicled by Charles Hobhouse, Grey's future Cabinet colleague, writing in his diary for 20 March 1893, 'Grey's speech on Uganda prompted no doubt by Rosebery made great stir in the Cabinet. Harcourt and others thinking it *too pronounced*.' The speech was a brave one as it contradicted Gladstone's policy of evacuation. It would be safe to say that Grey's imperialistic views were advanced under Rosebery's tutelage.

Through a combination of obstinacy and political stealth, Rosebery won the day. The Cabinet agreed to a compromise. A Commission of Inquiry headed by Sir Gerald Portal was despatched to Uganda, with the result that the country remained British. Public opinion, worried about a resurgence of the slave trade, was firmly in the Foreign Secretary's camp. Rosebery was always willing to play the resignation card, his colleagues knowing all too well that their fragile administration could not survive without him. We may assume that Grey learnt the arts of brinkmanship at an early stage under Rosebery's influence. As Foreign Secretary, Grey was indispensable to his own administration. Like Rosebery, he gained no pleasure from being in office and was always ready to offer his resignation. Both men had a hinterland outside politics and independent financial means. The threat of resignation made for a tricky bedfellow and more often than not provided the perpetrator with a trump card at the negotiating table.

Grey had passed his first parliamentary test with distinction, yet it had been a bumpy ride. It would have been all too easy for him to offend his Cabinet superiors, particularly the notoriously bad-tempered Harcourt. In the event he steered a deft course through the crisis, which did nothing but good for his career prospects. Sir Edward Hamilton on 25 July 1893 noted in his diary that Rosebery felt Grey 'possessed qualifications that might fit him for promotion some day from the Under-Secretaryship to the Secretaryship of

State'. Again on 5 October, after Grey's name had been suggested as a possible candidate for Viceroy of India, Hamilton noted that Rosebery refused to endorse Grey on the grounds that 'it would be a thousand pities if his parliamentary career were interfered with – probably with a peerage and with any rate position lost – while he was one of the very few men who might be regarded as making for a leader in the House of Commons.'

Grey was back alone at Fallodon for a rare summer weekend on 28 May, while Dorothy remained at the Hampshire cottage. He relishes the 'golden time', writing in his diary,

> hawthorn, lilac and laburnum in full flower; only one hawthorn in the Lands is a mass of it, but it is splendid; one can see nothing but flower on it. All the leaves are out and every tree is green except one or two old ashes, and even on them the green is showing at a distance.

He would not be back until the parliamentary recess, when summer would be over. Grey's wildfowl collection continued to be a source of joy and interest. He writes in the *Fallodon Green Book*,

> the un-pinioned Carolina duck nested in a hole about the depth of a man's arm in an old broken elm nearly opposite the house on the Lands: it is about thirty foot from the ground: today I found her, outside the wire with six birds about opposite the island of the old pond. I caught the young ones and put them over, the duck in great distress in the grass flapping round me: the next thing was to get her to join her brood over the fence, but she insisted on driving me away from the brood for about 150 yards before she would rise: then she flew to the new pond and then on to find them. Meanwhile they scattered in the long grass: four of them she found and took over: the other two I rescued and carried in my hat and restored to her on

the old pond. She had only six eggs and hatched them all; I wish I
had seen her bring the young ones down.

During his first tenure of office a few specific events made a deep
impression on Grey which would mould his future thinking on
foreign policy. For a number of years, friction with France and
Russia over a whole range of colonial issues had brought Britain
to the verge of war. The controversy over Siam in 1893 was, on the
face of it, of little importance, yet France and Britain came close to
conflict. The French made certain territorial claims on the Siamese
frontier and in doing so threatened Siam's independence. Britain
was keen to maintain an independent Siam as a buffer between her
Indian Empire and French Indo-China. Gunboat faced gunboat,
and the inevitable 'incident' nearly led to blows when a French
cruiser turned its guns on a British vessel at anchor. On top of
this there were constant boundary disputes in West Africa and an
ongoing argument regarding Newfoundland fishing rights. Most
significantly, the French had never really accepted Britain's occupation of Egypt. It is easy to understand why, a decade later, Grey
enthusiastically supported Lansdowne signing the Entente Cordiale
with France. It was essentially a colonial agreement that removed
potential sources of conflict around the globe. At a later date, Grey
would encourage the Unionists to pursue a similar agreement with
Russia in order to mitigate friction in the Far East, and no more so
than around the margins of the Indian Empire.

But there was another reason for Grey to welcome friendship
with France. As a junior minister he was to experience at first hand
the unattractive side of German diplomacy. He grew to dislike and
distrust their methods of doing business. It should be remembered
this was some five years before the Germans started building a fleet
'against Britain'. When the Liberals took office in 1892, Britain
was said to be living in 'splendid isolation', devoid of any international alliances. In fact, her isolation was far from splendid. For the

previous decade or so, Britain had leant towards the Triple Alliance of Germany, Austria-Hungary and Italy in a quest for diplomatic support over colonial disputes with France and Russia. Such support was particularly important in Egypt. It was in this connection that Germany would swiftly demonstrate she was not to be relied upon. In the early 1890s, British firms were competing with Germany for railway concessions in Asia Minor. Out of the blue, Britain received an ultimatum from Berlin demanding she cease to compete with Germany for such contracts in Turkey. Britain was abruptly informed that refusal would result in the German Consul in Cairo withdrawing support from the British administration in Egypt. Bearing in mind Britain's weak position with France, the Foreign Office had little choice but to back down, leaving Germany emboldened for future mischief. This action left a serious impression on Grey who was later to write, 'It was the abrupt and rough peremptoriness of the German action that gave me an unpleasant impression … the method adopted by Germany in this instance was not that of a friend, it left a sense of discomfort and a bad taste behind.'

Relations with Japan improved markedly during Grey's first tenure at the Foreign Office, culminating in Lord Lansdowne's Alliance of 1902. In 1894, Britain took a friendly and independent course following Japan's successful war with China. France, Germany and Russia pressurised Japan to surrender her fruits of victory, whereas Britain refused to interfere with Japanese claims. In addition, Britain signed an agreement whereby she relinquished all rights of jurisdiction over her subjects in Japan. These rights were retained by other European and American governments. Britain felt the time had come to treat the Japanese on the same basis as other great powers. These concessions smoothed the path for a full Alliance eight years later which was important to Britain in two ways. Britain badly needed an ally in the Far East to thwart Russian expansionism. For many years Russia had been viewed as a threat to the Indian Empire. At the turn of the century there was also a pressing requirement to protect British interests and

markets in China. After the signing of the Russian Entente in 1907,
the growing sea power of Germany replaced Russia as the major
threat to British interests. The Japanese Alliance enabled Britain
to rely on the assistance of their fleet when it came to policing
Pacific waters. At the same time, the Admiralty was able to transfer
warships back to the North Sea to meet the growing menace of
Germany. It is probable Grey's views on the importance of maintaining friendly relations with Japan were formulated in his early
years at the Foreign Office. In his 'City speech' of October 1905,
outlining Liberal opposition thoughts on foreign policy, Grey reiterated the importance of a 'defensive alliance' with Japan. As Foreign
Secretary he renewed Lansdowne's Alliance in 1911.

The parliamentary session of 1893 was particularly demanding. He
had few opportunities to pursue recreational interests and his spirits
were low. There were five days' holiday over Easter, after which
the House did not adjourn until the middle of September. It met
again in October and the session lasted into the new year, forcing
the Greys to spend Christmas at their London house in Pimlico.
Furthermore, come the spring, they were unable to leave for their
Hampshire cottage at weekends until Saturday morning. Here
was a passionate countryman chained to a desk in a cellar below
the floor of the House of Commons. It would be a misconception
to think Grey lazy just because he dreamt of his country pursuits
while a prisoner in the city. Previous writers have insinuated he was
always away fishing 'when the balloon went up'. This was quite
simply untrue. He had a strong sense of duty and a capacity for
hard work that matched his physical attributes.

But Grey was not to be denied his 'fix' of cottage life, however
brief the visit. Reminiscing later in life he wrote,

The spring and summer of 1893 were unusually warm and fine.
Every Saturday morning we left Grosvenor Road about half-past

five in the morning. We had no baggage and at that hour there were no hansom cabs so we walked across Lambeth Bridge, the river and houses presenting the same aspect of calm and quiet that inspired Wordsworth's sonnet 'On Westminster Bridge'. Thence our way went past St Thomas' Hospital and along the street that then led to the entrance of Waterloo. This street we called Wood Street; at that early hour it was deserted, the houses shut, the only sound in it was the vigorous song of a thrush in a cage that hung outside one of the houses. The thrush was always singing at that hour and the lines

'at the corner of Wood Street, when daylight appears,

Hangs a thrush that sings loud'

being familiar to us, we always spoke of the street as Wood Street, though that was not its real name. From this street the way led through the most unsavoury tunnel to the old Waterloo Station, and so we got away by the six o'clock train from Waterloo and to the Hampshire cottage soon after eight o'clock in time for breakfast. The start from London each Saturday morning was one of rapture and anticipated pleasure:

'Bliss was it in that dawn to be alive,

But to be young was very heaven'

– and week after week the Saturday and Sunday fulfilled anticipations. On Saturday, in hot summer weather, I would fish until about two o'clock and again from seven to nine in the evening. Sunday was not a fishing day then on that part of the Itchen and we spent it reading great or refreshing books, going on long walks in some of the most beautiful country in all the south of England, watching birds much in the spirit of Keats's sonnet, 'To one who has been long in city pent'.

All Grey's country pleasures are mentioned above: birds, fly fishing, walking and the Romantic poets, especially Wordsworth, who he sometimes charmingly refers to as 'Big Daddy'. But first and foremost The Cottage was a fishing lodge for Grey. His best fishing on the river was achieved in the early years. In *Fly Fishing* he writes of a memorable day in July 1892 when he caught six brace of trout, weighing 24 lb.

Most of the fish were caught on small flies during the morning rise before two o'clock in the afternoon. There is no doubt Grey was a brilliant fisherman. His ingenuity is demonstrated by another passage in *Fly Fishing* in which he recounts casting aside his usual dry fly and reverting to a 'black hackle', as if he were salmon fishing with a wet fly:

There was very little rise in the morning; a few fish were seen but as each one only rose about once in ten minutes, fishing with the dry fly was very intermittent and up till one o'clock nothing had been landed. It seemed that nothing more was to be done and I sat gazing listlessly at the water. A fairly broad straight bit of river was before me, smooth in places, but with small ripples of stream here and there. The thoughts of other rivers and salmon fishing came into my mind, until at last in a state of sheer despair and idleness it occurred to me that I would try a wet fly and in salmon fishing phrase 'put it over' the piece of water before me. 'The black hackle', a very favourite north country fly, was chosen and used as a salmon fly, that is to say it was cast across and down the stream at an angle and kept moving gently until the action of the stream brought it round to my own bank. The trout took it like salmon take a fly, sometimes under water, sometimes with a fair head and tail rise, sometimes with a plunge but for the most part either when the fly was midway across the stream or when it had come well round and was nearly straight below me; and the fish that rose took firm hold, hardly any being lost or pricked.

Grey landed ten trout in this manner by the end of the evening rise. He never managed the same success again using a wet fly on a chalk stream.

It was thoughts of this pastoral hinterland, providing such a contrast to the drudgery of Westminster life, that kept him going through the week, particularly in the spring and summer months. He writes,

Then, every Monday morning we went back to London, I, to spend the morning at the Foreign Office and the rest of the day after luncheon in the cellar-room under the House of Commons, in which I could hear the unpleasant sounds, when the obstruction in the House was very rampant and demonstrative, as it frequently was then, or when, as sometimes happened, there was open disorder in the House. Party feeling ran high in those days. We on the Liberal side felt we were right, that Unionist Government in Ireland had failed and would continue to fail, that till there was Home Rule there would be no peace and Ireland would be a source of perpetual weakness to us and a misery to herself.

Grey's love for innocent country pursuits not only allowed him to carry out his public duties so successfully but it is also what makes Grey such an attractive personality. He had reached the top of his profession in his early forties and certainly had no designs to become Prime Minister. Unlike most modern politicians, he was totally without ambition and social aspirations. All he wanted to do was to retire from office to the countryside, but in this he was fortunate: he had an estate and a private income to fall back on. One can think of several more contemporary statesmen, such as Neville Chamberlain and Alec Douglas-Home, who loved birds, but no other public figure wrote with such colour, passion and knowledge on the countryside as did Edward Grey.

Gladstone's Home Rule Bill passed its third reading in September 1893 and a few days later was thrown out by the Lords. This was the end of the line for Gladstone, who finally retired in the new year to be succeeded as Prime Minister by Rosebery. Although Grey was delighted at his old chief's appointment he would miss working with his political mentor on a day-to-day basis. Rosebery's successor at the Foreign Office was Lord Kimberley, a steady yet not top-class performer. Gladstone referred to Kimberley as 'the most long-winded man I have ever known in Cabinet'. Grey liked and respected the new Foreign Secretary as a gentleman and fellow countryman but at times found him frustrating to deal with, and never more so than over events in the spring of 1895.

Relations with France were deteriorating on the African continent. News was coming in of renewed boundary encroachments by the French on the Niger in West Africa. Additionally, rumours were circulating that they might also make a move on the Upper Nile. On 28 March, Grey received two questions in the House, one expected, on West Africa, and one unexpected, on the Nile Valley. Grey had earlier consulted Kimberley as to how he should respond to a parliamentary question on French activities in West Africa. Kimberley was non-committal, saying, 'You must do the best you can but I think you must use pretty firm language.' When asked in the House about the rumours of a French expedition heading for the headwaters of the Nile, and knowing he had the implicit support of the Prime Minister, Grey dismissed the rumours yet replied in the strong tones the Foreign Secretary had suggested he use for West Africa,

> The advance of a French expedition under secret instructions right from the other side of Africa into a territory over which our claims have been known for so long would be not merely an inconsistent and unexpected act, but it must be perfectly well known to the French government that it would be an unfriendly act and would be so viewed by England.

This statement became known as 'the Grey Declaration'. It would demonstrate its usefulness three years later, when General Kitchener accosted the Marchand expedition at Fashoda.

Grey's direct language caused a stir in Paris and in Cabinet. The French ambassador felt that the 'unfriendly act' was a warning that could only be followed by an ultimatum. Morley and Harcourt were horrified at what they saw as unnecessary provocation of the French. Kimberley was caught in the middle and Rosebery, ever the Imperialist, secretly delighted. The Prime Minister wrote to Kimberley,

Nothing should be done to diminish, impair, or reflect on the present position of E. Grey. He is one of the most important members of the Government for his being outside the Cabinet is the direct cause not of his failure, but of his great success as representative of the Foreign Office. Moreover he is persona gratissima to the House of Commons, popular, admired and respected.

In Rosebery's eyes, here was a man with a future; a Foreign Secretary in the making. If Rosebery was proving to be a disastrous Prime Minister, he had at least been an admired and successful Foreign Secretary. His government, lacking any sort of morale and the stomach for a fight, was defeated by an opposition motion in June and resigned. Rosebery, demonstrating his high regard for Grey, offered to make him a Privy Councillor. Grey declined on the basis that 'it would certainly be quoted and regarded as an undoubted pledge and earnest of future work'. The reluctant politician still had a country life at the forefront of his mind, as did his wife, who wrote to her friend Ella Pease in October, 'We have been so happy since the Government went out that I feel we could cheer anybody up unless they were set against us by the feeling that we were happier than we deserved.'

Just how much Grey disliked this self-imposed exile from the country can be seen in a diary entry for 23 June 1895 in *The Cottage Book*, which he kept at his weekend home on the Itchen, 'The Government were beaten on Friday night and we have spent these days in high hopes of an announcement on Monday, which will bring the end of this terrible time within sight.' Cottage leisure time had been drastically curtailed by his ministerial position. Another entry for 31 March states, 'Pruning Sunday. Disturbed by work and have to go up on Sunday evening.' This, of course, refers to the row over 'the Grey Declaration'. A maximum break of forty-eight hours was all Grey could manage over this stressful period, although on 28 April 1894, he did manage to sneak away on Friday night:

> I came by the last train on Friday night the 27th and walked out from Winchester at midnight. It was warm and soft: I heard a nightingale, and one sedge warbler was singing within hearing of the road just where a piece of the river could be seen, light at the end of a little dark path. I walked with my hat off and once a little soft rain fell amongst my hair: there were great forms of leafy trees and a smell and spirit everywhere and I felt the soft country dust about my feet.

This entry is so evocative of the days before tar-covered roads that the reader can almost hear a nightingale singing under a full moon enveloped in an aroma of new mown grass and damp dust.

That Grey was a romantic, there is no doubt, but he was also a serious Christian. There is a delightful entry in *The Cottage Book* for the weekend of 1 July 1894 on the subject of the local wrens which demonstrates this, Dorothy writing in their diary,

> The wren sang nearly all morning. We talked about it while we were at breakfast the first morning, and thought how nice it was that we knew enough to be able to love it so much, and how many people there were who would not be aware of it, and Edward said, 'Fancy if God came in and said, "Did you notice my wren?", and they were obliged to say they did not know it was there.'

The Greys had a special affection for the wren on account of its mighty voice in relation to its size and the fact that it is one of the only British birds that sings for most of the year. One of the Greys' favourite walks was beside Avington Lake; it was known to them as 'Wren Path', owing to the number of nests located along its course. Grey wrote that same weekend, 'When we arrived there was one wren singing most noticeably round the cottage; as I looked it flew happily over the cottage from the poplars to the limes, singing as it passed over the roof: "like a blessing", Dorothy said when I told her.'

Grey wrote in *The Cottage Book* for 21 May 1894: 'Dorothy went into the wild park [Avington Park] to hear nightingales at midnight.

There was a full moon and the grass was stiff with frost.' This was 'Nightingale Moon': the first full moon after the nightingales' arrival from Africa, when their singing was at a peak. Unknown to Grey at the time, all these diary entries in *The Cottage Book* would provide an invaluable larder of memories and facts which would be included in his bestseller, *The Charm of Birds*, some thirty-three years later. His brilliant comparison of the nightingale's song against that of the blackcap appears both as an entry for 30 April 1894 in *The Cottage Book* and again in the chapter on 'The Return of the Warblers' in *The Charm of Birds:*

> A nightingale's song is the most wonderful, but the most imperfect of songs. The long notes are divine, but they come seldom, and never go on long enough: the song continually breaks out with a burst, which promises a fine full spell, but it is always broken off in the most disappointing way. A blackcap's song, which comes next in quality, is short enough, but it seems finished in a way that no part of the nightingale's ever does, and one can't help thinking with some satisfaction of a good, steady old thrush singing right through from the beginning of February to the middle of June.

However idyllic their life together seemed at The Cottage, there must have been a serious flaw in Grey's relationship with his wife. That he was immensely fond of Dorothy will never be in doubt, but Dorothy was a solitary, often sickly person who could not satisfy her husband's physical needs. Grey was a handsome, healthy, active man in the prime of his life who was forced to spend much of his time on his own in the capital. Living alone in London was asking for trouble. Indeed, there is reason to believe that around this time he began an affair with a young woman in London. Grey was a reserved and discreet individual so it would not be surprising if he kept this relationship tightly under wraps. His parliamentary reputation was one of good judgement, firm character and trustworthiness; it would have shocked many of his colleagues if his complicated love life became public knowledge. In contrast, everyone seemed to know about Lloyd George's womanising. Over time the two men developed a strong dislike of each other and after Grey's death he would be heavily criticised by Lloyd George in his *War Memoirs*. It would be reasonable to suggest that Lloyd George had knowledge of Grey's private life and it perhaps explains Harold Nicolson's diary entry for Trafalgar Day 1932, in which he writes of Lloyd George referring to Grey's 'sham honesty'.

Certainly the lengths to which Grey would go to protect his reputation can be gleaned from an article published in *The Journal of Liberal History* written by Hans-Joachim Heller. In his article, he maintains that while working as a junior minister at the Foreign Office from 1892 to 1895, Grey had an affair with a Florence Annie Slee, the daughter of a south London family with an estate agency business in Hatton Garden. On 1 March 1894, Florence gave birth to a daughter, Winifred, in Bremen, Germany. On Winifred's birth certificate the parents are described as 'the British officer Charles Grey and his wife Florence Annie Slee, both of London'.

According to Heller, who as Winifred's younger son has spent years researching this aspect of the Grey family history, he is the grandson not of Charles, but of Edward Grey. He was brought up believing – and this belief is supported by some circumstantial evidence – that the real story was as follows. When his mother's pregnancy was confirmed, the Slee family and the Greys hatched a carefully considered plan to conceal the illegitimate birth and avoid a scandal. The deception was to be carried out with the assistance of two women of German origin, both employed by the Slee family for many years, as governess and piano teacher respectively. It was decided they would leave for the Continent with the pregnant Florence and once the birth had taken place the child would be brought up in Germany. Florence would meanwhile return to England and Charles, Edward's youngest brother, would then assume the role of sham husband of Florence. It is interesting that someone, maybe Edward Grey himself, deemed it important that the child should take her father's name. It so happened that Charles, then only twenty years old, was about to join the colonial service and leave for Africa, where he later died in a hunting accident.

Before their respective departures from London, a somewhat bizarre event occurred. Whether for reasons of conscience or religious sensibility, a secret, legally invalid marriage ceremony was held between Charles Grey and Florence Slee in an unlicensed chapel. Florence then spent several months in Germany while the pregnancy progressed. After the birth, she returned to her family in London. This is a very sad story, in that it appears she only rarely, if ever, saw her daughter again, did not marry, and died in 1957, having spent many years looking after the household of her estate agent brothers. We can assume that her relationship with Grey came to an end at the moment when, or soon after, the pregnancy became known. In 1895 the two 'guardians' moved with the baby to live on Borkum, a seaside resort on the North Sea coast of Germany, where they brought up and educated her as Winifred Grey, supported by a pension provided from England. In 1904 they received a lump sum of several thousand gold marks from the Greys, enabling them to purchase a boarding house called 'Haus Constance', possibly named after Grey's youngest sister, Constance, who could well have played an important part in the cover-up. Grey, with the prospect of high office in front of him, clearly felt the need to avoid the risk of scandal such as that experienced by Margaret Thatcher's close confidant and senior Cabinet Minister Cecil Parkinson.

During the Great War, in order to satisfy the German authorities over her nationality, Winifred was adopted by her governess, who kept the story of her true parents a close secret. She is known to have visited London at least once just before the outbreak of war. According to Heller, she was made aware of her parentage during a trip to England but never spoke of it directly to her sons or talked of what had happened while she was there. One can imagine that the news came as a great shock and may have brought with it a sense of betrayal. Many years later, Winifred married Captain Rudolf Heller, head of the military recreation home on Borkum, and in 1930 they moved to Berlin, where she miraculously survived the devastation of the Second World War with her two sons.

The evidence linking Winifred to Edward Grey, while hardly irrefutable, is compelling. It derives first from the birth certificate and other official documents linking her to the Grey family. It is strengthened by documents emanating from those close to Winifred and her guardians. For example, although these ladies carried the secret of what they knew about Winifred's background to their graves, the sister of one of them, a Mrs Behrmann of Bremen, later corroborated Heller's assertions. In a testimony to the police in 1937, as part of her requirement to prove Aryan credentials to the satisfaction of the Nazi authorities, she describes Winifred as 'the child of the famous English officer and politician in the Great War, Grey'. This is somewhat confusing as Grey was not an officer, but it does suggest she is not referring to Charles Grey.

In 1946–7 we find Winifred trapped in the Russian sector of Berlin, with many friends and associates of her German family writing to the British military authorities emphasising her English parentage, in support of her desperate efforts to obtain the right to live in what later became West Berlin. Many others were in a similar position and sadly she was unsuccessful. She was forced to live out the rest of her life and bring up her children behind the Iron Curtain. Perhaps most significantly, an examination of Heller's meticulously archived documents and photographs shows the remarkable physical like-ness of both Winifred and her son, Hans-Joachim, to Edward Grey. His distinctively patrician, pinched facial features, thin lips and large Roman nose are manifestly present in both mother and son.

In assessing whether Winifred was indeed the daughter of Edward Grey, or of his brother, one must also ask the following question. Would the Grey family have gone to such lengths, and expense, to conceal the illegitimate child of Charles, a younger son who was about to leave England for the African colonies? Everything about the sad story of Winifred Grey suggests there was far more at stake. An amusing tale is told by Ronald Storrs in one of his books. In May 1916, Grey was dining at Downing Street having just discovered that his favourite poet, William Wordsworth, had fathered an illegitimate child in France when only twenty-two years old. An animated Grey was recounting the story to his fellow guests and, according to Storrs, 'Balfour was shocked, Asquith delighted and Kitchener did not know who Wordsworth was.' Maybe Grey was secretly pleased he had more in common with his hero than he previously thought.

Winifred might not have been the only illegitimate child sired by Edward Grey at this time. There is a family legend amongst a minor branch of the Lascelles family that a boy raised amongst them was actually a love child of Sir Edward Grey born around 1890. In three successive censuses covering the late nineteenth century and succeeding Edwardian era, an Edmund Lascelles, then Edward Lascelles and then Edward Grey appears in the same Lascelles household, although no birth records of the boy have been found. He was raised in the household of Rowley Lascelles, the son of a chaplain who served in India. By 1911 he is named in the census as Edward Grey and no longer as 'Son' but as 'Visitor', with his profession listed as 'Private Means', while the other household members are employed in more humble occupations. There is no firm documentary evidence and no record beyond word of mouth from family members, but it does seem credible that he was the son of Edward Grey. If so, he would have represented the youngest of several Grey love children who were adopted or lived without recognition in other families in England or abroad.

If these stories are true then Grey must have lived with a deep sense of guilt throughout his life. It would have been a difficult cross to bear and suggests he would need to have been a much tougher character than many make out. No one of Grey's intelligence and integrity would want a fatherless child on their conscience, even if the best arrangements for its future had been made. Furthermore, he was a much respected public figure holding a ministerial position of great responsibility, and as such, any scandal in his private life would cause great embarrassment not only to his family but also to the Liberal Party. In later life, when Grey was saddened that he and his second wife, Pamela, could not produce an heir for Fallodon, he must have been aware of the cruel irony that he had illegitimate children he could not acknowledge. In *The Capital of Happiness*, Jan Karpinski writes that, 'Lloyd George is said to have accused Grey, in private and behind his back, of some scandal in his private life.' Maybe this explains why his private papers were destroyed shortly after his death.

Opposition Again

Grey spent Christmas 1895 and most of January 1896 with Dorothy at Fallodon, returning to London on the night sleeper on 2 February. The winter had been hard and six inches of snow fell at the end of January. He writes in his Northumberland diary, *The Fallodon Green Book*,

> The birds have been very hard pressed: there were weak redwings a few days ago, but I see none now: weak fieldfares and a few exhausted mistle thrushes are about. We have kept a supply of soaked dog biscuit and cocoa nuts in front of the library: more than twenty blackbirds, numbers of blue tits and some great tits have thriven well upon it and fed and quarrelled all day.

He also relates how much he enjoyed the presence of bramblings in the hard weather. Once the beech-mast had been exhausted they would swarm into the duck enclosure to feed on the corn.

The year 1896 was one of release for the Greys as it was for their political mentor, Lord Rosebery. Edward and Dorothy were still enjoying their first year of freedom when in the autumn an oversensitive, impetuous Rosebery finally resigned the Liberal leadership. Grey and Rosebery had much in common. They were both reluctant, retiring characters who privately expressed a hatred of public life. However, as with many politicians who have tasted high office, they found it hard not to return to the fray. Both men kept a weather eye on foreign affairs. With Rosebery leader of the party and Harcourt presiding over the Commons, the Liberal leadership was an uneasy truce. Grey remained close to his old chief and in February wrote to Dorothy from Mentmore, where he was attending a pre-session meeting of the Liberal hierarchy,

> I am in a large house and my room looks out on a courtyard with four walls and a huge iron gate. I heard the birds singing this morning but the sound came faintly from beyond the outer walls and I felt they were freer than I. Very large houses have their grounds so constituted as to keep birds at a respectful distance.

Early in the new year, events in South Africa were to heap untold embarrassment on the 'Imperial wing' of the party as details of the Jameson Raid began to trickle in. Dr Jameson and his private army of 'rough riders' invaded the Transvaal over the Christmas period hoping to provoke an uprising amongst the Uitlanders. The Uitlanders were English immigrant miners who suffered discrimination under President Kruger. This poorly organised adventure ended in disaster. Jameson and his fellow buccaneers were captured and handed over to the British to face trial. There was little doubt that Cecil Rhodes, English-born South African businessman, mining magnate and imperialist politician, was orchestrating events from behind the scenes in conjunction with 'the Rand Barons'. Two days after their capture, Rhodes resigned as Prime Minister of Cape Colony. The real question remained, what role did Joseph Chamberlain and the Colonial Office play in the drama? Questions were even asked of Rosebery. The Colonial Secretary was an admirer of Rhodes's 'imperial dream' and in early 1895 was behind Rhodes's appointment to the Privy Council. Jameson himself was found guilty and sentenced to fifteen months in prison, only to be granted early release due to ill health.

Although out of office, Grey maintained a strong interest in foreign affairs. During 1896 he would formulate a set of policy conditions to which he would hold steadfastly throughout his career. Events this year would mould his views on foreign policy, no more so than on the African continent. Grey had close family ties with South Africa. His cousin, Albert Grey, was Administrator of Rhodesia from 1896–8. His brother George was a colonial administrator and had taken part in the suppression of the Matabele rebellion in 1893. Dorothy wrote to her brother-in-law on 3 November:

> We are longing to hear what part you took in the great Battle of Bulawayo. We were, I think, ten days without any news of the columns at all, which was not nice, but we were very good and didn't worry at all. Edward said several times how awful it would have been if you had been conscripted and had not joined voluntarily and at any rate it was your wish to have some fighting.

Grey's strong Liberal views on conscription would take on a new relevance during the Great War a generation later.

With such deep-rooted family ties in Africa it is perhaps not surprising that Grey, who had a sneaking admiration for Jameson, was an advocate of an expansionist forward policy and thought the work of colonisation should be continued. Grey also had two cousins wounded participating in the Jameson Raid who within weeks had been elevated, along with their fellow conspirators, to heroic status by the British press. On 3 January, a sabre-rattling Kaiser, desperate for position on the world stage, sent a tactless telegram to President Kruger offering his congratulations for 'safeguarding the independence of the country'. The communication caused a convulsion of protest in Britain. The Raiders were feted by all and sundry and Jameson was much sought after in the drawing rooms of London society. Margot Asquith wrote, 'Dr Jim had personal magnetism and could do what he liked with my sex.'

Grey's deep-seated lifetime dislike for German diplomacy was moulded at this time. Many years later he would write,

The German Emperor's telegram, though it made no diplomatic incident, had its effect on British minds. Suspicion grew, later on, that Germany was encouraging President Kruger in order to make trouble for Britain in South Africa, and, though the dramatic demonstration of the German Emperor's telegram may not have initiated this suspicion, the recollection of the telegram strengthened it in later and more dangerous years.

Bismarck had always been non-committal in his support for the Boers but the Kaiser proved more impetuous. He had every intention of giving further encouragement to Boer aspirations and Grey was convinced Britain would soon have to intervene in South Africa. He wrote to Sydney Buxton after the news of the Jameson Raid,

> Germany will no doubt put on the screw in Egypt and be as nasty as she can everywhere. The fact is that the success of the British race has upset the temper of the world and now that they have ceased quarrelling about provinces in Europe and have turned their eyes to distant planes, they find us in the way everywhere. Hence a general tendency to vote us a nuisance and combine against us.

Grey's sentiments were echoed from the unlikely quarters of the Wilhelmstrasse. German Foreign Secretary Holstein wrote after his retirement in 1907, 'England, that rich and placid nation, was goaded into her defensive attitudes towards Germany by continuous threats and insults on the part of the Germans. The Kruger telegram began it all.' Ironically, the person who gained the most from this unfortunate episode was Admiral Tirpitz. Within months he would be introducing his new plans for the German Navy. It was obvious to the military authorities that they would be unable to move troops thousands of miles in support of the Boers while Britain controlled the sea lanes. Tirpitz wrote in his memoirs, 'The outbreak of hatred, envy and rage which the Kruger telegram let loose in England against Germany contributed more than anything else to open the eyes of large sections of the German people to our economic position and the necessity for a fleet.'

Other far-reaching views on foreign policy would be formulated at this time. One of Grey's most notable achievements as Foreign Secretary was to lay the foundations for Anglo-American friendship. Early in his career, nearly half a century before Churchill's close friendship with President Franklin D. Roosevelt, Grey saw the potential for a special relationship with America as vital to Britain's security and as a force for world peace. He understood the importance of a common language and culture. He was also sensitive to America's powerful economic position and her aspirations to become a major influence in international diplomatic circles. Like Britain, America was about to break out of her self-imposed isolation.

In 1895 the United States took an active interest in a boundary dispute between British Guiana and Venezuela. President Cleveland invoked the Monroe Doctrine stating that Britain should submit the boundary question to arbitration. As far as the Americans were concerned, a European power meddling in the affairs of a Latin American country was taking imperialism a little too far. (The Doctrine ran along the lines that the United States, controlling the American continent and being dominant in the western hemisphere, should have a right of interest in the affairs of any independent state in her sphere of influence.) On 11 January 1896, the Salisbury Cabinet reluctantly backed down, agreeing to negotiations with the United States. A pragmatic Grey was delighted, writing to Buxton, 'I have always felt that it was folly for us to argue about the Monroe Doctrine. The Monroe Doctrine is about whatever the United States says it is and what we have to consider is how far we can meet it.'

The Greys opened up The Cottage on Sunday 7 March. This was their first visit for eight months. The winter had been extraordinarily mild with 'no snow, hardly any frost and not one day's skating anywhere'. Bicycles, which would add so much to weekend enjoyment, were in evidence for the first time. The almost religious passion Grey felt for their little sanctuary overlooking the Itchen is obvious from the *The Cottage Book*:

> I am out of office, though not free of politics and we have learnt to ride bicycles and brought them with us meaning to get out at Alton and ride them here: a reckless and hard-hearted innovation which was stopped by the weather. We were prepared to rush into this dear place on bicycles for the first time in a way which I now see was inconsiderate and wanting in reverence to a place which has kept itself so unchanged for us. The rain obliged us to come down by train in the usual way and to walk the bicycles humbly down: they have remained unused since and out of sight and as great as the part they will play in our lives here, they will begin slowly.

In his mid-thirties Grey was not the highly polished ornithologist he became later in life. He was, however, learning fast under Dorothy's enthusiastic guidance. Two entries in *The Cottage Book* for 1896 demonstrate he has yet to hone his birdsong recognition skills. The weekend they opened up the cottage he writes, 'we heard a treecreeper and a golden-crested wren, at any rate one of them certainly'. When writing *The Charm of Birds* some thirty years later, he tells us how as a young man he used to confuse the high-pitched songs of a treecreeper and a goldcrest. He relates how the goldcrest's call-notes are 'like needle-points of sound' and that the song suggests 'a tiny stream trickling and rippling over a small pebbly channel and at the end going over a miniature cascade'. One of Grey's most impressive achievements in writing on birdsong is his ability to use an image to plant the individual song in form and sound in the memory. What is most moving about *The Charm of Birds* is that it is so evocative of one's own experiences and no more so than with the songs of the goldcrest and lesser whitethroat. On 18 May he makes another diary entry describing the frustration at his inability to recognise an unusual song:

A little bird with a monotonous and rapid song has plagued me all
these days; I have spent hours sitting opposite or under it without
ever getting a really good sight of it but I think it is a lesser whitethroat. It was often feeding among the young oak leaves and kept
'gabbling' its song but I could not catch sight of it. All sorts of other
birds would come and show themselves to me, close to it, but the
'gabbling' noise went on unseen.

In early October came the bombshell of Rosebery's resignation as
Liberal leader. To make matters worse Dorothy was ailing, experiencing bouts of lethargy and exhaustion. Although she was diagnosed
with Graves' disease, a condition caused by a thyroid deficiency, it
is more likely she was suffering from what we today would call ME.
Events left Grey even more disinclined to a political career. He had
written to Rosebery a few weeks earlier from the Shetlands where
he was fishing, 'up here politics seem less of a necessity than ever'.
Rosebery was neurotic, moody, riddled with self-doubt and too
thin-skinned for a political life. He was always going to jump ship.
Gladstone presented him the perfect opportunity with a speech in
Liverpool on the Armenian massacres. After sixty years of parliamentary service and four terms as Prime Minister, the 'Grand Old
Man' bounced out of retirement and advocated decisive, unspeci-
fied, unilateral action against Turkey in response to the atrocities
that were being committed against the Christian minorities. This
warmongering was too much for Rosebery, who believed Britain
should only respond through the Concert of Europe. The latter
had been formed in 1815 to enforce the decisions of the Congress
of Vienna. The major powers – Austria, Prussia, Russia, Britain
and later France – had agreed to maintain a balance of power in
Europe and to intervene if trouble arose in the smaller countries.

Rosebery felt Gladstone was being disloyal and, worse still, that
Harcourt was plotting behind his back. On Friday 9 October he
delivered his resignation address in front of an audience of 4,000

people at the Empire Theatre in Edinburgh. Ever the visionary, he warned of Britain being dragged into a terrifying conflict, 'You know what a European war means. It means massacre, the slaughter of hundreds of thousands of people; it means the ruin and destruction of the regions it invests.' Grey agreed with Rosebery that any protest to Turkey should be backed by the Concert of Europe. He was laying down a policy guideline that he would follow religiously throughout his career, climaxing in the July crisis of 1914 and further demonstrated by his campaign to establish a League of Nations after the war. A demoralised Grey despaired for the Liberal leadership and his party's lack of representation in Parliament. Both he and Dorothy secretly hoped for Rosebery's return. As late as August 1905, Dorothy wrote to a friend, 'When the crisis arrives my own eye will be fixed on the horizon looking out for the Rosebery star to come up.'

Grey was not present at the Empire Theatre for Rosebery's resignation speech as he was away in the Shetlands on an extended fishing trip. He had a passion for sea-trout fishing and that autumn, before Dorothy fell ill, he rented a house called Lunna: 'It was on a property of some 12,000 acres, remote from all hotels and so indented by small and large voes that the actual coast line was about thirty miles, all wild and rocky.' In the following passage from *Fly Fishing* he describes fishing for sea trout in Swining Voe. In doing so he delightfully captures the atmosphere of such sport in bleak, inaccessible wildernesses such as the Outer Isles where one might see seals on a rocky shore, a hen harrier gliding gracefully over the moor and in the far distance the barely discernible shape of a golden eagle soaring over the mountains, accompanied by the haunting croak of a raven.

> There was one voe some two miles in length with two small burns
> about a quarter of a mile apart at the head of it. It looked a likely place
> upon a large map and we walked over to it one Sunday afternoon to

see and hear what we could. There were a few crofters near the sea at the place and we were told by one of them that fish were seen jumping in the voe in September and that some one was supposed to have fished there once and caught nothing. We thought this hopeful, for where fish are seen in Shetland they may be caught, and one day I walked over to experiment. I seldom spent a more wretched and hopeless morning. There was no sign of a sea trout and to be wading amongst seaweed, throwing small flies in common salt water with a split cane rod, seemed quite foolish and mad. The burns were only large enough for minnows and I could see that there was nothing in them. Discomfort was added to hopelessness, for my mackintosh had been forgotten and some miles of rough peat hags and bogs were between me and the house. The morning had been fine but about ten o'clock a series of cold, pitiless storms began, which lashed the voe with heavy wind and rain. This would not have been intolerable, if it had not been for the long waders without which the deeper waters of the voe could not have been reached; but to stand in heavy rain with waders nearly up to the armpits, and without a short mackintosh, is to turn oneself into a receptacle for collecting fresh water. Desolate hills rose immediately behind, and as each storm came frowning up over the top of them, I retired from the water and crouched behind an old boat on the shore till the fury was past. After some hours of flogging the sea, hooking only seaweed, and dodging the storms, there was no spirit left in me. Blank despair overwhelmed me and I turned to go. My back was to the water, but I had got only a few paces from it when I heard a splash, and looking round, saw where a fish had jumped, the first sign of one seen that day. I went straight to the place and caught a sea trout almost at once and in the few remaining hours of the day landed sixteen pounds' weight of fish with a fly. It may not seem a very heavy basket, but it was something to carry over the moor in addition to heavy waders, and not to be despised as a contrast to the prospect of the morning.

In the autumn and early winter months, Grey spent as much time as possible at Fallodon. This was hardly surprising as he had just accepted to join a government commission which necessitated travelling to the West Indies in the new year. He was already experiencing the pangs of homesickness to come. At Christmas he wrote in *The Fallodon Green Book*, 'I see the winter outlook that is so well known, the pale green fields seen through bare brown trees. I love it all and wish I was going to stay in it till the leaves come.' The early autumn weather had been unusually poor. Grey, the maturing naturalist, was sure it had delayed the summer migrants on their long journey south. He tells us how he saw a summer warbler in the garden at Fallodon on 3 November and a swallow as late as the 15th.

Early in 1897, Grey departed for the West Indies on one of the very few foreign visits made over the course of his lifetime. Chamberlain invited him to join a Royal Commission examining the economic difficulties associated with the local sugar industry. Although advised by his close colleagues not to participate on account of the possibility of compromising his free trade principles, after an interesting meeting at the Colonial Office he decided to accept and take Dorothy along with him; it would be good for her health. The commissioners travelled from island to island gathering material for their report while Dorothy, with her passion for birds and books, spent most of March alone at Layou Park on Dominica. On her return to England she wrote to W. H. Hudson,

> I spent three wonderful weeks quite alone in a hut on the top of a tropical forest mountain, with Zeiss glasses and a lot of birds. I wonder if you have anything in South America at all like the solitaire bird there is there, a thrush with three out-of-tune notes, loud, slow and full of extraordinary feeling. I still feel haunted when I think of them.

Grey corresponded with Dorothy regularly by post and, unsurprisingly, birds featured prominently. He writes to Dorothy from British Guiana:

I used English birds as little pegs in my head on which to arrange and
sort the birds I saw. There were distinct pied flycatchers, very like the
pictures of British ones and behaving in the usual way. There were
cousins of sedge warblers, a wren of sorts for certain and the song
of a lesser whitethroat too hidden to get at.

The lack of a physical relationship in their marriage is suggested
by the following passage in the same letter:

Yesterday I read Richardson's *Pamela* and wondered whether it is
really possible for any two people to have their fill of the extremes
both of passion and a sympathy of interest and thought. Passion is
attractive but there is a love which is larger and stronger and has a
fuller life. Why didn't you see that I read *Pamela* before?

This letter reveals the extent to which Grey managed to compartmentalise his life. Having read *Pamela*, he now seems relieved that
he can more easily justify to himself his double life. If Grey was not
receiving love and sexual fulfilment from another quarter, surely
his relationship with Dorothy would have been under pressure?
She was suffering from a long-term illness, there was no sex and
they were more often than not hundreds of miles apart. The letter
tells us a good deal about their relationship, which was evidently an
immensely close platonic friendship bonded by common interests.
It also implies that Grey was a much tougher, more ruthless individual than that conveyed by the sensitive, romantic nature writer.
This in turn would also help explain how he managed to survive so
long at the top in politics.

Dorothy arrived at Layou on 27 February, having spent a few
weeks in Barbados. The strength of their relationship forged by a
shared delight in nature and books is obvious from this charming
letter written by Dorothy the next day:

I got up here last night at six, having started riding at one. It will
do very well for us. The ride up is perfect but the house is in a lime

grove and one sees no views. I have got a very good woman to do for
me, and a pony and boy. The night noises are splendid and there are
strange whistling birds which will have to be identified. I had a bird
at breakfast which was the size of a sparrow and all black except a
patch of red on its throat. I have brought heaps of books – two men's
loads. My things and servant all came in a boat to within two hours'
walk, and five men arrived carrying loads on their heads and with
flaming cocoa-nut torches in the dark last night. It's a fearful steep
climb up here, 1,000 feet above the sea. I have not explored yet but
there is said to be a very large lake close to. You would be amused at
this house. It is raised up on high legs and shakes a great deal when
you walk, but it is nice and clean and no drawbacks and Eva does
not mind the bad kitchen. I feel more adventurous and independent
now I am in the real wilds. I have summoned green cocoa-nuts and
shall drink nothing but them and tea. They have brought me limes,
bananas, eggs, breadfruit and green-stuff to boil and I have tinned
food and porridge and milk. One just does not want a blanket here
but it is heavenly cool. No insects of any kind and the mornings are
always misty till eleven when the sun comes over it. I long for you to
come and share things with me, the quietness, and the green things
and the fireflies and the blacksmith frog which is hard at work in the
dark. I read Carlyle all morning, Charles Lamb plays and poetry
till four, then tea and walk slowly about, looking at things until it is
quite dark. After dinner, write letters, and then read some letters of
Fitzgerald and go to bed smiling because of the humour in them.

Following the trip, the Royal Commission highlighted the dangerous
position of those islands where sugar was their only interest. Europe
was subsidising its own sugar beet industry by way of export incen-
tives and as a result, West Indian sugar was commanding a smaller
and smaller share of the British market. The report was published
in May and recommended an advance of £600,000 to improve
methods of cultivation and organisation. An Imperial Department
of Agriculture was set up the following year which helped the establishment of new industries, particularly encouraging the fruit trade.

The chairman of the Commission, Sir Henry Norman, recommended retaliatory duties on bounty-aided European sugar, but Grey, ever the free-trader, refused to back him.

The Greys arrived back England in early May and spent most of the spring and early summer at their Hampshire cottage before going north to Fallodon in late July. Having been out of the swim, Grey had to catch up with political developments at Westminster. When not speaking in the House on foreign affairs he would dash off to the Itchen to enjoy the mayfly season. Recovering from her affliction, Dorothy delighted in the quiet and solitude of Hampshire life.

An entry in *The Cottage Book* for 17 May reads:

> There were many wrens to be seen and I watched two who were climbing up trees and going along branches and taking notice of each other all the time. I felt very loving towards them, and when I began to read again I did not like the book, *Keats' Love Letters*; Keats and Fanny Brawn don't compare well with wrens.

This is a good example of Dorothy's prudish character. It was in her nature to prefer the cosy, homey relationship of the wrens to the obsessive, passionate, intense and hysterical letters written by Keats to Fanny.

There was no shadow foreign affairs spokesman as such on the Liberal benches, yet with his past ministerial experience it was not surprising that Grey continued to show a keen interest in all aspects of foreign policy. He was deeply sympathetic towards the oppressed Christians of Armenia and Crete. His speeches encouraged action through the Concert of Europe, demanding that Turkey introduce reforms. Early in the year there had been an uprising in Crete against Ottoman rule with the objective of a union with Greece. This resulted in a brief war between Greece and Turkey. In the peace negotiations during the summer, Grey applauded Lord

Salisbury for using the Concert as an agent for settlement. He also scored a few political points by reminding the Conservatives that it was their past policy of absolute support for the Turks, as a buffer against Russia, that so compromised the Ottoman Christian populations. On his return from the West Indies, Grey wrote to his close friend Munro Ferguson:

> My own opinion hitherto has been that Salisbury could do nothing by standing outside the Concert: and that, miserable as the Concert is, he may do some good inside it, if he insists upon the liberation of Crete from Turkish officials and Turkish administration. If he makes this an essential condition of all he does and brings it off, I really don't see why we should strike attitudes about whether Crete is annexed to Greece or not.

On 15 June 1897, Edward and Dorothy were back at The Cottage, having spent a few days at Littlecote, the home of their close friends the Watneys. Grey wrote in *The Cottage Book*, 'We are here again. Wild roses are fully out: sweet-briar showing freely and the chalk pit is sturdy with elderflower. Very cool weather and no roses out except one W. A. Richardson on The Cottage.' By this time Grey would have been busy on his first book, *Fly Fishing*, published in 1899. He was desperate to put his passion for nature into words and there was surely nowhere more conducive to writing such a book than The Cottage. Seeing the proofs, his friend Herbert Paul commented that the book was too good for a sporting library. Grey responded, 'I am possessed with the feeling that we live in a world, which in spite of much that is distressing, is beautiful beyond expression and to put across some of that feeling was what I most cared to do.' However, foreign affairs would never have been far from his thoughts as he walked out across the Itchen water meadows to check on the 'repulsive red-gaping, ill-tempered cuckoo chick' in the reed warbler's nest. He may well have pondered Kitchener's progress down the

Nile to destroy the Dervishes and avenge Gordon's murder at Khartoum. Also nagging at the back of his mind would have been the worry of German sugar beet flooding the British market, to the detriment of West Indian product. But little would he suspect that events this day in Germany would change his life for ever.

On 6 June, Admiral Tirpitz had arrived in Berlin to take up his recent promotion as State Secretary of the Imperial Navy Office. Within a matter of years this charismatic Prussian, with an unforgettable forked beard and bald, domed head, would become the most influential and effective minister in Germany since Bismarck. Tirpitz was born into a middle-class professional family, joined the Navy as a cadet aged sixteen in 1856 and quickly clawed his way up the ladder. He exhibited many of Jacky Fisher's characteristics. He was ambitious, energetic, aggressive, domineering and obsessive in his dream to build a fleet of German battleships to match the British, but he lacked the English Admiral's charm and sense of fun. Before his promotion to the top job he had been in command of the German cruiser squadron in the Far East, where he had set up a naval base at Tsingtao on the Yellow Sea. Back in Berlin, events were to move quickly. Just over a week later, on 15 June, he met the Kaiser in Potsdam to present a memorandum on the future of the German Navy. Tirpitz had determined to build a fleet of nineteen battleships against England, writing to a colleague, 'For Germany the most dangerous enemy at the present time is England.' The German ships would be well built and designed for operations in the North Sea, with stronger armour plating and less bunkering capacity than previous vessels.

This decision to expand the German Navy set the two most powerful industrial countries in Europe against each other, and would prove a turning point in modern history. Britain had lived in 'splendid isolation' for a century after Trafalgar, protected by the umbrella of the Royal Navy. Now Germany, the most powerful military force in the world, was aspiring to become a great naval power. The surest way of inducing insecurity into the British mentality was by threatening her naval supremacy. Alarm bells began to ring in the British psyche and slowly yet steadily Britain turned towards her two erstwhile enemies, France and Russia. As Winston Churchill was later to write, 'With every rivet that Tirpitz drove into his ships of war, he united British opinion. The hammers that clanged at Kiel and Wilhelmshaven were forging the coalition of nations by which Germany was to be resisted and finally overthrown.' Bismarck had always maintained that Germany should concentrate on being a continental power backed by a powerful army. Because of the Kaiser's fetish to emulate his English cousins and his jealousy of all things British, enormous financial and human resources were deployed on his pet project of building a navy which would otherwise have been allocated to the army. Two additional army corps on the German right wing in August 1914 would in all probability have taken Paris. As it turned out, the High Seas Fleet spent most of the war bottled up in port and did little to break the British economic blockade. Germany then turned to the submarine, which would eventually be responsible for bringing America into the war. The rest is well known.

Norman Stone writes in his *Short History of World War One*: 'The last thing that Germany needed was a problem with Britain and the greatest mistake of the twentieth century was made when Germany built a Navy designed to attack her.' In the decade before the outbreak of war, Grey would be defeated time and again in his quest for an understanding with Germany over naval armaments. Without such an agreement, the best chance for peace vanished. Algernon Cecil writes dramatically in his book, *British Foreign Secretaries 1807–1916*:

'Without a fleet' says a German critic who has made his name, 'Germany could get on with England – with a fleet it was out of the question.' That elementary fact was beyond William's capacity as a statesman to see and beyond Bülow's tact as a courtier to state. Hence flowed a sea of tears upon which all the ships in Europe might have found space to sail.

But this was not the first disastrous diplomatic blunder initiated by the Kaiser. Back in 1890, without the guiding hand of Bismarck on the tiller, he failed to renegotiate the three-year Reinsurance Treaty with Russia. The Russian bear then looked to France for solace, and so began Germany's self-imposed insecurity of encirclement.

During the summer, Kitchener's forces advanced steadily up the Nile and in August the Mahdist garrison at Berber surrendered without resistance. Ever since Grey had made his declaration in the Commons on 28 March 1895 on Anglo-Egyptian claims to the upper waters of the Nile, he had maintained an interest in Egypt and the Sudan. Grey was an advocate of a forward policy on the Nile for purely practical reasons, which brought him into conflict with the new Liberal leader, Harcourt. Grey wrote to Ronald Munro Ferguson,

If we do not push Egypt forward, we leave interests on the Upper Nile open to others; indeed by standing deliberately aloof now, we almost invite others to go in, to our prejudice and to the prejudice of Egypt for whom we are trustee; for while our interest in the matter is important, that of Egypt is vital.

Ominously, while Grey was opening up The Cottage in March 1898 for another season's fishing, Tirpitz pushed his Navy Bill through the Reichstag with a margin of 212 votes to 139. Bearing in mind he had only arrived in Berlin less than a year before, this was a considerable achievement. A grateful and euphoric Kaiser elevated the Admiral to sit in the Prussian Ministry of State. No doubt the German public had been roused by events across the Channel the previous summer. At Queen Victoria's Diamond Jubilee Review, the Royal Navy displayed 165 warships in five lines stretching over thirty miles. In June, Tirpitz formed the German Navy League, an interest group designed to develop popular pressure on the Reichstag to approve the expansion of the Imperial Navy and its related costs. Its membership quickly rose from 78,000 in 1898 to 1.1 million at the outbreak of war.

By the end of the year, Grey had completed his classic book *Fly Fishing*. It would be no exaggeration to place this work alongside Izaak Walton's *Compleat Angler* in terms of technical content; however, the excitement of landing a fish was only half the attraction for Grey. What he really appreciated was the beauty of the associated countryside and its birdlife. Grey's overriding achievement is that he succeeds in communicating this message to the reader through the quality of his writing. In the 1930 edition, Grey added a chapter, *Retrospect*, which concludes evocatively:

> Thus as the angler looks back, he thinks less of individual captures and days than of the scenes in which he fished. The luxuriance of the water meadows, animated by insect, bird and trout life, tender with the green and gay with the blossoms of early spring: the nobleness and volume of the great salmon rivers: the exhilaration of looking at any salmon pool, great or small; the rich brownness of Highland water: the wild openness of the treeless, trackless spaces which he has traversed in an explorer's spirit of adventure to search likely water for sea trout: now on one, now on another of these scenes an angler's mind will dwell as he thinks of fishing. Special days and successes he will no doubt recall, but always with the remembrance and the mind's vision of the scenes and the world in which he fished. For indeed this does seem a separate world, a world of beauty and enjoyment. The time must come to all of us who live long, when memory is more than prospect. An angler who has reached this stage and reviews the pleasure of life will be grateful and glad that he has been an angler, for he will look back upon days radiant with happiness, peaks and peaks of enjoyment that are not less bright because they are lit in memory by the light of a setting sun.

Grey was a brilliant fisherman, his skills honed on the crystal clear chalk stream waters of the Itchen when at Winchester College. In later years April would witness him enjoying the spring salmon fishing on the Cassley. Then came the mayfly at The Cottage and finally in late summer he would go north back to Scotland in search of sea trout and salmon. When the water was low and the weather unfavourable for fishing, there were other compensations. In the summer he wrote to Dorothy from the Highlands,

> The weather has been extraordinarily bad for fishing. But there are other things. Last night I walked up above the lodge and lay down on the top of a little hill out of sight, and listened to the sound of the streams from everywhere. I never felt the great impersonal personality of inanimate nature so before, nor understood so well before why Wordsworth lived in this sort of country and went out so much at night.

Grey's lifelong friend and future Cabinet colleague Sydney Buxton wrote of his dry-fly skills:

> Fisherman, rod, line cast and fly were all in unison. Without apparent effort, the line went out straight as an arrow, as light as thistledown, or the drag would be overcome by the exact amount of slack – it all looked so simple and easy. He fished with a stiffish rod, the better to control the hooked fish in a stream abounding in weed beds. He confined himself mainly to four flies plus the Mayfly. Curiously enough he could not fish with his left hand, but made up with greater dexterity in the right.

When at The Cottage, Grey delighted in cross-country walks and bicycling around the local Hampshire countryside. Dorothy's inactivity, which resulted from her illness, must have been a source of frustration to them both. Grey acquired a trailer for his bicycle and whenever possible took Dorothy along with him. Her health had deteriorated early in the year, which meant she was often alone at

The Cottage. On Sunday 3 July, Grey went on a long bicycle ride with close Northumbrian friend Ella Pease who wrote,

> Sometimes it was hard to leave her lying under the trees and go for a long bicycle ride with Edward, when formerly she had always been keener and stronger than I; but she never minded, she was always absolutely serene. I remember once, when we returned late from a ride in the Test valley, and I was full of the beauties we had seen, she contended that she had had the best time, because she had been watching a beautiful white owl flitting in and out of the woods on the opposite side of the Itchen.

It would be no exaggeration to rank Grey as one of England's most accomplished countrymen. Firstly, he was quintessentially English. He came from one of Northumberland's oldest land-owning families and was educated at Winchester and Balliol. A Member of Parliament, he sat on the board of one of his country's most famous railway companies and later in life played his part in directing the fledgling National Trust. He was a real-tennis champion, worshipped the Romantic poets, was quietly religious, sensitive to the beauty of nature, had a good sense of humour, was reserved, 'straight as a gun barrel' in his dealings with people and had a colourful love life but was always discreet. Above all, he was a well-balanced countryman. He participated in all country sports, foxhunting and shooting as a young man, and then continued to fish into old age when virtually blind. He kept his own wildfowl collection, was a pioneer conservationist and ecologist, and his observations on bird behaviour and migration a century ago were as sophisticated as anything emanating from a modern-day ornithologist. His writing on the countryside is ranked with England's best. In many ways he was the forerunner of Peter Scott, who founded Slimbridge and the Wildfowl and Wetlands Trust. Scott painted whereas Grey wrote, both men putting aside the gun for the binoculars in middle age.

In July, Grey was elected a director of the North Eastern Railway at a very welcome salary of £400 a year. In terms of mileage, gross receipts and balance sheet, the NER ranked amongst Britain's four biggest railway companies. Its geographical spread covered the prosperous industrial area of north-eastern England from the Humber to the Tweed, a district enjoying substantial mineral resources. Grey writes in *Twenty-Five Years*,

> The work was interesting; the conditions under which it was done were exceedingly pleasant and congenial. The full board consisted of twenty members; twice a month they assembled, generally at York, on a Thursday, and remained till after the board meeting on Friday, working in committees on Thursday and spending the evening together.

He was about to experience the world of business for the first time. This would complement his political career and make him an expert in the relatively embryonic field of industrial relations. It was not an easy time for railway labour relations and a workforce of over 30,000 at the NER was lobbying for improved working conditions. Although Grey was an imperialist on matters of foreign policy, he had surprisingly strong ties to the radical wing of the party when it came to domestic social reform. He was proud of the fact that the NER was the first railway company to recognise the trade unions. He wrote with great foresight to a friend who was a director of another railway company,

> I think your directors are wrong in not recognising the Union to the extent of letting the men be represented by the man or men of their choice. The NER always met the officials of the Union. No doubt the Union kept putting forward demands on the NER but the Union was strong, and did what other Unions do, and the trouble would have been made worse between directors and the men, if the NER had not recognised the Union. I suppose the other Lines think they can smash the Union or prevent its being formed in their systems,

but I believe the Unions will form anyhow and that in the long run
you can deal better with organised than unorganised labour.

It was about this time, through a mutual interest in fishing and
Liberal politics, that Grey developed a close friendship with Eddy
Tennant. It was a relationship that would last until Eddy's death in
1920 and in time would blossom to include Tennant's wife, Pamela
Wyndham. The two men probably first became acquainted when
Grey was a junior minister and they were immediately attracted
to each other by a common love of the countryside and country
sports. Eddy Tennant stood unsuccessfully as a Liberal candidate
for Partick in 1892 and Peebles & Selkirk in 1900. He was elected
as Member for Salisbury in 1906 and, with a good push from his
sister, Margot Asquith, was sent to the House of Lords as Baron
Glenconner in 1911. We know from their correspondence that the
Greys were dining with the Tennants in 1893 and in a few years'
time were regularly staying with each other in the country. On 6
November 1896, Grey writes to Eddy thanking him for an invitation to stay in Wiltshire and describes his recent fishing holiday in
the Shetlands: 'The Arctic and Richardson's Skuas had just finished
their breeding season and were common. Black Guillemots which
I had not seen before were very common and changed from their
black to grey plumage during my stay.' For his part, Grey asks Eddy
to stay at The Cottage to fish on 20 July 1897, suggesting his luggage
is forwarded to Itchen Abbas by train and that they bicycle across
country from Salisbury, 'We would then bicycle a really fine road
via wild downs. It is about twenty-five miles but we can break the
journey a bit at Stockbridge which is about halfway'.

On 2 September, Kitchener's Anglo-Egyptian army defeated
60,000 Dervishes led by the Khalifa at Omdurman, thus avenging

the massacre of Gordon's garrison some ten years earlier. He then proceeded to Fashoda on the Upper Nile, where it had been known for some time that a French expedition was heading across the continent from the west coast. When he arrived on 19 September, Kitchener found Captain Marchand and a handful of marines had already run up the French flag. The French had been warned by the Grey Declaration of 1895 that such an incursion would be viewed as an unfriendly act by England. Public opinion in Britain grew increasingly bellicose and the two countries came close to war. As the drama unfolded, Grey found himself back in the public eye; he reluctantly took down his fishing rods and came south.

Grey had supported the Kitchener expedition, as he felt inaction would create a vacuum on the Upper Nile which would be filled by other European powers. When the French expedition led by Marchand arrived at Fashoda, Grey and his fellow Liberal Imperialists gave the government stout support in taking a hard line. On 27 October, he stated: 'Egypt is the Nile and the Nile is Egypt.' Even Rosebery came out of hiding to lend Kitchener his support. On 12 October at a dinner held by the Surrey Agricultural Association, the former Prime Minister let rip:

> If the nations of the world are under the impression that the ancient spirit of Great Britain is dead, or that her resources are weakened or her population less determined than ever it was to maintain the rights and honour of its flag, they make a mistake that can only end in disastrous conflagration.

This punchy, patriotic performance, which perfectly captured the public mood following the Jubilee, no doubt raised Grey's hopes that the great man might one day return to leadership contention. The Liberal Party was split over the Fashoda issue, with its senior members, Harcourt and Morley, isolated in the 'Little Englander' camp. On 10 October, Harcourt wrote to Morley: 'As to official Liberalism its mouth is closed by the estoppel of Grey's speech.'

At the Mansion House on 4 November, a triumphant Salisbury

announced that the French had backed down. Rosebery spoke at
the same event and completely upstaged Harcourt. Coming on top
of unauthorised speeches from other members of the Imperialist
wing of the party, this was the last straw. On 14 December, Harcourt
resigned the leadership. On 16 December he was most magnanimous when he wrote to Grey:

> For you, my dear Edward, I have always felt the strongest attraction
> derived not only from hereditary attachment, but from esteem of
> your character and admiration of your ability. I have had my full
> share of the nineteenth century and the twentieth belongs to you.
> You have already established for yourself a first place in the regard
> and respect of the House of Commons – the only solid foundation
> of a public career.

Harcourt went even further when writing to Fowler: 'I have
certainly done all I can to bring Grey forward, feeling that he is the
young hope of the party.' If some thought Grey should put himself
forward for the leadership, Grey himself certainly did not. Tiring
of waiting for Rosebery to show his hand, he wrote to Haldane in
the middle of December,

> Far and away the best thing would be for Asquith to give up the
> Bar and throw himself into this position, and in the work of it, his
> qualities and powers would develop, and by the next Election he
> would have gained an influence far greater than he has ever yet had.

The Greys spent Christmas alone at Fallodon with their squirrels,
which had the habit of entering through the open library windows
to take nuts from Grey's desk. On 21 December he wrote in his diary,

> A very sad thing has happened. Our tame squirrel never came to
> be fed last Saturday and we felt anxious about it: the next day it

never came and we felt sure something was wrong and on Monday we found its mangled body on the garden path not too far from the window. We think it has been killed by the others. It had been a daily pleasure for us for about two years and had become so tame that it would come right in to us to take nuts and the last time I saw it sat on my knee and ate its nuts one after the other. It was also very clever at opening the box in which we put nuts for it and went freely about the room. The male squirrel used to be kept away by this one but he has known his way in for a long time and comes occasionally now: but he is a suspicious wild fellow and hates us and is not clever with the box, like our dear dead one, though he can open it.

The squirrels were, of course, red squirrels as the rogue grey squirrels had yet to reach Northumberland from the south. The photographs taken in Grey's old age by Seton Gordon, with robin and mandarin duck perched casually on his head, demonstrate Grey's remarkable ability to tame wild creatures. They also tell us much about his calm, patient and reassuring personality, qualities which would prove such an asset later in his career when he was Foreign Secretary.

The Boer War

Early in the new year, the political temperature in South Africa was rising fast. The discovery of gold in the Transvaal meant that the balance of power was shifting to the Boers, with the result that Britain became increasingly determined to protect her local supremacy. Across the globe, Britain was finding herself uncomfortably isolated in a world where her aggressive attitude to the Boers would soon generate enormous hostility. A surprising sense of insecurity was creeping into the British mentality, shortly to manifest itself in Colonial Secretary Joe Chamberlain's approach to Germany. Russia was sabre-rattling in the Far East. The Manchu Empire in China was in a state of decay. Russia, with her acquisition of Port Arthur in the north, now threatened Britain's substantial trade interests in the centre and south of the region. Chamberlain argued that British sea power alone could not halt Russian expansionism in the Far East. An ally was needed and Germany seemed to fit the bill, for she could of course also exert pressure on the Russian frontier in Europe. Grey disapproved of the Colonial Secretary's involvement in foreign affairs and took the opposite view of a German alliance. Experience had taught him to distrust German diplomacy. He was keen to settle outstanding differences with France and felt that a rapprochement with Germany would upset the French, who still hankered after the return of Alsace-Lorraine.

Sir Alfred Milner was a passionate imperialist who had been sent out to South Africa as High Commissioner in 1897 to sort out the mess following the Jameson Raid. He was a great advocate of Rosebery's new doctrine of Liberal Imperialism embracing 'state action at home and colonial strength abroad'. It would be the High Commissioner's job to promote 'imperial unity' and 'consolidate the Empire' in South Africa. Like Grey, Milner had been an undergraduate under the tutelage of the charismatic Dr Jowett at Balliol. Unlike Grey, Milner had graduated with honours, before going on to build a reputation as a sound and reliable civil servant. He began his career as private secretary to George Goschen, the Conservative Chancellor of the Exchequer. He then broadened his horizons by moving to Cairo as financial secretary to Lord Cromer, where he successfully sorted out the mismanaged finances of the Khedive, nominal ruler of Egypt. On his return home he was appointed Chairman of the Inland Revenue Board, where he controversially introduced death duties as a lucrative component in Sir William Harcourt's 1895 Budget.

By the end of March 1899, Milner had collected 21,000 signatures from the disenfranchised British miners, the Uitlanders, calling on the British government to intervene on their behalf. When gold had been discovered on the Rand a decade or so earlier, President Kruger, wanting to preserve the Boer character of the Transvaal amongst the influx of largely British miners, raised the franchise requirement for these recent immigrants from five years' residence to fourteen. The debacle of the Jameson Raid, coupled with the embarrassing cover-up at the subsequent enquiry which exonerated the Colonial Secretary, Chamberlain, from any blame, left a nasty taste of suspicion and distrust surrounding Britain, both internationally and in South Africa. The Raid had a number of important consequences in South Africa. It united the volk behind the Transvaal government and raised the status of a tired, old President to that of hero. Perhaps more importantly Jameson rallied the volk outside the Transvaal, particularly in the Orange Free State, culminating in a military pact signed in 1897. This had the potential to add 15,000 burghers to the Transvaal army of 25,000. President Kruger then took the decision to re-equip his army, purchasing 37,000 Mauser magazine rifles from Germany and the latest artillery pieces from Le Creusot in France.

Milner was an intellectual and brilliant administrator but also a hardliner. Cecil Rhodes's attempt to solve the Transvaal problem by way of the Raid had failed, as had the imperial government's forward policy some years earlier, resulting in defeat at Majuba in the First Boer War. Milner calculated he needed to force a showdown with Kruger; either the Boers would agree to introduce political reforms or it would come to war. He was convinced the latter was the most likely option. As far as reforms were concerned, Milner was a match for Kruger as a tenacious and unyielding negotiator. If war materialised, Milner would need the support not only of the Cape loyalists, but also that of Chamberlain, the Colonial Office and most importantly, British public opinion. As the weeks passed Milner became more hawkish. He was determined to provoke a war and annex the Transvaal for the Empire. By contrast, Chamberlain wished to achieve a settlement over the franchise question and negotiate a new convention guaranteeing the Transvaal's internal independence. Milner determined to turn the screw on Kruger. He would be unreasonable in his political demands and then provoke the Boers by demanding troop reinforcements from Britain. At the Bloemfontein Conference at the end of May, Milner rejected Kruger's concessions. The Boers had agreed to halve the residence qualification for the Uitlanders from fourteen to seven years. The gap was small but Milner had upped the stakes. Troop reinforcements followed and in October Kruger issued an ultimatum calling for their removal. Her Majesty's Government failed to reply within the stated forty-eight hours and the Boers invaded Natal. Milner had delivered his war together with favourable public opinion.

At first glance it is difficult to understand why Grey stood by the Conservative government over one of the blackest periods in British history and in the process was such an ardent supporter of

Milner. Grey was a sensitive man who always professed to hate war. He wrote to his friend Katherine Lyttelton in October 1899,

> I am depressed about this war: I admit the necessity of it and that it must be carried through but it has no business to be popular and the cry of 'Revenge Majuba' dishonours us and destroys our reputation for good faith. I should like to break the heads of all music halls first and then go out and teach the Boers gravely and sternly the things they do not know.

At the end of the day, Grey believed in equal rights for Boers and British; he wanted self-government for South Africa. A few years later he fully realised he had misjudged Milner – 'the most ideological of pro-consuls' – and was writing to Helen Munro Ferguson:

> I don't think I can talk about the colonies with Milner. He always says such rasping things, and he cannot keep his attacks upon the Government's South African policy of self-government out of his speeches, a policy he says that the people of England should have spat out of their mouths.

It is not certain how well Grey knew Milner. Although they were both Balliol men, Milner had gone down from Oxford some time before Grey arrived. Milner does, however, claim to have been close to Asquith and Haldane, and was also a great supporter of Rosebery, all three being Grey's closest political allies.

Closer inspection reveals that Grey's family had strong imperial ties with Africa. His cousin, Lord Grey, had taken over as chairman of the Chartered Company in 1896 when Rhodes was forced to resign. Grey's brother George had just returned from Bulawayo, where he was central to a forward policy. Dorothy wrote to their friend Herbert Paul in November 1899, 'George seems to have been annexing territory or making spheres of influence of some sort. I am glad he should enjoy himself but I daresay there will be a horrid little war about it someday.' Given his association with the African continent coupled with the Boers' intransigence, it is perhaps not surprising that in these early days Grey took such a strong line in seeing Kruger as the offending party. He wrote to Ronald Munro Ferguson on 1 October:

> Kruger has put himself altogether in the wrong by refusing the five-year franchise proposal made to him on 8 September by the Government. I suppose he will have another chance this week of accepting something moderate, and if he still refuses we must either enforce our demands or drop them. We cannot drop them. And the demands are admitted even by Morley to be reasonable. In July I was afraid we might be hurried into war before we believed war to be inevitable; since then the situation has changed and I really don't see what more the Government can do to avoid war, if Kruger persists in refusing the five-year franchise. I fear the younger Boers think they can beat us and if so they won't give way.

In reality, it was Milner who would prove the more dogmatic and Machiavellian. Grey's strong imperialist views at this juncture would lead his more radical Cabinet colleagues to mistrust his dealings with Germany a decade later.

While the drama was unfolding in South Africa, Dorothy fell ill again. She wrote to Mildred Buxton in March from Fallodon,

> I am much better thanks. The air made me feel different at once, and the weather has been gorgeous ever since I came. I have driven a slow pony up to the moors to hear the curlews making their lovely spring cry, which ought to cure anyone, it is so lovely. I also drive down to the sea and sit in the sun. I am a little weak still, of course.

In April she experienced a bad attack of flu on top of her heart disease. This resulted in a serious collapse and for a few hours she was thought to be dying. Luckily she soon regained her health and opened up the Hampshire cottage on 27 April. Apart from a week at Littlecote with the Watneys in early June, Dorothy spent the rest of the summer on the Itchen. So successful was her recovery that she and Edward took to sleeping out at night. In *The Cottage Book* she writes,

> We have taken to sleeping out at last, having always meant to and never bringing it off. I wake up a nice lot and enjoy my night. When a trout jumps and splashes flat it sets all the sedge birds noising. A heron has croaked both nights and coots sounds are very various. I got the little breeze that says 'the dawn – the dawn' and died away.

Happiness in life is so dependent on contrast and Grey had it in abundance with London politics, the Hampshire cottage, Fallodon and fishing in the Highlands. His broad range of interests had been further extended by his recent directorship of the North Eastern Railway. In March he wrote to Dorothy from the Station Hotel in York where he was attending a board meeting,

> I have had a walk alone in a fine March wind and sun up the Ouse and watched the ripples and wondered whether I could have put a salmon fly as far as the opposite bank, and at last I came to quite open country, larger than Battersea Park, with no people, and felt as if having seen the wide fields and free sky I had looked God in the face and been refreshed, and I thought I would write and tell you.

Like his hero, William Wordsworth, Grey saw God through the beauty of nature; unlike his favourite poet, salmon fishing was never far from his thoughts. It was in the Itchen valley under the tutelage of Dorothy that Grey became an accomplished ornithologist and developed a deep love of the British countryside. By the turn of the century he was beginning to display the knowledge that would make him celebrated as author of *The Charm of Birds* a generation later.

The Liberal Party was hopelessly split over South Africa. Radicals such as Harcourt, Morley and Lloyd George were stigmatised as 'Pro-Boer' and 'Little Englanders'. In January 1898, the steady, clever and unglamorous Scot, Henry Campbell-Bannerman, had become the fourth leader of the Liberal Party in five years. Henry Campbell came from an affluent commercial background and enjoyed a gilt-edged education in languages and classics at Glasgow University and Trinity College, Cambridge. He was elected to the Commons as the Member for Stirling in 1868 after a decade of business experience, and three years later received a substantial inheritance from his uncle, Henry Bannerman. In 1885 he finally entered the Cabinet as Secretary of State for War. He had no ambition to accept the leadership. His health was poor and his wife's even worse. He did so out of a sense of duty. Even though he was against the South African war, he led from the centre and did a remarkable job keeping the party together over these troubled times. When elected, it was thought he would provide the space needed for the Liberals to convalesce and recover. This is exactly what he achieved, and more. The *Manchester Guardian* reported: 'Here was an easy-going creature that would keep the nest warm for a bird of a more brilliant plumage to be welcomed back to its natural home in good time.' The newspaper was of course referring to Lord Rosebery, who still enjoyed a massive following across the country. Although weak in opposition, Campbell-Bannerman would prove an adroit and successful Prime Minister.

The war began disastrously for Britain. The towns of Ladysmith, Kimberly and Mafeking were besieged in the autumn. On 15 December, a force under General Sir Redvers Buller was defeated at Colenso with the loss of 1,100 killed while endeavouring to relieve Ladysmith. The next few days became known in England as 'Black Week' and witnessed British defeats at Stormberg and Magersfontein. The mobile Boer infantry equipped with the latest magazine rifles were proving more than a match for the complacent British.

It was against this gloomy background that Chamberlain made a speech in Leicester on 30 November proposing an Anglo-German Alliance. He declared that, 'the most natural alliance is between Britain and the German Empire'; he then went even further, suggesting, 'a new Triple Alliance between the Teutonic race and the two great transatlantic branches of the Anglo-Saxon race would become a potent influence on the future of the world'. The offer of friendship was met with a deafening silence in Berlin. When Chancellor Bülow rose to speak in the Reichstag on 11 December, there was no mention of an understanding with Britain – only of Tirpitz's Second Navy Bill. Bülow told his audience: 'Without power, without a strong army and a strong navy, there can be no welfare for us: in the coming century the German nation will be either the hammer or the anvil.' Germany danced around Chamberlain's proposal precisely because the Kaiser was desperate to see the Navy Bill pushed through the Reichstag. Until this was achieved, Britain had to be presented as a threat to German interests.

The Germans were never really serious about an alliance and they miscalculated the strength of Britain's desire for such an arrangement. As Grey had discovered a few years earlier, their diplomacy was clumsy and heavy-handed. Their strategy was to frustrate, delay and then endeavour to extract a higher price, usually in the form of more substantial colonial concessions, at a later date. The Germans always seemed to demand too much for their cooperation, seeking to use rather than to assist potential allies. Chamberlain decided his alliance should be placed in cold storage. Although Lord Salisbury was Prime Minister, he kept the foreign policy brief for himself; on account of his age, however, he tolerated the Colonial Secretary's 'overlap' into foreign affairs. The German diplomatic élite led by Bülow and Holstein were suspicious of Salisbury, who had always been a believer that Britain's security

lay in isolation. More significantly, the Germans failed to understand or appreciate the British system of parliamentary democracy.
They suspected that Parliament would throw out an alliance and,
even if proved incorrect, they were convinced any future government would reverse the policies of its predecessor.

Grey was deeply sceptical about an alliance with the Germans.
He understood all too well that an alliance with Germany would
incur the wrath of France, thereby making the peaceful resolution
of colonial disputes, particularly on the Nile, impossible. Grey
especially disapproved of the Colonial Secretary meddling in the
Foreign Secretary's brief, writing to Haldane on 4 December 1899:

> Joe's speech about the German alliance (unless it was expressly
> dictated by the German Emperor, which I can't believe) was disas-
> trous. I never read anything which struck me as being more of a
> mess. He really must be kept out of foreign politics or he will make
> everything impossible, even friendship with America.

On the same day he wrote to Ronald Munro Ferguson, 'Joe seems to
have made a most extraordinary speech about a German alliance:
unless what he says has been sanctioned by the German Emperor,
it seems to me most unwise to speak as he has done, in face of the
fact that German public opinion is all against us.'

During the period of the South African War, Grey the politician came of age. He took a tough stance on the war, becoming
leader of those Liberals who backed the government's position. By
making a series of speeches in favour of the war both inside and
outside Parliament, he raised his public profile to such an extent as
to make himself indispensable to the Liberal leadership. In doing so
he displayed a surprising degree of arrogance and disloyalty, which
would incur the ire of Campbell-Bannerman, then desperately
trying to keep a hopelessly divided party together. All the while Grey

unashamedly and openly canvassed for the return of Rosebery to lead the Liberal Party. He wrote to Rosebery on 26 July 1900,

> If you were to make the great sacrifice of coming out as leader of the party, with Asquith as leader of the House of Commons, I think a strong and successful Opposition would be built up. All I need say for the moment is that if you take the lead I shall recognise an obligation to make more sacrifices for politics than I have done since you retired.

These obstinate personal characteristics would surface again in the future in the guise of resignation threats when Grey, in his role as Foreign Secretary, had to defend his policies against the radical wing of the party.

For the first time in his career, Grey actually seemed to be enjoying the cut and thrust of political life. Although Britain was deeply shocked by the death of Queen Victoria in January 1901 – she had been on the throne for sixty-three years – the accession of Edward VII to the throne had given the nation renewed confidence and hope for a better future. The war in South Africa seemed to be drawing to a close and even the Kaiser was popular in Britain following his unusually dignified behaviour at his grandmother's funeral. Contrary to the advice of his ministers, the Kaiser rushed to Victoria's deathbed and, showing unusual sensitivity and genuine sorrow, won his English relatives' affection. Grey was now taking more of a leading role at Westminster, writing on 7 July 1901 to Louise Creighton, 'Politics have suddenly become very interesting to me because I think I may be in the beginning of new things – even fishing has gone to the wall.' Although Grey voted with the government over entry into the war, he did not hold back from criticising the Unionists for their provocative diplomacy during the lead-up to the crisis, their failure to clear the nation's name after the Jameson Raid, and the military's incompetence during the initial months of hostilities. Haldane and Fowler supported Grey in his endeavours, yet his two shining lights for the future, Asquith and Rosebery, were a constant source of disappointment. Asquith had an annoying tendency to keep his head down, while Rosebery demonstrated little enthusiasm for the leadership.

In the summer of 1900, events had taken a turn for the better in South Africa. Mafeking and Ladysmith were relieved and the Boer capital occupied. The government decided to call an opportunistic election. During the 'Khaki Election', the Liberals surprisingly held their own at the polls, yet Rosebery remained frustratingly detached from the fray. It was all wearing a bit thin for his long-suffering followers. Grey wasn't going to hold his breath, writing to Munro Ferguson on 18 October:

> I think my word to R. will be that if he doesn't come out into the open in the next two years his chance will be gone anyhow, and that he may at any time get an ultimatum from some of us that we are not going on any more without him.

Rosebery was still in the same mode the following summer, when he famously announced to a City audience, 'I must plough my furrow alone.'

Grey and his fellow Liberal Imperialists did, however, continue to wait patiently for the genius of Rosebery to provide the impetus for new ideas. They were beginning to despair, when, on 16 December 1901, his Lordship suddenly descended from his lofty tower. Amidst a sounding of trumpets from the national press, Rosebery spoke to an audience of 4,000 in a snow-covered railway shed at Chesterfield. He was flanked on the platform by Grey, Asquith and Fowler. The whole country awaited his deliberations in a fever pitch of excitement. Rosebery's private secretary, Edward Hamilton, wrote in late November: 'I doubt if the prospect of any speech has ever created more excitement. It is a striking testimony to the immense interest taken in the man. There is no one else on whom people hang in

the same way.' A cynical Campbell-Bannerman was not so generous, writing to his colleague James Bryce, 'Outside Potentate says
he must save the country – urgent and critical – hang the plough;
can no longer stand aside; will in six weeks be ready to utter the
words that will save us from ruin. Takes some time, naturally to
think what will be most popular.' Campbell-Bannerman had a
well-developed sense of humour and much enjoyed applying
nicknames to his colleagues. Grey and Haldane were seen as the
main mischief-makers and were referred to as 'Master Grey' and
'Master Haldane'.

For once, Rosebery did not disappoint his many supporters. He
delivered two hours of his celebrated oratory, leaving many spell-
bound or even in tears. The speech called for 'a clean slate' of new
policies, particularly in connection with Ireland, and advocated a
programme of 'national efficiency', promoting commerce together
with reform of the armed forces. Grey, displaying disloyalty and
insolence in equal measure, wrote to Campbell-Bannerman stating that the speech had forced him to follow Rosebery as leader.
Rosebery also attacked the government for demanding unconditional surrender from the Boers. He blamed the absence of a
negotiated settlement on the rigidity of Milner and called for
representatives of both sides to meet at 'a wayside inn' to reach an
agreement. The country was sick of war and his plea created the
climate for the peace negotiations six months later. Interestingly,
at this stage Grey differed from Rosebery with regard to his views
on Milner. Many people were demanding Milner's recall, yet in
Grey's eyes he could do no wrong; he wanted Milner to remain
in South Africa as an administrator. It is odd that Grey gave the
speech his whole-hearted assent, as Rosebery was also demanding
a break from the Irish alliance. Grey was an ardent 'Home Ruler'
and consequently, within a couple of years their political separation
would be complete.

The euphoria of the Liberal Imperialists was short-lived.
Chesterfield proved a false dawn. On 28 January 1902, Grey wrote
to Munro Ferguson, 'Things seem pretty quiet. I hear nothing from

R. and what I hear of him is rather tiresome and petty.' Rosebery retreated back into his shell, leaving the Liberal Party more divided than ever. Grey became a Vice-President of the newly formed Liberal League, created to promote a Rosebery leadership, but the great man never came forward to grasp his prize. Thankfully, when peace came in May 1902, the wounds in the Liberal Party quickly began to heal. Not before time did this talented young group of politicians begin to focus their attack on the government. Grey had earned his spurs on the national stage, but not without making errors of judgement along the way. He had misjudged the two great Imperialists, Rosebery and Milner, but, more significantly for the future, he had also underestimated the tenacity and subtlety of Campbell-Bannerman.

In March, Balfour introduced his controversial Education Bill abolishing the multitude of old school boards and granting responsibility for education throughout the country to local government. The Bill alienated many Nonconformist Unionists who saw it as a violation of the rights of parents to educate their children in their own faith. As well as splitting the Unionist party, the Bill had the long-overdue and welcome effect of uniting the opposition; most Nonconformists voted Liberal. The Liberal leadership came out in force against the Bill – which gave Rosebery's doctrine of 'efficiency' a hollow ring, as the aim of the legislation was to rationalise the existing outdated system. Interestingly, two senior Liberals, Haldane and Munro Ferguson, both close friends of Grey, supported Balfour's reforms. No doubt under their influence, Grey approved of the core reform but spoke in favour of Nonconformist grievances for party political reasons.

Grey's energised commitment to his political career meant that time at The Cottage was curtailed in the summer of 1901. On 7 July he writes in *The Cottage Book*, 'my time has sadly been broken by politics'; on 29 December, Dorothy writes to her friend Miss Soulsby,

'You see Edward has lately taken to politics and things have been raspingly difficult to manage.' The Cottage was not opened up until the end of April. The Greys went north in March for the spring salmon fishing on the Novar estate, the home of Ronald Munro Ferguson, Dorothy writing to Captain Barton, 'We are having a wildly expensive time up here – a £400 salmon river shared with Mr Watney. London and the House of Commons got unbearable.' It was a great success, so much so that he returned the following year, writing to Dorothy,

> I feel Scotch hills in every muscle already. The Alness comes out of a most wild mountain loch – a long one amongst mountains. I began to fish where it leaves the lake and as I put up my rod there came from the birch trees opposite a well-known and much loved voice, or rather two voices known to belong to one thing. Nothing – except your whistle – could have so surprised me with tenderness. It was a wood wren; both song and plaintive notes; so strange in far north mountains.

The fact that Grey could distinguish the two distinct songs of the wood warbler demonstrates that by the turn of the century he had become an accomplished ornithologist. Grey still, however, deferred to Dorothy, writing,

> I hardly dare write anything about birds; I am so overshadowed by Dorothy. I went with her on Tuesday to be shown the stone curlew's eggs – we spied and stalked and crept and saw a stone curlew standing by a lonely whin bush on the down like a sentinel. As we got nearer, it trotted off with the step of a ghost in the evening light, passed the nest and disappeared.

In the summer of 1901, when not fishing, Grey spent some of his limited time at The Cottage, bird nesting. He writes on 5 June,

> A spotted flycatcher is sitting over my dressing room window; it flies off when it hears the window open underneath it and then comes

hovering in the air to see what the noise was: in a walk up wren path we found a blackcap, a dunnock, a bullfinch, a sedge and a cock wren nest, very large and half lichen, half moss with one egg in it, which we took to be a cuckoo's.

As usual, Dorothy left for Fallodon in the middle of July. Grey made one further visit to the Itchen on 14 August, when he wrote a moving letter to Dorothy demonstrating his passion for The Cottage:

> It's one o'clock and I have just got here and I feel as if my heart was too full and might burst; the place is so sacred. I move about it in the most touching way. I feel as if I must keep coming in every half an hour to write to you. I have been on the bridge and eaten my figs on it and thrown the stalks into the river. I can hardly breathe for the sacredness of the place. It is very strange that you aren't here; stranger than I thought but I suppose it wouldn't be so strange to you as I am so often away. What wonderful days you must have here without me!

In 1902, the Greys let Fallodon to supplement Edward's small parliamentary income and as a result they had the compensation of spending more time at The Cottage. They travelled north the second week of August to fish in Scotland, not returning until late in October. Their departure date must have been determined by the rescheduling of the King's coronation on 6 August. It had previously been set for 26 June, but the King had developed acute appendicitis, with the result that an abscess burst in his intestine. However much they disliked formality, one must assume that the Greys attended the 1,000-year-old ritual, as Edward had been made a Privy Councillor in the King's coronation honours list.

Grey was at The Cottage the day the Boer War ended and wrote in *The Cottage Book*,

> About nine o'clock in the evening we heard the Cathedral bells faintly in the distance, then presently a small cheer in Itchen Abbas,

then the Itchen Abbas bells began and soon afterwards the Avington bells: there were big guns in the direction of Portsmouth and it is clear that some excitement is about. We suppose it to be news of peace.

A Government in Waiting

These three years were characterised by a series of increasingly significant by-election victories which suggested the Liberals would soon be back in power with Grey playing a leading role. He continued to articulate his Party's foreign policy both inside and outside the House of Commons, which was to prove a delicate task. In the summer of 1905, Russia was militarily humiliated by Japan over a war that had grown out of rival imperial ambitions in Korea and Manchuria and which was waged thousands of miles away from St Petersburg. At home she was further debilitated by internal revolution. Germany was determined to take advantage of Russian weakness and to reassert her authority in Europe. Grey believed that it was now time for Britain to view Russia as a friend in Europe rather than as an antagonist in the Far East. Over in the west, France needed an even more delicate touch. She was to feel increasingly insecure over Germany's aggressive diplomacy and began to look to her new Entente partner across the Channel for reassurance. It was during this period that Grey became convinced that Germany represented the main threat to European peace, but the last thing he wanted was for Britain to antagonise her. This was difficult in itself as Germany's growing commercial and industrial might led her to crave a fleet to match Britain's and construction was moving forward apace. When Berlin decided to threaten French dominance in Morocco by despatching the Kaiser to Tangier, Grey persuaded himself that the full weight of British diplomacy should be thrown behind the French, thereby strengthening the Entente.

These last years of opposition were amongst the happiest of Grey's life. His political career was not all-consuming and although the unofficial Liberal spokesman for foreign affairs in the Commons, Grey had significant time for other activities. He thoroughly enjoyed his railway work and still found the space for his leisure interests. He had developed an intense enthusiasm for spring salmon fishing following his visits to the Alness. In April 1903 he rented Rosehall, the lowest beat on the Cassley, a spate river that rises in the region of Ben More in Sutherland and then runs into the head of the Kyle of Sutherland, not far from Bonar Bridge. With the exception of 1906–7, he was to fish Rosehall, with his brother Charlie, every year until 1926.

On occasions the Greys would lend W. H. Hudson The Cottage, which he would use as a base for both working on his books and exploring the local countryside. Hudson had just completed his bestseller, *Hampshire Days*, which he dedicated to his friends 'Sir Edward and Lady Grey, Northumbrians with Hampshire written in their hearts'.

The Greys came south at the beginning of May to open up The Cottage, Dorothy writing on 2 May, 'It is wonderful to come here in full spring straight from Rosehall where no spring was. It is like sinking down into a delicious pool.' 1903 was a season of mixed fortunes at The Cottage. The spring and early summer weather was cold and wet; it was a record year for rainfall and the Itchen flowed full and strong. A great blizzard in April wreaked havoc with the garden, killing the iris flowers and the lilac. The chestnuts were left frostbitten and the hawthorn flower was scanty. Rats living in the cottage roof destroyed many garden nests, and the stone curlew and whinchat did not return to the surrounding downland. On the positive side, Grey acquired a new bicycle and trailer and towed a weak Dorothy around miles of the local countryside. On leaving The Cottage at the end of July, Grey wrote in *The Cottage Book*: 'The trailer has been a great thing to us this year: we have seen many miles and wide stretches of country together, light green and dark green and under the summer sun.' As Fallodon was let for another year, they returned to The Cottage for a warm and sunny autumn and set about redesigning their garden. New rose beds were laid out in November, chalk flints removed and loamy soil bought in from afar. Even their beloved chalk pit was embellished with lilac, honeysuckle and pink may trees.

On 18 July the Greys went to Wilsford, near Salisbury, to spend the weekend with Edward and Pamela Tennant. To Pamela and all those who visited, Wilsford was a paradise. The mock Jacobean manor was built of local stone and knapped flint and designed by Detmar Blow, reflecting Pamela's taste for the William Morris Arts and Crafts Movement. Surrounded by idyllic gardens and the cool water meadows of the river Avon, the house was located just below the wild open grasslands of Salisbury Plain. Pamela was a disciple of John Ruskin. She was a hugely rich romantic dreamer who, when not entertaining in London, loved to play the simple life in her beloved Wiltshire countryside. There was nothing she adored more than to roam in the moonlight amongst the pollarded willows of the Avon valley to catch a glimpse of a 'white owl', or to traverse the chalk downlands in a gypsy caravan encompassed by the strange wailing calls of 'the thick-kneed bustard'. Pamela Tennant was one of the three Wyndham sisters, granddaughters of Lord Leaconfield and immortalised in John Singer Sargent's portrait 'The Three Graces'. Her sister-in-law Margot married the then Liberal Home Secretary Herbert Asquith in 1894.

Pamela was an aristocrat, a pampered society beauty with a liking for poets and artists. She was a member of The Souls, an élite fun-loving, aristocratic group with a passion for art and literature. Arthur James Balfour was their 'high priest' and they flourished in Britain from the 1880s until the outbreak of war, when many of the younger generation were killed. In addition she had politics in her blood; her brother, George Wyndham, had been the Conservative Chief Secretary for Ireland. Her marriage to Edward Tennant was one of convenience, the Tennant family having made a vast fortune from chemical dyes in Glasgow. At the time of her marriage, Pamela was in love with Harry Cust, a highly intelligent society figure who never really fulfilled his potential. After being Captain of the Oppidans at Eton and a scholar at Trinity College, Cambridge, he was a member of The Souls, one-time editor of the *Pall Mall Gazette* and a Liberal MP. Cust was forced to marry another woman whom he had supposedly made pregnant. This broke Pamela's heart, so she decided to marry for money. Not unexpectedly, her marriage to Eddy Tennant was an unhappy union and, being a passionate woman, she took a number of lovers. Cust is perhaps best remembered as being the father of Lady Diana Cooper through his lover, the Duchess of Rutland.

There is a strong likelihood that Grey was in the relatively early stages of a deep and long-lasting love affair with Pamela at this time. In her book *Strangers*, Pamela's granddaughter, the author Emma Tennant, tells how her uncle, Colin Glenconner, always said that most of Pamela's children were by men other than her husband. Simon Blow, Pamela's great-grandson, writes in his book *Broken Blood*,

> Grey was at first a good friend of Eddy's but Pamela found him more sympathetic. He had a passion for birds, could talk about books and was generally Eddy's intellectual superior. A relationship started between them, but whether it became physical or remained purely spiritual, has never been definitely known. No love letters survive, though strong suggestions have been made that it was more than platonic.

Grey had given Pamela's third child, Christopher, who was born in 1899, his name and consented to become a godfather, yet it is more likely that David, Pamela's fourth child, born in 1902, was fathered by Grey. As we have seen, Grey and Eddy Tennant became very close friends in the 1890s so perhaps one can explain why Pamela and Eddy decided to give Christopher a second Christian name of 'Grey'. After all, Christopher didn't look like Grey and David's second Christian name was equally unusual – 'Pax', following the peace treaty signed with the Boers at the end of the war. Nicholas Courtney writes in his recent biography of Colin Tennant, Christopher's son and the celebrated proprietor of the island of Mustique, 'Colin always maintained, but with no proof, that Grey was the father of his uncles, David and Stephen, but not of his own father, Christopher.' Again, through close examination of the dates in the visitors' book from Wilsford, Colin was certain that his biological grandfather was Ivor Guest, cousin of Winston Churchill who became 1st Viscount Wimborne. With his dark, masculine good looks, thin lips and strong nose, David, on the other hand, had certainly developed a striking resemblance to Grey. In his biography of David Tennant, Michael Luke writes,

> Grey might well have been David's true father. David himself felt he had detected certain clues to support this possibility, one which did not displease the dark romantic in his nature. However that might be, the two Edwards and Pamela formed an amicable *ménage à trois* embracing Pamela's five children during the last years of Glenconner's life.

It would have been natural for Grey to crave a physical relationship with another woman, as his previous relationship, with Florence Slee, had been over for a number of years. He adored his wife Dorothy, with whom he shared many common interests, yet in Pamela he found another soulmate who could also satisfy his physical desires. Grey spent much time in London while Dorothy remained in the country. Pamela, with her secure aristocratic family background, was at ease with herself and therefore the complete opposite of Dorothy, but she also adored the countryside, birds, poetry and books. Mrs Belloc Lowndes writes in *A Passing World*,

> Grey told his second wife, Pamela, the widow of Lord Glenconner, that after he and Dorothy had been married a considerable number of years, she suddenly suggested that they should lead a normal

married life. He demurred, giving as the reason that they were both happy and satisfied in the life they had agreed on leading.

This would make perfectly good sense if, at the time, Grey was having an affair with Pamela, which he no doubt justified on the grounds of his wife's reluctance to have sex.

As Dorothy spent so little time in London, it is likely that the two women had limited contact before Grey became Foreign Secretary. This is borne out by Dorothy's thank-you letter to Pamela following the weekend at Wilsford:

> I am so refreshed by the dip into your life. You do so supremely know how to live; and I don't believe even politics can interfere or make your life dusty. There are so many fretful porcupines about that the view gets prickly sometimes. We have our own brand of quietness but yours is better and has far more beautiful things in it.

Nevertheless, it seems the two women became in a short time reasonable friends, bonded by a mutual interest in birds, books and verse. Pamela wrote of Dorothy: 'I thought her beautiful to look at and interesting to listen to. She had a charming voice so that even if all she had said had been less good to listen to, the voice would have secured one's notice.'

Eight weeks before the Greys stayed at Wilsford with the Tennants in mid-July 1903, Chamberlain made a speech in Birmingham Town Hall that would radically change the course of British politics. The heart of his message was that the Empire was in danger of disintegrating unless held together economically. This would necessitate the introduction of tariffs on goods imported from outside the Empire, such as American wheat, which in turn would push up the price of bread and become political dynamite. The issue of free trade was to complete the unification of the Liberal Party and split the Unionists down the middle. By the end of the summer, Chamberlain had sent a letter of resignation to Arthur James Balfour, who had taken over as Prime Minister from his uncle Lord Salisbury in July 1902. The government also lost two senior free trade ministers in Chancellor of the Exchequer Charles Ritchie and the Duke of Devonshire. On the morning of 16 May, Margot Asquith records in her autobiography that her husband came into her bedroom at 20 Cavendish Square waving a copy of *The Times* in his hand, saying, 'Wonderful news today, it is only a matter of time when we will sweep this country.' Grey was as surprised as anyone at the speedy turnaround in the fortunes of the Liberal Party. Earlier in the year he was all gloom and despondency, writing to Katherine Lyttelton:

I hate politics as much as ever and can't write about them. I think this Government will flicker out in a year or two and a Ministry will be reformed under Chamberlain. I see no prospect of the Liberals coming in before 1910 and I have no more thoughts of office than for the last several years; but I have a Railway Board and other business which is definite work, at which one can sit with one's feet on the ground, instead of standing on one's head hurrying with one's heels which is almost all one can do in Opposition.

Asquith took the lead in the Liberal free trade campaign and in the latter part of the year followed Chamberlain around the country rebutting his concept of protectionism. Grey played his part over this long, drawn-out two-year debate, making a number of lively pro-free trade speeches. On 15 February 1905, Grey spoke in favour of free trade in the House, the *Westminster Gazette* recalling the following day, 'Sir Edward dwelt on the danger of exploiting the Imperial idea for party purposes', and 'they cheered Sir Edward Grey as he put his points in that clear but off-hand way of his, as if he were slightly ashamed to be so young and yet possess so much knowledge'. Again in early April he spoke in the army debate and the same newspaper reported, 'Members listened to Sir Edward

Grey with great attention as he pointed out with Russia's power greatly weakened there was no necessity to maintain a large army to reinforce India.'

Grey may not have spoken as much in the House as, say, the ultra-ambitious Churchill, but when he did he was listened to. On 28 February the same year, he reiterated that a future Liberal government would stand by Britain's existing agreements with France and Japan. On 31 May he gave a speech to the Eighty Club, of which he was President, warning that the proposed Colonial Conference, to be held the following year in front of an election, would be a farce as the present government was not in touch with the country on free trade. He was back on his feet again in the House on 25 July, leading a vote of censure. He urged the government to go and, 'in that cool collected way', pointed out that the Prime Minister had lost not only the confidence of the country but also of the House of Commons. Grey made one final assault against Balfour in the House on 15 November, when he accused the Prime Minister of having no convictions of his own and giving no lead on tariff reform.

Lloyd George was most critical of Grey's role in opposition, accusing him of 'shunning the political battlefield' and of not playing his part speaking in Parliament and on platforms across the country. In his *War Memoirs* he writes of Grey:

> Even when he was busily negotiating faction inside his Party he preferred to remain behind the lines leaving the actual fighting to Lord Rosebery, Asquith and Haldane. He thus succeeded in attaining high position in Party Governments without incurring any of the risks of active engagement in Party struggles. The only office he ever held was by tradition deemed to be immune from the slings and arrows of partisan warfare. In opposition he substantially confined his sparring activities to impartial comments on foreign affairs. His administration in office and his allotted function out of office alike were therefore not subjected to the fierce onslaughts that test the quality of political leaders.

Although there is some truth in these accusations, it is evident Lloyd George had a chip on his shoulder. Grey came from an old-fashioned Whig background. With good looks and a name, he did not have to get his hands dirty in the same way as Lloyd George, who came from working-class stock. But Grey had spoken out on the great issues of his opposition, such as tariff reform and the Education Bill. In addition, as we have seen, he was particularly outspoken in his views over the Boer War, which were diametrically opposed to those of Lloyd George. Moreover, at this particular time, Grey was one of the few ministers who went to speak for Lloyd George in his constituency. The *North Wales Observer* recorded that the speech he delivered was 'a eulogy of Mr Lloyd George'. Grey later gave away his true feelings by writing rather patronisingly to the Liberal Chief Whip, 'Caernarvon appears to be on the fringe of the Celtic fringe and very remote.'

Lloyd George's views are full of contradictions. Sir Robert Perks, Liberal Imperialist Member for Louth, wrote to Rosebery in December reporting on a conversation with the Welshman:

> Lloyd George had little to say in favour of Haldane or Asquith as the former and also in some measure the latter is under the influence of people with whom they 'spend weekends' – that neither of them is a real 'democrat' – that personally he has much more confidence in Grey than in Asquith.

Here is a resentful, socially inferior Lloyd George on show, one that had little time for 'society' or the upper classes. Lloyd George almost certainly developed his specific dislike for Grey at a later date, when they disagreed on the future direction of the Liberal Party after the war.

Grey did leave himself open to attack at times as more often than not he was not prepared to forgo his fishing holidays. He did, however, sacrifice his spring salmon fishing to public duties in his first two years as Foreign Secretary. The government crisis over tariff reform was coming to a head in August and September as Grey departed for Rhiconich in north-west Sutherland. Dorothy wrote to Francis Buxton on 27 August:

> The Loch Garbet Beg which we have had to ourselves every other day has given Edward four salmon in five days, so he is quite satisfied. I don't seem to get salmon now, however hard I work, but I don't mind much. We have to have one meal a day with the Bishop and the Colonel and the casual traveller, but have a sitting room of our own and lots of books.

He was still flogging the water on 18 September when Dorothy wrote to Captain Barton, a friend she had made when in Barbados and who would later become Administrator of British New Guinea, 'Edward has got twelve bitter cold salmon in thirteen bitter cold days' fishing here. I only fish occasionally so have caught nothing. The only way to get fish is never to stop fishing for one moment of the day.'

The following summer the Greys returned to Sutherland to fish at Rhiconich and the Creighton family borrowed The Cottage. Dorothy still pined for her cottage, writing in *The Cottage Book* when back for the autumn:

> I walked down Chilland meadow towards a splendid sunset and walked back facing a full moon and a very good star. Foinaven and Arkle [two mountains on the Reay Forest estate in Sutherland owned by the Grosvenor family who were to give their names to famous racehorses] are very fine but this place is the dearest.

That autumn brought sadness to the Itchen country as Grey's kinsman Lord Northbrook died at Avington Park in late November. It was he who provided the fishing on the Itchen and allowed the Greys to build The Cottage beside the river. Dorothy wrote, 'nothing will ever be quite the same as it was. He was the reason of our having come here and his kindness made a shelter for us.'

Prime Minister Balfour once famously referred to Grey as an odd mixture of 'an old-fashioned Whig and a Socialist'. If Lloyd George felt his colleague was a caricature of the former then Grey's political leanings were a good deal closer to the latter. In 1903 the fledgling Labour Party was starting to win by-elections. The Labour Representation Committee, combining both trade unions and socialist societies, won Barnard Castle. Grey was delighted, stating publicly that Labour should have more direct representation in the House of Commons. After the Labour victory at Woolwich, Grey told an audience at Edinburgh University, 'I look upon the result with the greatest satisfaction, because it seems to me to prove that the wage-earning classes, who are numerically far the greatest of the population, are gaining in power and strength and concentration and organisation and political purpose. This is what should happen.' Grey had always been sympathetic to the unions. He represented a north-eastern constituency and by now had a good five years of railway experience under his belt.

1904 was the Jubilee year for the North Eastern Railway and also the year Grey became its chairman. He adored his railway work and found it a marked contrast to the frustration of political opposition. On 31 July there was a celebration dinner at the York Station Hotel, which Grey attended. It was fifty years before to the day that the Amalgamation Act spawned the NER by way of a merger of the York, North Midland and Leeds Northern Companies. The Jubilee year was one of great technological development for the NER, bringing the establishment of an electric train service between Newcastle and Tynemouth together with the installation of power and automatic signalling. The Jubilee represented a half-century of remarkable progress. In 1854 the system comprised 703 miles of railway open for traffic; by 1905, this figure had risen to

1,670 miles. The authorised capital had grown from £23 million
in 1854 to £87 million in 1905. Over the same period, revenues
grew from £1.6 million to £9.3 million. In 1904 the NER carried
55 million passengers, 13 million tons of general merchandise
and 42 million tons of minerals. Grey was elected chairman on
16 December, following the death of Lord Ridley. Dorothy was
very excited about the handsome salary of £2,000 a year, writing to Munro Ferguson: 'Most of the salary will have to be saved
to replace past election expenses, but I have ordered a new tea
table and some extra bulbs. It may even be that we shall want one
of the better sort of Grosvenor Road houses.' Grey himself relished
the challenge, writing to Buxton:

> It is a big job, but interesting. It will make a hole in my time: I can't
> help that. I have done nearly twenty years of political work, mostly
> in Opposition. I am not prepared to spend the next twenty years
> doing the same sort of thing to the exclusion of definite and useful
> work like the railway.

By the summer of 1904, the political prospects for the Liberals were
becoming brighter by the day. The party had pulled itself together
and was winning by-elections across the country. They had even
managed to recruit a few Unionist 'free-traders' to their ranks, the
most notable being the young Winston Churchill, who on 31 May
finally crossed the floor of the House, following the example of
his old friend and fellow 'hooligan' Jack Seely. A greater number
of Unionists would have deserted to the Liberal opposition were
it not for the lacklustre leadership of Campbell-Bannerman. He
was considered to be on the left of the party and his 'methods of
barbarism' speech when he criticised Britain's use of concentration camps during the Boer War was still fresh in people's minds.
Campbell-Bannerman's leadership was again in doubt as his wife's
health deteriorated. The Chief Whip, Herbert Gladstone, having
met Campbell-Bannerman back in October 1903, had reported
to Asquith that his leader was concerned he would not be able to

take on the heavy responsibilities looming in the future. A peerage would be more to his liking. Asquith was still trying to entice
Rosebery out of his self-imposed exile while Grey and Haldane
were plotting for an Asquith leadership in the House of Commons.
Gladstone's interview with Campbell-Bannerman should be taken
into account before one judges too harshly the Liberal Imperialists'
disloyal behaviour with regard to their leader.

The Anglo-French Entente was signed on 8 April 1904. The
ground had been prepared by King Edward's state visit to Paris in
May of the previous year. The trip proved a diplomatic triumph
for the King. His charm and bonhomie won over a city still seething from both Fashoda and Britain's treatment of the Boers. On
1 June, Grey made his most important parliamentary speech to
date in the foreign affairs debate. He replied to Lord Percy in 'his
quiet decisive way', following Lord Lansdowne's announcement of
the signing of the Entente Cordiale with France. He welcomed the
Entente, which was presented as a colonial agreement effecting
the settlement of various long-running disputes around the world.
The most notable example was 'Morocco for Egypt', the recognition of France's special rights in Morocco in return for French
assent to British rights in Egypt. There were no suggestions of any
kind of military alliance but, most significantly, no one seemed
to appreciate the significance of the last article of the convention, where the respective countries 'agreed to afford one another
their diplomatic support to obtain execution of the clauses of the
present declaration regarding Egypt and Morocco'. With Russia
foremost in his mind, Grey encouraged the government to make
the Entente a working model for other cases where possible, and
cheerfully concluded by reminding the House that 'we had happily
moved from a glacial epoch with France to a genial one' and that
he 'trusted that the Government would keep the fire of friendship
burning which they had lighted so well'.

Any hopes that Grey might have had for a closer relationship
with Russia were dashed by events in the North Sea on a dark
stormy night at the end of October. Admiral Rozhdestvensky's

Russian Baltic fleet, en route to relieve Port Arthur 20,000 miles away, and unwittingly to face annihilation some seven months later at the hands of Admiral Togo's Japanese fleet at Tsushima, fired on some British trawlers off the Dogger Bank, causing fatalities. The Russians had mistaken the fishing boats for Japanese torpedo boats. Conflict between Britain and Russia was narrowly avoided by an official apology and a substantial cash sum paid in compensation. The Kaiser, of course, could not resist causing mischief. As an ally of Japan, Britain declined to provide supplies for the Russian fleet. Germany, in defiance of neutrality, offered the Russians coaling facilities in home waters and in German south-west Africa. Senior officials at the Foreign Office were convinced that if the Russians had not already been allied to France they would have tied themselves in with Germany. German influence prevailed in both court and government circles.

Violent anti-Russian feeling now spread across Britain. Rumours were circulating in Whitehall that the Kaiser was encouraging the Czar to make trouble for Britain on the Indian frontier. The Foreign Office was convinced that the Germans would try and capitalise on the situation by calling for the formation of a continental league against Britain which would include the French. They need not have worried. Delcasse, the French Foreign Minister, was determined not to overturn years of hard work cultivating British friendship and he positioned himself as mediator between his new Entente partner and the Russians. He duly persuaded the Russians to set up an official inquiry which granted compensation to the British government. The Entente Cordiale had survived its first test.

Grey's views on foreign affairs were developed independently in opposition and not at a later date under the influence of anti-German Foreign Office officials, as some people suggest. His first biographer, Trevelyan, notes that Grey spoke in the House as early as January 1902 in favour of an agreement with Russia on Asian matters, most importantly in connection with Persia. Keith Robbins, a later biographer, quotes a private letter from Grey to Henry Newbolt a year later demonstrating a desire for closer relations with France and Russia: 'I have come to think that Germany is our worst enemy and greatest danger. As a matter of fact the German Government have behaved very badly to us in China.' Grey continues, 'I believe the policy of Germany to be that of using us without helping us: keeping us isolated that she may have us to fall back on. Close relations with Germany mean for us worse relations with the rest of the world especially with the US, France and Russia.' Grey had demonstrated to the French at Fashoda that he could be as tough and uncompromising as any when British interests were threatened across the globe. Given her enormous professional army, modern fleet and aggressive diplomacy, he now saw Germany as the danger area.

Just as Grey was dusting off his fishing tackle for his annual April visit to Rosehall, events in Morocco would prove his suspicions of Germany were not misconceived. On 31 March 1905, the German Emperor made an ill-considered and highly provocative visit to Tangier, yet again evidencing Germany's insensitive and clumsy diplomacy. With the signing of the Entente Cordiale, Britain had recognised France's special interests in Morocco and granted her a free hand in that country. France was now eager to incorporate Morocco into her North African empire. Lawlessness in Morocco had reached such a point that in late February the French demanded the Sultan hand over responsibility for the police and army to their own representatives. As a signatory to the Madrid Convention of 1880 guaranteeing the independence of Morocco, the Germans were justifiably upset not to have been consulted in advance. It was a fault of British and French diplomacy that Germany had not been presented with the contents of the Anglo-French Entente on signature. However, Chancellor Bülow's ham-fisted reaction was to despatch the Kaiser with a message of support for the Sultan. It was seen by Britain and France as abrupt, rude and aggressive behaviour.

Germany's pride was at stake. She wished to demonstrate to the French that a powerful neighbour was not to be trifled with. Yet it was obvious that such a challenge was not merely a defence of German treaty interests but also an attempt to disrupt the Anglo-French Entente. France was militarily unprepared and Russia drastically weakened by her war with Japan, so now was the perfect time for Germany to put Britain's support of France to the test. Grey always found it difficult to read the Germans. Who was actually calling the shots on foreign policy? Was it the Kaiser, Chancellor Bülow or the éminence grise at the Foreign Office, Holstein? The Germans probably did not know themselves. The Tangier incident was almost certainly the result of Bülow bullying the Kaiser into making a rash move. The British Foreign Office had no doubts. Sir William Tyrrell, Grey's future private secretary, wrote to Cecil Spring-Rice a year later, 'The real cancer in Berlin is Bülow, who lacks all moral sense in no ordinary degree. I despair of decent relations with Germany as long as he has a finger in the pie.'

Germany was well within her rights to call for an international conference to settle the future of Morocco, but she later backed it up with threats of war. Delcasse, the French Foreign Minister and the driving force behind the Entente Cordiale, declined but was then over-ruled by his spineless Cabinet colleagues. This in turn would lead to his resignation in early June. France had been humiliated and, on the face of it, Germany had won a significant diplomatic victory. Germany should have let matters stand but Bülow was determined to pressure the Entente, insisting on a conference in the new year, at which he would make the serious mistake of under-estimating Britain's resolve to stand by her Entente partner. As the summer wore on, German diplomacy with France became more heavy-handed. Berlin dragged its feet on agreeing the conditions of the conference and in August the Germans rubbed salt into the wounds by announcing that they were making a loan to the Sultan, which the indignant French saw very much as their own brief.

The Germans had another tilt at transforming the European alliance system in July. This time the Kaiser was responsible rather than the Chancellor, and his target was the Franco-Russian alliance. It yet again demonstrated their thoroughly amateur and unco-ordinated approach to foreign policy. On 24 July the Kaiser met the Czar on his yacht at Björkö Sound in the Baltic. The Kaiser encouraged the Czar not to be weak with his domestic reform party and suggested closing the Baltic to all warships except those of Russia and Germany. Worse still, he persuaded the Czar to sign a treaty which would nullify the alliance with France. The docu-ment provided for mutual assistance between Germany and Russia in the event of either being attacked by a third party. The Czar insisted on the agreement only applying to Europe. It excluded the Far East, where Germany was looking for Russian cooperation to counter Anglo-Japanese ascendancy. Bülow, having read the draft agreement, threatened to resign if the treaty was signed, and Count Lamsdorff for the Russians, not willing to upset the French, prevailed upon the Czar to change his mind. This diplomatic fiasco resulted from insecurity on both sides. Russia was preoccupied with domestic revolutionary problems and severely weakened by the war with Japan. Germany, for her part, was developing a paranoia over 'encirclement' and saw enemies on every frontier.

Affairs far away in North Africa were hardly likely to interrupt Grey's customary spring salmon fishing holiday on the Cassley. There was deep snow and high winds for the first fortnight but even with the poor conditions, Grey caught seven fish and Dorothy four. On her last day, 27 April, Dorothy wrote to Ronald Munro Ferguson,

> Edward is pleased with himself and the world, having now in half the number of days, got only two fewer fish than he got on the Conon … Very much better fish too. In his few intervals indoors he sits by a window which overlooks a good pool and murmurs, 'What a nice word "river" is.' He goes out every day meaning to fish the less likely pools as well as the best and comes in without having

the heart to leave the favourites. The keener he gets, the smaller the
rod he uses, and it may be heard making a sharp whistling sound up
and down the banks, quite different to the usual sound of casting.

In the same letter Dorothy continues, 'long-tailed tits and grey
wagtails abound, and curlews do one's soul much good'. The beautiful spring notes of the curlew enveloped the Greys when fishing
around the estuary. Their music was one of Grey's five favourite
bird songs and he writes lyrically of their song in *The Charm of Birds*:

> The notes are uttered on the wing to the accompaniment of a grace-
> ful flight that has motions of evident pleasure. The notes do not
> sound passionate; they suggest peace, rest, healing, joy, an assurance
> of happiness past, present and to come. To listen to curlews on a
> bright, clear April day with the fullness of spring still in anticipation,
> is one of the best experiences a lover of birds can have.

The following day Dorothy was back in her beloved Itchen country
opening up The Cottage. She wrote in *The Cottage Book* on arrival,
'The grass everywhere seems very thick and soft after the little
wiry Scotch stuff. The wind was blowing cuckoo notes from tame
park and a chiffchaff spoke in a settled way in the chalk pit.' Dorothy
much preferred the softness of the Hampshire countryside to the
harsh wilderness of the far north, writing to Grey, 'Oh the splendid tufted grass and the cuckoos and the water buttercups and the
plumey green hedges. It's an enchanted land ... it's all very fine to
have your salmoning and your great Scotch country. I like lesser
things and flatter things and greener grass at this time of year.'
    In contrast to the previous year, May was a disappointing month,
with cold winds and frosts. Dorothy was miserable as she could not sit
out under the full moon and listen to the nightingales, writing in their
diary for 28 May, 'The nightingale moon of last week was wasted by
clouds and wind and could not be sat out under.' The nightingale was
Grey's totemic bird. He thought the song bewitching and wonderful,
yet, he says, 'It is a song to listen to, not to live with.'

Following the death of Lord Northbrook, the month of June brought further sadness when Grey's mother died at Bellshill in Northumberland. They arrived back at The Cottage from the funeral on 14 June, Grey writing: 'The death of Mother brings mortality home to one more than anything I have known. It is like a landslide in my past. My life would not have been without hers and hers is gone.' To make matters worse, perhaps Dorothy had not completely recovered her strength, as the bicycle and trailer was much in evidence again that summer. In early July he trailed Dorothy up to Morn Hill to listen to the stone curlews: 'We walked into the warren on the top and lay in the dusk listening to the stone curlews: they have a melancholy cry as if they knew they belonged to an age that is gone and were the last of their race.' These were prophetic words from Grey, as by the turn of the century the stone curlew was well on its way to becoming a breeding rarity in Hampshire. Grey had a real affection for this weird wader of the dry, flinty downlands. With its large yellow eye and its strange wailing cries usually heard soon after dusk, he believed the stone curlew to be an almost ghostlike bird. As Fallodon was still let, Dorothy remained at The Cottage throughout the autumn, with Grey joining her at the weekends.

Grey's patience finally ran out in the autumn of 1905 when he split from his political mentor Lord Rosebery. Rosebery had been speaking out against the Entente for some time, warning that 'this unhappy agreement is much more likely to promote rather than to prevent unfriendliness'. He prophetically told Lloyd George that it would eventually lead to war with Germany. Rosebery was not an anti-French Germanophile. In fact he much preferred France, as shown by his visits to Paris, his love of French literature and his much acclaimed biography of Napoleon. He thought the Kaiser was a dangerous fool. Rosebery was convinced that Britain should seek out the strongest ally, whereas the Entente policy was based on

the opposite idea: that of the balance of power. At a dinner given
at his Berkeley Square home on 12 July, Rosebery said to Admiral
Fisher of the Entente, 'You are leaning on an aspen and the German
Emperor has 4 millions of soldiers and the second best Navy in
the world.' On Blenheim Day (13 August), Grey wrote to Ronald
Munro Ferguson, 'I think more and more that Rosebery is wrong
about Germany and I feel so strongly that if any government drags
us back into the German net I will oppose it at all costs.' Grey was
determined to protect French independence. He was well aware
that if France was destroyed, Germany would establish dominance
in Europe, leaving Britain isolated.

As far as his fellow Liberal Imperialists were concerned, the final
nail in Rosebery's coffin came with a disastrous speech given on
25 November at Bodmin denouncing Home Rule. Two days before,
Campbell-Bannerman had made a speech at Stirling outlining a
compromise on Irish policy hammered out with Asquith. For practical reasons – namely the need to keep John Redmond, leader of
the Irish Nationalists, happy – and, most importantly, for reasons
of conviction, it was impossible for the Liberal Party to abandon
Home Rule. The Nationalists were informed that Home Rule
remained a major policy objective for the Liberals, yet it would not be
given the priority of previous governments. Home Rule stood in the
way of important social reform and as a result, full self-government
for Ireland would have to wait. But in the meantime, a step-by-step
devolution policy would be enacted. Unfortunately nobody seemed
to have informed Rosebery who, with one foot in politics and one
outside, never bothered to consult his colleagues. Rosebery's speech
made the newfound unity of the Liberal Party appear pretty frail,
especially with a general election only weeks away. Grey saved the day
by immediately speaking up in favour of the Stirling compromise at
Newcastle-under-Lyme. Not unnaturally, Dorothy was heartbroken
that her husband's political separation with Rosebery was complete.
There was some consolation in that their personal friendship was
not broken. The Greys accepted an invitation to spend Christmas
with Rosebery at his stud, The Durdans, near Epsom.

Grey as a handsome young Parliamentary Under-Secretary at the Foreign Office in 1894. The Prime Minister, Lord Rosebery, wrote to the Foreign Secretary, Lord Kimberley, of Grey's 'great success as representative of the Foreign Office', adding, 'Moreover he is persona gratissima to the House of Commons, popular, admired and respected.'

The old three-storey Fallodon Hall, taken from the pond bench where Grey presided over the evening 'duck dinner'. Grey's wildfowl collection provided him not only with an enormous sense of interest and happiness throughout his life but also with a welcome buffer against the strains of public life.

Edward and Dorothy Grey in 1886, shortly after their marriage, when they shared Fallodon Hall with the Grey family. The honeymoon surrounded by so many family members must have been fairly inhibiting.

Lord Rosebery looking worse for wear on opium as Prime Minister. When an undergraduate at Oxford, he was famously quoted as saying, 'I shall marry an heiress, win the Derby and become Prime Minister.' He accomplished all three and much else besides.

King Edward VII and Queen Alexandra. A playboy prince, Bertie became an immensely popular and effective constitutional monarch. Grey wrote of his King, 'He read all his important papers and not only accepted the constitutional practice that foreign policy be that of his Ministers but he preferred that it should be so.'

The Hampshire Cottage on the river at Itchen Abbas, with Dorothy sitting in the doorway. W. H. Hudson wrote, 'It was an ideal spot for a nature-lover and an angler to pitch his tent upon.'

Sir Edward and Lady Grey with a young Winston Churchill and Richard Haldane in 1901 at Guisachan, the home of Lord Tweedmouth in the Scottish Highlands. Tweedmouth would become First Lord of the Admiralty in 1906 and was married to Winston's aunt, Fanny Spencer Churchill.

ABOVE LEFT Henry Campbell-Bannerman.
In opposition during the Boer War he presided
over a divided Liberal Party, yet he became a
most effective Prime Minister and headed one
of the most brilliant administrations ever to
grace Westminster. Huge crowds at his funeral
demonstrated the affection and respect in
which he was held by his country.

ABOVE RIGHT David Lloyd George, the young
Radical. Although opposed to the Liberal
Imperialists' support for the Boer War, he
worked well with Foreign Secretary Grey when
he was Chancellor of the Exchequer.

LEFT Arthur James Balfour. A brilliant brain
and high priest of The Souls, he took over
the Foreign Office from Grey in 1916. He once
famously said of Grey, 'He is a curious mixture
of an old-fashioned Whig and a socialist.'

The author's great-grandmother, Consuelo Marlborough, flanked by Richard Haldane (left, Secretary of State for War) and by John Morley (right, Secretary of State for India). These two political allies of Grey look rather out of place weekending with 'the racing set'.

The fastest train in the British Empire on its 43-minute run from Darlington to York in 1904, at the time when Grey was chairman of the North Eastern Railway.

Winston Churchill and his wife Clemmie on British Army manoeuvres at Aldershot in 1910. In September 1911 Grey wrote to his close friend Katherine Lyttelton, 'The Winston Churchills have been at Fallodon for a Sunday and I liked it. They are so exceedingly nice to each other.'

HMS *Dreadnought*, Jacky Fisher's revolutionary new battleship launched early in 1906, made all other battleships redundant and immediately intensified the international naval arms race. Her state-of-the-art turbine engines carried a formidable gun platform of ten 12-inch guns through the water at 21 knots.

Winston Churchill and Admiral Fisher. 'Yours till charcoal sprouts.' Winston brought Jacky Fisher back to the Admiralty in 1914. Fisher had dragged the Royal Navy into the modern age during his first stint as First Sea Lord from 1904–10.

David Tennant. Quite possibly Grey's son by Pamela. The physical resemblance is most striking: thin lips, strong nose and high forehead.

Christopher Tennant. Pamela's eldest son. Although he was christened Christopher Grey Tennant and Edward Grey was a godfather, it is unlikely Christopher was fathered by Grey.

Winifred Heller. Born in 1894, she lived her entire life in Germany. There is a strong possibility she was Grey's first illegitimate child. Her son, Hans-Joachim Heller, who now lives in Berlin, certainly bears Grey's distinctively patrician, pinched facial features, thin lips and large Roman nose.

Dorothy Nelson of Boston, Massachusetts, born July 1911, claims her father was Sir Edward Grey and her mother was 'a lady-in-waiting'. Again, an uncanny physical resemblance.

LEFT Count Paul Wolff-Metternich. German ambassador in London 1901–12. He was a popular ambassador who played a straightforward and honourable role in keeping the peace between the two countries. Grey wrote, 'I regretted his departure and the farewell dinner given to him at the Foreign Office was not a political gesture but a genuine expression of personal regard.'

BELOW The beautiful Wyndham sisters, 'The Three Graces', painted by Sargent in 1910. Lady Elcho, long-term lover of Arthur James Balfour, on the left, Pamela Glenconner, the love of Edward Grey's life, centre, and Mrs Adeane, right.

✤

In early September Grey took the fishing at Relugas, on the river Findhorn, south of Inverness. Dorothy wrote to her friend Captain Barton, 'It is the most beautiful and various river in Scotland and we catch salmon in deep dark brown pools with a line of white foam curling down the middle and steep green rocks leading up to the birch trees against the blue.' Asquith had rented a house for the summer holidays at Glen of Rothes in the north-east of Scotland and Haldane was at home in Perthshire. Haldane decided that he and Asquith should drive to Relugas to formalise their understanding with Grey that they would not take future office under Campbell-Bannerman if he remained in the House of Commons. Haldane was selected to communicate the content of the Compact to the King. The basis of the agreement which would become known as 'the Relugas Compact' was that Campbell-Bannerman would go to the Lords as Prime Minister, with Asquith leading the Commons in the role of Chancellor of the Exchequer. Grey would become Foreign Secretary and Haldane was to be Lord Chancellor. It seems most arrogant and presumptuous for two men who had never held high office to act in this fashion but, as witnessed by Herbert Gladstone's comments, their doubts about Campbell-Bannerman's ability to survive in the Commons were genuine enough. Haldane, rightly viewed as the arch-plotter by his leader, was the one who made the running over the Compact. The 'old-fashioned Whig' in Grey was loath to put his head above the parapet, Haldane writing in his autobiography, 'Asquith and I were more practical than Grey, who hated to make any move.' Although all three men were ambitious, they had much to lose if they accepted office. Asquith and Haldane were very successful barristers and Grey, certainly the least aspiring of the three, was greatly enjoying the chairmanship of the NER, with its attractive salary.

Once back from Scotland and with the break-up of the Balfour ministry imminent, Grey dived back into the rough and tumble of political life. He made several important speeches that autumn, often exposing his strong liberal views on domestic matters such as the necessity of improving state education. On 13 October he attended a large Liberal rally in the Manchester Free Trade Hall. He spoke from the platform in support of Winston Churchill, who was standing as a Liberal candidate for North-West Manchester. The *Westminster Gazette* compared Grey's political leanings to the Tory Lord Hugh Cecil, and reported the next day:

> Sir Edward Grey seems to be the ideal of the Conservative-Liberal who appeals to the moderate, sober-minded, sensible body of opinion that governs the country, who dislikes jingoism and desires a preservative and not an aggressive foreign policy, who objects to demigod methods and will not lead the public to expect more from Parliament than Parliament can give.

However, the suffragettes arrived in force and turned the Manchester meeting into a street brawl. Christabel Pankhurst and Annie Kenney were arrested and taken off to Strangeways prison. Grey and Winston were howled down for not committing themselves on female suffrage. Grey was not prepared to deal with the issue on this occasion as it was not a Party question. The treatment they received was possibly unjust as, encouraged by his wife, Grey had made his positive views on 'votes for women' known on several occasions, although he hated the perpetual disturbance the suffragettes caused at public meetings.

On 21 October, Grey made a major speech on foreign affairs in the City of London. Balfour's administration was on its last legs and good money was on Grey to take over at the Foreign Office. The speech was of great importance, not only because it outlined the thinking of an incoming Liberal administration but also because it steadied a few nerves across the Channel, where the French were being threatened by Germany over Morocco. The speech demonstrates

yet again that Grey had his own strong views on foreign policy long before he could have been influenced by his officials at the Foreign Office. As both extremes of the Liberal Party had advocated better relations with the Germans, many people thought a future Liberal government would revert to 'splendid isolation' rather than pick a fight with Germany. On 19 October Grey wrote to J. A. Spender:

> The impression that has been spread abroad with some success by those interested in spreading it, is that a Liberal Government would unsettle the understanding with France in order to make it up to Germany. I think we are running a real risk of losing France and not gaining Germany, who won't want us if they can detach us from France.

Grey's key message was one of continuity. There would be little change from the policies of Lord Lansdowne, which delighted officials at the Foreign Office. A 'special relationship' would be cultivated with the USA, the Anglo-Japanese alliance would be renewed and the Entente Cordiale strengthened. As far as the latter was concerned, although there had been diplomatic problems since its inception, 'the spirit of the agreement is more important than the letter of the agreement'. Finally, he touched on his desire to seek a new friendship with Russia by settling differences around the frontiers of the Indian Empire, in much the same way as Britain had done with France in Africa. He hoped France would act as a bridge between Britain and Russia. Grey knew that securing an entente with Russia would be no easy task. Not only were the Russians notoriously difficult to deal with but also, back home, the radicals in his party had an aversion to doing business with an autocrat like the Czar. There was, however, light at the end of the tunnel. In mid-October, Russia edged towards a constitutional democracy, promising progressive social reform and establishing the Duma as the sole executive body for her Empire. A move towards parliamentary democracy could only be a force for the good when it came to Britain establishing closer ties with Russia.

Grey always craved improved relations with Germany, but he realised how difficult it would be to achieve his aim without upsetting the French. The last thing he wanted at the current time was an alienated France, as this would upset 'the balance of power' on which the peace of Europe depended. As it was, that 'balance' had been altered a few months previously by Russia's defeat at the hands of the Japanese. He was well aware of the difficulties presented by a hostile press and unfavourable public opinion both in Germany and Britain. The *Westminster Gazette* echoed Grey's views: 'The Teutophobe in England plays all the time into the hands of the Pan-German in Germany. Germany becomes more and more insecure. Our threats and complaints just increase the German fleet and check our diplomacy. There are certain English writers who are worth a battleship a year to Germany.' Grey knew that Britain had no right to complain about Germany building a fleet and in any case did not have the means of preventing it. He also understood that such a fleet presented a threat to British interests, necessitating a competitive construction programme at home which would prove unpopular with his Liberal colleagues. As far as Germany was concerned, Grey felt that what was needed was a change of feeling rather than of policy. There were no outstanding points of issue, only deplorable relations with the press and public that resulted in an atmosphere of suspicion between the two countries.

As part of the Liberal Imperialists' programme of 'efficiency', Grey had always counselled reform of the Army and Navy. He saw the establishment of the Committee of Imperial Defence by Balfour as a step in the right direction, but felt that too much was still being spent on the Army in an inefficient manner. In terms of reform, the Royal Navy was five years ahead of the Army, entirely thanks to Britain's greatest sailor since Nelson, Admiral Fisher. Jacky Fisher was short and stocky with a youthful face which, complete with quasi-Oriental features, led to his enemies accusing him of being 'the son of a Cingalese Princess'. His droopy eyelids and large grey eyes set far apart in a face of yellowish complexion gave his appearance an eastern flavour. He was a human dynamo: brave, energetic, ambitious, quick-witted, self-confident, charming, passionate and patriotic. His only form of exercise was pacing the deck, and his single relaxation dancing. But Fisher was not a fighting sailor like Nelson. Certainly he had seen some action in China and Egypt but first and foremost he was a reformer and administrator. He brought the Navy into the twentieth century with a bang, and that it had badly needed. Prior to Fisher's reforms, promotion was gained by seniority rather than merit. There were too many outdated ships scattered across the globe. Complacency had crept in over a century of peaceful 'splendid isolation'. Flying the flag across the Empire meant that the paintbrush had superseded gunnery practice in terms of importance to the Royal Navy.

Fisher was the first to demand reforms in technology, personnel handling and tactics at sea. He re-concentrated the fleet on home waters, improved naval gunnery and introduced modern ships, including the Dreadnought battleship, destroyers and submarines. He began the substitution of turbines for reciprocating engines and urged the use of oil fuel rather than coal. He even introduced ovens into ships' galleys to produce fresh-baked bread on a daily basis. The Dreadnought, launched in February 1906, was of revolutionary design. She was turbo-driven with a cruiser's speed and better armoured, with ten twelve-inch guns in five turrets. All these reforms not only brought greater efficiency to the Navy but also produced greater economy in naval expenditure. The Navy estimates actually began to fall, giving credence to the Liberal Imperialist cry for 'efficiency'. Even Dorothy was impressed, writing to Captain Barton from Rosehall on 13 April,

Edward went to see the naval cadets at the great Fisher-created college at Osborne. Their training sounds like a thing out of an H. G. Wells book and another world. Ideal conditions of health, a scientifically blended day of book-learning and engineering and the most excellent food possible. There is no restriction on the amount of jam eaten!

Jacky Fisher was First Sea Lord from 1904 to 1910, that crucial period before the outbreak of war, and was later pulled out of retirement by Churchill in 1914 to serve a further year. He came from humble origins and worked his way to the top through hard work and the excellence of his creative mind. After spells at sea across the world, he ran the Navy's Gunnery School, where he developed an independent research centre for torpedoes. He then achieved promotion to gunnery officer on HMS *Warrior*, Britain's first ironclad, before taking over as Director of Naval Ordnance. Fisher had a tempestuous personality which made him enemies in the service, but he also had a wicked sense of humour and great charm which gave him the ear of politicians and royalty alike. Outside the Navy he had no real interests except dancing – an activity which he introduced onto his all-male ships – yet he was worshipped by his men. Grey was also a great fan. In opposition he was a staunch supporter of Fisher's naval reforms and chaired a committee of enquiry into the best method of manning the new Navy. Throughout this momentous period of reform, Grey and Fisher would become invaluable to each other. Long before Grey had experienced at first hand many heated Cabinet discussions over the naval estimates, he had been a 'big Navy' supporter. He believed that a powerful navy assisted the execution of a successful foreign policy and was delighted to see naval reforms being pushed through under a Conservative government. For his part, Fisher, like Grey, increasingly saw Germany as the threat to European peace and accordingly shuffled his ships around the globe to strengthen the North Sea Fleet.

Grey showed his mettle again in December. He had ditched Rosebery as a possible future leader and was now determined to openly signal his disapproval of his current leader, Campbell-Bannerman. He was still holding rigidly to the Relugas Compact, whereby Campbell-Bannerman's move to the Lords had to be a condition of his inclusion in the new government. Grey also felt, wrongly as it turned out, that although there was a meeting of minds over Ireland, there were still policy differences between Campbell-Bannerman's wing of the Liberal Party and the 'Imperialists'. He therefore wanted the government spokesman in one of the two Houses to be from the right wing of the party. By digging in his heels in such a manner, wasn't Grey risking a split in the party on the eve of a general election? Was this not the action of a hypocrite? After all, it was only two weeks before that Grey had chastised his friend Rosebery for risking a party split over his Home Rule speech at Bodmin. Asquith had recently detached himself from the Compact on the grounds that the new government was being formed *before* the election rather than after, as originally supposed.

The Conservative government finally fell, having lost a vote in the House on the question of the introduction of Chinese labour in the South African mines. On 4 December, the day that Balfour announced his resignation, Grey had two meetings with Campbell-Bannerman at his house in Belgrave Square. Grey attended the first interview with Asquith. An amicable discussion on Irish policy took place, during which all parties found themselves in agreement on a 'step-by-step' policy for Home Rule. Later in the evening, Grey returned alone and stated he could not serve unless Campbell-Bannerman went to the Lords. The Liberal leader described Grey as arriving 'all buttoned up and never undoing one button', presumably because he failed to give satisfactory reasons for his demands. Campbell-Bannerman had known for some time that a plot was afoot to turn him out to grass in the Lords, 'a place of which I have neither liking, training or ambition', masterminded by that 'ingenious person, Richard Burdon Haldane'. At a meeting on 13 November, Campbell-Bannerman had told Asquith that 'nothing except the point of a bayonet would induce [him] to go to the Lords'.

Grey realised he was behaving badly, but stubbornly believed he was right about Campbell-Bannerman's leadership capabilities. On 6 December he cheekily offered his leader an alternative: that Haldane, who was not the leader's favourite colleague, should go to the Woolsack to lead the Lords while Campbell-Bannerman remained in the Commons. Grey knew he was putting Asquith in a difficult position as demonstrated by a letter to Dorothy:

> If I stay out Asquith will have to decide what he does; if he goes in without me his position will be horrid and people will say he has abandoned me in order to have office. If he stays out with me it is considered that the Liberal Party will smash and Free Trade may be beaten at the Election.

Campbell-Bannerman was reasonably relaxed as he had the key figure, Asquith, secured as Chancellor. The new Prime Minister was not worried about excluding Haldane; he had never warmed to him, although he thought it would be a shame to lose Grey. Nevertheless, with Lord Elgin booked for the Colonial Office, Campbell-Bannerman telegraphed Lord Cromer in Cairo, offering him the Foreign Office. The great man declined by return. Grey would not consider joining the team without his closest political ally, Haldane.

Asquith broke the deadlock on the afternoon of 7 December by encouraging the Prime Minister to include Haldane, who in turn would then reel in his reluctant friend. Grey was finally persuaded to accept the Foreign Office by Haldane over a fish dinner in a private room at the Café Royal; Spender and Arthur Acland had been called in earlier to exert their influence. The new Cabinet list was ready for the King the next day. When his closest political friends agreed to serve, Grey knew the battle was lost and it was his duty to the Liberal Party to accept office. They had both been granted their preferred portfolios, Asquith as Chancellor of the Exchequer and Haldane, with the Lord Chancellor's office already allocated, more than happy to become Secretary of State for War. Grey had once again demonstrated the obdurate side of his character. Roy Jenkins writes in his biography of Asquith, 'in some respects of his temperament Grey was like Rosebery. He loved creating situations in which he could say no.'

Douglas Hurd starts an essay on Grey in his book, *Choose Your Weapons*, with the lines, 'No one was delighted, no one was appalled when Sir Edward Grey was appointed Foreign Secretary in December 1905.' This is quite simply not true. Margot Asquith writes in her autobiography, 'The Foreign Office adored Edward Grey and was in a state of trembling anxiety lest he should stand out.' Margot promised to send Louis Mallet (Grey's future private secretary) a telegram when the whole matter was settled. The good news having been received, he wired back, 'Thank you and God. Suspense awful.' Grey was well known to the Foreign Office, having spent three years as an Under-Secretary in the early 1890s, when he had shown the French his teeth with the 'Grey Declaration'. He had recently made two sensible speeches on foreign affairs, demonstrating continuity with the policies of Lord Lansdowne, and above all he was sound on Germany.

Grey evidently returned to the Foreign Office with an excellent reputation. In December 1905, Lord Hugh Cecil wrote to Winston Churchill, warning him that, 'Shining as a firework on a platform or in the House was all very well but the further steps require a reputation as a good administrator, a skilled and industrious official – the sort of reputation Edward Grey eminently has'. The influential Liberal journalist J. A. Spender was also delighted at Grey's appointment, writing in *Life, Journalism and Politics*,

> My relations with Grey were rather those of friend than a journalist. We had been at Oxford at the same time and at the same college; I had seen him continuously from the time that he was Under-Secretary for Foreign Affairs, argued freely with him in the days of the Liberal League and kept in touch with his mind in foreign affairs in subsequent years. Failing Rosebery, I greatly wished him to be Foreign Secretary and was much troubled when he made difficulties, or seemed as he often did, to be in flight from public life.

In her autobiography Margot Asquith also chronicles a meeting on 13 November between Campbell-Bannerman and her

husband when the latter advocated Grey for the position of Foreign
Secretary: 'He said that he was the *only* man and that it was clear
in his mind that Grey's appointment as Foreign Minister would be
popular all over Europe.' The fact that Grey was highly thought
of in Europe at this early stage is interesting, as he had never
travelled on the Continent. His suitability for office is reinforced
by a letter from Cecil Spring-Rice to Ronald Munro Ferguson
in 1898:

> Last night I saw Metternich, the Kaiser's favourite diplomat. He
> talked of Grey with great admiration as having a real talent for
> foreign affairs. You see that everyone says the same thing and you
> and Lady Helen ought to see that he spares a little time from his
> ducks to learn French.

On the afternoon of 11 December, Grey drove to Buckingham
Palace with Henry Fowler and John Morley to receive their seals
of office. They departed into one of the worst fogs London has
known, Grey writing in his autobiography,

> We had got but a little way from the gates when the brougham came
> to a stand, completely lost in the fog. Thinking I could do better on
> my feet, I left the brougham; in a few steps I had lost my way and
> sense of direction. I walked into the head of a horse and felt my way
> along its side until I found a hansom-cab attached to it. The driver,
> when asked if he could find his way to Birdcage Walk, said he had
> just come from it and would try; he succeeded after some time and it
> was then easy to follow the curb at a foot's pace to the Foreign Office
> where I then took over the work.

On 21 December, when Campbell-Bannerman was making a
formal statement to the effect that the Entente with France would
be maintained, Dorothy was writing to her friend Ella Pease:

The last fortnight has been quite the most horrid we have ever had and it is a great grief to both of us that Edward is in a government without Rosebery. But I am very glad he should have work that interests him so much. There is a lot of flummery about the Foreign Office and I try not to think about how badly I shall do my small part of the work. But I shall try very hard.

In his biography of Grey, Trevelyan tells us that at the time the government was formed, Dorothy kept repeating, 'this is separation'. It is difficult to decipher whether she was referring to Rosebery or her husband. She was dreading playing the political hostess and was devastated by Rosebery's self-imposed exclusion from government. We must assume she was referring to her husband, as the Greys joined Rosebery at The Durdans for Christmas.

Christmas at The Durdans would have been a welcome release for the Greys. Dorothy, who invariably preferred animals to people, would have relished her conducted tours around the stud. Grey, for his part, had the use of a squash court and a 'pro' to play with. Indoor activities included hours of perusal in the great library and, fortified by his Lordship's Madeira, enlightened conversation on such diverse subjects as racing, nightingales, Liberal politics and the European diplomacy. With his formidable insight, Rosebery forecasted a momentous breakthrough for the Labour Party at the forthcoming elections which would have far-reaching consequences for the Liberals. With the recent growth in the power of organised labour, Rosebery foresaw the Labour Party taking up the radical cause on the left wing of British politics. He anticipated that the Tories on the right would continue to champion Empire and democratic capitalism. Meanwhile, the Liberal Party would split in the middle and wither on the vine.

The twelve months from April 1904 to April 1905 under Lansdowne were a significant period for British diplomacy, setting a course that

Grey would follow through to the outbreak of war nearly a decade later. Rosebery foresaw that the Entente Cordiale would eventually lead to war with Germany. The Germans were in the right over French actions in Morocco, yet the Kaiser's appearance in Tangier was ill-judged and provocative. However, Britain was determined to stand by her French ally and demonstrate the Entente had substance, thereby relegating the importance to Britain of good relations with Germany. In addition, because of the close ties between France and Russia, the Entente Cordiale implied improved Anglo-Russian relations. As the drama unfolded, Germany would become increasingly paranoid about her own isolation, which over time would raise the political temperature across Europe to fatal levels.

The Entente Cordiale Bedded Down

1906 was the most momentous year in Grey's life. As soon as his feet were under his desk at the Foreign Office he was faced with crucial decisions that would confirm his country on a diplomatic course which, nearly nine years later, would result in the despatch of the British Expeditionary Force to France. The first few weeks of the new year represented some of the toughest in Grey's long career. He entered office at a time of international crisis as Germany tested the Anglo-French Entente over Morocco. The Algeciras Conference which had been called to review the Moroccan situation was now at hand and the French were keen to ascertain from the new Foreign Secretary the level of support they could expect from Britain, not just at the conference but also in the last resort of an armed conflict with Germany.

New Year was a stressful time for Grey as he had to settle in at the Foreign Office and fight a general election at the same time. On 1 January he wrote to Dorothy,

> I am up to my eyes in work and have a settled sadness at being in office. I think of it every morning when I wake and feel just as I did about being back at school. The electric light has gone out suddenly and I have nothing but two quiet candles to work on within this large room. It is very cold.

He spent the first three days of the week in London, leaving for Northumberland on the Wednesday night sleeper. The balance of the week was taken up with electioneering in his large rural constituency, which stretched from Berwick to Alnwick. The contents of the dreaded red boxes that followed him from the Foreign Office had to be read before breakfast. On top of all this pressure was to come more personal tragedy.

On 3 January, Grey had his first official meeting with the German ambassador, Count Paul Wolff-Metternich. It was important to brief the respective ambassadors of Germany and France at an early stage as to what they could expect from the incoming Liberal administration in terms of foreign policy. Grey informed the ambassador that the new friendship with France and the removal of old colonial quarrels by way of the Entente were most popular in Britain. He told Metternich that Britain had no intention of making any trouble for Germany at the Morocco Conference but would not leave the French in the lurch as a result of a question arising out of the Anglo-French agreement. Metternich reported on the meeting to Berlin,

> Later in the conversation Sir Edward Grey said he had found among his predecessor's memoranda a conversation with me the previous summer in which Lord Lansdowne indicated that, if there was war between Germany and France on account of Morocco, public feeling would force the Government to fight for France. He, Grey, believed that the British people would not stand France being involved in a war with Germany on account of the Anglo-French agreement and that, if it happened, any British Government, whether Conservative or Liberal, would be forced to help France.

So began the first of many warnings to Berlin of Britain's likely position with France if war was forced on her by Germany.

Grey was most conciliatory towards Metternich and expressed a general wish for improved relations between the two countries. In a letter to the Prime Minister on 9 January he wrote,

On behalf of the Government I have said that we shall not use
the Anglo-French Entente against German policy or interests: that
though at the Conference we must keep our public engagement to
France, we shall not egg on France against Germany; and that if
things go smoothly at the Conference it will be possible to use our
influence with effect to ameliorate the tone of the press and public
opinion here respecting Germany. Also that we wish to improve relations between France and Germany.

In the same letter he mentions the diplomatic benefits that might
arise from helping Germany acquire a coaling station on the west
coast of Morocco. This demonstrates a degree of *naïveté* from an
inexperienced Foreign Secretary, as the Admiralty, let alone the
French, were dead set against such a plan. He also hints at the fledgling military conversations between Britain and France, 'but the
War Office ought, it seems to me, to be ready to answer the question, what could they do if we had to take part against Germany if,
for instance, the neutrality of Belgium was violated'.

The relationship that soon developed between Grey and
Metternich was excellent. It was one based on mutual respect. In
the same communication with Berlin, Metternich reports favourably on the Foreign Secretary's greatest asset, his personality: 'I will
first say that Sir Edward Grey gives me the impression of being a
frank, straightforward man, that one knows where one is with him.'
Grey for his part writes of Metternich in his autobiography:

He had been rigid in upholding the German view against ours ... But
I always felt that whatever I said would be faithfully reported by him;
that no chance and unintentional slip of mine would be distorted
or misrepresented. In the whole of our transactions I never found
reason to complain of any unfairness. It was also my impression
that, however stiff Metternich might be in upholding the views of
his Government to us, however little disposed he seemed to concede
anything, yet in his own reports to Berlin he put the British view in the
most favourable light that he thought could fairly be placed upon it.

On 10 January it was the turn of the French ambassador, Paul Cambon, to meet Grey at the Foreign Office. Cambon was an agreeable, sagacious, professional diplomat who had been sent to London nearly ten years earlier by Delcasse to work up the Entente Cordiale with Britain. He came straight to the point. Would Britain provide France with armed support in the event of an attack by Germany arising out of the Morocco situation? Grey was on the back foot as he was unable to consult the Prime Minister or his Cabinet colleagues during the election campaign. He replied that in his opinion British public opinion was likely to be sympathetic but all he could promise was 'benevolent neutrality'. Grey explained that everything would depend on the manner in which a war broke out. Furthermore, a commitment to provide France with support in advance of such aggression would effectively be transforming the Entente into an alliance. As Cambon departed, Grey promised to consult his colleagues and agreed to meet the ambassador again when the election was over.

Cambon was not, however, to leave the Foreign Office empty handed. At the end of the meeting he raised the question of continuing unofficial military conversations which had been taking place between the respective naval and military experts under the last Conservative government. They focused on sending an Expeditionary Force of over 100,000 men to France within two weeks of the outbreak of hostilities. If Britain did indeed decide to take France's side in a future armed conflict with Germany, it was only sensible that there should be a military strategy in place. In an age of strategic railways, mobilisation would move at a rapid pace. Grey agreed that these conversations be put on a more formal basis, writing in his autobiography,

> Plans for naval and military cooperation had, I found, begun to be made under Lord Lansdowne in 1905, when the German pressure was menacing. The naval conversations that had already taken place had been between experts yet the military conversations had hitherto been through an intermediary. Henceforth it was decided

they too, would be direct. But it was to be clearly understood that these conversations or plans between military or naval staffs did not commit either Government and involved no promise of support in war.

To avoid any misunderstandings, the new Secretary for War, Richard Haldane, arranged for a letter to be signed by the Director of Military Operations, General Grierson, and the French military attaché in London, Major Huguet, stating that the talks did not commit Britain.

There has been much criticism of Grey over the years about the 'secret' nature of the military conversations. His decision to author- ise the talks without the matter being discussed at Cabinet would prove one of the most controversial actions of his tenure at the Foreign Office. Grey discussed the whole concept with Haldane in his constituency on 12 January. Haldane then gave Grey the neces- sary authorisations for the conversations to proceed and they were placed on an official footing on 15 January. The Prime Minister was not informed of the conversations until he arrived back in London on 26 January, when he gave his blessing for their continu- ation. While there was no legal commitment attached to these talks, they obviously implied moral support. The Prime Minister was concerned about the interpretations which might be put on the conversations, as witnessed by a letter to Lord Ripon dated 2 February: 'I do not like the stress laid upon joint preparations. It comes very close to an honourable undertaking and it will become known on both sides of the Rhine.' His concern was obviously not serious enough for him to insist that he or the Foreign Secretary should raise the issue at the first Cabinet meeting on 31 January.

It is very likely that Grey for his part expected opposition over the conversations from the radical wing of the Cabinet and one can only assume he was keen not to involve them if at all possible. The radicals were shocked when they heard of the talks for the first time some five years later during the Agadir crisis. The concealment contributed to an atmosphere of suspicion and encouraged the post-Agadir critics of Grey's foreign policy. As Douglas Hurd writes in his essay on Grey, 'If the military talks with France had been concealed for five years, what else might be going on behind their backs?' However, it was common practice for Foreign Secretaries throughout this period to have two circulation lists for certain documents on foreign affairs. In Grey's early days in office, the Cabinet was far too involved in its domestic programme to give much time to foreign policy. 'Limited' circulation would normally include the Prime Minister, Asquith, Haldane, Ripon and sometimes Morley, the only radical amongst the group. Grey almost certainly exonerated himself in the knowledge that the military planning was taking place on a hypothetical basis without any commitment. In addition, not being an expert on military matters, he could justifiably detach himself from their content. He left the whole exercise to the experts without checking on their progress. General Grierson and his assistant, General Robertson, attended French Army manoeuvres that summer, selected ports for landing troops and areas for deployment along the border on the basis of a German invasion through Belgium.

On 27 January, the Greys joined the Prime Minister for the weekend at Windsor Castle, where it is thought the King was fully briefed on the military conversations with France. In his personal correspondence, Cambon states that the three men decided to keep silent and the Prime Minister confirmed the Cabinet would not be informed. If this is the case, the Prime Minister should take as much blame as his Foreign Secretary. If the conversations were considered 'secret' in London, they were open knowledge in Berlin, as demonstrated by this passage from Prince Lichnowsky's *Heading for the Abyss*: 'The Anglo-French naval pact as well as other agreements of a defensive nature which had arisen out of the Morocco crisis, although for a long time known to the German Foreign Office through reports of their secret agents, had not been communicated to the German

embassy in London.' In fact, it seems the military conversations were also open knowledge amongst many opinion formers in Britain. J. A. Spender always felt that high-ranking soldiers were indiscreet, writing in *Life, Journalism and Politics*:

> I myself knew nothing of the critical conversations between Grey and Cambon during the month of January and I am afraid was thinking much more about the Liberal triumph than the Algeciras Conference. In the course of the next few months I learnt – though not from Grey – that our military advisers were in touch with the French and that they had roughly agreed about their method of cooperation, if circumstance should compel them to act together.

Spender understood, as did many others less informed than he, that diplomatic action without the back-up of military support would be of little use in checking an ambitious Germany. He found it hard to believe that so many members of Cabinet claimed ignorance of the talks, even though they were doubtless distracted by their domestic responsibilities. It was widely known that Britain might become involved in a continental war, hence Haldane's plans for an Expeditionary Force that could be mobilised at a few days' notice with the Territorial Army in reserve behind it. Spender writes, 'There was no concealment; the military correspondents and those of us who expounded the scheme in leading articles spoke quite frankly about its assumptions and the emergencies it was intended to meet.'

Lloyd George must take some of the blame for the hype surrounding Grey's 'Machiavellian secret diplomacy'. In his *War Memoirs*, Lloyd George is highly critical of Grey in his role as Foreign Secretary. He accuses him of being aloof, insular and almost entirely out of the clash of party conflicts. His disingenuous commentary centres around the lack of an 'early warning' to Germany regarding the circumstances under which Britain would enter the war. He remarks on the general secrecy of foreign affairs and the lack of discussion on such matters in Cabinet, particularly

when it came to the subject of the military conversations which
he claims he first heard of in 1911. He goes so far as to say that
the French and Russians regarded these talks as tantamount to
a commitment to aid France if she was attacked by Germany.
While there was no doubt some truth attached to the latter, Grey
and others, including the King, had on countless occasions stated
to Germany that while Britain was at no point legally committed
in such a situation, public opinion in Britain would be so sympathetic to France that it would be impossible for any government to
remain neutral.

There was unquestionably a moral commitment to France
implied by the military conversations and the French authorities
must have been greatly encouraged by their initiation. In July 1914,
Eyre Crowe, the Assistant Under-Secretary, prepared a memo for
his chief arguing the case for intervention, writing,

> The argument that there is no written bond binding us to France is
> strictly correct. There is no contractual obligation. But the Entente
> has been made, threatened, put to the test and celebrated in a
> manner justifying the belief that a moral bond was forged. I feel
> confident that our duty and our interest will be seen to lie in standing
> by France in her hour of need. France has not sought the quarrel. It
> has been forced upon her.

Grey was well aware of the moral aspect and stated many times
that he would resign if the Liberal government did not stand by
France in the event of an attack by Germany, writing,

> If there is a war between France and Germany it will be very diffi-
> cult for us to keep out. The Entente and still more the constant
> and emphatic demonstrations of affection (official, naval, political,
> commercial and the Press) have created in France a belief that we
> shall support them in war. If this expectation is disappointed, the
> French will never forgive us. There would also I think be a general
> feeling that we had behaved badly and left France in the lurch …

On the other hand the prospect of a European war and our being
involved is horrible.

Grey was walking a tightrope and he knew it. So did the Prime
Minister, who stated the military conversations created at least
'an honourable understanding', but even if he wanted to, a legal
commitment could not be given, owing to his 'parliamentary
straitjacket'.

It could be argued that to create a moral commitment on an
issue as important as this and then not to discuss it in Cabinet
or Parliament was bordering on deception. With hindsight Grey
regretted not having had a wider debate at the time and admitted that 'with more experience [he] would have shared the Prime
Minister's apprehension'. He himself was very clear as to the defini-
tion of any 'honourable understanding' with the French. He writes
in his autobiography, 'But the honourable understanding between
myself and Cambon was very clear, and it was that nothing that
passed between French and British military authorities was to entail
or imply any obligation whatever on either Government.'

Grey admits that he created a rod for his own back by not calling
for a full Cabinet discussion on the subject of the military conversations, but the Prime Minister and other senior Cabinet colleagues
who were privy to the information must equally share the blame.
They all took advantage of the fact that the radical section of the
Cabinet were too preoccupied with domestic reform and their own
briefs. Grey's retiring character did not promote extensive debate in
an open forum; he hated confrontation. Zara Steiner writes in *The
Foreign Office and Foreign Policy 1898–1914*,

> Part of the Cabinet's ignorance over the full extent of the existing ties
> between Britain and France was due to lack of interest and domestic
> preoccupations but part was also due to Grey's reserve and reluc-
> tance to discuss policy questions in Cabinet. Grey's high reputation
> in the country assured him a large measure of freedom in his office.
> Unless openly challenged he preferred to avoid open debate. Yet the

radicals in the Cabinet knew far more about Grey's diplomacy than they later admitted. If they could not move the Foreign Secretary on fundamental issues they could and did force him into unwelcome paths. Lloyd George's contention that 'the Cabinet as a whole were never called into genuine consultation upon the fundamental aspects of the foreign situation' is neither accurate nor just.

J. A. Spender certainly thought that the charges against the Foreign Secretary of secrecy and deception were grossly misleading. In his autobiography he writes,

> The reader who has had it hammered into him that 'secret diplomacy' played a great part in those times, will, perhaps, be pulled up by hearing me say that secrets were of no importance. So let me pause for a moment to testify on this point. In after years it fell to me, in helping Grey to write his own narrative, to read through the chief part of the British diplomatic record of the time. Again and again, when I came to the principal transactions, I asked myself whether there was anything unknown to me before which would have changed the general judgement, if it had been known at the time, and whether there was anything withheld which ought to have been known. And invariably I found myself answering that there was nothing. There were many interesting new details, much that helped to make real and vivid the story of Grey's own part, but the picture in broad outline remained as before, and none of its main features needed to be repainted or seriously modified. Grey's policy stood as a perfectly straightforward handling of the known facts and material, and whether he was right or wrong, neither supporters nor opponents have cause to say that if they had known more they would have judged differently. British action at all important moments was what it seemed to be and its motives what they were supposed to be, and if others were deceived it was because they imagined the reality to be different from the appearance, and imputed to Grey Machiavellian designs of which he was entirely innocent.

❦

While all this drama with the French was unfolding in Whitehall, Grey's Cabinet colleagues were away in their constituencies preparing for the election. Polling was spread over three weeks, commencing on 12 January. Grey's own result in Berwick was announced on 25 January and represented his best ever, topping 5,000 votes. The Liberals' overall majority nationally was 132, the opposition returning only 157 members, including 132 Conservatives and twenty-five Liberal Unionists. The Labour Party allied to the Miners Federation won forty-three seats. This was the revolution in British political history that the brilliant and visionary Rosebery had foreseen. The working classes were even represented on the Liberal benches. John Burns, a former working-class agitator, was given the Local Government Board. He tells a charming story of how, when arriving at Court for the first time in his Privy Councillor's uniform, he was saluted by the guardsman who a few years before had prodded him in the backside with a bayonet at a demonstration.

Meanwhile Grey had received a forceful despatch from his ambassador in Paris, Francis Bertie, in reply to his Cambon memo of 10 January. The ambassador pleaded with the Foreign Secretary to promise France more than simple neutrality in the event of a war initiated by Germany. Bertie was encouraged in his endeavours by Grey's new private secretary, Louis Mallet, who was an enthusiastic Francophile. Grey's appointment as Foreign Secretary coincided with the arrival of a group of extremely able men who occupied key positions at the Foreign Office. The new Permanent Under-Secretary, Sir Charles Hardinge, took up office a few weeks after Grey and became an invaluable friend and adviser. Hardinge was the elder of the two, and with Grey coming from the conservative wing of the Liberal Party, the two men would work well together, Hardinge writing in *Old Diplomacy*,

> With Grey I was able to discuss everything with the utmost freedom, more as two equals than as chief and subordinate, and he allowed

me the greatest freedom of action ... I always look back on those
five years of work and cooperation between Sir Edward and myself
as five of the most fruitful and happiest years of my life. They were
ceaseless sunshine without a shadow.

Like many of his contemporaries at the time, Hardinge was very
much 'old school', having been educated at Harrow and at Trinity,
Cambridge. He was immensely well connected, knowing Curzon,
St John Brodrick and the King, in addition to his wife being one
of the Queen's ladies-in waiting. He was an energetic and efficient
diplomat whose abilities were quickly recognised by those at the
top. His career was greatly assisted by Edward VII, who could still
persuade the Foreign Office to accept his recommendations for
senior diplomatic posts. Being an ambitious man, after a series of
minor diplomatic postings, Hardinge returned to London, where
he joined the camp of those associated with reform at the Foreign
Office. Under the new administrative system, responsibility would be
diffused down to an extremely able team of senior officials who were
all concerned about German ambitions and anxious to strengthen
Britain's ties with France and Russia. In 1903, the King used his
influence to secure Hardinge the top job in St Petersburg, where he
would lay the groundwork for Grey's Entente four years later.

Grey, Hardinge and Bertie feared a restless Germany and were
always looking for ways to shackle her power, hence they strove for
friendship with Russia and were determined to give backbone to
the Entente Cordiale. On 20 February, Hardinge wrote to his chief:

It is generally recognised that Germany is the one disturbing factor
owing to her ambitious schemes for *Weltpolitik* [on the back of
Germany's rise as a major industrial and trading nation, a call arose
for overseas expansion through the acquisition of colonies] and for a
naval as well as military supremacy in Europe.

Grey was his own man but, as Steiner writes in *The Foreign Office
and Foreign Policy, 1898–1914*, 'The strength of Hardinge's conviction

influenced the already uneasy Grey and gave a distinct focus to British policy.' Grey's experiences of the Germans during his last spell at the Foreign Office had left a nasty taste. Hardinge was one of the first diplomats to grasp the growing threat of the German Navy and the problems it would generate for future Anglo-German relations. In the coming years, Grey would always throw his weight behind the 'big Navy' group in Cabinet discussions over the naval estimates, which set a ceiling for annual expenditure on the Navy.

Sir Francis Bertie and Louis Mallet were the two most avid anti-German officials in Grey's employ. Bertie was the most accomplished of Grey's ambassadors. He was convinced that Germany would involve Europe in a world war and that the only course for Britain's safety was to turn the Entente with France into an alliance. Mallet would do everything in his power to bolster Grey's support of France in the impending Moroccan discussions at Algeciras. While generally sympathetic, Grey kept a weather eye on his officials at the Foreign Office. The new head of the Western Department was Eyre Crowe, a leading German expert and a celebrated Germanophobe. Crowe had married a German and had many high-ranking connections in that country. He, too, was worried about the growth of the German Navy and believed that Germany would upset the balance of power in Europe. He writes in a Foreign Office minute, 'My impression gained from much personal intercourse with Germans of all classes and from the study of German periodicals and literature, is that the necessity of an all-powerful Navy has become an act of faith with the whole mass of the German population including a large number of socialists.'

The Algeciras Conference opened on 16 January and the British delegation was in the good hands of Sir Arthur Nicolson, an experienced diplomat with strong anti-German leanings. Grey was determined to give the French maximum diplomatic support and thereby bolster the Entente. There was no better man for the job than Nicolson. Like Crowe, he saw Germany as the only threat to the European balance of power and passionately believed that Britain's security lay in her entente with France. In fact, if he had his own way, the Entente would be turned into an alliance. His son Harold describes him at the opening of the conference:

> Already bent with rheumatism and arthritis, he would bend even lower over his papers. A shy person, one would say – a small, frail figure with a finely shaped forehead. Diffident, apparently, and engagingly honest. Suddenly he would raise his eyes – those blue and piercing eyes – from his papers. In fluent Oxford French he would state his case: fact upon fact: moderately, calmly and with an authoritative certainty which hushed all interruptions. He had about him a sense of control which was something more than self-control. They did not accost him when he left, small and smiling, for his villa.

In later years, the German ambassador, Prince Lichnowsky, writes of Nicolson, 'He was no friend of Germany's, but his attitude towards me was scrupulously correct and courteous.'

As soon as the elections were over, Cambon was back in Grey's office on 31 January, seeking the reassurances for which his government was so desperate. Would Britain come to France's aid if she was attacked by Germany? This was to become one of the most controversial meetings of Grey's political career. What sort of commitment did Grey give Cambon? The revisionist historians, and particularly Niall Ferguson, in his book *Empire*, refer time and time again to Grey's 'commitment' to France. On many occasions Grey stated his personal opinion that if Germany forced war on France, Britain should go to her assistance. He also stressed that in these circumstances he felt public opinion would be on the side of France but he knew Cabinet and Parliament would not bind themselves in advance of the specific reasons for war. When criticising the pro-French officials at the Foreign Office, who were desperate for a firmer commitment to France, Douglas Hurd writes, 'What Sir Eyre Crowe and others had to accept, despite their own upbringing and studies, was that in Britain, in the last resort, policy is made not by professionals but by a Cabinet responsible to Parliament.'

Grey told the French ambassador in no uncertain terms that he could not give France a blanket assurance on the war issue as it would effectively mean transforming the Entente into a defensive alliance, which would not be favourably received at Cabinet or by Parliament. To soften the blow, he related how he had recently informed Metternich that in the event of the Germans forcing war on France, British public opinion would most likely come out in favour of intervention on France's side. Lord Lansdowne had stated as much eighteen months ago. He then reiterated to a relieved Cambon that Britain would honour her Entente commitments, leaving France a free hand in Morocco and promising continued diplomatic support at Algeciras. Finally he confirmed that much progress had already been made with the military conversations but, of course, on a totally non-binding, uncommitted basis.

Cambon was desperate to take something more substantial back to France than Grey's personal words of comfort, but in his heart of hearts he realised the impossibility of receiving a firm commitment from the Foreign Secretary. He understood that the radical majority in Cabinet and a Liberal-dominated Parliament would never give their assent to a formal alliance. It was a tricky meeting for an inexperienced Foreign Secretary. The following day, Grey sat down and wrote to Dorothy: 'I had tremendously difficult talk and work yesterday, and very important. I do not know that I did well but I did honestly.' This was his last letter to his wife. A few hours later in the lanes around Fallodon, she was thrown from her dog-cart as the horse shied. She landed on her head, was rendered unconscious and never recovered.

On 1 February, Grey lunched with John Morley, Secretary of State for India, at the Foreign Office. In the afternoon he was attending the Committee of Imperial Defence when his private secretary Louis Mallet brought in a telegram conveying the tragic news of Dorothy's accident. Grey took the night train from King's Cross. He reached the schoolhouse in Ellingham where Dorothy lay

unconscious in the early hours. She died on Sunday 4 February. *The Times* obituary column described her life as 'so private and so retired that it seems almost an impertinence to write anything of it for public perusal'. The enigmatic Dorothy was portrayed on the one hand as 'a woman in a million' to those who knew her well, and on the other as cold, unsympathetic, reserved, self-centred and severe to those who didn't. She was a maverick, one who never courted popularity, detested publicity and had little time for society.

Mrs Creighton, an intimate friend of both the Greys, hurried north to be beside Edward in his hour of need. She writes in her memoir of Dorothy,

> They carried her body back to Fallodon that afternoon. It lay in the library at Fallodon, beautiful in death, with a smile of perfect peace. The sun streamed in through the open windows and the squirrel came in as usual to fetch its nuts from the box. The first snowdrops from the garden were laid upon her breast. The sun shone, too, when we carried her body to Darlington to be cremated according to her wish. It was a day of fresh wind and blue sky and bright sun such as she would have loved. We, a little band of not more than seven friends, followed her body across the cemetery in the sunshine, the soft wind blowing back to us the scent of the flowers that covered the coffin and we left the fair covering of the noble spirit to be returned to the elements whence it came.

Although there was no physical side to the Greys' marriage, their love and affection was close and immensely strong. They shared common tastes and interests. Dorothy's counsel was much valued by Grey in his political career, as evidenced by this passage from *Twenty-Five Years*:

> Through all our married life I had been in the habit of discussing public affairs and sharing all thoughts with my wife; and she had been interested in discussing these with me. Her interests and outlook on life were wide and her opinion on what came before her

and on all that we talked of was always fresh and independent, some-times so original as to penetrate new aspects and throw new light on the subject; never was it commonplace or second-hand, never the outcome of conventional or party or class thought. All this was now withdrawn from me. We had acquired knowledge and shared thought together and developed tastes and pursuits in common.

While not doubting for one moment Grey's feelings for Dorothy and his reliance on her judgement, one can be forgiven for thinking her death may not have left him as friendless as his words suggest. If Grey was in the process of a long-standing affair with Pamela Tennant at the time, he would have received all this support and maybe more from his mistress.

After the funeral on 7 February, Grey had to catch up with the contents of those daunting red boxes that followed him remorse-lessly from the Foreign Office on his travels. They were full of news from the Algeciras Conference, where the highly capable Sir Arthur Nicolson was executing his chief's instructions to the full: 'to help France carry her point at the Conference'. Nicolson was given a long rein by Grey. He wrote to his wife, 'I find the Conference most interesting. The Government leave me entirely alone. I work alone happy and untrammeled.' The conference can be split into two distinct periods. A period up until early March when Germany was on the offensive, displaying all her natural aggression, and a period thereafter when she was isolated and in tactical retreat. There were two main issues at stake: the control of the Moroccan police and the internationalisation of the State Bank. France was willing to be flexible on the shareholder structure of the Bank but in no circumstances would she agree to compromise on the police question. She was insistent that control be shared between herself and Spain, while Germany proposed alternative schemes to prevent it happening.

In the early weeks Germany tried her best to isolate France. On 3 February, Count Tattenbach, one of the German delegates, met Nicolson to persuade him to put pressure on the French to make concessions. Nicolson held his ground, describing Tattenbach to Grey as 'a rasping, disagreeable man, not straightforward or truthful'. Throughout this period German diplomacy showed itself in its worst possible colours. Germany's game plan was to sow distrust of Britain in the minds of the French. To this end, she circulated rumours that Britain was planning to cease diplomatic support for France. The German delegates bullied and lied their way through the proceedings and in the process lost the confidence of other European countries and, more worryingly, America. There was no need to behave in this fashion, but it was all too often the nature of German diplomacy. Germany had a good case to argue but, as usual, she failed to handle it correctly. There never seemed to be any structure, consistency or concrete goals to German foreign policy. Nicolson wrote to his wife:

> I don't at all like the look of things. Germany is playing a double game, false and contradictory. She says one thing at Berlin, another at Washington, another at St Petersburg, another at Rome and Madrid. And Radowitz [the first German delegate] says different things to every person he talks to. The reason is that Germany does not know what she wants.

The turning point in the conference was the vote of 3 March. The Germans had persuaded Austria to propose that Casablanca should be excluded from the Moroccan ports to be policed by Franco-Spanish officers. The French dug their heels in and refused to give way. The conference then began to discuss the State Bank issue, when it was suggested that proceedings be suspended for a few days. Sir Arthur Nicolson immediately proposed that the delegates should revert to discussing the police issue. It was decided to put the matter to a vote, where Germany found herself isolated by ten votes to three. Only Morocco and Austria sided with her. Grey had yet to develop his close relationship with President Roosevelt but he must have been encouraged by the stance of America. Although the President had persuaded France to agree to a conference the previous year, when proceedings opened he firmly supported the French, as he believed their interests in Morocco were more significant than those of other powers.

The German Chancellor, von Bülow, who was determined at the outset to avoid isolation or any kind of humiliation, signalled a general retreat. On 6 March he agreed to accept a compromise on the police question and von Holstein was removed from the case. A month later the Act of Algeciras was signed, with Germany receiving the small consolation of an international police force being stationed at Tangier. With his resolute support of France, Grey had strengthened the Entente, which significantly had not gone unnoticed in the capitals of Europe. On 12 April, Spring-Rice wrote to Grey from St Petersburg:

> May I express the very warmest admiration for your conduct of affairs in the last few weeks? Your absolutely straight unwavering and frank declaration of your intention to stick to Lord Lansdowne's engagement has made a deep impression both here and at Paris. I don't believe the Russian Government would have quite come up to the mark without your example. The ally couldn't do less than the friend.

Grey was subtly preparing the ground for a future friendship with Russia. As early as 19 February he had written to Spring-Rice explaining his Moroccan policy: 'Meanwhile I am impatient to see Russia re-established as a factor in European politics. Whether we shall get an arrangement with her about Asiatic questions remains to be seen: I will try when she desires it and is ready.'

Grey's foreign policy was not anti-German. He always maintained that the Entente Cordiale should not prohibit friendly relations with Germany. However, he was not prepared to cultivate a rapprochement with Germany at the expense of the French. Even after Algeciras, France was edgily insecure and unfairly felt that Britain was on the verge of abandoning her commitments under the Entente. German diplomacy revelled in mischief-making and played on these insecurities. The Germans did not fear the Entente but they disliked it. In the past it had suited them for Britain to be on bad terms with France. Hence, during the summer they cultivated a rumour in Paris that Britain was planning an entente with Germany, citing the King's visit to the Kaiser at Kronberg and Haldane's invitation to attend German Army manoeuvres as evidence. On top of this, in May, Britain received a glut of official visits from German burgomasters, artists and newspaper editors. Grey had a most delicate path to tread with French sensitivities. He was constantly needing to pour oil on troubled waters. The King's visit went ahead despite the Foreign Secretary's misgivings and Haldane was told by his friend in no uncertain terms not to attend any German military parades celebrating the anniversary of the Battle of Sedan.

Later in the year Grey began to work on his relationship with Theodore Roosevelt. In December he wrote to the President thanking him for American support at Algeciras and outlining his foreign policy:

> It is not anti-German. But it must be independent of Germany. We wish to keep and strengthen the Entente with France, who is now very peaceful and neither aggressive nor restless. She also plays the game fairly and as long as she trusts one she is a good friend. The weak point is that she might some day have a scare that we intended to change. I think Germany has already tried more than once to make her imagine this.

Later in the letter he touches on Germany's aggressive plans for *Weltpolitik* with an accompanying arms build-up for the domination of Europe. Grey would never forget the history he had been taught at Winchester: that England always opposed any power which tried to dominate Europe.

The Foreign Secretary's workload was frightening. He would rise at 7 a.m. and resume work on his red boxes until breakfast at nine o'clock. After breakfast he would review the newspapers and work on private correspondence before arriving at the Foreign Office at 11 a.m. In the morning he would deal with overseas telegrams and papers sent to him by his Under-Secretaries. Then in the afternoon he would meet with officials and have appointments with foreign ambassadors. After tea he would work on his red boxes and return home about 7 p.m. He often had an official dinner, which meant working on his boxes again before bed. In his autobiography he characterises the worst type of day for a Foreign Secretary as one which included a debate in Parliament, as he then somehow had to make up for the time taken from his Foreign Office work:

> One of the most depressing moments is after a long Foreign Office debate in the House of Commons. The debate may have begun at four o'clock and ended at eleven. It will have been necessary for him to sit through it and to speak, possibly to make a difficult and important speech. When the debate is over he enters his room at the House of Commons and sees the pile of red boxes that have accumulated.

Grey made his first important appearance in the House as Foreign Secretary on 5 March, when he spoke on the reform of the Consular Service. The *Westminster Gazette* reported the following day: 'The Foreign Secretary made an excellent impression on the House, his manner cool and collected and his voice modulated to the pitch of cold impartiality which seems to remove every question he touches far from party passion into the clear light of pure reason.'

Poignantly, there were no further entries in *The Cottage Book* after Dorothy's death. The last entry in his 'northern diary', *The Fallodon Green Book*, was in early February:

> On the 1st of February Dorothy was thrown from her dogcart near Ellingham; she was never conscious afterwards and died in the schoolmaster's house between three and four on Sunday morning, two days and three nights afterwards. I am left alone with no wish to live. Fallodon as it is today is what she made it; the planning and the taste is all hers. I cannot even keep it beautiful without her. It is my wish presently to make a record of all that she did in the house and in the garden, in the hope that someday when I am gone the place may again belong to someone who will love it and be grateful to her. In the meantime I shall do what I can to keep it all as she left it and shall come here to rest and live in the happy past; if indeed I live for all my mind is clouded with a doubt.

When work permitted, Grey took the night sleeper north to Fallodon. One can imagine the pain and loneliness he must have felt on those first few visits after Dorothy's death. He returned home for the weekend on 17 February, writing to Mrs Creighton, who he had asked to undertake a memoir of Dorothy,

> I am having a hard struggle. Every day I grasp a little more of all that it means. Just when I have got my spirit abreast of life, I feel and understand more sorrow and sink again. Sometimes it is like a living death; and the perpetual heartache which has set in wears me down. I have gained time by work; I did it all this week and did it well and could give my mind to it. But sorrow keeps pace with time; it gets fuller and makes itself more felt and realised.

He was back at Fallodon two months later and embarked on one of his favourite bicycle rides over the moorland road from North Charlton. He then proceeded to climb Ross Camp and was invigorated by the spring notes of the golden plover and curlews. His

friends were worried about his solitude; on 15 April he wrote to
Katherine Lyttelton:

> There need be no fear of my being alone here. It is true that I am
> alone but in that way I learn what sorrow teaches and that is to
> the good. For instance, I ask if Dorothy joined me again should I
> be more or less loving now? And the answer is more loving. I had
> learnt all that happiness could teach me and now I have learnt more,
> for sorrow and happiness both teach love, only each leaves so much
> untaught which only the other can give. And so I am learning and
> growing, my spirit is becoming more fit to meet hers or to go, when
> the time comes, wherever hers has gone. These thoughts come to
> me in solitude. We both had an unusual gift of solitude, the power
> to enjoy being alone, but she had used it more than I had done and
> in the last ten years she had grown more than I had, partly by illness,
> partly by being many days alone, partly by strong friendships; while
> I had always been more hustled and bustled by public life and work
> and business so that I was getting left behind. Now in a time like this
> when I am constantly thinking and longing, love goes on growing
> and I would not have it disturbed by anyone else with me just now.
> Much of each day is very sad. But I am used to that and before each
> day is over there come thoughts, which turn to peace and at the
> worst I am never angry or impatient or in despair.

That Grey needed both his friends and his work is demonstrated
by this touching letter to his great political ally Richard Haldane
immediately after Dorothy's death:

> It is over and we are companions in sorrow now until life ends. I shall
> feel the need of friends, a thing I have never felt while I had her love
> every day and could give all mine to her. If I could realise at once all
> that this means I could not live but I suppose nature will dole out to
> me just the suffering every day which I can bear. My best chance is
> to begin work again at once and I have told them to begin sending
> Foreign Office work to me tomorrow. Will you have me in your flat

if I come to London next week and have all my things moved down from the flat above?

The Germans were not the only thorn in Grey's side in the spring of 1906. The traditional Anglo-Turkish friendship that went back to the Crimean War had been reversed and in recent years Britain had lost influence in Constantinople. Turkey was ruled by the degenerate, mentally deranged Sultan, Abdul Hamid, who was responsible for the Armenia massacres in 1895. The persecution of these minority Christian groups in the Turkish Empire had caused great indignation in Europe and particularly in Britain, yet as ever it was proving difficult for the powers to act in harmony over their protest. Ever since Britain's occupation of Egypt the Sultan had found it hard to resist meddling in local affairs. Grey and Hardinge both suspected that Turkey was being encouraged by Germany in her intrigues. German influence, backed by her military prestige and a complacency to the Sultan's atrocities, had become predominant in Constantinople, Grey writing,

> German policy seems to have been based upon a deliberate belief that moral scruples and altruistic motives do not count in international affairs. Germany did not believe that they existed in other nations and she did not assume them for herself. The highest morality for a German Government was the national interest; this overrode other considerations and as such she pursued it at Constantinople. Her policy was completely successful; ours was deadlock and failure. Germany pushed her commercial interests in Turkey; the wealth of Asia Minor was passing into her hands, but she gained these advantages by acting on the belief that morals do not count in policy.

In April, Turkish troops occupied certain areas at the base of the Sinai Peninsula and demanded that Egyptian troops be withdrawn from the island of Tiran, the only satisfactory anchorage in the Gulf of Aqaba. Lord Cromer was not amused, as there had been a long-standing arrangement with Constantinople that the Khedive had the right to administer the Sinai Peninsula. Grey was quite willing to establish a proper boundary in Sinai but only through friendly negotiation, which would take time. He was certainly not going to be bullied, as the aggressive line taken by the Turks menaced the Suez Canal. With Grey's blessing, the British garrison in Cairo was reinforced, a gunboat sent to Aqaba and the Mediterranean fleet steamed eastwards. The Sultan was presented with an ultimatum on 3 May which expired ten days later. He backed down as the clock struck twelve. Grey was pleasantly surprised by the attitude of Germany over the crisis. Although there was a good deal of suspicion in Britain at the time over their railway construction activities in the Ottoman Empire, the Germans gave the Foreign Office an assurance they would not support the Sultan in this disagreement. Meanwhile the Foreign Secretary was quietly acquiring substantial support for his firm, common-sense approach to the crisis and he was congratulated in the press for handling the situation with 'dignity and fairness'.

In his autobiography Grey charmingly describes his personal predicament on the final day of the ultimatum. That day, 13 May, was a Sunday and Grey had to spend the morning at his London residence in Queen Anne's Gate with Charles Hardinge and Eldon Gorst, awaiting the Sultan's reply. The second Sunday in May was known in Grey's calendar as 'Beech Sunday', representing that time of the year when the young fresh beech leaves were at the peak of their beauty. He writes,

It was my habit on that morning each year to bicycle to a beech wood some nine miles from The Cottage. There I lunched once every year on that day at the foot of a certain tree. The wood was entirely of beech; the trees standing far apart, the grey boles grew up straight and clear and smooth for some distance above the ground. High overhead the branches touched and made a canopy; the blue sky just visible here and there; the sunshine coming through the

tender, light-green leaves; a breeze stirring them now and then, but
very gently, such was the vision of what I had seen and known year
by year that was present to me in the Foreign Office in the second
week in May. I thought of it, looked forward to it, counted on it.

Thus the Sultan ruined Grey's 'Beech Sunday': 'I now had to wait
another twelve months to see the great beech wood as I knew it in
its greatest beauty.' The Sultan's reply was received at midday. That
same afternoon Grey, not to be put off by second best, took the train
to Guildford and walked some of his favourite Surrey countryside,
arriving back in London that evening refreshed for the coming
week's work.

Grey had shown his teeth to the Turks in Sinai. A few weeks
later, another incident took place in Egypt which necessitated
a firm response from the local administration on the ground. In
the middle of June a group of British Army officers were pigeon
shooting at the village of Denshawai when they were attacked
by the inhabitants. One of the party was killed and several injured.
The death sentence and life penal servitude were served on those
responsible. The excessively harsh sentences were badly received
both in Egypt and back in London by the radicals in the Liberal
Party. Understandably, Grey and the Prime Minister did not want
to undermine the authority of the local administration, but it was
a political embarrassment. The radicals at home remembered only
too well Grey's imperialist views over the Boer War and his forward
foreign policy at the headwaters of the Nile. Grey's biographer
Keith Robbins views the Denshawai Incident as one of the decisive
moments in the evolution of modern Egyptian nationalism: 'It
provided just the kind of issue to unite discontented urban journal-
ists and intellectuals with the peasant masses.' Grey himself was
always embarrassed by the severity of the sentences and eighteen
months later he instructed Eldon Gorst, Lord Cromer's replace-
ment, to release the prisoners.

The incident had caused quite a stir in the press and on 5 July
Grey was called upon to defend the executions in Parliament. The

qualities of trust and calm reassurance inherent in his character were badly needed in this instance. He told the House that the punishment was carried out in a humane fashion with no callousness or thoughtlessness demonstrated. The *Westminster Gazette* reported the next day:

> If anything was needed to prove Sir Edward Grey's ability to handle the difficult and delicate questions that fall within the sphere of his department, the admirable discretion and tact which he displayed in the debate on the Foreign Office vote yesterday would have afforded a triumphant endorsement of the special qualities he possesses for the post.

Fresh from his successes at Algeciras, Sir Arthur Nicolson was despatched by Grey to St Petersburg on 28 May as the new ambassador. His brief was to initiate talks on arrival with Izvolsky, the Russian Foreign Minister. With Nicolson on the ground, the last building block was in place for Grey to achieve his dream of an agreement with Russia. At the Foreign Office, Sir Charles Hardinge was also desperate for an understanding. His knowledge of Russia and experience with Russian officials would be vital in securing a deal. Hardinge writes in his autobiography,

> I have been so imbued with the importance of an agreement with Russia that it was one of the reasons which induced me to give up the embassy in St Petersburg since I felt that I could do more by impressing my views on people at home and I promised Lamsdorff and the Emperor that I would do my level best to bring it about.

In the same way as Britain ironed out colonial differences with France in 1904, Grey entrusted Nicolson with the task of reaching an Asiatic agreement with the Russians. He was to negotiate specifically on Tibet, Afghanistan and Persia, three countries where

Britain had been quarrelling with the Russians over the right to protect states that had no real wish to be protected. There was a general need to ease tensions in the Middle East and also to reduce the military burden on the government of India but, as with the French Entente, Grey saw the real benefit in Europe. Both Hardinge and his chief believed that Russia provided the vital continental check to the German threat, although they well understood that patience would be required. The Russians were still licking their wounds from defeat at the hands of the Japanese.

Patience and sensitivity would be essential for success, as the concept was to generate detractors on both sides. There was a strong prejudice against Britain in Russia following the alliance with Japan; moreover, a powerful element at the Russian court and in government circles favoured a deal with Germany. The rulers of Russia were not only suspicious and hostile but also unstable. Nicolson foresaw the cataclysm around the corner. To make matters worse, public opinion in Britain was running against an understanding at this time. The radical wing of the Liberal Party viewed Russia as a barbarous country that denied her subjects such liberties as trade unions, and one that existed under the constant threat of social unrest and revolution. Grey was even being criticised by his own supporters for allowing the fleet to visit Kronstadt, as the massacre of Jews in Russia was causing an outrage in Britain amongst the Liberal élite. The Foreign Secretary, with a weather eye on his Russian agreement, demonstrated his tough, uncompromising side. He claimed that the massacres were not the responsibility of the Russian government and, what is more, to cancel the fleet's visit would upset the Reform Party. Looking at the big picture it was difficult to see what Nicolson could offer the Russians. When negotiating with the French, Britain offered the carrot of Morocco. Free passage through the Dardanelles was a possibility, but this concession required agreement from all the powers and in any case hardly seemed desirable. The prospects were far from promising, yet Grey and Hardinge at the Foreign Office and the trusty Nicolson on the ground were not to be dissuaded.

Nicolson began formal negotiations with Izvolsky in early June, Tibet being the first issue on the agenda. Harold Nicolson writes in his biography of his father, 'Nicolson was not by nature a patient man. In the small affairs of life he would fidget at a momentary block in the traffic, at the slightest hesitation or stumbling in a person addressed. In public affairs, however, his patience was phenomenal.' Events would quickly prove how badly he needed this quality. Socialist revolutionaries continued to spread anarchy and terrorism across the Empire. Between the outbreak of the revolution in January 1905 and May 1909, nearly 1,500 provincial governors and state officials had been murdered by terrorists. On 22 July the Duma was dissolved and a state of martial law was introduced, which produced an outburst in Liberal Britain. The Prime Minister concluded a speech to a Russian parliamentary delegation in London with the words, 'La Duma est morte, vive la Duma.' This in turn caused much agitation amongst government circles in Russia. Both Hardinge and Grey suggested that negotiations be suspended. To his eternal credit Nicolson kept the discussions alive, even though they proceeded at a snail's pace.

Just before Parliament rose for the recess, Grey experienced the first of many battles over the naval estimates, which would cause a serious split in Cabinet for some years to come. The radicals, who were pushing for an expensive social reform programme, were desperate to reduce naval expenditure. At the Foreign Office, Hardinge, well aware that a successful foreign policy depended on a strong Navy, was understandably worried about Germany's recent naval build-up. At a Cabinet meeting on 10 July covering the 1906/7 estimates, Asquith asked for the four proposed Dreadnought battleships to be cut to two. After much argument the Prime Minister decided to set up a committee to resolve the issue, comprising himself, Asquith, Grey, Fisher and Tweedmouth. Grey was in an unenviable position. On the one hand he was committed to an agenda of social reform, while on the other he had to ensure that the Navy kept ahead of the German construction programme. On 9 May he had supported a motion in the House on the reduction of armaments, arguing that Britain should currently give a lead 'as her naval superiority had never been so undisputed'. A compromise was reached by cutting £1,500,000 from the naval estimates. One battleship was dropped and another was made conditional on the outcome of the Hague Conference for Disarmament taking place the following year.

Grey's detractors have been all too ready to accuse him of putting his leisure interests before his parliamentary duties. In his first year at the Foreign Office he only managed to fish the Itchen on two Saturdays all season. On 2 June he wrote to Eddy Tennant lamenting his lack of fishing: 'I have not put a rod up yet. I calculate it is thirty-seven years since I let June arrive without having caught a trout!' Finally, on the morning of 4 June, he fished the Top Water Beat taking five trout, and on 14 July he fished 'Jaw Hatches' in the afternoon only, catching a solitary fish. What is more, in April he had sacrificed his real passion, a fortnight's spring salmon fishing on the river Cassley. In later years, as pressure of work built up and his eyesight weakened, this annual spring holiday became sacrosanct, with either Haldane or Morley providing cover at the Foreign Office. If giving up his only holiday in the far north of Scotland was not bad enough, turning his back on his beloved Itchen was even worse. 1906 saw the novice Foreign Secretary taking his new responsibilities very seriously indeed.

Even Saturdays were consumed by work. At the end of the year he described his life to his friend Henry Newbolt: 'Foreign Office work is like the Greek Furies, it pursues one incessantly and one may not rest and read. I fly from it every Saturday evening but it catches me up on Sunday morning.' Grey was one of the most accomplished real-tennis players in the country, playing twice a week at Lord's. He now found it impossible to stay match-fit and keep the fixed times necessary for competitive matches, so he gave up the sport altogether. He did, however, institute a new regime for Sundays in the autumn and winter. He would stay at the Forest Park Hotel in Brockenhurst and on Sunday mornings, after he had opened his red boxes, would set out into the New Forest with a sandwich in his pocket, only to return under the moon and stars.

Grey returned to Fallodon around the beginning of August for the parliamentary recess. On arrival he felt very low and tired. He missed Dorothy dreadfully yet he was delighted to be back in the bosom of his home. He wrote to Mrs Creighton,

> I am glad to be here. There is something of the parent about one's home; and how few people can have a home in which they have been brought up as children and which remains their own and their home. It strikes me as a very rare thing. At first I was very low on coming back here. Now I am better than I have been. A feeling has come over me that love is going on unimpaired.

Later in the month his spirits and sense of humour revived with visits from close friends such as Haldane and Spring-Rice. He delighted in the company of both men yet was disappointed neither could contribute on the card table, writing to Lady Helen Munro Ferguson,

> It is a pity that one should love Bridge and then find that one has collected for friends the only people in the world who dislike it, though I agree generally in disliking the people who like it; which suggests a doubt whether if one liked Bridge one is really fit to be a friend of anyone who dislikes it. Happily I play it badly.

The autumn session proved an uphill struggle for the Liberal Party. Although they had been returned with a massive majority, the House of Lords continued to wreck their business programme.

The government's major Bills on Education and Plural Voting were rejected by the upper chamber, while the Agricultural Holdings Act received a severe mauling. The Education Bill was basically Balfour's Act of 1902 but tailored to remedy some of the grievances of the Nonconformists, while the Plural Voting Bill was designed to end the antediluvian practice of landowners who owned land in more than one constituency receiving more than one vote. If it was the object of the Lords to delay badly considered legislation then there was a case for rejecting the Trade Disputes Bill. However, their lordships cynically let it through as they were not willing to confront organised labour. The overwhelmingly Tory House of Lords, aptly known as 'Mr Balfour's Poodle', was acting in a thoroughly unconstitutional fashion and seemed only interested in causing maximum damage to the government. So began the long, drawn-out war between the Lords and Commons which finally ended with the Parliament Act of 1911. Lloyd George was desperate for battle to commence, as was Grey, who had always longed to abolish the hereditary peers and substitute an elected chamber.

Against this dire parliamentary background there were renewed concerns for the Prime Minister's health, raised, ironically, at a time when he had finally won over the admiration of his colleagues. His wife, to whom he was immensely close, had died at Marienbad on 30 August. King Edward was visiting his favourite spa at the same time and showed real concern and affection. The King attended the simple service at the local cemetery and wrote to his Prime Minister, 'I know how great your mutual devotion was and what a blank the departed one will leave in your home. Still I feel sure that you can now only wish that your beloved wife may be at peace and rest and free from all suffering and pain.'

On 2 October, at Belmont, his home in Scotland, Campbell-Bannerman suffered the first of a series of heart attacks that would result in his death eighteen months later. At the end of the parliamentary session on 21 December, J. A. Spender wrote in his biography of Campbell-Bannerman: 'It was generally acknowledged and by opponents as well as friends, that the Prime Minister had established

a firm hold on Parliament and the country, and developed qualities of both intellect and character in his handling of great affairs
for which even his friends were hardly prepared.' Spender was no
doubt referring to Grey and his fellow Relugas conspirators.

In late December Grey went north to spend his first Christmas
alone at Fallodon. One can imagine the feeling of emptiness he
must have endured. He wrote to Mrs Creighton, 'It was very bad for
the first day or two at Fallodon; I don't quite know why – perhaps
it was because of the vivid memory of this time last year when
the election was beginning.' In *The Charm of Birds* he writes of an
event that took place on Christmas morning of such beauty that it
became etched on his memory for ever. He could not remember the
date, but relates how 'it was many years ago when my sight was less
impaired'. If one had to guess, it was probably his first Christmas as
a widower, but in any event it demonstrates not only how much his
wildfowl collection meant to him but also why he is ranked as one
of Britain's best nature writers:

> I went out after breakfast; the waterfowl had been fed rather later
> than usual: they were still finishing their meal under the big larch
> tree or were assembled at this end of the pond, which being much
> shut in by trees and shrubs, was still in dark shadow. I went to the
> other pond some two hundred yards away and sat on the garden seat
> on the farther side. The pond is more open: there are no tall trees
> on the east side and all the water was in full sunlight. There was
> not a bird on it; there was no stir in the air; the surface of the water
> was smooth and without motion. Presently pintail, widgeon, tufted
> ducks, pochard and one or two other kinds began to come flying
> over the intervening shrubs and trees from the pond where they had
> been fed. They came, some singly, some two or three together. None
> of them had yet seen the sun that morning and each and all, as if
> in greeting to it, began to sport and play. They threw the water over

their bodies, they raised themselves up on it and flapped their wings; they swam rapidly in all directions, low in the water with quick and eager forward dartings of the head and neck. They sprang from the water into the air and took headers from the air into the water; they made short flights in one direction, lit on the water for a moment and made another flight back in the direction whence they came. They dived unexpectedly, travelled underwater, came up in some new place, and then, as if surprised at what they saw, dived again with exceeding suddenness. They splashed for the sake of splashing; there was not a square foot of water that was not in constant agitation. For some time the scene was of motions of delight and exhilaration. At length, first one bird and then another flew up onto the bank that faced the sun or on to the south end of the little island; there they stood or sat, many of them side by side in pairs and rested motionless or slept. Some half-dozen birds only remained on the water and each of these was still, the head turned round and the bill resting in the feathers of the back. All was quiet; there was no sound or stir; the water again was smooth, the reflections in it were composed once more; the sun still shone; on the water and the birds; on the scarlet-barked willows and the delicate bareness of winter trees on the opposite side. Anyone who had come upon it now might have thought the place was under some spell. He would have seen a man on the seat sit motionless too, for a long time; entranced rather than asleep: the scene had indeed sunk down into his heart and 'held it like a dream'. There are times when man's consciousness seems laid to rest in one great whole, of which he has become a part. There are hours of which it can be said, 'thought was not, in enjoyment it expired'. So it was now and if anything stirred in the mind at all, it was an echo of the words 'and God saw that it was good'.

The famous ornithologist James Fisher said Grey 'wrote like a dream'. Just why was he such an accomplished nature writer? It seems incongruous that a successful politician who prospered in the rough-and-tumble of the House of Commons for a generation should also be able to write in an erudite and sensitive fashion about the loveliness of the countryside. Most importantly, he was born an English countryman, amongst the burns and hills of Northumberland, where as a boy he developed an immediate interest in country sports. Then, as a young man, he came under the influence of others, his wife Dorothy, the poet Wordsworth, the writer W. H. Hudson and finally his second wife Pamela. From this eclectic group he acquired a genius for bird observation, a love of verse and a special appreciation for the beauty of nature. Grey first discovered Hudson in 1893 when he was tied to his ministerial desk in London. One night Dorothy sent a message to Grey in the House, 'First about the Hudson book, I have read a good deal: it touches very fine notes for feeling for nature. I felt first sad because it was such a long way off from what we are doing.' Grey always longed to flee Westminster and join Hudson on his sylvan progresses around the English countryside, writing to a friend some years later, 'Some day when there is a storm and you are all hugging your houses and reading your *Times*, I shall take the road and be no more seen, and wander till I cease upon the midnight somewhere in the open air.'

Grey was an incurable dreamer who also displayed a strong religious faith, and like his mentor William Wordsworth, he saw God through the beauty of the world. Hence he wrote of a spring day in the Itchen valley:

The beauty has been overwhelming; pear and apple blossom overlapped and the profusion and splendour were more than human capacity could appreciate. I used to feel at this season of the year a sense of waste because I could not enjoy at once all that was spread abroad; till one day the overwhelming egotism of looking at it from this point of view occurred to me, and I thought that God might be contemplating it all. Then I ceased to be oppressed by the sense of waste. The sight of all this beauty and the feeling of response to it in oneself gives assurance that God rules in the Universe and that no evil can prevail.

Like his friend Hudson, he delighted in expressing his treasured rural experiences through the written word. But above all, it must have been the contrast in Grey's life that contributed most to his superb prose. So unhappy was he at the grind and monotony of political life that he longed for his weekend release to The Cottage or the New Forest. He must have lain awake night after night pondering an escape home to Northumberland or taking a fishing holiday in Sutherland. The stresses of office and the many tragedies in his personal life would have sharpened his pencil as he recalled the many happy memories of the past. Grey's nature writing will always remain a testament to the 'happiness that on balance outweighed the sadness' in a life full of both achievement and tragedy.

An Entente with Russia

G rey had negotiated his first crisis as Foreign Secretary with
honours. In doing so he had strengthened the Entente and
demonstrated to the international community that the cornerstone
of Britain's foreign policy was a close understanding with France.
Under Grey's stewardship Britain had discarded her self-imposed
Victorian isolation and could now be trusted as a friend. Britain's
steadfast support of France was not lost on the Russians, who would
be Grey's next target. Now that the Algeciras Conference was over,
many opinion formers in Britain looked forward to a much desired
détente with Germany. After all, they said, Britain had no need
to quarrel with Germany as there were no real parts of the world
where their respective interests clashed. Grey, however, remained
cautious. The Germans had taken no pains to cultivate Britain's
friendship and their traditional policy of playing off power against
power, in order that they should profit from the divisions of others,
had reared its ugly head again at Algeciras. Germany simply didn't
come across as a comfortable bedfellow and would need a careful
eye. Harsh German diplomacy, on display once again at the conference, had resulted in self-imposed diplomatic humiliation and Grey
was well aware Germany would not tolerate such a climb-down
again. The military conversations, rightly authorised by Grey but
rashly kept a secret from the majority of Cabinet colleagues, went off
the boil after Algeciras, when any immediate threat of war receded.
However, their initiation, coupled with the fact that Haldane was
currently working up his plans for a British Expeditionary Force,

meant that Britain was assured a sound strategy at the outbreak of hostilities in seven years' time.

The positive side to all this pressure was that it kept the new Foreign Secretary's mind focused. He still missed Dorothy dreadfully. As the anniversary of her death approached in early February, he retired alone to Fallodon. He wrote to Mrs Creighton on 2 February,

> I have been in London all this week and had to stay for a Cabinet yesterday. This morning I got home at sunrise. There were many of these winter morning homecomings and I always used to go straight to Dorothy's room and she had a fire lit and we sat by it and had a little tea while I told her all my news. I have the tea and the fire put ready for me now and go to sit there first. There I found your letter this morning and I am very grateful for it; it gave me comfort. What you have learnt by your own sorrow is a priceless gift to your friends when they have to tread the same path. My great prayer and struggle now is for strength; I cannot feel interest in politics at all, nor in my work as I should; it continues to die away and that makes things very hard for there is so much work and it is so incessant.

With the disarmament talks looming at the Hague Conference in June, Grey found himself in yet another uncomfortable position. Although the 1899 conference had completely failed on the arms limitation front, the new Liberal government felt they should take account of public opinion and push for some form of disarmament agreement. After all, they had shown the international community the way forward with cuts in their naval and military budgets during their first year in office. In February, Grey wrote to President Roosevelt urging that America should initiate a proposal for arms limitation at the Hague: 'I can't help feeling that if the two great strands of the English-speaking nations stand together for common sense and peace the rest of the world will follow.' The Prime Minister went even further, publishing an article in *The Nation* on 2 March concerning the importance of arms limitation to world peace. The Germans, needless to say, took it as an Anglo-French plot to frustrate their efforts in making good HMS *Dreadnought's* technological lead. As a result at the end of April, Bülow announced in the Reichstag that Germany would decline to discuss anything to do with disarmament at the conference.

King Edward disapproved of the forthcoming conference and was concerned that Grey 'might be carried away by sentimental ideas'. The King had met the Kaiser at Kronberg in the autumn. He remembered only too well how the German Emperor had praised militarism and poured scorn on the approaching conference. The King need not have worried. Grey, as Foreign Secretary, was only too aware of the importance of keeping ahead of Germany's construction programme, as were his officials at the Foreign Office. In fact, W. T. Stead, an enthusiastic peace campaigner and former editor of the Liberal *Pall Mall Gazette*, blamed Hardinge and his colleagues at the Foreign Office for the failure of the conference. Stead felt that Grey gave too much power to his subordinates. Zara Steiner in *The Foreign Office and Foreign Policy 1898–1914* writes, 'Stead's attack oversimplified a complex personal relationship. Hardinge was not Grey's master but his partner. A genuine concordance of views, particularly in the vital matter of Anglo-German relations, bound them close.'

Hardinge's subordinates shared his own suspicions of German motives, none more so than the Foreign Office's chief authority on Germany, Eyre Crowe. Early in the new year, Crowe had produced a classic memorandum on Britain's relationship with France and Germany which Grey circulated to the Prime Minister, Ripon, Haldane, Asquith and Morley. The memo covered the whole history of diplomatic incidents over the last decade. Grey saw it as a useful guide to policy. Crowe described the Entente as 'hardening' and in Britain's dealings with Germany he insisted that 'firmness pays'.

He demonstrated that German policy was dominated by hostility to Britain and that, prior to Algeciras, German aggression was met by concession after concession. He claimed that German policy was characterised by 'a total disregard for the elementary rules of straightforward and honourable dealing'.

Crowe argued that now Germany had become a great industrial and military power it was only natural that she should want to become a world power with a colonial empire. This expansion was unlikely to be peaceful and with the construction of a powerful battle fleet it would upset the existing balance of power in Europe. Crowe was part of the British delegation to The Hague and felt that the dominating influence at the conference had been a fear of Germany. He wrote to Charles Dilke,

> The most marked feature of the Conference to my mind has been the open hegemony exercised by Germany over the states of Europe; not only Austria and Italy but also Russia almost invariably voted with her. Our disarmament crusade has been the best advertisement of the German Navy League, and every German has by now been persuaded that England is exhausted, has reached the end of her tether, and must speedily collapse if pressure is kept up.

The Hague Conference ended in failure, with Germany and Russia in particular refusing to discuss arms limitation. Russia was still rebuilding her armed forces following defeat by Japan, and Germany continued in her quest to challenge British sea power. Trevelyan, in his biography of Grey, referred to the conference as 'another milestone towards Armageddon'. Not unnaturally, while fighting his Foreign Office corner, even Grey was lukewarm in his support for disarmament. Secretary Root of the American delegation stated that Grey's support was merely a gesture 'to satisfy English public opinion'. The whole conference seemed to unite against Britain on any question of naval warfare, with the right of capture of seaborne commerce as the central issue. A contest had developed between Britain wanting to uphold the prerogatives of sea power and the Continentals trying to reduce them. In the event of war with Germany, blockade of the North Sea and Channel ports was a vital weapon in Britain's strategic armoury. As a result, Grey was determined to preserve the right of capture from any restrictions. Against this pessimistic background and much general resistance, there was one ray of hope. When it ended in August, the Americans managed to push through a resolution calling for a third conference in eight years' time.

The new year saw negotiations for a British agreement with Russia proceeding slowly but steadily in the right direction. Izvolsky, who was anxious not to upset the Germans, had visited Berlin in the autumn to ascertain whether they had any objections. The Russian Foreign Minister received a greenish light from Berlin but his visit raised suspicions in London. It was only a year before that the Czar had met the Kaiser at Björkö. While the main aim of a Russian agreement was to secure the defence of India, Grey was adamant that Russia should not form a pact with Germany. In such a case France might then be forced to defect, thereby isolating Britain in Europe.

The easiest item on the negotiating agenda was Tibet, and agreement was reached by the end of January. Grey was only interested in securing the country as a sanitary cordon against Russian infiltration towards India. In the event, Nicolson secured full recognition of Britain's predominant position in Tibet together with a Russian agreement not to interfere in the affairs of that country. For her part Britain agreed to evacuate the Chumbi valley and both sides agreed not to send in scientific or geographical explorers for three years, thus tightening the isolation of Tibet.

Persia was the core of the agreement and the danger-point. Grey writes in his autobiography,

> The inefficiency of Persian Governments, the state of their finances, the internal disorders, not only laid Persia open to foreign interference,

but positively invited and attracted it. Tehran, the capital and seat
of the Central Government, was in the north of Persia; it was in
easy striking distance from Russia, it was quite out of British reach.
Russia had therefore a great and perpetual advantage in the struggle
that went on between British and Russian diplomacy in Tehran.

For some years the government of India had been concerned about
the possibility of Russian penetration in two areas: the Persian
Gulf and the province of Seistan, the eastern province of Persia on
the Indian frontier. Grey decided to pursue a policy idea of Lord
Curzon's: that of dividing Persia into spheres of interest. Russia's
interests would be prevalent in the northern zone, with Britain
occupying the south; a neutral zone would be formulated in the
middle. By the beginning of April agreement had been reached
as to the delimitation of the respective spheres of influence. The
Russians received the whole of the northern zone including
the capital, Tehran, together with important trade routes, while the
British zone comprised the important Afghan and Indo-Persian
frontier regions. A compromise was reached on the Persian Gulf.
The government of India disliked the fact that the majority of the
Gulf coast fell into the neutral zone. As a result, Grey received in
writing from the Russians an acknowledgement of Britain's special
interests in the Gulf. Although the agreement provided for the independence and integrity of Persia, the local government in Tehran
was not enamoured of the proceedings; for generations they had
played on the rivalry between Britain and Russia.

The Anglo-Russian agreement was finally signed on 31 August
after a last-minute compromise over Afghanistan. The Foreign
Office and government of India were delighted with the Afghan
section. Russia had recognised Afghanistan as outside her orbit,
promised to conduct future political relations through the British
government and agreed that her agents were forbidden to enter the
country. Nicolson had followed up Algeciras with another remarkable success. Grey was effusive in his praise, writing to him, 'Since I
have been at the Foreign Office I can say without qualification that

in everything in which you have been engaged you have made a success. I wish that you could be multiplied at will so as to be available at once in every place where there were difficulties.'

Grey himself was congratulated by the Prime Minister:

My hearty congratulations on the Russian agreement which is a great achievement. For a time at least it removes the danger of an Asiatic avalanche and will make things easier in Europe. Even if the respite prove comparatively brief, you have at least the honour of having secured it by your tact, patience and firmness.

Campbell-Bannerman was correct in his assertion that Russian dealings in Persia would cause Grey untold headaches in the future, yet the Indian frontier was now secure and Britain had an additional comfort against German ambitions in Europe. France was obviously well pleased with the outcome. Germany adopted an attitude of reserve, with an insecure and paranoiac Kaiser more convinced than ever that his country was being encircled by its enemies.

It is doubtful whether Grey could have concluded a successful agreement with Russia without the assistance of John Morley, Secretary of State for India. Rosebery had been Grey's mentor on Empire and foreign affairs, but it was Morley who moulded his domestic political views. Grey had always been fascinated by Morley's intellect and closely followed his articles in the *Pall Mall Gazette*. Grey's radical views on Home Rule and reform of the Lords, so unlike others from his privileged background, were formulated at a young age under the influence of Morley. Richard Haldane in his autobiography wrote how Grey differed from Asquith and the other Imperialists: 'Grey they found more difficult. He had a most attractive personality and embodied the best tradition of the Whigs. But he was advanced in his views and of a very independent mind. The Whips could not count on him as they could with Asquith.' It is interesting to note that the two men whom Grey leant on most in his early years, Morley and Ripon, both came from opposite wings of the party and reflected his views on domestic and foreign policy respectively. Ripon had been closely consulted over the military conversations with France and during his time at the Colonial Office came to appreciate the danger of German ambitions.

Grey wrote to the Prime Minister on 31 August, 'Without Morley we should have made no progress at all for the Government of India would have blocked every point: Morley has removed mountains in the path of negotiations.' To Morley himself, Grey wrote, 'If you had not taken the strong and clear line which you did, we should have had to go to the Cabinet time after time to get authority to overrule the objections of the Indian Government.' It is clear that these two Gladstonian elder statesmen, who would have known Grey's grandfather, the Home Secretary Sir George Grey, took a paternal interest in the young Foreign Secretary's career. It is also evident that whether in the Cabinet or the Foreign Office, colleagues liked and trusted Edward Grey. Morley greatly admired his abilities on the floor of the House, writing of Grey's performance in the Russian Agreement debate early in February 1908, 'He is a singularly attractive speaker. Grey followed Percy in that curiously high, simple, semi-detached style which, combined, as it always is in him, with a clean-cut mastery of all the facts of his case, makes him one of the most impressive personalities in Parliament.' Morley had always enjoyed a close interest in foreign affairs. In Grey's later years at the Foreign Office, Morley was only too willing to act as a stand-in while the Foreign Secretary recharged his batteries on the river Cassley.

While Grey was busy securing a fundamental strand of his foreign policy with an agreement with the Russians, he was not dilatory in other directions. In Europe he had recently signed an agreement with Spain which pledged both countries to maintain the status quo in the waters adjacent to southern Spain and north-west Africa. On the other side of the Atlantic, as demonstrated at Algeciras, America was emerging from a period of diplomatic isolation. Grey was determined to capitalise on this situation and establish more intimate relations with the United States. In Roosevelt, the 'rough rider' and conservationist, Grey recognised a kindred spirit.

He immediately commenced a written correspondence with the President, thanking him for his diplomatic assistance at Algeciras and urging him to support arms limitation at The Hague. Grey got on particularly well with the American ambassador in London, Mr Whitelaw Reid, and wanted to reciprocate in Washington, where Sir Mortimer Durand had not been a success as British ambassador.

The King was keen to send Hardinge but Grey was loath to lose his services at the Foreign Office. He then unsuccessfully tried to tease Rosebery, who was sulking at Dalmeny, out of his self-imposed retirement. In March he settled on James Bryce, the Secretary for Ireland, who was an intellectual and a distinguished author, having also written a classic work on the American Constitution. Grey wrote of Bryce in his autobiography, 'Probably no Ambassador was ever so qualified as Bryce, by a combination of great intellectual gifts and natural simplicity, to bring out the points of resemblance and sympathy between the two countries, and to recommend them to the Americans.'

Grey was not the only new minister who was up to his neck in work. His close friend Richard Burdon Haldane was engaged on a programme of reform at the War Office that would earn him his place in history as the most effective ever Minister of War. At the time of the Boer War the Army was in a chaotic state. The British Army was scattered across the Empire in small groups and at time of war, volunteers were recruited who lacked training, discipline and equipment. Haldane writes in his autobiography, 'Not only was there no General Staff to do the thinking, but the organisation in time of peace was different from that required of war, so different that there was hardly a unit that was capable of taking the field as it stood.' Although the Conservative government had failed to push through army reform, enhancements to the system had been implemented. By December 1902, Balfour had formed his new Committee of Imperial Defence to coordinate defence planning across both the Army and Navy. The following year the Esher Committee was set up to propose improvements in the operation of the War Office. Its major recommendation was that a modern command structure should be created under a new Chief of the General Staff. Lord Roberts would be the last officer to hold the rank of Commander-in-Chief.

When Haldane commenced his deliberations at the War Office in the new year of 1906, his position was not an enviable one. Conditions were now totally different from Victorian times. The two old enemies, France and Russia, were now benign. There was next to no chance of a French invasion across the Channel or a Russian incursion towards the Indian Empire. It was the Germans who currently made the British apprehensive. What did they plan to do with their rapidly growing modern Navy? A German invasion from the Channel ports was a distinct possibility, thus an Expeditionary Force was needed which could be rapidly mobilised and maybe come to the aid of France. To make life more difficult for Haldane, his radical colleagues were both screaming for budget savings and firmly set against conscription. There were also many people only too pleased to see him fail with his reforms. Even the Prime Minister remarked caustically on his appointment to the War Office, 'We shall now see how Schopenhauer gets on in the Kailyard.' Haldane achieved the impossible. He reconciled economy and efficiency and won over his critics in the process. He had the organisational and intellectual abilities for the task and demonstrated great tact in deal- ing with the Generals. Haldane characteristically buried himself in books on German military procedure and appointed an excellent military private secretary in Colonel Ellison, formerly Secretary of the Esher Committee. Grey's support was invaluable and, with his industry and energy, Haldane won over Campbell-Bannerman from the start.

Haldane introduced his Army Bill on 25 February. The basis of his plan was to reorganise the existing muddled mass of troops in the regular army, militia and volunteers into two distinct lines. For overseas service, he introduced a fully equipped professional

Expeditionary Force of 160,000 men, made up of six divisions, including a cavalry division that was capable of reaching France within fifteen days. A second-line army was then formed out of the Yeomanry and Volunteers, which would become the new Territorial Army. The Territorials would be earmarked for home defence, administered by local county associations. The militia was abolished and a Special Reserve created in its place which would be used to replace losses amongst frontline troops. Finally, to assist in the planning and execution of his designs, Haldane ordered the formation of a General Staff. All this was achieved with a saving of £3 million from the Army estimates. Haldane's Army Bill became the principal achievement of the 1907 parliamentary session. For all the criticism surrounding the 'secret nature' of Grey's military conversations, it is hard to argue with Trevelyan, who writes in his biography,

> The early arrival of the British Army in France in August 1914 just saved Paris and the Channel Ports from capture. But for the Haldane Reforms and the much-abused Military Conversations which Grey had sanctioned, the war would have been lost at the outset. For the Military Conversations had enabled the British and French authorities to lay plans together beforehand for the transport of our Expeditionary Force to France.

No one denied the Foreign Secretary's heavy workload, but many criticised him for not speaking enough both inside and outside the Commons. Unlike Churchill and Lloyd George, both brilliant self-publicists, Grey preferred to keep a low profile. He did, however, have to answer questions in the House twice a week and one columnist came to his support, writing, 'Those who know what his daily work is will bear the highest testimony to his steadiness and persistency in advancing good causes by quiet means.' On 10 April, Grey replied for the government in support of Haldane's

Army Bill, putting the detailed reforms into layman's terms and at all times reinforcing the hostility of the government to any form of conscription. The *Westminster Gazette* reported:

> His speech was a godsend to those Members who had not yet clearly grasped the outlines of Mr Haldane's scheme. Sir Edward employed the simplest language and thus brought the Government's proposals, stripped of all bewildering phraseology, clearly before the most unmilitary mind in the House. Across the quiet, clear stream of argument there flashed at times a gleam of humour, as when he reminded the Opposition that they should be the last to criticise the Government's scheme, after their notable failure to solve the problem of army reform.

These comments throw light on his speaking abilities and why he was considered such an accomplished parliamentary performer. Contrary to what his critics would have us believe, he had the intellectual firepower to assimilate a difficult brief but at the same time the ability to put across complex solutions in a clear and concise manner. His delivery was always calm, unemotional and totally devoid of any amateur theatricals.

The Russian agreement was one of the cornerstones of Grey's foreign policy. It was hardly surprising, therefore, that he felt it necessary to cancel his spring holiday salmon fishing on the Cassley for the second year running. One can see from his fishing diaries that he did however manage to fish the Itchen on eleven occasions throughout the season from May until August, nearly always on a Saturday. The Avington water, which was hosted by Grey's cousin Lord Northbrook, carried six rods. Vernon Watney, a close friend of Grey's, was a member of the syndicate, as was Grey's brother Charlie. During this lonely period of his life Grey delighted in the company of his younger brother, who often stayed at The Cottage when fishing the river. Grey's most successful day was late in the season on 3 August, when he caught eleven fish on a red quill gnat, the largest being 1 lb 12 oz. Grey felt that ten pounds' weight of brown trout should make the angler content, fifteen pounds would be considered good and twenty pounds exceptional.

The formality of official state receptions and banquets invariably curtailed the weekends, on which Grey relied for his sanity. The Colonial Conference opened in London on 15 April with Lord Elgin in the Chair and his Under-Secretary, Winston Churchill, characteristically making most of the running. On 22 April Grey wrote to Mrs Creighton:

I had to go to a dinner for the Canadian Prime Minister on Saturday, so half a Sunday and a Sunday night was all I had at the Cottage. It rained and I walked over Itchen Down to Abbotstone and enjoyed the rain. But to keep you in touch with the Cottage I send you a little news. The long-tailed tits' nest is safe but whether the eggs and birds are in it I do not know; it has a ruddy cock pheasant's feather in the mouth of it. The cock chaffinch still drags a wing but is in high spirits; both it and the rival are very tame. The wagtails have gone. A willow warbler has come but no nightingale yet. This morning was beautiful, blue sky and warm sun on moist earth; it was heart-rending to leave it. I see no signs that any of these Colonial Premiers care for these things and a Japanese Mission is being sent all the way from Japan on purpose to destroy by another official dinner my 'Beech Sunday' in May.

In late September, Grey departed for Scotland to spend two days with the King at Balmoral. He would doubtless have preferred to be alone at Fallodon, yet he was touched by the King's kindness and charm. Any formality of court life would have been alleviated by visits to the Dee to catch a salmon and walks on the hill to enjoy the golden eagles soaring above Glenmuick. Grey's father, Colonel George Grey, had been one of the first equerries to Edward VII when he was Prince of Wales. Grey appreciated the way in which the King recalled memories of Colonel Grey when he had been with him in Scotland. He also never forgot the comfort and sympathy Queen Alexandra demonstrated to his mother at the time of his father's death. Grey thought the Queen a beautiful woman who sadly suffered from increasing deafness. At the time of her death Asquith stated that Queen Alexandra was the one royal he loved. After dinner one night, the King and his Foreign Secretary discussed the failure of the Hague Peace Conference. The King demonstrated a distinct dislike of his German nephew and it was his view that the Kaiser's highly-strung and temperamental personality was largely responsible for Germany's aggressive and domineering foreign policy. The King ominously reminded Grey that when he met his nephew the previous year at Kronberg, the German Emperor had told Hardinge that 'any talk of reduction of military strength merely causes smiles in Germany'.

When the King met the Kaiser at Cassel as part of his Continental summer tour, Hardinge reported to Grey that there was no intimacy between the King and his nephew, yet relations between the King and the Emperor of Austria were most friendly. The King invited Clemenceau to meet him at Marienbad, which was well received in France. In addition, he extended an invitation to the Russian Foreign Minister, Izvolsky, as the Anglo-Russian talks were nearing a successful conclusion; Izvolsky was also taking the waters at Marienbad. For all his self-indulgence, King Edward was a natural diplomat and a great asset to his country. Grey fully realised this and being no control freak let the King have his head at times, yet always under the watchful eye of Hardinge. Grey writes in his autobiography,

A legend arose in the King's lifetime, which was perhaps more widely believed afterwards, that British foreign policy was due to his initiative, instigation and control. This was not so in my experience. He not only accepted the constitutional practice that policy must be that of his Ministers but he preferred that it should be so. He read all the important papers, and now and then a despatch would come back with some short marginal comment approving of something contained in it but comment of any sort was rare and I do not remember criticism or suggestion.

It is worth noting here that whereas Edward VII was able to exercise some diplomatic influence on behalf of his government in his meetings with foreign relations and heads of state, the Kaiser had the constitutional power to achieve his ends. As Emperor of Germany he had the power to appoint the Chancellor and thus influence internal affairs, in addition to having supreme command over the military.

Hardinge always accompanied the King on his foreign visits, conveniently relieving Grey of the burden of ceremony which he so disliked. Grey never resented Hardinge's close relationship with the King, maturely seeing it as part of a team effort. Hardinge wrote in *Old Diplomacy*, 'Our co-operation in the interests of the Foreign Office was so united and Sir Edward Grey's character was so frank and upright that he never felt any jealousy of my close political friendship with King Edward.' From the start of his career it was obvious to all parties that Grey's great asset as Foreign Secretary would be his character. He was so straightforward and honest that people trusted him. Lord Robert Cecil, Grey's Under-Secretary during the war, said of his chief,

> He was indeed, more than any man I have ever known, free from petty jealousies and personal vanities. Indeed, partly owing to his dislike for urban life and his consequent perpetual wish to get out of office, he was politically completely disinterested. For all the years in which he was connected with the Foreign Office, I don't think there was a single day in which he would not have welcomed resignation. He held office because he thought it his duty to do so and for no other reason.

The enormous volume of work and amount of time Grey spent in the Commons made it essential for him to delegate to his permanent officials. On 15 April, Grey wrote to Spring-Rice in Teheran,

> As for the bag I have given up writing at all. This year I have to attend royal dinners and so forth and the result is that I sometimes

work until 2 a.m. and begin work again at 7 a.m. My normal day
begins at nine and ends at midnight. The weekend I spend alone out
of London and that keeps me going.

Earlier in the year, Hardinge had applied pressure on Grey to allow
the King to invite the Kaiser on a state visit to Britain. Hardinge felt
it might reduce tensions while the Anglo-Russian talks were proceeding. The Liberal press welcomed the idea, claiming it would be seen
by all as much needed evidence of goodwill on both sides, and
although the Anglo-French Entente was set in stone no one wanted
Britain's relations with France to be given an anti-German colour.
Grey was nevertheless worried about the French reaction and, not
surprisingly, German efforts to break the Entente over Morocco a
year before still left a nasty taste. It did take place, however, and
on 12 November Grey attended a banquet for the Kaiser in St
George's Hall, Windsor, for 180 guests; it was just the sort of ceremonial occasion he detested. The capital afforded the Emperor a
warm welcome, particularly when he called for the maintenance of
European peace at the Guildhall. *The Times* was effusive in its praise
for the Kaiser, which was no doubt gratefully received bearing in
mind the court scandals prevailing back in Germany. 'The Kaiser
has never ceased during the nineteen years of his reign to touch the
imagination of Englishmen. His vigour, his directness and courage,
his whole-hearted patriotism and his devotion to the trust confided
in him have secured the regard of a nation.'

The visit had very nearly failed to materialise, some say because
of Grey's decision not to allow a proposed escort of German
battleships into Portsmouth Harbour. The Kaiser had first pleaded
an attack of influenza. It was much more likely that the impending trial of his close friend and adviser Philip von Eulenburg for
homosexual offences drained his self-confidence, thus adding to his
normal insecurity in his uncle's presence. King Edward could not
resist a mischievous reference to his nephew's supposed illness in his
speech. He told his audience he was delighted to see their Majesties
looking in splendid health and he hoped their stay in Britain would

improve it further. Lord Esher hit the nail on the head when he said
to Grey after dinner, 'Our King makes a better show than William.
He has more graciousness and dignity. William is ungraceful, nervous and plain; there is no atmosphere about him.'

Two days after the state banquet at Windsor, Campbell-
Bannerman suffered a severe heart attack following a speech at
Bristol. Grey had seen him the day before at a Cabinet meeting
and thought he looked exhausted. The British people had developed a real affection for their Prime Minister and enquiries as to his
well-being flooded in from the King downwards. Once his official
visit was over, the Kaiser went to stay with a Germanophile friend,
Colonel Edward Montagu-Stuart-Wortley, at Highcliffe Castle
near Bournemouth. Grey had two long meetings with the Emperor
during his visit. The Kaiser failed to impress. Grey thought he
talked a good deal of rubbish about Germany's ambitious new
construction project across Asiatic Turkey, the Baghdad Railway,
and he attacked the Jews in an aggressive, unattractive fashion:
'There are too many of them in my country, they want stamping
out.' The Foreign Secretary talked about German naval expansion
and the problems it caused Britain. The Kaiser vowed his Navy
was not built against Britain, but few believed him at the Foreign
Office. He longed for maritime and colonial vengeance on Britain
and had huge support at home, witnessed by the success of the
Navy League. On 1 December, Grey wrote light-heartedly to Mrs
Creighton from his favourite hotel in the New Forest:

> I had a good walk from 11 a.m. to 6.30 p.m., the last part of it in the
> dark. The German Emperor is perilously near but I know he can't
> find me in the Forest – people in motor cars are chained to the roads
> and there is no freedom like the freedom of one's own feet.

Before departing for a Scottish Christmas at Glen with Pamela and
Eddy Tennant, Grey made a speech summarising his foreign policy
in his constituency at Berwick. He told his audience that he had been
true to the policy of his Conservative predecessors by developing

the Entente with France, and indeed he had gone even further by adding new friendships with Russia and Spain. He would dearly love to add Germany to the list but this was more difficult as, unlike the cases of France and Russia, there was little scope for diplomatic concessions around the world. The recently announced increase in German naval estimates now made an agreement most unlikely. Even a good Liberal journal such as the *Westminster Gazette* saw an arms race ahead as inevitable:

> To whatever party we belong all of us are agreed that naval suprem-acy is a vital interest to this country and it follows therefore that whatever Government is in power it must always keep ahead, we will not say of German programmes, but of German performance. That is a fixed principle by which we must abide and it means no unfriendliness to our neighbours.

The Tennant family home lay to the south-west of Innerleithen and was built in Scottish baronial style by Sir Charles Tennant (Margot Asquith's father) in the late 1850s. Grey wrote to his friend Herbert Paul, 'It was just a happy children's Christmas which left the grown-ups free to walk about the hills and read and talk quietly.' Unsurprisingly, after Dorothy's premature death, Grey became even closer to Pamela but he was characteristically discreet. Mrs Belloc Lowndes writes of Grey in *A Passing World*:

> The fact that he had been for a long time – and by that I mean over years – on terms of intimate friendship with both Edward and Pamela Glenconner was not realised by certain of his friends. Propinquity is an old-fashioned word seldom used nowadays, yet it exactly describes the part that was played in the friendship of Edward Grey and Lord and Lady Glenconner from 1906 to when Lord Glenconner's death took place.

The Foreign Office is within a few minutes' walk of 34 Queen Anne's Gate, then the Glenconners' London home. Grey used to work on, long after he had sent his secretaries home, and then walk down Birdcage Walk to dine with the Glenconners. Again, Max Egremont, the head of the Wyndham family, writes in his biography of Siegfried Sassoon, 'Eddy proved a dull husband and the beautiful and self-consciously cultivated Pamela took up with Sir Edward before Tennant's death in 1920.' How much Eddy knew of Grey's relationship with Pamela will never be known but one must assume he was not stupid. Eddy, who remained close to Grey all his life, was not a jealous man. He was in awe of his wife's volatile personality and no doubt preferred the quiet life. In any case Eddy was purported to have a mistress in the Borders, so perhaps his wife's relationship with Grey suited him.

Emma Tennant is even more explicit in her book on the Tennant family, *Strangers*, writing, 'Eddy knows, without of course it ever being mentioned, that his wife will marry Grey and live at Fallodon should anything happen to him. He and the other Edward are already seen as Pamela's two husbands: sometimes he thinks it would not matter at all if he simply slipped away.' In the same book Emma Tennant also comments on the longevity of the relationship: 'The long-standing friendship between Grey and her [Margot Asquith's] brother Eddy – and the long love affair, so people say, between Grey and Eddy's wife Pamela – means it is highly likely that Grey will be a guest at Wilsford too.' Angela Lambert in her book *Unquiet Souls* also comments on the complex protracted relationship that existed between Grey and the Glenconners:

> The marriage that was hastily arranged between Edward Tennant and Pamela Wyndham turned out within a very short time to have been an obvious mistake. It made no difference. Pamela found the love of her life in another Edward, later Lord Grey of Fallodon, and the three of them lived in a discreet ménage à trois which lasted until Lord Glenconner's death.

It is interesting to note that all of Grey's personal papers and private correspondence with Pamela mysteriously disappeared after his death. In her book, Mrs Belloc Lowndes informs the reader that she was once asked by Pamela to assist with the editing of her correspondence with Grey, which was concerned 'almost entirely with verse, and with bird lore, subjects in which they were both deeply interested'. The request was taken no further. According to Mrs Lowndes, Grey asked Pamela not to publish anything in his lifetime and soon after his death the letters were destroyed. Being a deeply reserved person, this suggests he may well have had a secret or two to hide.

There was another guest at Glen for Christmas, a man who had become a great friend of Grey's and would remain so for the rest of his life. Henry Newbolt had been a contemporary of Grey at Oxford before developing into the classic all-rounder: lawyer, editor of the *Monthly Review*, novelist and poet. He had become celebrated for his patriotic ballads, the best known being 'Vitai Lampada' and 'Drake's Drum', the former describing a Clifton schoolboy cricketer who learns selfless commitment to duty in cricket matches at Clifton and goes on to fight in the Sudan as a member of Gordon's relief column. At Abu Klea in 1885, the British square was broken by the Dervishes and the popular Colonel Burnaby of the Royal Horse Guards killed, which inspired Newbolt's immortal lines 'Play up, play up and play the game'. Newbolt would later be recruited by Charles Masterman to help maintain public opinion in favour of the Great War and was knighted in 1915. Grey probably first met Newbolt at the 'Co-Efficients' dining club in the 1890s. Newbolt had been put up for the club by H. G. Wells and in 1907 he moved to Netherhampton, a few miles south of the new Tennant manor house at Wilsford.

Their friendship tells us a good deal about Grey, as the two men appear remarkably similar characters. Newbolt, like Grey, was a Liberal Imperialist. He was a loyal patriot, brought up on old-fashioned values, who believed in Empire and social reform at home. He was a lover of English literature and poetry – apparently people who read Newbolt's poetry also read Wordsworth – and he was a born countryman, having a particular passion for the water meadows and chalk downland around Salisbury. Above all he adored birds and for many years placed birds' nesting in *Who's Who* as his favoured recreation. Newbolt wrote in his journal that he usually talked to Grey about birds during dinner and wondered 'what he manages to talk to other people about while the servants are in the room – birds are a perfect passe-temps from the diplomatic point of view'. The two men even looked alike: handsome, a full head of hair, strong nose and thin lips. But most interestingly, behind that prim Edwardian exterior lay a complicated domestic life – yet again, a ménage à trois. Newbolt's wife had a long-standing lesbian affair with her childhood love, Ella Coltman, who joined the Newbolts on their honeymoon. Newbolt was also Coltman's lover and died in her house in Kensington in 1938.

An Eruption in the Balkans and Humiliation for Russia

Grey was satisfied with his performance over his first two years at the Foreign Office but as he travelled south on the night sleeper early in the new year, he still could not sleep. He was as restless as the Germans across the Rhine. He had cemented the Entente Cordiale and in the process reassured the French of Britain's friendship. He had long sought an agreement with Russia, the implementation of which in his view had now restored the balance of power in Europe. With the injection of French capital, Russia was quickly regaining her strength, thereby providing a welcome check on Germany from the east. There would be problems ahead – there always were when dealing with the Russians. However, the India Office was happy, as pressure was finally relieved from their frontier. Grey saw Germany as the main threat to European peace and was backed to the full in this view by the heavyweights at the Foreign Office. At the War Office his friend Haldane had reorganised the Army into a small but highly efficient force. Grey had done all in his power to prepare for the worst, now he saw his main responsibility as patching up relations with Germany and securing a moratorium on naval construction.

In the event, it was fortunate the Foreign Secretary had made such sound progress, for in the autumn the fuse for the outbreak of the Great War would be lit in the Balkans with an irreparable split between Austria and Russia. Back in 1897 the two countries had pledged themselves to cooperate on all Balkan matters. Again in 1903 they had signed the Mürzsteg programme, one of the objectives being to put an end to Turkish misrule in Macedonia. As a result it was agreed to implement local reforms, the most important being the organisation of a police force led by foreign officers. Grey and his officials at the Foreign Office had always been deeply suspicious of any dealings with the Austrian Foreign Minister, Baron von Aehrenthal. In late January 1908 their misgivings were realised when the Baron announced he had applied to the Turkish Sultan for permission to construct a railway through the Sandžak from Sarajevo to Mitrovica. This caused an immediate rift with Russia, who saw the action as a breach of the Mürzsteg Agreement and more importantly an attempt by Austria to upset the balance of power in the Balkans. The Austrians also disconcerted Britain and the other powers who viewed such action as disloyal when they were united in pressing Macedonian reforms on Turkey.

So began a decline in relations between Austria and Russia which would deteriorate further in the autumn with the annexation by Austria of Bosnia and Herzegovina. This expansionism and irreversible rift with Russia would eventually lead to the outbreak of the worst war in European history. The Ottoman Empire was slowly disintegrating with the pressures of Balkan nationalism and Austria was determined not to suffer from the same malaise. Slav minorities across the Balkans were being encouraged in their efforts by Serbia. The Serbs in turn looked to support from Russia, who saw herself as protector of Slav interests in the Balkans. Austria was keen to demonstrate to these breakaway groups that Russia, following her comprehensive defeat at the hands of the Japanese, was in no position to come to their assistance. Germany, paranoid that she would lose her one reliable ally, made the fatal error of encouraging Austria in her efforts to bully her Balkan neighbours.

On the domestic front the new year began with the first of a long list of crises over the naval estimates. Battle commenced at the Cabinet meeting of 21 January. The German supplementary law of 1907 had made it necessary for the First Lord of the Admiralty, Lord Tweedmouth, to ask for increases in the 1908/9 naval estimates. The radicals in the Cabinet, who were determined to push forward their expensive social programmes, were outraged. They were led by two young, ambitious and energetic ministers, Lloyd George and Churchill. The Cabinet radicals, who included heavyweights such as Morley, Burns, Crewe, McKenna and Harcourt in their number, claimed to carry a third of the parliamentary party, which would mean serious trouble for the government if it came to a vote in the House. The Admiralty, backed by the old Imperialist triumvirate of Asquith, Haldane and Grey, finally won the day but only after Fisher had threatened to resign if the estimates were not pushed through. Grey was Tweedmouth's most ardent supporter in Cabinet and would write to the King later in the year, 'If the German fleet ever becomes superior to ours, the German Army can conquer this country. There is no similar risk of this kind for Germany; for however superior our fleet was, no naval victory could bring us any nearer to Berlin.'

It always helped that in the background Grey had public opinion on his side, even a leading Liberal newspaper writing, 'It might help at this stage if it were understood in Germany that so far as the British Government is concerned, naval supremacy is a fixed policy which cannot be challenged however much it might desire economy.' This was, however, the first real challenge to Grey's authority in Cabinet. He was a supporter of a 'big Navy' yet he was also sensitive to his colleagues' feelings. He therefore decided to bring up the whole question of naval construction with both the German ambassador Paul Metternich and the Kaiser. The timing was excellent as King Edward, accompanied by Hardinge, was to make a royal visit to Kronberg later in the summer. As a result of the breakdown of the Hague Peace Conference, coupled with his own suspicions of Germany's aggressive ambitions, Grey was not optimistic as to the outcome.

For the first time since Dorothy's death, Grey did not spend the
anniversary at Fallodon. He stayed alone at the Forest Park Hotel
in Brockenhurst, the rural retreat that would play an important part
in his life in the stressful years running up to the Great War. He
wrote to Katherine Lyttelton on 4 February, 'I went to the hotel
that Dorothy found for me in the New Forest and was out in the
Forest for many hours on a beautiful day and came back by star-
light. That is the sort of thing I am really made for – not politics.'
In a letter to Mrs Creighton later in the year, his Christianity shines
through in his longing for an afterlife, where he craves a reunion
with Dorothy: 'I was thinking the other day what a secure possession the past is. The happiness and beauty that it had cannot now
be spoilt or impaired: having had it one cannot be pessimistic
either about this life or another.' Again to Katherine Lyttelton,
his preference for a solitary existence is evident as he speculates
what form his life would take if he were ever to leave politics:
'What I might do would be to do my railway work again and live
mostly in the country and be nice to a few friends when I saw
them or wrote to them, if they would remember that I was on an
ebb tide.'

Aside from the New Forest, the Itchen valley and his native
Northumberland, there was one other beautiful part of the English
countryside that occupied a special place in Grey's affections and
that was the Norfolk Broads. He first visited these famous wetlands
as a young man to shoot duck and then in 1908, with two Cabinet
colleagues, Bron Lucas and Edwin Montagu, he decided to set up
a bird sanctuary, acquiring a small section of the Broads known as
Ball's Corner. The following year Lucas also bought Hickling Broad
together with a lodge called Whiteslea which on his death in 1916,
serving with the Royal Flying Corps, passed to the Grenfell family.
The extensive reed beds played host to many of Grey's favourite
birds such as the bittern, bearded tit and reed warbler. There is
one passage in *The Charm of Birds* that delightfully demonstrates his
remarkable ability to convey in writing the atmosphere of such a
unique habitat:

Reed beds have a delicate beauty of their own: especially is this to be noted on a sunny day in February or March. There is no young green in the reed bed yet but last year's stems are cream-coloured; the dark feathery heads look silvery in the sunlight and nod like plumes as the wind agitates the innumerable reeds. The warblers have not come but this is the time when reed beds have a peculiarly delicate and graceful beauty. Imagine such a day on the Norfolk Broads where the spaces of open water between the cream-coloured reed beds are blue with the reflection of the sky. As the new reeds grow up green in May the reed warblers come and make their presence known. The time to listen to them is on a fine day in June, when there is just enough breeze to make a slight rustling in the tall reeds that blends with the continuous singing of the birds. Then we know the world in which reed warblers live and we feel the spirit of it.

At the end of February Grey displayed an uncharacteristic lack of judgement. He was a close friend of Lord Tweedmouth and for a number of years he and Dorothy had visited the First Lord's Guisachan estate at the mouth of Glen Affric in the Highlands, to stalk and fish for salmon. In order to support Jacky Fisher, who was threatening resignation over the naval estimates, Lord Esher had written a supportive letter to *The Times* stating, 'There is not a man in Germany from the Emperor downwards who would not welcome the fall of Sir John Fisher.' This provoked the Kaiser to write an undignified nine-page letter to the First Lord complaining of Britain's attitude to the growing German Navy. The Emperor insisted it was nonsensical and untrue to believe that it was being built to challenge British naval supremacy.

Grey approved his friend's reply to the Kaiser and also suggested that he include details of the proposed naval estimates, which was unconstitutional as they had yet to be approved by Parliament. Here was a conciliatory Grey taking an independent line from his own supposedly anti-German officials at the Foreign Office. The whole episode proved to be the final nail in the coffin for Tweedmouth, who would shortly be replaced at the Admiralty. The First Lord was so excited to receive a letter from the Emperor that he revealed its contents to every hostess in London. Tweedmouth had been ill for some time and his behaviour was becoming increasingly erratic. On top of these indiscretions, he had failed to support the First Sea Lord, Jacky Fisher, in his damaging, long-standing personal feud with Admiral Charles Beresford. The highly conservative Beresford was most critical of Fisher's naval reforms, which had the negative effect of splitting the Senior Service into two rival warring camps.

In mid-April, Grey took his first holiday in three years and went north to fish the Cassley with his brother Charlie, Haldane providing cover at the Foreign Office. They stayed in the Rosehall post office, which masqueraded as the village shop. Grey left his lodgings every morning after breakfast, returning at teatime only to find a huge pouch of Foreign Office papers which kept him busy until bedtime. Unfortunately the water was low and there was hardly any fishing. There is no loch at the Cassley's source and as a result the water drops quickly if not constantly topped up by rain or melting snow. Grey managed to catch only two fish but compensated for it by walking the moors in April sunshine listening to the spring song of the curlews.

As the Cassley leaves the open moorland and before it reaches the sea, it flows through a deep gorge which contains a steep waterfall. Below the waterfall lies the Falls Pool. It was not prolific in terms of fish caught but Grey loved to lie above the pool in the April sun and reflect on the work of his favourite poets. In *Fly Fishing* the romantic Foreign Secretary writes,

Poets under such benign influences of Nature are moved to soothing thoughts of how life may end. Keats' thought was *to cease upon the midnight with no pain* while listening to the song of the nightingale. Shelley's imagination was that death like sleep should steal upon him by the seashore where he might *hear the sea breathe o'er my dying brain its last memory*. Most peaceful of all is Wordsworth's description of the actual close of the life of an old clergyman in the Lake country. He was still able-bodied and hale, though in extreme old age, when *like a shadow thrown softly and lightly from a passing cloud, death fell upon him, as reclined he lay for noontide solace on the summer grass, the warm lap of his mother earth.* So to one whose work was done and whose strength had failed might the end come fitly and happily while he lay listening to the sound of the falling water, his last sight that of the splendid pool with the sun shining on it and his closing thought the exceeding beauty of the world in which he had lived.

When Grey had last been on the Cassley in 1905, Dorothy was at his side. One can only guess at what morbid thoughts were going through his mind as he lay looking down on the pool from the heathery bank above. Rosebery reported gloomily on a meeting with Grey a few months after Dorothy's death: 'He lives entirely in the past, describes himself as "waiting". Waiting for the door that closed behind her to open for him, hoping it will be soon.'

On account of ill health the Prime Minister, Campbell-Bannerman, had formally resigned on 3 April against a background of mounting pressure from a recent crop of by-election defeats. His death followed soon after and Grey returned south for the funeral at Westminster Abbey on 27 April, where Asquith gave a warm and moving address. The streets to Euston station were lined with dense crowds demonstrating the affection and respect in which he was held by the country. How the Liberal Imperialists initially misjudged the man. After overcoming Balfour in the House, he became a confident and successful Prime Minister as well as a much loved leader of the Liberal Party. Grey was man enough to write to Campbell-Bannerman on his resignation, 'The difficulties I made when the Government was formed were short-sighted and ill-judged and we all feel now that the troubles which your presence at the head of the Government kept in abeyance will have to be faced.' Grey had written to the Prime Minister in a similar mode on the death of Lady Campbell-Bannerman, 'All my forecasts before the elections were wrong, and your presence in the House of Commons has been not only desirable but essential to manage this party and keep it together; and so it continues to be; and I most sincerely wish you health and strength for the coming year.'

The Foreign Secretary must have been delighted that the French Prime Minister, Clemenceau, was present at the Abbey. He was looking forward to the forthcoming Anglo-French trade exhibition at Shepherd's Bush that would hopefully promote even stronger ties between the two countries. The *Westminster Gazette* echoed Grey's views: 'To every sincere lover of peace all the world over the Anglo-French friendship should be a source of unfeigned satisfaction; threatening no other power with a hostile coalition, the friendship of England and France constitutes the most solid of existing guarantees for the maintenance of European peace.'

On 10 June Grey was back at The Cottage fishing with his good friend and Cabinet colleague Sydney Buxton. Buxton was a keen fisherman and always joined Grey on the Itchen for the early summer fishing. Grey preferred fishing the river in June for two reasons. Firstly, the rise was quite different from that in May. The hatch of fly was not so frantic and was more prolonged, giving an extended day's fishing. Secondly, the trout were in their best and strongest condition, making the challenge of landing a fish all the more exacting. He adored the contrast of being on the river in June to the hot oppressive days in London. In *Fly Fishing* he writes,

> There is the aggressive stiffness of the buildings, the brutal hardness of the pavement, the smell of the streets festering in the sun, the glare of the light all day striking upon hard substances and the stuffiness of the heat from which there is no relief at night – for no coolness comes with the evening air and the bedroom windows seem to open into ovens; add to these hardships what is worse than all, the sense of being deprived of the country at this time and shut off from it.

It was in June that the water meadows were at their most colourful, when 'the common yellow iris, ragged robin and forget-me-not make rough damp places gay and the clear water in the little runnels among the grass sparkle in the sun'.

Another reason Grey loved to fish the river in June was that the birds were still singing, one of his favourites being the grasshopper warbler. This spring migrant has a song similar to the sound of a soft-running fishing reel which it rehearses late on into the summer. Grey writes in *The Charm of Birds,*

> In one mile of the Itchen Valley that had much rough tussocky ground, too rough and coarse to be mown, there used to be two and sometimes three pairs of grasshopper warblers; and just when the evensong of birds had ceased in the warm dusk of June and July evenings the grasshopper warblers would begin to sing. Thus to me the song became associated with failing light and the end of a day's fishing. The territory of each bird became familiar to me, the presence of each was greeted every year and noted evening after evening on the way home in the quiet twilight: my waders, brushing through the lush, soft growth on the river bank made a sound not out of keeping with that of the bird.

His love of birds also kept him sane when in London and on 3 July he wrote to his friend Katherine Lyttelton:

> Last week I went to the Horticultural Garden at Wisley with Mildred Buxton and Pamela Tennant. We went to see flowers and incidentally found a great spotted woodpecker's nest and saw both the old birds and heard the clamour of the young. There has been no such surprise since Saul went out to look for his father's asses and found a kingdom.

While Grey and Buxton were enjoying their weekend on the Itchen, King Edward, together with Hardinge and Nicolson from the Foreign Office, were in the Baltic attending a banquet hosted by the Czar and his ministers on the Russian royal yacht at Reval on the Baltic Sea. The purpose of the meeting was to 'bed down'

the new Anglo-Russian relationship and work up a package of Macedonian reforms with Izvolsky, the Russian Foreign Minister. Turkish misrule in Macedonia had continued unabated for years and there was a wave of humanitarian feeling in Britain for these disadvantaged Christian populations. Grey's efforts to induce the Concert of Europe to cooperate on the matter had been frustrated by Germany's unwillingness to upset the corrupt Sultan. The Anglo-Russian Agreement had been generally welcomed in Britain for the relative peace it had brought to India's north-west frontier, with a Liberal newspaper writing, 'The new Anglo-Russian Entente is a logical outcome of the Anglo-French Entente. Both make the Frenchman sleep sounder at night, the one appears to protect his household, the other his money.'

Needless to say, the King's visit to Russia generated a chorus of disapproval in Britain from both Liberal and Labour backbenchers who wanted little to do with such an autocratic regime. The recently elected Socialist MP Keir Hardie brought a motion against the visit before the House which was defeated by 225 votes to 59. The King was furious and banned him from future Royal Garden Parties. On 28 May, Grey had to reassure another Labour MP that 'no new convention or treaty is under discussion between the two Governments nor is it intended to initiate any negotiations during the visit', but even moderates were upset when the King made the Czar an Admiral of the Fleet without prior reference to the Admiralty or the Foreign Office. Grey recognised that this unconstitutional action could place him in an awkward position in the Commons. Asquith, for his part, suggested to Grey that on future royal visits the King should be accompanied by a responsible minister.

Grey was only too relieved to be represented by Hardinge at Reval. The weather crossing the North Sea was atrocious. There was much ceremony, dressing-up and huge quantities of bad food on the Russian royal yacht, everything he detested. The Foreign Secretary's absence from these royal visits would leave him open to criticism from his enemies and future historians, the sybaritic Roy

Jenkins describing Grey as 'a man of most remarkable insularity' in his *Gallery of 20th Century Portraits*. Did he really need to be present? Hardinge was, after all, an immensely experienced diplomat, his 'partner' at the Foreign Office and a close friend of King Edward. The Permanent Under-Secretary always submitted a detailed memorandum to his chief on his meetings and besides, a Foreign Secretary in the Commons didn't really have the time for these overseas royal jaunts where very little was achieved. Wasn't it better that he stayed at his desk taking a balanced view from above, particularly when the regime in question was so unpopular in Britain and there was also a very real possibility of upsetting the Germans? In the event, the meeting between the two monarchs and their officials turned out on balance to be a success and Admiral Fisher reported that the Czar was 'like a child in his delight' with his new appointment. Harold Nicolson writes in his biography of his father Lord Carnock, 'The Czar had returned from Björkö and Swinemunde frightened and humiliated: he returned from Reval flattered and reassured. The greatest diplomatic victories are gained by doing nothing: and King Edward, although too superficial to be a statesman, was a supreme diplomatist.'

Perhaps Grey was right not to join the cruise. The Germans were far from delighted or reassured by this regal assignation. They must have viewed it as the final collapse of the old Bismarckian policy of keeping Russia apart from France and both of them apart from Britain. In addition, the presence of so many senior officials such as French, Fisher, Hardinge, Izvolsky and the Prime Minister, Stolypin, aroused their suspicions. A few days after the Reval meeting, the Kaiser publicly stated at a military parade, 'They wish to encircle and provoke us.' He then threatened to break out of his supposed 'encirclement'. The idea that Germany was purposely being encircled by her enemies was widely believed by the German people. Furthermore, the whole policy was attributed to King Edward and his foreign visits. The latter, of course, was complete myth. It was Germany's own actions that drove her 'enemies' into each other's arms. Germany chose Austria as an ally, rather than Russia, after the fall of Bismarck; this resulted in Russia turning to France. When Germany commenced building a fleet to compete with the Royal Navy in 1898, Britain could not afford to remain isolated so she decided to settle her long-standing colonial differences with France. As Germany aggressively tried to break the Entente, Grey moved Britain in the same direction with Russia.

The fantasy of encirclement is no better explained than by the German ambassador to London at the outbreak of war, Prince Lichnowsky. He writes in his book *Heading for the Abyss*:

> Germany, although by far the strongest Power on the Continent, insisted on keeping the world in a constant state of nervousness with her everlasting new grants for the Army and Navy, with provocative speeches about 'mailed fist' and 'shining armour' and with swashbuckling rodomontades and fanfaronades of all descriptions. To crown all, she refused to listen to any proposals made at the Peace Conferences for the limitation of armaments. One crisis followed another, each leaving our neighbours no choice but to submit to humiliation or to fight. Abroad, these everlasting crises created the impression that a new appeal to arms would be by no means unwelcome to our rulers. We thus induced the other Powers to forgo their old differences and forced them to come to terms with one another in order to safeguard themselves against the 'German Peril'. This process led silly people to believe we were being hemmed in and encircled.

Grey himself writes in his autobiography, 'It seemed to me that Germans must understand this sequence of events and that the theory of the "encircling" policy was encouraged to keep German opinion up to the high-water mark in expenditure on German armament.'

While Grey regarded German claims of 'encirclement' as wild exaggeration, he was at all times sensitive to their feelings of insecurity and did not want to help create any false impressions. He was always keen to promote agreements that included Germany, thus not making her feel isolated or cold-shouldered. As a result, in

April he pressed his Cabinet colleagues to approve the signing of
the North Sea Agreement. The treaty guaranteed the status quo
of the North Sea, with Germany, Britain, Holland and Denmark as
the relevant signatories. At the same time, he was aware of French
sensitivities and was careful to see that they were informed of all
proceedings. On 13 December 1907 Grey wrote to Lord Ripon:

> I am not sure that Germany has any motive except to show she is
> not isolated; she may have intended to separate us from France but
> if so that is over, for she has now put the North Sea proposal before
> France. If Germany is set upon appearing before the world arm in
> arm with us and France, it will not do to affront her by refusing. If
> we did Germany would have some pretext for saying that we aimed
> at her isolation.

In the same mode he encouraged Nicolson to persuade the Russians
to join France, Germany and Britain in a deal on the Baghdad
Railway, thereby proving to the Germans 'that no ring was being
made against them'. Grey always wanted better relations with
Germany, but not at the expense of his Entente partners. It was an
exceptionally difficult balancing act in an atmosphere of distrust
and suspicion. D. W. Sweet in his essay on 'Great Britain and
Germany 1905–1911' writes:

> Conclusive evidence that Grey's policy towards Germany was not
> one of encirclement is provided by his response to the suggestion
> which was made from time to time (notably by the French) that efforts
> should be made to detach one or other of Germany's partners from
> the Triple Alliance. He always rejected the idea summarily, on the
> ground that the only effect of such an attempt would be to confirm
> the worst fears of the Germans and drive them to precipitate the
> general conflict which above all he desired to avoid.

Events in the late summer proved that Grey's general pessimism
over the government's efforts to limit the naval race with Germany

was not unfounded. Interestingly, initial contact was made not by Grey but by two of his colleagues, the Permanent Secretary at the Foreign Office and the new Chancellor in the Asquith administration, Lloyd George.

In the interests of domestic social reform, the Chancellor was desperate to cut the naval estimates. With this in mind, and with Grey's approval, Lloyd George met Metternich twice in July to try to achieve a relaxation in naval construction. The question was also raised by Hardinge with the Kaiser on the occasion of the royal visit to Kronberg in August. The King cannot have much been looking forward to the visit as he was viewed in Germany as the originator of the Entente and the protagonist of Germany's 'isolation'. The German press portrayed King Edward as an ambitious man with an antipathy to Germany, who from the beginning of his reign had set himself to form a European coalition for the isolation of Germany. Needless to say, the British delegation ran into a stone wall. The Kaiser stated that any discussion on arms limitation was 'contrary to the national dignity'. Of course Germany had the right to build what she wanted, but an expansionist policy didn't make for friendship and only sharpened antagonism. Following the failure of these talks the government decided to shelve further discussions and increase its own construction programme. Lloyd George and Churchill, with expensive social reforms such as the introduction of old-age pensions and national insurance in mind, continued to canvass publicly for an Anglo-German naval agreement and had to be reined in by the Prime Minister.

The summer also saw the first signs of trouble brewing in the Balkans. Izvolsky had swallowed his pride over the Sandžak Railway. In June he proposed a secret deal with Austria whereby Russia would agree to the annexation of Bosnia and Herzegovina if Austria in turn would agree to the opening up of the Straits to Russian warships. Turkey was to be given the Sandžak in compensation. At some point the other powers would have to be consulted in their capacity as signatories to the Treaty of Berlin, which governed these respective matters. Aehrenthal and Izvolsky were fortified in their machinations by the Young Turk revolution in July, which overthrew the corrupt regime of Sultan Abdul Hamid. The term 'Young Turks' referred to members of Ottoman society who were progressive, modernist and opposed to the status quo. The change of government was initially well received by Liberals in Britain and it was seen by the Foreign Office as a way of loosening Germany's commercial dominance at Constantinople. The new administration was committed to giving equal rights to all their subject nationalities, so for the present Grey could heave a sigh of relief and throttle back over his frustrating and long-standing ideas for Macedonian reform. The last thing he wanted to do was to offend the new administration by pressing for further reforms.

On 6 October, Aehrenthal announced the annexation of Bosnia and Herzegovina to an indignant Europe. The previous day, Bulgaria had declared herself a sovereign state. Both actions were a serious blow to Turkish prestige. Izvolsky had been deceived by Aehrenthal, who had announced his part of the bargain before the Russian Foreign Minister had consulted the powers about the opening of the Straits. The Kaiser was furious. He would now have to choose whether to upset his ally Austria or his new friends the Turks. Although no national interests were at stake, Grey took a firm line as the annexation represented a gross breach of international law. Britain could not recognise the right of any power to alter an international treaty without the consent of all the parties concerned. In any case, he was adamant that Britain would not recognise either action unless financial compensation had been secured by Turkey. Grey felt that Austria's action represented an untimely challenge not only to the new Turkish regime but also to Serbia. One million Serbs lived in Bosnia and Herzegovina.

Although Izvolsky had blundered, Grey knew he had to provide support. If the Russian Foreign Minister fell then the whole Anglo-Russian Agreement could be at risk. The British Foreign Secretary

was therefore facing a delicate situation. He had nailed his colours
to the mast in support of Turkey but he must at all costs avoid
upsetting the Russians. He did not want to give the impression that
he was reverting to the old Victorian policy of propping up Turkey
as a bastion against Russian expansionism. Izvolsky visited Grey at
the Foreign Office on 9 October and insisted that he had not given
his assent to the annexation. Desperate to save face, he immediately
raised the question of opening up the Straits. He wanted right of
passage for Russian warships out of the Black Sea without the right
of entry for foreign vessels. (Ever since the Treaty of London in 1871,
the Straits had been closed to all foreign warships.) Although Grey
was sympathetic to a course of action that freed up Russia's access
to the Mediterranean, he was against a one-sided arrangement and
moreover felt it was not the right time to press the fledgling Turkish
administration for concessions.

Grey knew from Nicolson that Izvolsky was in fact barking up
the wrong tree. Russian public opinion was much less concerned
about the Straits than the interests of Slavs in the Balkans. The
Foreign Secretary reminded Izvolsky that Russian aggression in
Persia was currently having a negative effect on public opinion
in Britain, but he did agree to a Russian call for an international
conference to regulate matters, a policy he would revert to on a
number of important occasions in the future. Grey saw the primary
role of the conference as supporting the new Turkish government
and placing it in such a position that it could accept peace with
honour. D. W. Sweet in his essay on the Bosnian crisis writes, 'It was
an undoubted success for Grey's diplomacy that he had averted a
collision between his Russian and Turkish policies, by persuading
Izvolsky to subordinate his aspirations at the Straits to the British
policy of support for the Young Turk regime.'

By December it was obvious the idea of a conference was not
going to work. Germany was not keen to risk another diplomatic
defeat such as she suffered over Morocco and, although angry
at Austria's independent line, she decided to support her 'ally in
shining armour', in the emotive words of the Kaiser. In the event

of war, Austria was needed to relieve Germany of some of the burden on her eastern front. Austria, emboldened by Prince von Bülow's support, realised that Russia was in no position to call the shots. After all, Russia had received absolutely no support from her French allies and the British were more interested in appeasing Turkey. An arrogant Aehrenthal did not see himself discussing compensation for Serbia over a conference table. He decided to reach an agreement with Turkey by way of a cash payment and ask the powers to ratify the annexation. Russian humiliation was complete. Henceforth her policy would centre around the creation of an anti-Austrian bloc in south-east Europe. At the end of the year, the long fuse to a cataclysmic confrontation in the Balkans was very much alight.

The humanitarian side of Grey's tenure at the Foreign Office was demonstrated not only by his quest for Macedonian reform but also by his actions in the African Congo. Involvement in both cases ran counter to British interests. By raising the question of reform Britain alienated Turkey, driving her further into the arms of a grateful Germany. Macedonian reform provided Britain with an opportunity to work with a new ally but, as witnessed in Persia, Russia was an uncomfortable bedfellow. While the Russians were keen to press reforms on Turkey, they also jealously guarded their position of influence in the Balkans. In the Congo, Britain had even more to lose. For many years the Congo had been owned by King Leopold of Belgium, who had encouraged slaving. The general atrocities had stirred the indignation of the British public. Grey was on dangerous ground. None of the other powers, except the distant United States, showed any interest in involving themselves. There was always the danger that Belgium might look to Germany, who had colonies adjoining the Congo, for support. In the event, thanks to Grey's tactful yet firm involvement, the Belgian state was persuaded to take over the Congo from King Leopold and reform was accomplished before the outbreak of war. After three years at the Foreign Office, Grey was fast becoming one of the most respected statesmen in Europe. In November, Hardinge wrote to a colleague of Grey's growing stature at home: 'I am glad to say that Sir Edward Grey's position has recently become enormously strengthened and I think that no Liberal Party could do without him. This has had an admirable effect on the confidence which it has given him.'

In the middle of the Bosnian crisis a diplomatically clumsy Kaiser found himself in deep water yet again. The discussion with his friend Colonel Edward Montagu-Stuart-Wortley after his state visit to Britain the previous November suddenly appeared in the *Daily Telegraph*. In the article, the Kaiser pronounced his main goal was to improve Anglo-German relations. No one disbelieved him but he made a fool of himself by claiming, 'The prevailing sentiment among large sections of the middle and lower classes of my people is not friendly to England. I am therefore in a minority in my own land.' He even claimed the credit for resisting a scheme to prevent Russian intervention against Britain during the Boer War. Grey never thought the Kaiser was a fool but he genuinely believed he had a streak of madness in his make-up. He once told Henry Newbolt, 'Germany has the most powerful army in the world and it is at the command of a madman.'

The proceedings were received with disbelief and even amusement on both sides of the North Sea, but many Germans felt humiliated by their Emperor's behaviour. Nicolson reported from St Petersburg that the Czar was furious. Grey wrote perceptively to Ella Pease from The Cottage on 8 November:

The German Emperor is ageing me; he is like a battleship with steam up and screws going, but with no rudder, and he will run into something some day and cause a catastrophe. He has made a fool of Germany. All the world is laughing at him and he has the strongest army in the world. The Germans don't like being laughed at and are looking for somebody on whom to vent their temper and use their

strength. After a big war a nation doesn't want another for a generation or more but after forty years of peace, if a nation is strong it
begins spoiling for a fight. It is thirty-eight years since Germany had
her last war and she is very strong and restless like a person whose
boots are too small. I don't think there will be war at the present
time but it will be difficult to keep the peace in Europe for another
five years.

These were prophetic words from Grey, who believed a European
war was now a very real possibility. Under Germany's constitution,
the Kaiser had overall responsibility for diplomacy and the military.
By 1908 his personal rule was on the wane. A leading article in a
Liberal newspaper in Britain had written of the Kaiser, 'We have
been taught to regard him as wilful and autocratic, as the irresist-
ible warlord who grinds his opponents to powder and will brook
no opposition from his advisers. Now the part changes and he is
presented as wax in the hands of a clique of morbid and effeminate
conspirators.' The Kaiser had an immensely complicated personality that originated from a childhood inferiority complex as a result
of being born with a withered arm. While adoring his grandmother,
Queen Victoria, he was deeply jealous of his English relations,
especially King Edward. The Kaiser was a strange mixture, being
intelligent and kind one moment, yet headstrong, conceited and
a bully the next. Coming on top of the court scandals, the *Daily
Telegraph* article enraged both the Reichstag and the Foreign Office.
The Kaiser lost his self-esteem and his people in turn lost confidence in him. This left a dangerous vacuum at court that would
soon be filled by the military.

There was an outcry in the British press. Fleet Street felt that
coming on top of the Kruger telegram and the Kaiser's visit
to Tangier, 'enough was enough'. The *Pall Mall Gazette*, referring to
the 'blazing indiscretion' of the German Emperor and the 'casual
carelessness' of his foremost statesmen, called for some 'coher-
ence and consistency' to be injected into German foreign policy
if Europe was to remain at peace. There had been mass meetings

around Germany to protest against the Kaiser's prominence in foreign policy, and the newspaper could not see how the relationship between the German nation and its Emperor could ever be the same again. As the sympathetic newspaper saw it, the problem lay with the fact that the feudalism of Prussianised Germany was becoming intolerable to the German people and current so-called German socialism represented 'the resentment of the belated survival of a medieval political system'. The *Pall Mall Gazette* saw a silver lining amongst all this embarrassment: 'As it happens the publication in the *Daily Telegraph* has given a much needed stimulus to the driving force of public opinion with regards to the needs of the Navy, a most timely and valuable effect, and one of which we are profoundly grateful.'

Although Grey was immersed in work at the Foreign Office, he still found the time to take an interest in domestic matters. With his north-eastern background coupled with direct experience in the railway industry, he had always been a champion of the trade unions and a strong supporter of the Liberal programme for social reform. That curious combination of 'the old-fashioned Whig and the Socialist' came to the fore as the House of Lords continued to savage the government's legislative programme. The Unionists only had 147 Members in the Commons but, supported by 500 peers, they were making it impossible for a democratically elected body to govern. In late November the Lords threw out the Licensing Bill, which was designed to reduce the number of public houses selling liquor by 30,000 over fourteen years by cancelling licences. Grey had been committed to constitutional reform for many years but realised the government were on thin ice. He wrote to James Bryce, 'I am afraid of a breakaway in our party for a Single Chamber and that would mean a split. I want a Second Chamber but I do not like entrusting real powers to one unless it is elective.'

If Grey felt he was due a peaceful run-in to Christmas, he was to be gravely disappointed. At a Cabinet meeting on 8 December the new First Lord of the Admiralty, Reginald McKenna, gave his colleagues another nasty shock. He informed Cabinet that the

Admiralty had acquired information that proved the Germans were accelerating their construction programme by placing contracts and accumulating materials for their Dreadnoughts in advance of their official start dates. To make matters worse, Britain was short of suppliers to manufacture gun mountings and had no dry dock facilities for her Dreadnoughts on the east coast. As Germany had recently increased her capacity to build battleships, the First Lord announced he would be asking for six new ships in the 1909 estimates rather than four. This would necessitate an increased expenditure of £3 million. Once again the Cabinet radicals led by Churchill and Lloyd George were horrified. By 1908 Britain had twelve Dreadnoughts either built or under construction. To placate the radical wing of their party, who were desperate for more social reform, the Liberal government had axed four battleships from the 1906–8 estimates. As it turned out, the new British naval attaché in Berlin and the Admiralty had got their sums wrong. Germany would only have eleven Dreadnoughts by 1912 and not seventeen, as originally thought. Based on the evidence put forward, Grey was determined to support McKenna and defend Britain's naval superiority, but not before he had initiated another discussion on construction cutbacks with the German ambassador, Count Paul Wolff-Metternich. A meeting was set for early in the new year.

The tragedy in Anglo-German relations was that there was no part of the world in which the two countries were really opposed. The one material question that divided them was naval construction. Stoked up by a press campaign in the respective countries, Britain believed the German Navy was directed at her and the Germans believed Britain's Entente policy was aimed at them. Britain had of course made a rod for her own back by introducing the Dreadnought. The Germans would now have to build new battle-ships of their own, and their technology was amongst the best in the world, particularly in the fields of armour protection and gunnery.

The country at large was feeling especially insecure at this moment through the lack of discipline being demonstrated by naval officers in the two warring camps of Fisher and Beresford, the *Westminster Gazette* writing in its leader column:

> The ability of the Navy to retain the command of the sea and to protect our supplies in time of war belongs to the life and death of the nation. If it is equal to the task we shall keep our commerce; if it is unequal to it we shall lose our commerce and a lot else besides.

In Germany, public sentiment was right behind their naval policy, which in turn was reinforced by the virulently anti-British Navy League, which enjoyed an income of £50,000 a year and the most successful monthly periodical in circulation. It would be almost impossible for ministers to make a public withdrawal from the arena, as German naval policy was fixed by past Naval Laws and there could be no revision until the existing programme expired in 1911. There was therefore no alternative for Britain than to continue to build and for the taxpayer to foot the increased bills.

'Big Navy Man'

G rey had his promised meeting with Metternich regarding the German construction programme on 4 January. It was always going to be an uncomfortable confrontation as more often than not Metternich was kept in the dark by Tirpitz and, even when he had information to hand, the ambassador was told not to pass it on to the British. The Foreign Secretary explained that the Admiralty had evidence that Germany was accelerating her construction programme. Grey informed Metternich that if this was the case, Britain would have to base her own requirements on Germany's shipbuilding capacity rather than on her stated Navy Laws. When Metternich denied the rumours, Grey suggested that the respective naval attachés should be given permission to inspect the shipyards to ascertain the facts for themselves. The ambassador insisted the Kaiser would never approve such a course of action. Grey was no more successful at a second meeting a month later. Metternich did, however, confess to the fact that German yards were accumulating certain materials in advance of the construction dates. Grey in turn impressed on the ambassador the enormous significance of the Navy to Britain. He rammed home the point that the Navy was to Britain what the Army was to Germany; supremacy at sea guaranteed the security of the Empire.

While these deliberations were taking place, the Admiralty increased its estimates from six to eight battleships, causing blood pressure to rise amongst the 'economists' in the Cabinet. Grey and Haldane supported McKenna. The Foreign Secretary would go to any lengths to maintain Britain's lead in Dreadnought construction; it was essential to his foreign policy. When pushed, Grey could be most obstinate and he was only too willing to proffer his resignation. Charles Hobhouse, a Cabinet colleague, wrote in his diary, 'Edward Grey is clear, narrow and obstinate when convinced of the soundness of his case, but convincible up to that point. He carries great weight in Cabinet and is apt at finding solutions of difficulties, very conciliatory and with plenty of humour.' In the event, it was the Prime Minister who came up with the compromise solution at Cabinet on 24 February. Four battleships would be laid down in the 1909 estimates with four more to be laid down by 1 April 1910 if the German construction programme warranted them. Asquith was particularly irritated by the antics of Lloyd George and Churchill, writing to his wife in the middle of the naval crisis, 'There are moments when I am disposed summarily to chastise them both.' Their shrill cries for defence cuts created a tense atmosphere that complicated Anglo-German relations. The Foreign Secretary on the other hand was the Prime Minister's 'rock': 'E. Grey is a great standby, always sound, temperate and strong.'

It was not just the naval scare that occupied the Foreign Secretary's attentions at the beginning of the year. Ominously, Conrad von Hötzendorf, the Austrian Chief of General Staff, had recently met his German counterpart to work up an operational strategy in the event of a war with Russia. The situation in the Balkans began to slowly unravel in January, providing in the process some successes for British diplomacy. On the 11th the Austro-Turkish settlement was signed, providing financial compensation for Turkey in respect of the annexation of Bosnia and Herzegovina. Grey had taken a strong stand against the annexation and was adamant that Turkey receive satisfactory compensation after the event. By advising the Turks to hold out for their just deserts he had a decisive influence on the outcome without being directly involved in the negotiations. On 22 January in a speech at Coldstream, Grey was cautiously confident that matters were resolving themselves in the Balkans, but he was still concerned about the position of Serbia and the size of the indemnity payable to Turkey over Bulgarian independence: 'We have been through some months of gloom and anxiety; it would be too much to say the sky is clear but there is now a most gladdening appearance of some blue sky.' Three months later, on 19 April, a Turco-Bulgarian agreement was signed compensating Turkey for the loss of Eastern Roumelia and for the forfeiture of revenues from the Oriental Railway, seized on Bulgarian independence. The settlement represented a double success for Grey as he had worked closely with Russia in providing both advice and support for Turkey.

These diplomatic successes were short-lived. They were all too soon negated by the Austro-Serbian crisis and by the inclination of the Young Turks to move back into the German camp. Serbia had demanded territorial compensation from Austria following the annexation of Bosnia and Herzegovina. She rightly felt she was being strangled by her larger neighbour geographically, politically and economically. Serbia needed above all some measure of economic freedom and an outlet for her trade, preferably a port on the Adriatic coast via Bosnia or Montenegro. The Austrians were loath to grant any concessions, as a subservient Serbia represented a guarantee against the racial ambitions of the southern Slavs. Anyway, there was next to no chance of Austria agreeing to territorial compensation as the most interested party, Turkey, had recognised the annexation on 26 February. With Serbia persisting with her demands, the mobilisation of the Austro-Hungarian Army was approved on 29 March. Two days later Serbia, lacking Russian support, climbed down. Aehrenthal was now convinced of the value of a military threat in Balkan diplomacy. The British press were well aware of the seriousness of the situation in the Balkans and the associated consequences for European peace. The leader column in the *Pall Mall Gazette* stated as early as 8 March:

There is a powerful war party in Vienna as well as an excited population in Belgrade with two armies on a war footing which neither
state can afford to prolong indefinitely, in order to realise that, if
peace seems the more probable issue today, it is by no means certain
that war may not be the picture that will finally be presented to us
by the Balkan Bioscope.

Grey had been worried for some time about an escalation into a full
European war. He perceptively wrote to Cartwright at the embassy
in Vienna about Aehrenthal's reckless and irresponsible behaviour:
'A breach of the peace will provoke a conflagration greater than
anyone can foresee: he is living in a fool's paradise. It is dangerous to light a fire out of doors when there is a lot of combustible
material about.' Berlin had used the 'mailed fist' and supported
Austria, firstly in order that Teuton rather than Slav interests might
gain the upper hand in south-east Europe and secondly to prove
to the Triple Alliance that she was strong enough to repay Austria
for her steadfast support at Algeciras. Germany and Austria had
won a great diplomatic victory in ensuring Russia and Britain gave
up their demands for a conference, but at what cost. There were
prophetic words in the *Pall Mall Gazette*:

> Russia for the moment lies prostrate at the feet of Germany but that
> humiliating position will, assuredly, not be permanent. Gradually
> Russia will arise and as she gathers strength and heals her grievous
> wounds, military and social, she will again stand erect and forget her
> present humiliation. Her indignation will not die away: on the contrary
> it will spread through the nation and will accumulate at compound
> interest until the day comes when Russia can look for revenge. And
> with Russia there will be the Slav race, not Serbia and Montenegro
> alone but within the dominions of the Dual Monarchy, the Slavs,
> Czechs and Croats who have been flouted even as she has been.

Over in St Petersburg, Arthur Nicolson was full of gloom. He felt
the Russians might try and seek an accommodation with Berlin,

bearing in mind the lukewarm support they had received from their Entente partners. Nicolson saw the balance of power in Europe as seriously threatened. He was convinced that the only way forward was to turn the ententes into alliances, but the Liberal government would not countenance the idea. He wrote pessimistically to a friend:

My firm opinion is that both Germany and Austria are carrying out a line of policy and action carefully prepared and thought out. Algeciras had to be revenged: the 'ring' carefully broken through: and the Triple Entente dissipated. The Franco-German Moroccan agreement was the first step. Russia is temporarily weak with a timorous Foreign Minister. She had to be frightened out of the Entente and the first step toward this has been eminently successful. The Franco-Russian alliance has not borne the test: and the Anglo-Russian entente is not sufficiently strong or sufficiently deep-rooted to have any appreciable influence. The hegemony of the Central Powers will be established in Europe and England will be isolated. The activity in building up the German Navy here is also significant: and the sudden entry of Germany on the scene here is also significant. When we have passed through the present 'Sturm and Drang' period, I should not be surprised if we were to find both France and Russia gravitating towards the Central Powers, as neither of the former, distrustful of each other, feels that she can stand alone against the power of the central combination.

On 13 February King Edward arrived safely back at Buckingham Palace following a state visit to Germany. He had been dreading the visit and Queen Alexandra greatly disliked both the Kaiser and the Empress. Alexandra had detested the Prussians ever since they went to war against the country of her birth, Denmark, in 1864 and took over the duchies of Schleswig and Holstein. When Prince George had been awarded the Order of the Black Eagle by the

Kaiser some years earlier, Alexandra had written to her son, 'And so my Georgie boy has become a real live filthy blue-coated *Pickelhaube* German soldier!!!' It was hoped in the press that the royal visit would alleviate the feeling of suspicion surrounding the two countries thanks to Germany's paranoia over 'isolation' and Britain's concern over the naval build-up. Once again the Foreign Secretary decided to stay at home, excusing himself on a concern that his presence might signify a new special relationship with Germany which would upset the French. As Germany's behaviour over the Serbian crisis would show, there was little chance of that. The trip was not without drama, as the King collapsed at a dinner in the British embassy. He was suffering from bronchial problems brought on by an excess of cigars and found it difficult to climb the stairs.

It had been finally decided that Hardinge would accompany the King to Berlin. At Grey's insistence, Hardinge congratulated Bülow on the signing of a pact on 9 February with France over Morocco. Looking on the bright side, the signing was an admission on the part of Germany that Britain's friendship with France need not imply hostility towards Germany. The back-slapping was a magnanimous action by Grey, as Germany had agreed to recognise French political interests in Morocco in return for a partition of all economic concessions between France and Germany. This smacked of a breach in the 'open-door' policy to Britain and America. Bülow then informed Hardinge how he had disapproved of Aehrenthal's behaviour over Bosnia and that Germany had a strong desire for peace in the Balkans. To complicate matters, the Kaiser told the King in confidence that he no longer trusted Bülow's judgement and he blamed his Chancellor for the disastrous *Daily Telegraph* interview. Little wonder that German foreign policy was so muddled.

Grey must have felt a degree of guilt over the King's health, as it was he who insisted the visit went ahead in the cause of Anglo-German relations. He saw it as the best way of demonstrating to the Germans that the King's many foreign visits were not intended to encircle their country. Bridges did, however, urgently need to

be rebuilt following the King's recent meeting with the Czar at
Reval. The poor quality of Anglo-German relations was yet again
demonstrated later in the autumn, when the Foreign Secretary,
backed by Hardinge, forbade a visit by a band of the Coldstream
Guards to Cologne for fear of upsetting the French. The King,
who had given his prior approval, was furious. The episode demonstrates what a delicate balancing act Grey faced. Better relations
with Germany were to be encouraged but not at the expense of
snubbing the French. It also proves that Grey was a much more
tenacious operator than many suspected. He was his own man
and he didn't seem to mind upsetting the King if he felt he was
acting correctly and in the best interests of his country. Again,
when Lord Esher, King Edward's adviser and close friend, asked
the Foreign Office for a certain memorandum on behalf of the
King, he was told in no-nonsense terms by Grey that it could only
be released if requested by the King's private secretary. Perhaps it
was Grey's intransigence that had led the King to turn down the
Prime Minister's submission a few months earlier that the Foreign
Secretary should be given the Garter. The King excused himself by
maintaining that there was no precedent since Sir Robert Walpole
for granting such an important honour to a commoner.

On 29 March Grey made an important speech in the Commons,
replying for the government to Balfour's censure motion on naval
construction. His aim was to convince the British public that as long
as he remained in the Cabinet, Britain's national security would
not be endangered. He found the general expenditure on arms in
Europe abhorrent, yet he promised a strong Navy which would
form the cornerstone of British defence. The Foreign Secretary told
a shocked House that 'Germany has set herself the task of building
the most powerful fleet of Dreadnoughts the world has ever seen
and that imposes on us the necessity of rebuilding the whole fleet.'
At one stroke he had denounced the value of all Britain's ships of

a pre-Dreadnought type. He went on to inform his audience that he would not consider any unilateral disarmament. Britain would follow suit if Germany took the lead, and a first step to common sense could be an exchange of shipyard information between naval attachés. As for Anglo-German relations, he wanted them to remain friendly and at no point would he encourage the isolation of Germany. Grey concluded his speech by reminding the House that a friendly relationship with Germany was a key component of his foreign policy, but reiterated that it could never be at the expense of France and Russia. At the same time he refused to contribute to Britain's own isolation by sitting back and watching a single power establish a dominance over Europe, something which had been the basis of British foreign policy for many centuries past. The speech was well received by all sides in Britain, Herbert Gladstone writing to the King that Grey's 'cool, impressive delivery kept the House in closest attention from beginning to end'.

The German ambassador, Prince Lichnowsky, certainly believed Grey's claim, writing:

> The British statesman, after having settled all outstanding points of difference with France and Russia, wished to make similar agreements with us. It was not his object to isolate us, but to the best of his power to make us partners in existing association. Just as he had succeeded in removing Anglo-French and Anglo-Russian differences, so, too, he wished if possible to eliminate Anglo-German differences, and by a network of treaties – which would no doubt in the end have led to an agreement on the thorny question of naval armaments – to ensure the peace of the world, after our previous policy had led to an association – the Entente – which represented a mutual insurance against the risk of war.

On a Sunday morning in mid-April, Grey was back at Rosehall on the Cassley. He wrote to his friend Henry Newbolt, 'I walked up a lonely glen and lunched by a burn. The air vibrated with the wonderful spring notes of many curlews and from far up the hill came the croaking of ravens.' On Monday morning the river was in perfect condition. He was full of anticipation for some excellent sport. The day turned in a personal record for the refreshed Foreign Secretary. He had five salmon on the bank by teatime before returning to the little post office to check his red boxes. There was disturbing news from Constantinople: a military revolt had overtaken the Turkish government and was developing into civil war. He took the decision to return to London – but not before catching another fish.

In *Fly Fishing* he writes of his intense disappointment and frustration:

> The next morning I left: the river was still in good order; there was the prospect of a week of good sport if only I could stay: there was the certainty that I must wait a whole year before I could spring salmon fish again. And there was not even the compensation of feeling a martyr to duty. If the disturbances at Constantinople became dangerous, British action must be limited to protecting lives and property. The measures necessary for this would be taken by the diplomatic and naval authorities on the spot whether I were at the Foreign Office or not. If I stayed at the Cassley until something really happened I could be at the Foreign Office in plenty of time to deal with political complications that might arise later on, the public interest would not suffer if I awaited developments. But the fear of what would be said in the House of Commons and in the Press, if something did happen and I were absent from my office, destroyed my equanimity: I went back to London feeling cowardly rather than noble, and not at all convinced that the sacrifice made was necessary. The event proved that it was unnecessary.

Grey managed to fish the Itchen for six days in May, including three over the Whitsun bank holiday when he caught twenty-four trout with Eddy Tennant as his guest. Unless his brother Charlie was fishing, Grey was usually alone at The Cottage and because of his workload he was never there for long. He wrote to Mrs Creighton, who was staying at The Cottage in September:

> The spirit of the Cottage is peculiar and unfailing. I wish I didn't have it for such short periods. There isn't time in the two or three days of a weekend to sink down into it: it is after two days that one is thoroughly in tune. And for these last four years there has been disturbing work to do at the Cottage and that must be so as long as I am in office. Foreign Office things are always a mess: they are not as if one was doing constructive work or writing a book or a lecture or reading up a subject and they can never be put aside for a day. Nevertheless Cottage is a refuge always and there is quiet.

May was also a good month on the Itchen, but the rise was much shorter than June; two hours was normal, four hours if you were lucky, and it rarely began before eleven o'clock. But then May was Wordsworth's 'golden time'. There was more time to enjoy 'the glory of the month': the birdsong, the blossom and the fresh green leaves. Grey writes in *Fly Fishing*:

> There is so much to be seen and heard in May. There are the separate and successive greens of the fresh young leaves of different trees, perhaps the most tender and the most transient of all the colours that leaves or flowers give to any season. Then there are the great blossoms of May, of which I especially value six, all so conspicuous in colour as to compel attention and three of them wonderful in perfume. They are lilac, hawthorn, gorse, horse-chestnut, laburnum and broom. Not to spend time in the country while all these things are at their best is to lead a dull life indeed; and yet, if we are not to miss some of them, we must spend a part at least of every week of May in going about the country with attention free and eyes afield. Dry fly fishing leaves many hours free for this. The first half of May, too, is the most favourable time for making the discovery of birds. The summer birds have nearly all arrived and all the birds are singing; but the leaves are not thick yet and

both in brushwood and in trees it is comparatively easy to see the different species.

In mid-July, two important events took place on the naval front. On 26 July McKenna announced in the Commons his decision to build the extra four Dreadnoughts. Asquith had finally been won over by the news that Austria and Italy had initiated construction programmes of their own. Grey was largely responsible for the fact that eight battleships were finally ordered. He carried great weight in Cabinet and had made the acceptance of the naval estimates a condition of remaining in office. Grey's support of the 'big Navy' group did not make him an extremist. He was always prepared to enter into talks with the Germans to try and solve the naval problem. If he could engineer a cut in naval expenditure, he was well aware of the advantages that would follow in domestic politics, and that is why he confirmed his desire for some sort of understanding with Germany in his speech to the Commons on 29 March. The recent appointment of Bethmann Hollweg, replacing Bülow as Chancellor, gave cause for fresh hope. He genuinely sought friendly relations with Britain and understood that the size of the German fleet was the main obstacle to a breakthrough. On 21 August he informed Sir Edward Goschen, the British ambassador in Berlin, that he was willing to initiate talks of a general nature with Britain. Grey welcomed the idea but, much to the irritation of the Germans, he insisted on keeping the French and Russians informed of developments.

The complete German proposals were received on 4 November. In return for a naval understanding, the Germans sought a political agreement that would give them security in Europe. Grey was to be disappointed on two fronts. Firstly, the Germans were not prepared to reduce the size of their own naval programme, only to slow down the rate of construction. Secondly, they wanted a neutrality agreement. If either side went to war with a third country, the other would remain neutral. This effectively meant leaving France and Russia at the mercy of Germany. Hardinge and Crowe were disgusted although not really surprised at the German approach. The forthcoming elections in January were a convenient excuse for putting further discussions on hold and a dispirited Grey was happy to keep the door ajar if only to keep the radicals in Cabinet at bay.

On 3 August Grey was invited to Cowes to take part in the ceremonials surrounding the state visit of the Russian imperial family. It also gave him the chance to reacquaint himself with a more humble Izvolsky. The Foreign Secretary was not looking forward to the proceedings. The visit was most unpopular amongst the Liberals in Britain. The prejudice against an entente with such an autocratic regime had deepened since Russia's military intervention in northern Persia in April. Grey had to overrule the Prime Minister's suggestion that the visit be merely a family affair; Asquith would have been far happier if Stolypin and Izvolsky had stayed at home. The royal party steamed down the lines of the fleet, which looked reassuringly magnificent. In the evening, against a background of gaily illuminated battleships, the King gave a banquet on the *Victoria and Albert*. Grey's dinner companion was a rapidly ageing Nicolson, who also hated these state occasions. Right now the ambassador had to be thankful for small mercies. The government had refused to contemplate his suggestion of a full alliance with Russia, but at least his Entente, and indeed Izvolsky, had both survived the humiliation of the Bosnian annexation. Little of importance was discussed. Izvolsky complained about Aehrenthal and then urged Grey to do all in his power to support the Young Turks. He feared that the dissolution of the Turkish Empire in Europe would increase Austrian influence in the Balkans. On the sticky subject of Persia, he expressed a desire 'for a frank and full interchange of views between the two governments on all questions'.

The visit of the Czar sparked rumblings from the back benches about Grey's foreign policy, suggesting the shape of things to come; apparently his approach was 'not Liberal enough'. Arthur Ponsonby, who led the critics of Grey's policy, thought the Foreign

Secretary showed 'too much conscience on the Austro-Turkish question, too little on Russia and not enough zeal on the Congo question'. In July, Grey found himself constantly on his feet in the House answering questions on Persia. As the local Liberals struggled for constitutional government, Russian troops were moved across the border into northern Persia to counter rioting. Grey had to reassure the House that the Russians were keeping the Foreign Office informed of their actions and that there had been no reports of any British lives in danger.

❧

Throughout the summer there was an outcry from the landed classes over the land taxes and death duties introduced in Lloyd George's 'People's Budget' on 29 April. Rosebery had been characteristically effective in speaking out against the Budget in Glasgow, accusing the 'Vulture State' of introducing 'a Revolutionary Socialist Budget'. The Duke of Northumberland was particularly vociferous, complaining in a letter to *The Times* that his enforced economies would mean inflicting great hardship on his retainers. Grey bravely took up the challenge laid down by his powerful Northumbrian neighbour, replying in a letter to the newspaper:

> Is that really so, have you looked round the whole field of your expenditure and come to that conclusion? Have you no sporting rights in Scotland or other amenities which you could let to somebody else who would take on your servants and gamekeepers? Have you no superfluous house or property for which you could find a tenant? Is it not even possible you have talents hidden in a napkin which you might turn to account by earning a little money? Or failing that are there no economies possible in your acquisition which would save you from the sad necessity of reducing labour on your estate?

When Grey spoke out, people listened. He commanded considerable cross-party respect because of the 'continuity' attached to his foreign policy. The *Westminster Gazette* hit on his winning ways: 'It is the simple and direct form which makes the writer so effective in controversy and it does not attempt to deny that the national requirements call for a real sacrifice from those who enjoy the lion's share of the nation's wealth.'

Although up to his neck at the Foreign Office, Grey played his part in the great debate over the Budget, speaking out across the country against the unconstitutional behaviour of the House of Lords. At Trowbridge on 24 November he reminded his audience of the historic importance of the House of Commons as guardian of Britain's democratic rights:

> It is by claiming the right to withhold and grant supplies that the House of Commons gained its position in the country. Those who value the liberties of this country must insist that power shall not be filched from the House of Commons and that as the House of Commons and not the House of Lords is the guardian of the liberties of the people and has won those liberties for us, so in the hands of the House of Commons that power must remain unimpaired.

Ten days later he was at it again:

> I am in favour of a Second Chamber, but precisely for that reason one of my grievances is that we have no Second Chamber. When a Conservative Government is in power, well, of course, that is the time when I being a Liberal should most like to see a Second Chamber. This is precisely the time when we have only a Single Chamber and those who accuse us on the Liberal side of tending towards a Second Chamber ought to realise that is why under the present system we have the grievance of living under a Second Chamber Government, because whenever the Tory Government is in power, what is the House of Lords? – a voice, a dummy. Well, it is not a Second Chamber. It is a sleeping partner. Is it a Second Chamber when a Liberal Government is in power? No it is not. It is an Opposition which is a very different thing. That is the issue.

Whenever Grey found the time outside the dry-fly season, he went home to Fallodon. Occasionally he would stay with friends such as the Tennants at Wilsford or the Buxtons at Newtimber Place in the Downs north of Brighton. He spent much of his time alone, reading, walking or writing to friends. On 5 September he wrote to Mrs Creighton from Hatfield:

> I am reading *Forgotten Tales*, a selection of cautionary and improving stories at the end of the eighteenth and the early nineteenth century; E. V. Lucas has dug them up and they have many delightful expressions. 'The boys' father though a labouring man had a generous heart' and two little boys writing to their sister say 'Our rabbit has kindled' which apparently means that it has young.

In the spring he wrote to Katherine Lyttelton of a weekend at Fallodon when he undertook a favourite walk over the moors and up Ross Camp with its panoramic views,

> I went over the moor to Ross Camp to-day and lunched and read and slept a little in the heather. I see the wonderful beauty of the world as it still is and I think of the happiness I have had and I do from my heart say Oh! That men would therefore praise the Lord for his goodness! For I have had that which is worth being born for or dying for or waiting for; and others may have it all too. The beauty of the world at any rate is for all who have eyes to see and hearts to feel. I shall die grateful for what I have had, whether I die soon or late. And whatever happens to me between now and then.

Grey never lost his sense of community and relished attending his local church at Embleton, which formed such an important part of his youth with the Creighton family. On 24 October he wrote again to Katherine Lyttelton, demonstrating both his deep sensitivity and a sharp sense of humour:

To-day I went to church unintentionally, by which I mean that I
put aside the church-going clothes when I got up and put on the
others intending not to go. Then after breakfast I changed my mind,
though not my clothes and went and enjoyed it. It seemed to be
harvest thanksgiving when I got there: the Church was decorated
with chrysanthemums and oats, and an occasional beetroot or
carrot; and we had four harvest hymns? They make me wriggle and
purr with enjoyment.

> And keep us in His grace,
> And guide us when perplexed
> And save us from all ills
> In this world and the next.

The simplicity gave me such a *douce attendrissement* that I felt as if I
could kiss the whole choir for singing it. But they missed out one
verse of 'We plough the fields and scatter' and I nearly made a fuss
and interrupted the service then. We had too the 118th Psalm and a
fine chant for it: do you know that psalm? It is splendid and buoyant
and says things two or three or four times over because it is so glad.

The August Bank Holiday was spent with the Buxtons in Sussex.
A fellow guest, Lucy Masterman, recorded in her diary, 'We spent
the whole of the first evening playing tip and run with the Buxton
children, a game into which the whole house party got gradually
absorbed.' Sydney Buxton, along with Haldane, ranked as Grey's
closest friend in the Cabinet. The two men were closely linked by
a love of country pursuits, particularly fishing and ornithology.
The Newtimber visitors book records his name twenty-one times
between 1904 and 1932. The Buxton family adored Edward Grey,
and Dorothy had been their 'dearest and certainly most interesting
female friend'. Mildred Buxton wrote of Grey, 'I hope I shall see
him Prime Minister before I die.' She also wrote to her son describing Grey as 'a wonderful combination of simplicity with a really
great character and a particularly lucid mind'. Some years later in

South Africa, she compared Louis Botha to Grey: 'His character is like Sir Edward Grey's, I think, in many ways – great simplicity and a great sense of duty, and he also hates politics and longs to get back to his farming.'

The Budget was finally sent to the Lords on 4 November. It was radical by necessity, in order to finance both old-age pensions and the Dreadnoughts. The supertax of 6d in the pound on incomes of over £3,000 a year caused relatively little comment. However, the Prime Minister was correct in his assumption that the new land taxes would do most 'to set the heather on fire'. Grey agreed, telling the house party at Newtimber that the new land taxes would cost him £70 a year including insurance against death duties. Over many weeks of sensitive Budget discussion, the Chancellor managed to carry his Cabinet colleagues. Haldane and McKenna were always critical of Lloyd George's methods and style, while the landed interests such as Crewe, Harcourt, Runciman and Grey disliked the substance of some of the Chancellor's proposals. In the end everyone fell into line in the cause of Cabinet unity. At this stage Grey and Lloyd George would appear to have had a good working relationship, although they were on opposite sides of the fence when it came to naval matters. According to Trevelyan, Grey replied to a correspondent who had abused the Chancellor,

> I cannot agree with what you say. Mr Lloyd George is a colleague with whom I have always been on the best of terms personally and the Budget raises money required in a way which presses much less, I believe, upon the poorer classes than any alternative that could be devised.

Lloyd George was respected but not liked by many of his colleagues and it is interesting to note that he was afraid of Grey. Charles Hobhouse writes in his diary,

Lloyd George has humour – great quickness of thought, and a wonderful power of managing men for a short time. He knows no meaning in the words *truth* or *gratitude*. Asquith is afraid of him, he knows it, but he likes and respects Asquith. He is a little afraid of Grey – and of no one else, and treats Winston Churchill like he would a favourite and spoilt naughty boy.

Trevelyan tells us that Grey 'disliked the shrill Limehouse note in Lloyd George's speeches'. In early August the Chancellor made a speech in the East End attacking members of the land-owning aristocracy for protesting about his Budget. He claimed that 'A fully equipped Duke costs as much to keep up as two Dreadnoughts and is less easy to scrap!' The King was furious and complained to the Prime Minister that Lloyd George was inciting class warfare. Henry Newbolt agreed with the monarch and wrote angrily to *The Times*, disassociating Grey, 'with his lofty simplicity of character', from Lloyd George and the radicals, with 'their destruction of sympathy between rich and poor'. This in turn upset Grey, who wrote to his friend, 'I think it very unfair to my colleagues to put me on a separate pinnacle. Asquith and Haldane are just as entitled to your praise as I am. What you have said about me could separate all of us.'

The Lords threw out the Finance Bill by a majority of 350 votes to 75 on 30 November, necessitating a general election in the new year. Grey knew the government was in for a long fight with the Lords and was keen for battle to commence. The King, who was angry and miserable with Balfour and Lansdowne for having placed him in an unpleasant constitutional position, dissolved Parliament on 3 December. The Cabinet had been discussing for some time ways of emasculating the powers of the Lords. They had considered a permanent transfer to the Prime Minister of the Sovereign's prerogative for creating peers, but felt it might finish off King Edward. They finally settled on an approach whereby they would pass a Bill to curb the power of the Lords, having in advance secured a pledge from the King that he would create a sufficient number of peers to ensure the Budget's passage through the upper chamber. The King's private secretary, Lord Knollys, was sounded out privately and warned that the King might abdicate rather than agree to swamping the Lords with new peers which in his opinion would be tantamount to its destruction.

❧

A lonely Christmas at Fallodon would have afforded Grey much time for sombre reflection. Not only was the constitutional battle with the Lords intensifying at home, but the storm clouds were also gathering in Central Europe. Austria's relations with Serbia were on a fast downward track. The people and army of Serbia had not been in sympathy with their government's actions in backing down in face of Austrian threats, and that in turn lent power to revolutionary movements such as 'Black Hand', committed to a greater southern Slav empire. Austria's Chief of General Staff, Count Franz Conrad, was desperate for a war with Serbia. Russia would not allow herself to be humiliated again, and the next time Austria issued arrogant threats, the Russians would stand by her Slav friends. The Balkan region as a whole was becoming volatile and unstable. Recent Austro-Russian antagonism was now providing encouragement for the newly emergent Balkan states to break away from a crumbling Ottoman Empire.

At the same time, Germany's foreign policy was undergoing a reorientation. Managing the Reichstag was proving increasingly difficult for the German Chancellor in light of the budgetary demands of Tirpitz's fleet. As a result there was a gradual shift away from playing on the world stage – the policy of *Weltpolitik* – to a consolidation of Germany's position as the major continental power. This would tie Germany even closer to her insecure Austro-Hungarian ally and would soon necessitate additional resources being allocated to the Army. More ominously, and perhaps unknown to the Foreign Secretary, the sound of jackboots and clinking swords belonging to high-ranking Prussian officers was now to be heard in

the long cold stone corridors of the Kaiser's palace in Berlin. In
his heart of hearts Grey knew a European war with Germany lay
around the corner and, despite the misgivings of the radicals in his
own party, he would do his utmost to prepare his country for such
an eventuality.

Two General Elections

The election was over by the end of January. The Liberals' huge independent majority had evaporated and Grey was left drained and in low spirits. On 28 January he wrote to Mrs Creighton, 'The Election was dreadful, Foreign Office work all morning and three meetings an evening.' He was not optimistic about the Liberals' chances of remaining in office with the constitutional issue at the forefront of parliamentary affairs. He feared for his foreign affairs brief, which was being eclipsed by domestic problems. Despite Grey's pessimism, it was not all bad news. Even though the Unionists had gained 116 seats, the Liberals still enjoyed a healthy majority with Irish Nationalist and Labour support included. Grey himself had polled the same number of votes as in 1906 although his opponent increased his count by 500.

On 7 February Grey wrote a firm letter to Asquith outlining his views on the current political situation. He wanted the constitutional issue tackled as a matter of priority. He was not prepared to watch the Lords wreck the government's legislative programme a moment longer. The Cabinet was split on the way forward. Harcourt led the group wishing merely to curb their Lords' power of veto, while Grey was the most powerful advocate for reform. Grey, ever the radical, wrote to the Prime Minister, 'It is the constitution of the House of Lords and not its powers which are an anomaly.' He wanted the hereditary peers swept away and replaced by 'a new Second Chamber, much smaller in size than the House of Commons, based upon the elective principle, with, if desired, a minority of distinguished life-members'. Hardinge informed the King that a melancholy Grey was convinced there would be a Cabinet split over both the constitutional issue and the naval estimates.

The stubborn, uncompromising side of Grey showed itself again in March when a Cabinet committee reported that the government should merely move against the Lords' right of veto. The main resolutions agreed by the committee were that the Lords could not tamper with a Money Bill and that the power of the Lords to delay all other legislation should be limited to two years. In addition, the maximum length of a parliament was to be reduced from seven to five years. Grey promptly sent in his resignation to the Prime Minister, supported by Runciman. McKenna stated that if Grey went, he would too, and there were question marks over Haldane and Crewe. The Prime Minister was well aware that a Grey resig-nation could mean the end of his administration, such was Grey's standing in the Liberal Party. For once, Asquith was upset by Grey, writing to Crewe, 'I have had a tiresome letter from E. Grey.' A compromise was finally reached by inserting a preamble into the Parliament Bill whereby the government declared its intention to reform the Lords at some future point. Tactically, Grey was almost certainly wrong to push for full reform of the Lords instead of clipping its wings. Resulting delays in the legislative programme, particularly over Home Rule, may well have lost the Irish vote and split the Liberal Party.

By the end of April, government morale had improved beyond recognition. Lansdowne was true to his word that the result of the election would settle the Budget issue. The reintroduced Budget had a successful passage through both Houses, obtaining a majority of 100 in the Commons. Asquith re-established his authority in the Commons on 14 April, making a commanding speech on the constitutional issue. He told the House that if the Lords rejected the veto resolutions, the government would either resign or accept a dissolution. Importantly, if a dissolution was granted, the King would, if necessary, create a large number of peers to push the required legislation through the Lords. As Parliament adjourned for a short recess at the end of the month, a relieved Prime Minister set off for the Mediterranean on the Admiralty yacht, *Enchantress*, while the Foreign Secretary was already back at Rosehall on the Cassley for his annual fix of spring salmon fishing. He wrote to Katherine Lyttelton, 'It might seem rather scandalous that I should have come here while there is a political crisis but I feel very pleased at having bolted.' He no doubt deserved his holiday and, after all, he knew that the Budget had been sent back to the Lords unchanged. The government had held their ground in the face of fierce Irish opposition to the whisky tax!

The ten-day break with his brother Charlie on the Cassley was the highlight of Grey's year and he had no intention of letting their Lordships ruin his fishing holiday. The more confident the Foreign Secretary grew in office, the more disinclined he was to have his spring break threatened by work. Grey always thought the glory of salmon fishing was in the spring. A river was usually in good condition owing to a combination of autumn rains and recent snow-melt. As every angler knows, there are two aspects to salmon fishing that are particularly exciting: the anticipation of catching a fish in a river the angler knows well and then the actual hooking of a fish. Grey describes both most graphically in *Fly Fishing*. He informs the reader that the full joy of salmon fishing cannot be appreciated unless the angler knows his river really well:

> Anticipation, the knowledge of what to hope for or what to expect, is an important factor without which the fullest pleasure cannot be. The prospect of salmon fishing in an unknown or little-known river is good, but it is much better when we can in imagination fish the pools before-hand, dwelling with the mind's eye on what experience has told us is the best spot in each pool.

Likewise, he writes of that culminating moment when the fisher-man experiences a gentle tug on the line and thrills to the few initial clicks of the reel as the fish takes the fly to the bottom of the pool:

> To me there is nothing in all sport equal to the glory of success in salmon fishing, but the supreme moment is undoubtedly the actual hooking of the fish. However great my expectation and keenness, the feel of the fish when it hooks itself comes upon me with a shock of surprise and delight and there is a sudden thrill in having to do with the weight and strength of a salmon. A sense of complete achievement and satisfaction is felt merely in the hooking of it.

His lack of satisfaction in playing a salmon, as described in *Fly Fishing*, is perhaps surprising:

> I remember being a little disappointed even with the first salmon which I played on a salmon rod. I have never yet had a fish in play on a salmon rod for more than half an hour or landed one more than 200 yards from the place where it was hooked.

Sydney Buxton, in his tribute to Grey, *Edward Grey, Bird Lover and Fisherman*, saw things slightly differently, writing of his blind friend in later life, 'I remember his saying to me that one of the thrills in playing a salmon, now obliterated, was the sudden sight of the scattering spray that marked the line as it cut the surface of the water when tautened by the hooked fish, or in a subsequent rush.' Grey certainly found a sea trout or a wild brown trout, with their agility and speed of movement, much more exciting to play than a 'stately' salmon.

King Edward died just before midnight on 6 May at Buckingham Palace. Britain had lost a wise and worldly monarch at a time of grave constitutional crisis. Grey had taken an early train to The Cottage for the weekend when he received a message from Hardinge that the King was seriously ill. He returned at once to his house in Queen Anne's Gate, where he sat up late into the night with his brother George, waiting for news. The silence of the night was broken by newspaper sellers crying 'Death of the King'. He wrote in his autobiography, 'I felt like something irreparable, like a landslide had happened.' Grey, unlike the King, had no love of the ceremonial or of life in the fast lane, yet over time he developed a great respect for his monarch. The King had a splendid capacity for enjoying life, always managing to combine bonhomie with great dignity, and his people loved him for it. Most importantly, when abroad the King was the perfect ambassador, always full of charm and tact. It is true he disagreed with his Foreign Secretary at times, usually over minor issues, such as Edward making the Czar an Admiral of the Fleet at Reval, yet the King was a sympathetic supporter of the general direction of Grey's foreign policy.

Edward VII was a great constitutional sovereign whose indirect role in smoothing the waters for Britain's policy of entente with France and Russia was much appreciated by his Foreign Secretary. Grey was well aware of the benefits that his monarch could bring to the team effort, so he put him into play but always under the protective wing of Hardinge. Following the death of the King, the *Pall Mall Gazette* leader column stated on 7 May:

In one respect the late Sovereign played an invaluable part which cannot be severed from the political history of our times. He came to the throne at a time when our foreign policy was bankrupt, when we stood without a friend in Europe and when our relations with the nearest geographical Power were perverted by the memory of outworn rivalries and meaningless traditions. In the change which has so happily replaced those conditions it is needless to say the King did not work alone. The ideas and forces from which the Entente was to be born were in existence and steadily germinating. But it was the Sovereign who realised the significance and value of the new movement, arranged its opportunities and smoothed its path. Without the aid of his gracious personality and diplomatic skill the

fruition of its hopes must have been deferred and its untold services
to the cause of peace during recent years might have been impossible. No English Sovereign since William III has left a stronger or
more beneficial mark upon the international policy of Great Britain.

The Prime Minister, in particular, would miss the late King's counsel at this dangerous time. There was a general feeling in Cabinet,
led by Harcourt, that owing to the new King's inexperience it
would be most unfair to force on him a major constitutional decision such as obtaining a guarantee to create new peers so soon after
ascending the throne. Thus, in an attempt to solve the crisis, it was
decided to set up a Constitutional Conference with the opposition
leaders, with the government represented by the Prime Minister,
Crewe and Birrell, and the opposition by Balfour, Lansdowne,
Austen Chamberlain and Cawdor. The opening meeting was set
for mid-June.

The funeral of King Edward took place in brilliant sunshine on
20 May. Enormous crowds watched the procession. The King's
terrier, Caesar, led by a kilted Highlander, followed the gun carriage
and cut more of a dash than the army of European royals. The
Kaiser, who had come to bury his wicked uncle – the man supposedly responsible for encircling Germany – was staying with his
cousin George at Windsor. For once, his kindly and sympathetic
demeanour would be much appreciated by the British public. It
would be the last time such a gathering of rank and royalty would be
seen in public. The pomp and ceremony of the funeral represented
the end of an era. Within a few years monarchies would be swept
away by war and revolution, the rule of the aristocracy in Britain
terminated by the introduction of the Parliament Act, and millions
of ordinary people around the globe would be annihilated by the
modern technologies of battle. That clever and sophisticated courtier who knew everything and everybody, Lord Esher, felt something
was in the air, writing in his diary, 'There never has been such a
break up. All the old buoys which have marked the channels of our
lives seem to have been swept away.' A quarter of a million people

filed through Westminster Hall for the lying-in-state, demonstrating the love and respect the British people had for their monarch. He was buried in St George's Chapel and afterwards Grey attended a formal luncheon in the Waterloo Chamber at Windsor Castle.

Before lunch, Grey managed to snatch a few words with Colonel Theodore Roosevelt. Although they had corresponded regularly, this represented Grey's first meeting with the ex-President of the United States. Roosevelt was on a world tour and had just arrived from Africa, where he had been big-game hunting. Well acquainted with Grey's delight in the countryside, the Colonel asked to be taken on a guided bird walk in the New Forest and a date was duly fixed before his return journey in early June. At lunch Grey sat next to Hardinge, who was distraught at the death of his friend and master. He was most touched when his Permanent Secretary thanked him for never showing any kind of jealousy over his close personal relationship with the King. Hardinge was due to leave for India in October to take up the position of Viceroy. Grey dreaded his departure. For over five years, Hardinge had provided the Foreign Secretary with his learned professional advice. What is more, the working relationship had been that of close friends.

On 22 March, Metternich called on Grey at the Foreign Office to resurrect naval discussions and the possibility of a political agreement. The Cabinet radicals, led by the Lord Chancellor, Loreburn, were snapping at the Foreign Secretary's heels for some sort of settlement and the French were now less sensitive to Anglo-German dialogue, having recently settled their differences with Germany over Morocco. The present appeared as good a time as any for a settlement but the Foreign Secretary held his ground, insisting on a slackening in German naval construction as a prerequisite for a deal. This, needless to say, fell on deaf ears. With encouragement from the Cabinet, Grey decided to keep the door open for further negotiations, even though Germany's proposed political settlement

insisted on a neutrality formula in the event of war with France. Grey was determined to steer such conversations away from France and towards the Baghdad Railway.

Construction had commenced on the Baghdad Railway in 1903, the intention being to connect Berlin with Baghdad, thus increasing Germany's influence in Asiatic Turkey. Britain felt that the railway was a threat to India and her interests in the Persian Gulf. By building the railway, the Germans would gain access to the oilfields of Iraq. In addition, with a line to the port of Basra, they would secure better links to the eastern parts of the German colonial empire and bypass the Suez Canal in the process.

The Foreign Office was appalled at the possibility of selling out France. Eyre Crowe wrote scathingly of the Germans, 'But to ask for the abandonment of France and make, in addition, onerous conditions about the Baghdad Railway and Persia, is a plan to characterise which it is really difficult to find the appropriate adjectives.' As usual, Grey was under intense pressure in Cabinet and early in the new year the pro-German radicals persuaded the Prime Minister to set up a committee consisting of Grey, Asquith, Crewe, Runciman, Morley and Lloyd George to coordinate talks with Berlin. The Foreign Office was shocked. They believed the Foreign Secretary was being marginalised and saw the whole process as an attempt by the left wing of the Cabinet to force through a political agreement with Germany at whatever cost.

Railway negotiations were conducted by the late King's friend Sir Ernest Cassel, who managed to persuade the Germans to accept that the southern section of the Baghdad Railway would be placed in a new company in which Britain would receive a 50 per cent stake. D. W. Sweet in his essay on Anglo-German relations writes,

> The British Government, taking the view that the railway would be constructed eventually with or without British assistance, was chiefly concerned to secure British participation on the terms most favourable to its own interests; it also wished to concert its policy with the French (who for financial and commercial reasons wanted

to participate) and with the Russians (who, fearing the intrusion of Turkish and German influence towards the Caucasus and northern Persia, did not).

When the Kaiser had visited Windsor in 1907, Haldane had explained how Britain needed a 'gate' to protect the Indian Empire from troop movements along the line. This could best be achieved by Britain controlling the southern section from Baghdad to Basra. The Kaiser had been reasonably happy with the suggestion but back in Berlin, Bülow had shot down the proposition, causing deadlock.

In the course of these events, the Russians manifested themselves once again as difficult bedfellows. The Czar met the Kaiser at Potsdam on 5 November. Behind the backs of their allies the Russians agreed with Germany to construct a branch of the Baghdad Railway in Persia before any agreement had been reached with Britain on the southern section. In return, the Germans agreed to respect Russia's special interests in northern Persia. The Foreign Office regarded the whole exercise as a typical German ploy to upset the Entente powers. The Russians became the first power to reach an agreement with Germany over the Baghdad Railway, leaving Grey resentful of the new Foreign Minister, Sazonov, and his abandonment of the principle of collective negotiation. As if problems with the Baghdad Railway were not enough, back at home Grey's beloved NER had been on strike, paralysing the northeast of England. Ten thousand railway workers had stopped work, forty collieries were closed, 20,000 miners idle, a fleet of steamers incapacitated and 5,000 ironworkers at Middlesbrough laid off. The strike had been called by freight workers and had luckily been settled relatively quickly under the new Conciliation Conference set up in August 1908 to iron out disputes between the company and its staff.

At the end of the year all German negotiations seemed to have hit the buffers. Back in July Grey had been persuaded by his radical colleagues to drop the idea of obtaining an actual reduction in the German naval programme, and some ground for optimism was justified in October when the Germans agreed to an exchange of technical information between the two Admiralties. They still, however, insisted that as a quid pro quo for any undertakings about their naval programme they would require a general political formula. Here was a classic case of the Germans responding to a softening of the British position with their own hard line, but in the agreement to exchange information Grey at least had something for the radicals. It was a policy he had been advocating for some years.

Meanwhile, the armaments race continued apace. The First Division of the German High Seas Fleet, made up of four of the latest Dreadnoughts, moved their base from Kiel on the Baltic to Wilhelmshaven on the North Sea. At the same time the Reichstag voted funds for four additional battleships, bringing the total ordered to seventeen. Back in Britain, the First Lord asked Parliament for five extra Dreadnoughts, taking the naval estimates to over £40 million. Hardinge believed that Britain was the only stumbling block to Germany's domination of Europe and wrote to Bertie in Paris on 1 April, 'The only thing we can do is to go on building and to make our position so absolutely secure that no sane man could ever dream he would gain an advantage by attacking us.'

Amidst such frantic activity at the Admiralty, the British Army suddenly awoke from a period of dormancy. In August, a tall, energetic Francophile cavalry officer, General Henry Wilson, was promoted from running the Staff College to become Director of Military Operations. The military conversations with the French were immediately reactivated. Wilson was convinced that the injection of six British divisions into the French line could protect Paris and immediately began working on the logistics of transporting an Expeditionary Force to France. There were at this time no plans in place for supplies, suitable port facilities, railway capacity or the method of deployment of the troops. Wilson spent the balance of the summer on his bicycle studying the Franco-Belgian and Franco-German frontiers. He was a fluent French speaker and met with Foch and his General Staff every time he visited the Continent.

Haldane had provided the tools back in 1907 and luckily Wilson was now in the saddle to ensure they were correctly utilised.

On 3 June Grey was back at The Cottage fishing the Chilland beat with his friend Edward Tennant. They caught eight trout between them, including one that broke the local record at 2 lb 3 oz. He returned to the Itchen a week later, but this time with Theodore Roosevelt, the ex-President of the most powerful nation on earth. The long-awaited day of the bird walk in the New Forest had finally arrived. On 8 December 1919, Grey gave a lecture to the Harvard Union recalling how:

> Several years ago when I was at the Foreign Office in London, I got a letter from Mr Bryce, who was then the British ambassador in Washington, saying that President Roosevelt intended to travel as soon as he was out of office. He wanted it to be arranged that somebody who knew the songs of the English birds should go for a walk with him in the country, and as the songs were heard to tell him what the birds were. It seemed to me very attractive that the executive head of the most powerful country in the world should have this simple, healthy, touching desire to hear the songs of birds and I wrote back at once to Mr Bryce to say that when President Roosevelt came to England I should be delighted to do for him what he wanted. It is no more a necessary qualification for the Secretary of State for Foreign Affairs in London than it is for the President of the United States that he should know the songs of birds and it is an amusing coincidence that we should be able to arrange this little matter satisfactorily between us as if it were part of our official duties, without feeling obliged to call in the experts.

They met at Waterloo and took the train to Itchen Abbas, driving on to the little village of Tichborne. Having spent some time walking along the banks of Grey's spiritual home, they moved off to

Stoney Cross in the heart of the forest. They then proceeded down a forest stream, the Highland Water, towards Brockenhurst, where they spent the night in the Forest Park Hotel. The Foreign Secretary was a little apprehensive at first as the best of British birdsong was over, but he need not have worried. Their safari was a complete success. Roosevelt was fascinated to watch the skylarks springing into the sky from the grass. He agreed that they exactly fulfilled Wordsworth's description, 'they soared but did not roam'. They reached the inn in Brockenhurst just before nightfall and were entertained on their arrival by a nightjar. Grey felt an immediate natural affinity for the Colonel. He was fascinated by this dynamic man of so many parts.

After the walk Grey wrote to Mrs Creighton,

> I have liked Roosevelt immensely and really enjoyed the walk and the whole day. We saw forty different species and heard the songs of twenty of them and his knowledge and interest in birds is that of a real lover of birds. We had a good talk too about politics and books, including poetry, of which I found he knew by heart several of the things I have learnt. He has a peculiar faculty with it all of imparting healthy courage and vigour. I have loved him.

Roosevelt, for his part, warmed to Grey's straightforwardness, describing him to a friend as, 'a kind of high-minded public servant, as straight in all private as in all public relations, whom it is essential for a country to have'. The ex-President had met a number of senior politicians on his visit to London and it is interesting to note that he refused to meet Churchill, whom he regarded as rude and bumptious. He made a speech at the Guildhall on 31 May praising British rule in Egypt. He declared that 'Britain had given Egypt the best government it has had for 2,000 years but weakness could ruin this work'. Lord Crewe, the Colonial Secretary, was not as pleased with the compliment as Grey. Eldon Gorst had just been sent out to Cairo to replace Cromer as a liberalising influence.

Roosevelt had a unique knowledge of natural history. He had a thorough understanding of British birds but had lacked the opportunity to hear them sing. He at once picked out the blackbird as his favourite. He was most indignant that he had not heard more of its abilities in this area before. The Colonel wanted to know why everyone talked so much about the thrush; maybe the blackbird's dull name detracted from its reputation? In his same address to the Harvard Union, Grey told his audience:

> One more instance I will give of his interest and knowledge. We were passing under a fir-tree when we heard a small song in the tree above us. We stopped and I said that was the song of the golden-crested wren. He listened very attentively while the bird repeated its little song, as its habit is. Then he said, 'I think that is exactly the same song as that of a bird we have in America'; and that was the only English song that he recognised as being the same as any bird song in America. Some time afterward I met a bird expert in the Natural History Museum in London and told him of this incident and he confirmed what President Roosevelt had said, that the song of this bird would be about the only song that the two countries had in common. I think that a very remarkable instance of minute and accurate knowledge on the part of Colonel Roosevelt. It was the business of the bird expert in London to know about birds. Colonel Roosevelt's knowledge was a mere incident acquired, not as part of the work of his life but entirely outside it. I remember thinking how strange it seemed that the golden-crested wren, which is the very smallest bird we have in England, should be the only song bird which the great continent of North America has in common with us.

The foundations of the 'special relationship' with America can be traced back to the close friendships Grey established with Ambassador Page and Colonel House, President Wilson's roving ambassador, over several years before the outbreak of war. Yet there is something symbolic about Grey and Roosevelt, bonded by a mutual love of conservation and natural history, from different sides of the Atlantic, walking together in the New Forest. The friendship struck up between these two famous statesmen marks a significant point in the history of Anglo-American relations. Their close bond, cemented by common interests, spawned other, less obvious benefits. For example, it paved the way for one of the most successful international conservation measures: the Migratory Birds Treaty was negotiated by the Foreign Office and the State Department and was finally signed by the British ambassador in Washington in 1916.

Grey's detractors, clustered around their bible in the form of Lloyd George's *War Memoirs*, have found it all too easy to carica-ture him as a nice insular Northumbrian, lacking in imagination and intellect, who enjoyed the simple things in life. But it was this very presence of a hinterland, of pursuits outside his main career, that kept him going through such a difficult decade at the Foreign Office compounded by more than a fair share of personal adver-sity. Theodore Roosevelt certainly proved that many celebrated statesmen have sought solace in outside interests. These pursuits could be of a literary nature, as practised by Disraeli, or, in the case of Rosebery, both of a literary and sporting bent, or indeed merely social, as manifested by the country house weekend activi-ties of Asquith and Balfour. Sydney Buxton was convinced that Grey's passion for the countryside 'kept his brain clear and his mind unclogged'.

Contrary to Lloyd George's accusations of laziness, on 25 August, at the height of the holiday season, Grey was speaking at Tillmouth Park in the far north of his constituency on matters outside his foreign affairs brief. Referring to the Constitutional Conference, he told his audience: 'The government will not abandon anything that is vital in their case against the present Second Chamber.' He reassured his constituents that the government would not accept a settlement that placed it in a similar position to which it found itself in 1906 – a government with an enormous majority yet without the means of overcoming the deadlock between the two Houses. He emphasised the government's commitment to free trade, warning the assembled company that 'protection is likely to prove the short cut to Socialism' and reminding them that under free trade, Britain's trade account had continued to grow, whereas 'protectionist countries' had witnessed increased agitation as a result of a higher cost of living, with a corresponding increase in the socialist vote. Although a great champion of radical policies, Grey constantly spoke out against the dangers of socialism and excessive state control. On 28 October he was on his progressive feet again, giving the David Dale memorial lecture on industrial relations, stressing the importance of conciliation and arbitration between employers and employees.

Back at Westminster the Constitutional Conference reconvened in the autumn. Proceedings had moved at a snail's pace and in November seemed to be on the verge of complete breakdown. The King, Prime Minister and most of the Cabinet were keen for a compromise solution, as opposed to the Irish and radical left, who viewed the conference as a means of watering down the government's constitutional aims. In the end it was Home Rule and the intransigence of Lord Lansdowne that buried a settlement. The Unionists wanted constitutional matters, if twice rejected by the Lords, submitted to a referendum, whereas Asquith preferred that a list of certain proposals be excluded from the operations of the Parliament Act and thereby continue to qualify for their Lordships' power of veto. Lansdowne, a prominent southern Irish landlord, was determined Home Rule should be on that list.

Lloyd George, exasperated by the lack of progress, put forward the idea of a coalition government. The idea fell on fertile ground at the feet of the Foreign Secretary. A typically dejected Grey was convinced that if the conference failed in its objectives the Liberal government would fall and the country would dissolve into chaos. Asquith, who was often irritated by Grey's pessimism, described him as 'dolorous and despondent', writing to Crewe, 'I have a letter from E. Grey from which it appears that Lloyd George has been extending his missionary operations into that quarter and apparently not without producing an impression.' The Chancellor's creative thinking made no more progress than the conference. At the 10 November Cabinet meeting it was decided to dissolve Parliament. An immediate general election was to be called, but not before the Prime Minister underwent the unpleasant task of securing, if the situation arose, the King's guarantee to create sufficient peers to see the Parliament Bill through the Lords. A battle of the private secretaries ensued and the new King grudgingly agreed on the condition that his 'guarantee' need not be made public until the event happened. The King sensibly accepted the sound constitutional advice of his father's private secretary, Francis Knollys, rather than following the more conservative lead of his own adviser, Sir Arthur Bigge. The scene was now set for an all-out battle with the Lords.

The election was over by Christmas. The voters gave the government the result it was looking for. The Liberals lost three seats but effectively increased their overall majority from 124 to 126. On a smaller poll Grey's majority went up by three votes. The country was tired of the continuing constitutional struggle and wanted the matter settled. Grey would have been relieved if he had known that this would be his last election. He hated electioneering as much as he disliked political life, writing to Katherine Lyttelton on Boxing Day,

I have been through the furnace of an election once more. It was a short nightmare this time. I heard one or two of my colleagues; one only this time, I think, shrieked rather loudly while he was suffering from it, but I hope we shall all meet with our nerves steadied by the Christmas holidays and our tempers soothed by plum pudding. Arthur Balfour looks as if he didn't eat enough plum pudding. I thought he got rather wild in the Election. Elections consist of saying that the proposals of the other fellow mean something which he says they do not mean. I am weary at the thought of another spell in office. All last year I kept loosening the straps, thinking I might soon put the burden down. Now I have to buckle it closer without having put it down at all. But one must take life as it comes.

Over the course of 1910, foreign affairs had unwittingly been relegated to the back seat. It was a year that witnessed two elections, the death of a King, serious labour unrest, terrible weather conditions with violent storms and floods, technological advancement with people learning to fly in earnest (which would revolutionise warfare) and, more positively, the 1909 Budget had been placed on the statute book, incorporating the introduction of a state pension. An exhausted Foreign Secretary spent Christmas at Fallodon with his brother George. He told Katherine Lyttelton that they played draw-bridge together from dinner to midnight. George had spent much of his life in Africa as a colonial administrator, explorer and passionate big-game hunter. Grey was delighted his brother's visits to Fallodon were becoming more frequent. He particularly liked the fact that George took a great interest in estate matters. George was unmarried and Grey hoped he would retire to Northumberland, making Fallodon a joint home. It was not to be. The curse of personal tragedy was soon to strike Edward Grey yet again. George returned to Africa after Christmas, never to return. He was mauled by a lion and died a few days later.

The Agadir Crisis

At the beginning of February Grey received news of his brother George's death in Africa. After Dorothy's death Grey had become much closer to his two brothers. He was proud of George's achievements as a colonial administrator and his grief was so severe that he felt it didn't sit well with a career in politics. Lord Selbourne wrote, 'I doubt if in the whole history of the Empire any Englishman has ever performed a more tiresome and intricate piece of administrative work than the dismantlement of European and native rights in Swaziland by George Grey.' Grey felt like resigning but once again drew on his inner resources, writing to his friend Ronald Munro Ferguson, 'George had the great qualities and also those that made him endearing and lovable. I feel as if the loss of him must finish what was left of me: but he wouldn't have liked that and I must try to be worth something. He judged me so generously.'

As April approached, Grey was desperately looking forward to his annual fishing holiday on the Cassley, but first he had work to do. He had been having a torrid time with his own backbenchers, who had become restive at the lack of any naval agreement with Germany. On 8 March he made a statement to the House on the Baghdad Railway. He felt he should clear the air as the railway had become a pawn in the European diplomatic game. He was particularly keen to eradicate any Anglo-German misunderstandings over the railway, for example, British suspicions that Mesopotamia might be flooded with German emigrants. Grey reminded the House that the railway was a German concession in Turkish

territory in which Britain had no right to intervene. However, if
in approaching the Persian Gulf, the railway went outside Turkish
territory and prejudiced British interests then involvement would
be justified. Germany was keen for British participation and the
Foreign Secretary viewed a deal as a means of furthering Anglo-
German friendship. There had been 'dry runs' in 1903, when Lord
Lansdowne declined to participate, and further problems in 1909.
Before any involvement could be contemplated, two obstacles had
to be overcome. Agreements had to be reached both on equality
of treatment for British and German goods and on the ownership of
that section of line running to the Gulf. It was essential that this strategic stretch should be under British control. Grey believed that the
construction of the railway would benefit all nations but in that
vital Gulf section of the line, Britain had to protect her interests.

The parliamentary party was still desperate for defence cuts and
the issue culminated in a Commons debate on 13 March. Fighting
his corner, Grey wound up for the government, making one of the
most important speeches of his life. He agreed with the House as
to the futility of international arms expenditure but reiterated that
unilateral disarmament would be a mistake. He told the House
that every country was feeling the burden of taxation to fund
armaments. Taxation only caused discontent and in Germany it
had encouraged socialism. He went on to relate how relations with
Germany had improved in the last two years and that the two countries had no reason to quarrel. He explained to members how the
German Navy Law dictated a lower level of construction at the end
of the year, at which point Britain could reduce her expenditure. He
would continue to strive for an agreement with the Germans, but at
the same time he warned the House that Germany perceived her Navy
Laws as sacrosanct. Only a week before, the Cabinet Committee on
Foreign Affairs had put forward a paper outlining the framework for
a simultaneous political and naval agreement with Germany. Grey
had concurred, but only on the basis that it contained nothing that
would upset the French and Russians. The document would be delivered to the German Chancellor by the British ambassador in Berlin

at the end of the month. In the meantime the Foreign Secretary's speech was most favourably received in Germany.

One of Grey's foremost achievements as Foreign Secretary was overseeing the establishment of a diverse group of international allies. 1911 witnessed the development of closer ties with both Japan and the United States. The original 1902 Japanese Alliance, negotiated by Lansdowne, was now due for renewal and with Europe in a state of potential turmoil Grey was determined to push through an extension. The two powers agreed to provide mutual support in the maintenance of their rights and interests in Eastern Asia and India, to champion the independence and integrity of the Chinese Empire and to assist each other in the case of any unprovoked attack. The presence of a Japanese fleet in the China Sea had allowed Britain to withdraw naval units closer to home. What is more, Australia and New Zealand had recently informed Britain they were not willing to accept the responsibility for policing the Eastern oceans. Although the new treaty, approving a continuation for ten years, was signed on 3 April, a complication immediately arose with America.

President Taft had suggested Britain and America should sign a General Arbitration Treaty, binding themselves to bring to arbitration every possible dispute between the two countries, 'however vital, however closely affecting national honour or feeling'. Bryce, in Washington, had built an excellent relationship with the Taft administration and Grey jumped at the chance of further cementing Anglo-American relations. He saw other benefits and wrote excitedly to Ambassador Bryce, 'The effect of such agreements upon disarmament and the morale of international politics should be considerable.' In the Commons debate of 13 March, Grey endorsed the President's arbitration scheme but at the same time emphasised to the House that it was not intended as a defensive alliance against a third party; America at this time was desperate

to avoid any sort of formal European entanglements. Grey's statement was well received on the other side of the Atlantic but before
negotiations could commence, steps would have to be taken to
ensure that the proposed treaty did not conflict with the Japanese
Alliance. The Japanese annexation of Korea in August 1910 was not
well received in America. Japan had declined the offer to become
a party to the Arbitration Agreement, but confirmed they had no
objections to the Anglo-American treaty as long as the provisions
of their alliance with Britain were excluded. A revised alliance was
signed with Japan on 13 July. Although the Anglo-American treaty
was signed in Washington in August, it was not to be ratified by the
Senate for another year and even then in an emasculated form.

The Foreign Secretary must have known that the river was in perfect
order, for he departed for Sutherland at a dangerous time. Yet again
there was disquiet in Morocco. Early in the year a revolt had broken
out against the Sultan and by April he was besieged in Fez. On the
17th the French ordered their troops into the capital – a dangerous
move as the Germans would rightly view such action as a breach of
the Act of Algeciras. The drama unfolding in North Africa was not
going to deter Grey from his spring break and in the latter part of
April he set off for the Cassley, where he was about to experience
the best salmon fishing of his life. He caught fifty salmon in ten
consecutive fishing days when heavy showers had kept the river at a
perfect height. The best day produced eight fish and the worst four.

On the penultimate day, Sydney Buxton, who was now at the
Board of Trade and had been detained in London by an industrial
dispute, came up to join him. Grey had promised his friend he
would leave the two best pools quiet until he arrived and then watch
him hook a fish in each of them. He writes in *Fly Fishing*,

My friend arrived shortly before two o'clock and when he had
lunched and put up his rod went straight to the Big Lazy Pool. He

rose and touched a fish half-way down the pool but it came short;
a few yards lower down he hooked and landed a salmon. In the
Round Pool his fly reached 'the glass' [an area of clear water] without touching anything and then covered the place on which I relied
to give him a fish. I feared the second half of my promise had failed.
I urged my friend to cast again and a fish did come and was landed.
It is seldom that anything in salmon fishing goes so entirely to plan.

On his return to the Foreign Office, a discouraging reply from
Bethmann Hollweg was waiting for Grey on the question of a naval
agreement. The Germans were not prepared to offer a reduction
in the tempo of naval construction. Both parties were also miles
apart when it came to a political agreement. Britain was only
offering a settlement of the Persian and Baghdad Railway questions, whereas Germany was still seeking a neutrality agreement
in the event of war with France. The negotiations now seemed
deadlocked. Throughout the early summer, the Foreign Secretary
had repeatedly tried to persuade the French to withdraw their
troops from Fez. He was uneasy about German and Spanish reac-
tions yet was only too well aware that his hands were tied by the
Entente Cordiale. The Germans were already unhappy with their
1909 Moroccan agreement with France, as it had reaped little in
the way of economic benefits. At the end of May they gave their
reluctant approval to the French occupation so long as it was of
a temporary nature. June saw the French still entrenched in Fez
and to make matters worse, Spain had occupied her own sphere of
influence in Morocco. It was only a matter of time before Germany
would make her move. Grey was not worried about the
Germans pressing France for concessions in equatorial Africa, but he
would be concerned if they tried to acquire a port on the Moroccan
Atlantic coast.

At the Foreign Office, Nicolson and Crowe felt the Entente was
in danger. There was much goodwill in the press following the

Kaiser's visit to London in May for the unveiling of the Victoria Memorial. The country at large rejoiced that Anglo-German relations seemed to be improving, the *Westminster Gazette* naïvely reporting, 'We believe him to be absolutely sincere when he declares to maintain peace and friendliness with Britain.' Grey and his officials took a different view. Whenever friendship was on offer, the Kaiser assumed he had Britain in his pocket. They saw the whole public relations exercise as a softening-up campaign designed to give the Germans a free hand in their dealings with France. In this instance, as events unfolded in Morocco, they were shortly to be proved correct. Grey's anti-Russian colleagues in Cabinet and Parliament were much encouraged by the new atmosphere and were pushing hard for a political agreement with Germany. Nicolson and Crowe, on the other hand, being seriously worried about the 'German menace', were all for converting the ententes into alliances. They believed that the German Army and Navy were much stronger than was necessary for mere defence. They were convinced that in the wrong hands these powerful forces would be used to subdue Europe. Grey's top officials feared that the ententes were sufficiently binding to encourage Paris and St Petersburg but not sufficiently binding to discourage the authorities in Berlin. The radicals in the Liberal Party would never agree to a more formal arrangement. Once again Grey was encased in a straitjacket. At the Foreign Office, only his new private secretary, William Tyrrell, was truly sensitive to his predicament.

On the domestic front, the summer saw the conclusion of the constitutional issue. The Parliament Act was passed by a large majority in the Commons in the middle of May. There were unbelievable scenes in the Commons on 24 July when Asquith rose to move that the Lords' amendments to the Parliament Bill be considered. The Prime Minister was howled down for a full half-hour and was unable to speak, F. E. Smith and Lord Hugh Cecil being the ringleaders.

Margot Asquith was in the Ladies' Gallery and sent Grey a note
that stated, 'They will listen to you, for God's sake save him from
the cats and cads.' When Grey rose, he was uncharacteristically
flushed and angry. The House fell silent as he asserted that: 'If
arguments are not to be listened to from the Prime Minister, there
is not one of us that will attempt to take his place.' He sat down to
cheers from his own side before all hell broke loose once again. The
Speaker suspended the session.

The Lords finally voted for the Parliament Bill by a majority of
seventeen on 10 August. Temperatures inside the House were nearly
as hot as outside, where it was ninety-seven degrees in the shade.
Lord Halsbury and his 'backwoods' peers lost their battle, and the
King was spared the humiliation of creating new peers. The diehard peers, led by Halsbury, were known as 'ditchers' and were
said to have three talents: they knew how to kill a fox, get rid of an
unwanted mistress and evict a bad tenant. Apart from the drama
over the amendments, Grey played little role in the crisis, unlike his
former chief Lord Rosebery, who swung the vote by taking twenty
or so undecided peers with him in the lobbies. Rosebery had dined
at Buckingham Palace the previous night and the King was thought
to have asked him to speak in favour of the Bill. It was Rosebery's
last speech in the Lords. So ended the brilliant, yet ultimately disappointing, political career of a man so often seen as the potential
saviour of his nation.

June represented the calm before the Moroccan storm. On the
anniversary weekend of the bird walk with Roosevelt, Grey retraced
their footsteps, writing to his friend later in the year,

> I did at various times – on Sundays mostly – go all over that ground
> again this year. It was a hot dry year and the birds ceased their songs
> sooner in consequence – owing probably to the difficulty of food
> supply that made it harder to feed their young and made them less

well fed themselves. I noticed this year that, at the time corresponding to that of our walk the year before, there was much less singing.

On Saturday 10 June he fished at The Cottage with Edward
Glenconner. Although they caught six trout between them it was
one of only a handful of occasions he was able to fish the Itchen in
1911. The forthcoming crisis in Morocco was to severely curtail his
summer leisure activities.

On 22 June, Grey attended King George's coronation at
Westminster Abbey. He was delighted to be hidden away amongst
the Colonial Premiers. Unusually for Grey, he found the pageantry
of it all, embodying 1,000 years of history, most moving. The Chief
Whip, the Master of Elibank, remarked that the King behaved
on his great day 'with the calmness and quiet dignity of a perfect
English gentleman'.

The Foreign Office's worst fears were realised on 1 July when the
German cruiser *Panther* moored off Agadir on the pretext of
protecting German commercial interests. The British press were
quite relaxed and not surprised by the German decision. By
acting unilaterally in Fez, the French had clearly been in breach
of the Algeciras Agreement. However, under the Franco-German
Convention of February 1909, the Germans had agreed to disin-
terest themselves politically in Morocco in return for economic
concessions. The Germans had every right to be involved in any
deliberations but this clumsy, tactless, sabre-rattling behaviour was
typical of German diplomacy and smacked of the heavy-handed
tactics employed by Bülow and Holstein in 1905 when the Kaiser
landed in Tangier. The whole episode was also guaranteed to
provoke Britain, who saw the proceedings as yet another attempt
by Germany to smash the Entente and particularly resented the use
of its Navy in the process. Germany was looking for a prestigious
diplomatic success and demanded substantial territorial concessions

in the French Congo as compensation. While both Grey and the new French government were sympathetic to concessions in return for a German agreement to give France a free hand in Morocco, the former was determined at all costs to uphold the Entente with full diplomatic support. Nicolson, not unexpectedly, saw a silver lining to the crisis. It was an 'eye-opener' for those in the Cabinet who had been clamouring for an understanding with Germany.

An emergency Cabinet was called on 4 July to discuss the crisis. Against the advice of his officials, Grey took a moderate line, refusing to send a gunboat to a Moroccan port. It was agreed that British interests should be safeguarded in three areas: no German port would be tolerated on the Mediterranean nor any fortified port on the Atlantic coast. An 'open-door' policy for British trade had to be maintained and the French were to be told that as they were partially responsible for the crisis, they should grant concessions to Germany. These would preferably be in the Congo but compensation in Morocco itself was not ruled out. The Germans were then informed in no uncertain terms that Britain would not recognise any Moroccan settlement about which it had not already been consulted. At the end of the first week Grey had left both his officials and the French angry at what they considered a faint-hearted response.

Following an 11 July Cabinet, Grey agreed to Franco-German discussions exclusive of Britain as long as any compensation agreed was outside Morocco. He also rejected another French suggestion for joint action to remove the *Panther* from Agadir. Germany then characteristically overplayed her hand at the negotiating table, demanding the whole of the Congo, and the talks faltered. At a further Cabinet a week later, Grey called for an international conference to solve the crisis and announced that in the event of Germany refusing to attend, Britain would take steps to protect her interests. This was too much for the Lord Chancellor, Robert Loreburn, and the radicals, who claimed that such action might result in war with Germany. What is more, the impasse was developing against a wall of silence from the Foreign Office in Berlin, who had refused to acknowledge Britain's communication of 4 July. Tensions had reached such a level that Grey warned McKenna to place the fleet on full alert, as it might be attacked at any time. It was at this moment that Lloyd George decided to intervene, not only unlocking the door to a settlement but also ensuring one of the most significant events in pre-war Anglo-German diplomacy. The Chancellor of the Exchequer, previously seen as leader of the pro-German group in Cabinet, was about to crack the whip.

On the evening of 21 July, Lloyd George was to give a speech at the Mansion House, where, in the words of Violet Asquith, he would 'shed all the trappings of a Little Englander'. That same afternoon he visited Grey at the Foreign Office and asked whether any reply had been received from Berlin to the communication of 4 July. Grey replied in the negative. The Chancellor then asked whether he could include a passage on foreign affairs in his speech that night in the City. Grey then approved the contents. Although no mention was made of Morocco, the implication was plain to all:

> But if a situation were to be forced upon us in which peace could only be preserved by the surrender of the great and beneficial position Britain has won by centuries of heroism and achievement, by allowing Britain to be treated, where her interests were vitally affected, as if she were of no account in the Cabinet of nations, then I say emphatically that peace at that price would be a humiliation intolerable for a great country like ours to endure.

Britain had placed her full diplomatic weight behind France and insisted on being a party to any Moroccan settlement. The speech had the immediate effect of breaking Berlin's silence. Although negotiations dragged on for many weeks, a settlement was finally agreed, with France obtaining a free hand in Morocco and Germany receiving territorial concessions in the Congo. Grey writes in his autobiography,

The speech was entirely Lloyd George's idea. I did nothing to instigate it but welcomed it. The effect was much greater than any words of mine could have been. There was a section, and a considerable section, of opinion in this country that looked upon the Foreign Office in general, and myself in particular, as being unduly anti-German, just as in 1893, for instance, they looked upon Rosebery and the Foreign Office as being anti-French. Anything that I said was therefore liable to produce a certain reaction of antipathy in this section. The Germans knew this well enough and no doubt prepared to make discount of what I said but Lloyd George was closely associated with what was supposed to be a pro-German element in the Liberal Government and the House of Commons. Therefore when he spoke out, the Germans knew the whole of the Government and House of Commons had to be reckoned with. It was my opinion then, and it is so still, that the speech had much to do with preserving the peace in 1911.

The Mansion House speech also had far-reaching domestic implications. The radical hero of the left had supported Grey's foreign policy, thereby assuring him additional support in Cabinet and in the party which would be vital in fending off his critics in the immediate future.

Grey's relations with Winston Churchill were also cordial at this time and would become closer still when Churchill was promoted to First Lord of the Admiralty in the autumn. On 28 May, when Clementine gave birth to a baby boy, Randolph, Grey, together with F. E. Smith, was appointed godfather. Churchill saw a good deal of the Foreign Secretary over the long hot summer of 1911 and not just in an official capacity. Grey writes in *Twenty-Five Years*:

One other colleague, not tied to London by official work, kept me company for the love of the crisis. Winston Churchill was then at

the Home Office but he followed the anxieties of the Foreign Office
with intense interest and, I imagine, saw much of Sir Henry Wilson,
then at the War Office – at any rate, he insisted on taking me to
see Wilson and their talk was keen and apparently not the first that
they had had. Let me not be supposed to imply that Churchill was
working for war, or indeed desired it: he followed all the diplomacy
closely, but never either in Council or in conversation with me did
he urge an aggressive line. It was only that his mettlesome spirit was
exhilarated by the air of crisis and high events. His companionship
was a great refreshment and late in the afternoon he would call on
me and take me to the Automobile Club which was but thinly popu-
lated, like other clubs, at this season. There, after what had been to
me a weary, perhaps an anxious day, he would cool his ardour and I
revive my spirits in the swimming-bath.

On 18 September, Grey wrote to Katherine Lyttelton from Fallodon
demonstrating a real fondness for the Churchills: 'I have no time to
write for the time that I do not give to shooting, bridge and sleep
must be given to Foreign Office work. The Winston Churchills have
been here for a Sunday and I liked it. They are so exceedingly nice
to each other.'

When the Moroccan affair was finally resolved in the autumn,
Europe found herself badly shaken. The Continent had come
within a whisker of war and was a less stable place than prior to the
Panther setting sail. The Agadir crisis represented a serious diplomatic
defeat for the Germans. They had received no economic concessions in Morocco and next to no support from their Austrian allies.
The Kaiser and his Chancellor lost further credit and the military
party tightened its grip. The German press and militarists saw it as
a national humiliation and were baying for blood. Nicolson feared
the worst; he thought Germany would seize the first opportunity
for revenge and in the meantime Britain would have to increase her

naval estimates. Grey writes in *Twenty-Five Years*, 'The militarists in Germany were bitterly disappointed over Agadir and when the next crisis came we found them with the reins in their hands at Berlin.'

Once again Grey had been determined to support the Entente and by doing so he had inadvertently elevated a colonial dispute into a European crisis. Germany, however, had no intention of going to war at this time as the Army and Navy were not ready. She merely saw the Moroccan situation as yet another opportunity to test the Entente. Germany wrongly believed that because Grey's foreign policy was under attack from the radicals in Parliament, he would not be as forceful as he was back in 1906. As it was, Grey had to plot an uncomfortable course between incurring the wrath of the radicals on one side for upsetting the Germans and his own officials on the other, who felt he had not gone far enough in his support of the French. In fact, Grey had been the voice of moderation over the crisis. While standing firmly behind the French, he encouraged them to make concessions to Germany and forbade the despatch of a gunboat to the Moroccan coast.

M. L. Dockrill in his essay on 'British Policy during the Agadir Crisis of 1911' writes approvingly of Grey's calm and measured approach to the crisis, writing,

> That the Agadir incident was solved without war had been partly a result of Grey's efforts. He had steered a narrow course between the pressure of the faint-hearted in the Cabinet, like Loreburn, who wanted Britain to have as little to do with the dispute as possible, and the fire-eaters in the Foreign Office, and later Lloyd George and Churchill who pressed Grey to go further in support of France and in opposition to Germany than he thought wise. Grey was determined to go to war to support France if Germany tried to humiliate or force war on her. But he insisted that all means must be exhausted before Europe was plunged into war. He wanted Britain to take all possible precautions in case Germany went to war, while, at the same time, supporting from the sidelines efforts to achieve a reasonable settlement of the dispute.

Grey kept his new friend Theodore Roosevelt fully informed on current European developments. The following extract from a letter to America demonstrates how much he desired better relations with Germany:

> The Germans, or rather the Prussians – for the south Germans are of different ideals and temperament – are a very difficult people. Their way of beginning a conversation is to stamp on your foot to attract your attention when you aren't looking and then they are surprised and very annoyed when the conversation doesn't go smoothly afterwards. Nevertheless I wish we could get on better with them: it may be easier, if they have really settled the Morocco question as far as they are concerned. But to get on well one must feel that one is dealing with someone who can be trusted not to take some untoward turn.

Unfortunately, Germany's diplomatic defeat at Agadir had driven the Kaiser away from Bethmann Hollweg and into the camp of Tirpitz and the militarists. Harold Nicolson writes in his biography of George V, 'The consequences, Grey wrote in his melancholy wisdom, of such a crisis, do not end with it. They seem to end but they go underneath and reappear later on.'

As the weeks of negotiation between France and Germany over Morocco dragged on, Anglo-German relations took a big step backwards as an anti-British press campaign intensified in Germany. The German press perceived Britain as a mischief-maker who encouraged France to take aggressive and unreasonable attitudes, while in reality she was a steadying influence encouraging France to offer Germany satisfactory compensation. The German press were convinced that Britain was thwarting their foreign policy and weighting the balance of power against Germany in Europe. In fact, the way Britain had stood by her ally was totally different from the method of support Germany had given Austria, her ally 'in shining armour', over the annexation of Bosnia-Herzegovina, when a great diplomatic victory had been secured at the expense of Russia. This sour atmosphere demonstrates how Britain's colonial agreement with France in 1904 had within a few years taken on a distinctively European dimension. At the end of the crisis the *Westminster Gazette* lamented the sad state of Anglo-German relations:

> There is no material cause which prevents friendly relations between Britain and Germany. We may look all round the world and fail to discover any conflict of serious interests which weighs an ounce in the scale against the things that unite the two countries. We are each other's best customers, our power is so distributed that it ought to be complementary and not antagonistic, we have ideals in common and characters very similar.

The irony was that the unnecessary antagonism was being stoked up by the German press and would only lead to a resumption in naval competition which Grey was trying his best to curtail.

In early August Grey managed to escape the oppressive heat of London and the tense atmosphere of the Foreign Office by taking a short holiday with the Tennants at Glen. On 22 August, he wrote his thank-you letter to Pamela: 'I have enjoyed the shooting and the hills but without that or any outside thing it is always a pleasure to be in your house and in your presence.' Pamela must have been looking forward to his visit, for all was not well in the Tennant household. It is evident from a letter written to Grey by Pamela on 3 August that she was suffering from depression and 'bouts of discontentedness'. There is strong evidence that her marriage to Eddy was going through a difficult period, with statements such as, 'If only I had somebody in the house who gave me a little praise', and 'I cannot do anything right' and again, 'Think what it would be like to live in a house where one was of no value.'

Although always in the background, Grey brought a degree of stability to Pamela's highly-strung life, without which she might well have experienced a breakdown. He certainly knew how to keep her spirits up, writing to her later in the year, 'I wonder how much you know of the pleasure you gave me on Friday. I was feeling so tired and flat that I half shrank from your coming but I knew I should like to see you. Are you not more than Mary Queen of Scots beautiful!' He then moved on into a typical piece of Grey prose: 'I went for a walk and lunched under a gorse bush in a thick Scots fir wood and saw some redpolls and a charm of goldfinches ... There was no sun to steer by so I steered in the forest by the direction of the wind and the slant of the rain.' Pamela no doubt saw herself as a tragic character in the same mould as Mary, Queen of Scots, locked as she was in an unfulfilled marriage to Eddy. It is interesting to note that Simon Blow writes of his mother, Diana Bethell, (Pamela's granddaughter) in *No Time To Grow: A Shattered Childhood*, 'And my mother sits on her bed swaying and telling us she's Mary Queen of Scots. Whenever Mummy compares herself it's always with someone tragic. She draws wild and unhappy comforts from the tragedies of others.' Blow could as well have been writing about his great-grandmother.

One can see from their correspondence that Grey was deeply in love with Pamela, but his workload and her country-orientated family commitments meant that they would have had limited opportunity to enjoy each other's company. The widowed Foreign Secretary in middle age was still a fit and good-looking man, both influential and charismatic. Like his colleague David Lloyd George, he enjoyed the company of women, the only difference being that Grey was secretive, reserved and discreet. There is little reason to suppose that Grey was not seeing other women at this time and in the summer of 1911 we have evidence from across the Atlantic, albeit of a tenuous nature, to support this theory.

On 26 August 1912, a baby, born on 23 July 1911 and named Janet Lincoln, was adopted by a well-to-do family in Worcester, Massachusetts. At the same time the child was renamed Dorothy May Nelson and records of her name change exist while the actual adoption records are sealed. The adoptive parents were advised

that the child's birth father was Sir Edward Grey and her mother
was a well-born Englishwoman with royal connections, possibly
a lady-in-waiting or a maid of honour. William and Cora Nelson
kept the secret of Dorothy's adoption from her until after Grey's
death, when she married and gave birth to a daughter of her own.
By an extraordinary coincidence, Dorothy had decided on the
name Janet for her new baby. Cora then finally revealed the secret
of Dorothy's parentage, telling her she couldn't possibly call the
child Janet as that was her own name. Dorothy compromised on
the name Janice for her child, and in turn kept the secret from her
husband during his lifetime, only revealing the truth to Janice after
his death. When Dorothy wished to travel overseas in later life, she
tried to track down her original birth certificate in order to obtain
a passport. She was given brief sight of a document which named
the mother as Mary Della Lincoln of Washington DC.

Janice Babbitt is a retired teacher, living near Boston,
Massachusetts. She is trying to get access to her mother's original
birth certificate from the authorities in Washington but it seems that
even after 100 years, a sealed adoption record is just that – sealed.
From Janice's collection of photographs of her mother, we can see
the physical resemblance between Dorothy Nelson and Edward
Grey is truly remarkable. Grey exhibited several distinctive physical
characteristics that were all inherited by Dorothy: a strong aquiline
nose, pinched lips, a high forehead and piercing blue eyes. When
the photographs are placed side by side one would imagine they
were brother and sister.

Along with the extraordinary physical resemblance which gives
this story credibility, there are one or two other coincidences which
add credence. It is interesting that the child's name was changed
to Dorothy, perhaps somehow in tribute to Dorothy Widdrington,
with whom Grey had no children? The name Lincoln is also interesting. There is an obvious Washington connection with the name
and perhaps Grey's new close friend, ex-President Roosevelt could
have helped him find a 'safe house' for Mary Della Lincoln to give
birth to her illegitimate daughter? It is pure speculation, but the

first foundling home and hospital in Washington DC was housed
in the old British embassy building on K Street and its patron had
been Abraham Lincoln. In 1912 it may have been an obvious choice
for a young upper-class Englishwoman who had become pregnant
and travelled abroad to give birth in secrecy, as was quite normal
at the time. In his long tenure as Foreign Secretary, Grey never left
Britain until the spring of 1914, when he participated in a state visit
to France. His first visit to America was in 1919, so we know that any
child of his could only have been conceived in Britain. Adoption
records in the United States are currently sealed in certain states.
It may well be that at some time in the future, if these regulations
are relaxed, we shall be able to solve the riddle of the mysterious
'lady-in-waiting'.

However, having examined the list of those in service to Queen
Alexandra, the spotlight falls on Violet Vivian, sister of Lord
Vivian, who served as a maid of honour at various times during
this period. Violet was no stranger to transatlantic travel. Her sister
Dorothy, in her biography of her husband Field Marshal Earl
Haig, noted that Violet had (unusually) in 1908 asked the Queen
for a leave of absence to visit America. Then in both 1910 and 1911
passenger manifests show her travelling home from Canadian ports.
Contemporary gossip columns suggest that Violet was extremely
well connected in America and that her circle included at least one
influential Bostonian. She would have had little problem in making
discreet arrangements for a clandestine birth and adoption. It is
worth noting that the Vivians were not an unexciting family. Lord
Vivian was reported in the *New York Times* in 1907 as having been
granted a decree and custody of his children on the grounds of his
wife's 'misconduct with Mr Curphey both in Egypt and England
while the peer was big-game shooting in Canada'.

Unable to enjoy a physical expression of the deep love and partnership he had with his first wife, Dorothy, Grey was obliged to turn
elsewhere for sexual intimacy. In that era, well before the dawn of
contraception, it is hardly surprising that there should have been
at least one and in all probability several children born to different

women with whom Grey had affairs. As he destroyed his private papers, we can only speculate, but it does seem that Grey, with the probable assistance of members of his family, did his best to do right by his love children. They all appear either to have received financial support or to have been adopted into comfortable households.

On 23 August, prompted by the worsening international situation, Asquith called a special all-day session of the Committee of Imperial Defence (CID). The purpose of the meeting was to review British strategy in the event of a war with Germany. It would turn out to be one of the Committee's most effective sessions and would have important repercussions. Present at the meeting were the Prime Minister, Grey, Haldane, Churchill, Lloyd George, McKenna and the service chiefs. Radicals such as Morley and Harcourt were not invited. Convinced that a European war was inevitable, Sir Henry Wilson had been busy with his French military counterparts for the last twelve months. The General pressed home three vital points on his audience. The British Expeditionary Force must join the French armies on the Belgian border, it must mobilise the same day as the French and it must despatch all six divisions. The Army's case was therefore well researched with a specific role on the Channel flank of the French Army.

Sir Henry Wilson gave a thoroughly professional presentation in the morning. The afternoon session developed into farce when the First Sea Lord, Sir Arthur Wilson, put forward the Navy's case. The Admiral began by informing the Committee that the Navy was not in a position to transport the BEF to France, which brought gasps of incredulity from the committee. His next effort, a preference for military operations inside the Baltic along the coast of Pomerania, induced laughter from Lloyd George and Churchill. Grey, not being interested in military strategy, had little to contribute but even he could see the Navy needed its own General Staff to coordinate its activities with the Army. Grey saw Asquith alone after the meeting and the Prime Minister whispered, 'McKenna must go.' Haldane threatened to resign if nothing was done. He had his own agenda and was desperate to get his claws into the Admirals as he had the Generals. Unfortunately for Haldane, he had been made a Viscount in April and the Prime Minister wanted his First Lord in the Commons. In late September, Churchill was given the Admiralty. Aside from his energy, which would prove invaluable in bringing the fleet to a state of readiness, it was a clever move as it detached Churchill from the 'economist wing' of the party. Now both Churchill and Lloyd George were of the same mind as Grey with regard to readiness for war.

When Morley and the Cabinet radicals learnt of the secret defence meeting, they were furious. The idea of British troops being despatched to France to join an army on the Meuse was, in the words of Harcourt, 'criminal folly'. They were also worried about the balance in Cabinet now that Churchill and Lloyd George had changed sides. The radicals were not the only people frightened by Britain's commitment to the French. The Prime Minister himself had become alarmed. Asquith was concerned that the military conversations were dangerous in that they might encourage the French to assume British support in any circumstances. Grey was adamant that the communication should continue since the conversations implied only moral support. On 8 September, he wrote to the Prime Minister, 'It would create consternation if we forbade our military experts to converse with the French. No doubt these conversations and our speeches have given an expectation of support. I do not see how this can be helped.' Lord Esher saw things rather differently, telling the Prime Minister that the talks 'certainly committed us to fight whether the Cabinet likes it or not'.

On 29 September, colonial ambition coupled with a jealousy of France's position in North Africa led the Italians to declare war on Turkey and they duly occupied the Turkish provinces of Tripoli

and Cyrenaica. They cunningly made their move when the other powers were preoccupied with the Moroccan negotiations. Grey was concerned that the Italian aggression would make Turkey look weak and thereby encourage other nationalistic enterprises in the Balkans. He therefore encouraged Italy to pay Turkey compensation and unsuccessfully tried to persuade her not to seek a complete annexation of Libya. He was well aware that Turkey had a large army which she might feel compelled to use elsewhere.

On 6 October, Grey enjoyed some well-earned respite from the stresses of the Foreign Office when he received the freedom of Berwick-upon-Tweed in his constituency. He had been the local Member of Parliament for twenty-five years. Alderman Plenderleith, speaking in front of the Mayor, paid the Foreign Secretary a warm tribute and summed up what the country as a whole thought of one of its most respected public servants,

> Sir Edward was the bearer of an honoured name, a statesman by inheritance, by instinct, by natural bent of inclination; in his public utterances calm, judicial and convincing; in private utterly unostentatious, frank, genial and brotherly. We are not surprised to see such a man associated with the memorable announcement regarding the possibility of cementing the nations of Europe and of the world in a happy brotherhood by providing the means whereby the cruel arbitration of the sword should give place to honourable and peaceful arbitration.

One can well imagine what was going through Grey's mind as he took the applause: 'If only this obsequious and verbose fellow really knew what was currently going on in Europe and just how hard it will be to prevent a future world war.'

Grey soon found himself back in the bear pit of Westminster life when the subject of the military conversations was raised at a heated Cabinet meeting on 1 November. Haldane had the unenviable task of explaining the history of the talks. Grey himself assured his colleagues that at no stage had Britain's freedom of decision of action in the event of war between France and Germany been compromised. Morley led the charge against Grey and the Cabinet split with fifteen ministers against the talks and only five in favour. This demonstrates the near impossibility, even if Grey wanted to, of converting the Entente into a full alliance, as advocated by Nicolson. Luckily, Asquith had a genius for finding a way through the undergrowth. He constructed a formula that allowed talks with the French to continue while at the same time safeguarding the Cabinet's future freedom of action. It was agreed that no talks could take place between the General Staffs which might, 'directly or indirectly, commit this country to military or naval intervention'. Grey now had his back against the wall both in Cabinet and in Fleet Street. Relations with Germany after the Agadir crisis had become more strained and the radicals claimed that Grey had nearly taken Britain into war for the sake of French interests. The British press was ranged against his foreign policy, C. P. Scott of the *Manchester Guardian* being particularly scathing of his Persian policy. Grey was quite indifferent to their attacks and was ready to quit if pushed. His view was always that he would be far happier out of office and that he had no reputation to nurse in view of a future career.

Grey counterattacked with a foreign policy speech in the House of Commons on 27 November. He took immense trouble with the content, discussing it in advance with Asquith and Haldane and even consulting the new Leader of the Opposition, Andrew Bonar Law. The government had been facing criticism that not enough debating time in the House was given over to foreign affairs, even though for the first time in living memory there was a Foreign Secretary in the Commons answering questions twice a week. Having recounted the Moroccan crisis in detail, as well as his dealings with the German ambassador, he touched on Persia, where Britain was encountering problems with Russia. He assured the House that the government would never make any secret arrangements that committed Parliament to obligations of war. From the German point of view, he explained how Metternich saw the future as being 'a clean slate', with the goal being improved relations between the two countries. Grey was insistent that Britain could never embark on a war without the support of public opinion. He summed up his views on foreign policy as 'a readiness to make a new friend whenever we can without losing an old one'. He would seek a rapprochement with Germany, but not at the expense of existing friendships with France and Russia. The Entente, he said, was the best guarantee that neither country would practise a provocative policy towards Germany.

Although Asquith described the speech to Crewe as 'a great performance and having the effect on the House which Grey alone was capable of producing', it failed to placate his backbench critics, such as Arthur Ponsonby and Noel Buxton. The latter desperately sought a distinct Liberal foreign policy. They felt Grey's policy was too Tory in outlook and that their party's foreign policy was in the hands of the Liberal League, that it was merely an extension of Lansdowne's ideas a decade before. For all the criticism Grey received in Cabinet, Parliament and the press, he was convinced he had public opinion on his side. He had no intention of changing his style of diplomacy but he would continue to reach out for an Anglo-German détente. To that end he met with Metternich again on 20 December and raised the possibility of a revision of the Anglo-German agreement on the Portuguese colonies.

Grey had little time to enter into the festive spirit in the run-up to Christmas. On 5 December he was speaking in Plymouth, where he reaffirmed Metternich's views: 'The Morocco depression is passing away and we may legitimately expect the diplomatic barometer soon to rise.' On the 14th he was on his feet again in the House, batting away further criticism over his handling of foreign affairs. He emphatically repudiated the charge that the Cabinet was not kept informed on matters of foreign policy. He told the House that the Cabinet was briefed on a daily basis, remarking, 'I can only say that if I was as well informed about the business of the Departments of all my colleagues as they are about mine, I should be a great deal wiser than I am.' He went on to make a statement about Persia. There was concern in Britain that Russia was impairing the sovereignty and independence of Persia. Grey reassured the House that Russia's military occupation of Persian territory was of a temporary nature. In addition, the Russians had undertaken not to recognise the ex-Shah. The Foreign Office had also agreed with the Russians to extend a joint loan to Persia and to recruit a new financial adviser at the earliest opportunity. In summary, he told the House that the Anglo-Russian agreement had been a great service to the Nationalist cause.

The quest for some sort of naval understanding would continue into the new year, but it would prove a thankless task. Tirpitz had greatly increased his influence in Berlin and the Kaiser took an intense personal interest in the development of the fleet. Trevelyan relates how Ambassador Metternich, who would shortly become a victim of the Agadir debacle, wrote to his friend Maximilian von Hagen:

> About Christmas time in 1911 I had the last interview with the Kaiser and Tirpitz in the Berlin Palace about our relations with England and I laid emphasis on the favourable feeling in England. Tirpitz declared that he knew from a trustworthy source that at the time of the Morocco crisis, when the Kaiser was on his yacht in Norwegian waters, English torpedo boats had been ordered in the event of hostilities to sink the imperial yacht. As the Grand Admiral gravely stroked his beard while telling this fairy tale and the Kaiser turning to me cried: 'And you want me to come to an understanding with these people?' – I realised that the Navy Bill had already been decided on by the two and further arguments were useless. I was tired of the lonely struggle with Berlin, where I could find no support whatever.

If Grey's critics believed the Foreign Secretary too conservative in his foreign policy, the same could not be said of his leanings in domestic politics, where he was closely aligned with Lloyd George. This radical tendency, coupled with the fact that the Chancellor had recently joined Grey's camp over the Morocco crisis, made it frustratingly difficult for Grey's critics to evict him from office. In August, Grey had been effusive in his praise for Lloyd George's role in ending the railway strike. Two-thirds of Britain's railway workers had walked out for the first time, posing dire consequences for the nation's economy. It was called off within forty-eight hours, largely thanks to the Chancellor's communication skills. Grey was most critical of Churchill's decision to declare martial law. He felt the days of treating workers in this fashion were now over. In November, Lloyd George publicly stated his readiness to move an amendment to an adult suffrage bill in favour of women. Grey was a firm supporter of votes for women, as he was of the Chancellor's National Insurance Bill. This working alliance with Lloyd George, developed across the political spectrum, makes the Welshman's barbed pre-war criticism of Grey, recalled in his *War Memoirs,* all the more surprising.

The sweltering summer of 1911 was to prove an important milestone on the road to Armageddon. Grey had once again given France his unwavering diplomatic support over the Agadir crisis and was interestingly cast as the moderate against the background noise of his more bellicose officials at the Foreign Office. After all, even Lloyd George at the Mansion House had given an unveiled hint to the international community that Britain might go to war to protect her national interests. Germany had lost face again on the world stage and local public opinion hardened against Britain, who, through her support of France, had turned a colonial dispute into a European crisis. Britain had been on the verge of war, which frightened her ruling élite. The crisis spawned the highly significant Committee of Imperial Defence 'war council' meeting, whereby Britain's foreign policy would adopt for the first time a coordinated Continental strategy. A significant consequence of the meeting was Churchill's move to the Admiralty, which would provide Grey's pro-Entente policy with much needed reinforcement in Cabinet. At the same time, opponents of Grey's foreign policy, both in Cabinet and on the back benches, who felt that Britain had adopted an unnecessarily provocative stance towards Germany, sharpened their knives. Over the next few months the Foreign Secretary would show admirable backbone in fighting his corner in the face of considerable domestic opposition.

Grey Under Attack and a Naval Agreement with France

Returning from his all-too-short Christmas break, Grey was well aware that Cabinet harmony could only be maintained if a fresh attempt was made to reach an agreement with Germany. Although sceptical of any success, he welcomed a new initiative as long as it didn't upset the relationship with France. After all, both the French and the Russians had dealt separately with the Germans, so why not Britain? Anglo-German discussions always seemed to hit the same brick wall. The Germans wanted a neutrality agreement from Britain in return for minimal naval cutbacks, whereas Britain hoped for a substantial reduction in German naval spending in return for minor colonial concessions, preferably in Africa. Negotiations with Germany for a political solution would splutter on for a few months, with Grey refusing to go beyond an offer of a non-aggression formula. As long as the stalemate continued, Britain's diplomatic support for France would become more pronounced, as would her acceptance of Russia's aggressive policies in Persia.

As soon as the dust had settled over Agadir, the recriminations began and the French Foreign Minister, De Selves, was pressured to resign by the Senate Committee for his handling of the crisis. Across the Channel there were many only too keen to remove Grey from the Foreign Office. His enemies were convinced he maintained a deep-rooted hostility towards Germany and above all they hated the way he continued to placate Russia over her high-handed action in the Far East. Russia had taken advantage of Britain's Moroccan problems to consolidate her influence in both Mongolia and Persia.

Even the Liberal *Westminster Gazette* criticised his communication skills:

> Sir Edward Grey, we think, would do well to devote a little more time to explaining himself in detail to the public. It is true he has made useful and important speeches on foreign affairs during the last few weeks but unlike his predecessors he seldom publishes papers and the inner history of the last few years has been reconstructed from newspaper reports or worse still, gossip.

Elements of the Tory press went much further, one publication accusing Grey of benefiting from an army contract, facilitated by Haldane, for the supply of stone from a local quarry in Northumberland under his ownership. It was quickly discovered Grey didn't own any stone quarries!

Grey's critics concentrated on his Persian policy. His appeasement of Russia's forward policy in northern Persia had infuriated the radicals. An American, Morgan Shuster, had been sent to Tehran to reorganise the chaotic Persian finances. He had made himself most unpopular locally by going too far, too soon, and the Russians demanded his removal. For fear of rocking the Entente, Grey agreed to Shuster's dismissal. A prime goal of the Anglo-Russian Entente was, after all, to preserve Persian independence. In addition, Grey believed an American citizen supported by the British government would look bad in the eyes of the other powers and be seen as a symbol of British supremacy. Grey fully realised the immense frustration and difficulty attached to doing business with the Russians, but he would not pick a fight with them over Persia and he was not alone in that view. Over a decade before, Lord Selborne, the Tory First Lord of the Admiralty had written to Curzon:

Compared to our Empire, Russia's is invulnerable. We must be on the defensive in a contest because there is speaking generally and roughly no part of her territory where we can hit her. The expansion of her empire does not involve her in the responsibilities which the expansion of ours does us – her standard is much lower; her communications are secure; she has not even to keep one eye behind her – defeat, diplomatic naval or military matters mean less to her than any other Power – absence of education, parliament and press is not an unmixed evil – consequently I would always much rather not quarrel with her if I could honourably or wisely avoid it.

Grey was determined to make the Entente with Russia work, whatever his critics argued. He was nothing if not resolute and at times, downright obstinate. He had been used to getting his own way for many years and he wasn't going to give up now. His father had died young and the twelve-year-old Edward suddenly found himself in charge of a predominantly female household. As a newly married politician he spent much time alone in London, and then Dorothy tragically died within weeks of him becoming Foreign Secretary. Grey deserves much credit for his steadiness and consistency in support of an entente policy which originally was not of his making. He had to fend off the slings and arrows of the radicals in his own party, who disliked any sort of European entanglement, but he always felt public opinion was on his side. The British people hated the bullying nature of German diplomacy and were apprehensive of their growing fleet. Although he harboured no aggressive intentions towards Germany, for his part the Foreign Secretary had his eye firmly fixed on the European benefits of the Russian Entente. He was also far too strong a character to rip up his hard-earned convention with Russia because of domestic pressure from the left wing. After all, if it had not been for the Anglo-Russian Entente, the Persian Nationalists would have been wiped out and the ex-Shah reinstated as a vassal of Russia.

In February the King made Grey a Knight of the Garter. Asquith intended it as one in the eye for his Foreign Secretary's critics and wrote admiringly to Grey, 'I only send you a line to assure you that after four years of what is called power, this is the one thing which, in a personal sense, has given me deep and abiding pleasure.' Although Grey disliked decorations and ceremony, he was genuinely pleased to have been awarded the Garter, but was typically terrified it would pull him deeper into public life. He wrote to Katherine Lyttelton,

> It will make life a little more conspicuous and complicated and it gives me a feeling of being still deeper in. I do long to be in the country and free to go and look at the sun and be out for the day without having to work early before I go out and late after I come in to make up for having spent a day out of doors.

Grey's relationship with Katherine Lyttelton poses interesting questions and one might be forgiven for thinking it was more intimate than just good friendship. Originally the friendship was between Dorothy and Katherine, but after the former's death Grey and Katherine became very close friends, as witnessed by the many letters written by Grey over a period of thirty years and kept by the recipient. After Dorothy's death, most of the letters contained invitations from Grey to lunch or to dine on a regular basis, nearly always quietly at home. Only on a few occasions was her husband Neville asked and there is little evidence to suggest that Grey enjoyed a close friendship with Neville in the same way as he did with Eddy Tennant. In the summer of 1912 Grey used his influence with Haldane to secure Neville Lyttelton the Governorship of the Royal Hospital at Chelsea, complete with a grace-and-favour residence. On 2 August an obviously smitten Grey replied to a letter of thanks from Katherine, 'The man who has your gratitude is but one degree less proud than the man who has your love. You are now safely "Chelsea-ed". It is such a permanent thing and dignified too.' Pamela was always rumoured to have had a number of lovers before the war and in this particular decade she was spending much of her time with her children in Wiltshire, so Grey would have had the flexibility to see other women.

❦

The next round of Anglo-German discussions were initiated through an unorthodox source: two businessmen of German-Jewish birth with royal connections, who feared the economic consequences of a European war. Sir Ernest Cassel was a City banker and close friend of King Edward. Albert Ballin was chairman of the Hamburg-Amerika Line and an associate of the Kaiser. The initial approach is thought to have come through Ballin. Cassel then took a memorandum to Berlin drafted by the Prime Minister, Churchill and Lloyd George. The document suggested recognition of British naval superiority with an agreement by Germany to cut back her naval programme. In return, Britain would assist Germany with her colonial aspirations and endeavour to draft a satisfactory political formula. Britain would not, of course, go so far as neutrality, but the formula would contain wording that ensured Britain would make no unprovoked attack on Germany or pursue aggressive policies towards her.

The minister chosen to spearhead the mission to Berlin was Haldane. He had the most knowledge of Germany and the best contacts; he was known to be sympathetic. Cassel first suggested Churchill but he declined to go, as did Grey. The Foreign Secretary was not optimistic of success and felt that it would be sensible if exploratory talks took place at a less official level. The French were, not unnaturally, worried about the visit and the mandarins at the Foreign Office were nearly as hostile as Tirpitz and the German naval authorities. Grey fully realised that both in the national interests and in the interests of Cabinet unity, a final effort had to be made to secure a naval agreement with Germany. He was also completely comfortable with his close friend Haldane filling his shoes. He writes in his autobiography:

I agreed without demur and with goodwill to Haldane's visit. I
always felt that the pro-German element here had a right to demand
that our foreign policy should go to the utmost point that it could
to be friendly to Germany. That point would be passed only when
something was proposed that would tie us to Germany and break
the Entente with France. Not only were people entitled to demand
this of British foreign policy but it was essential that those who set
the most store by the Entente with France should concede it. To do
so was the only way to preserve unity of support in the Cabinet and
in the Liberal Party for the Anglo-French Entente.

On 8 February Haldane met the German Chancellor, Bethmann
Hollweg, at the British embassy in Berlin. He made a number of
important points. He admitted that Germany had every right to
increase the size of her fleet but in doing so it left Britain with
no alternative other than to increase her own naval expenditure,
as well as encouraging her to draw closer to other European
powers in the interests of her own security. Grey was to write after
the event,

> Germany was undoubtedly within her rights in challenging our
> sea power but in doing so she compelled us to find safety both by
> increasing our naval construction and by a policy which would not
> leave us exposed to the hostility of other naval powers. A desire for
> peace and friendship entered largely into our relations with France
> but German action made them in this sense a practical necessity.

Significantly, Haldane also informed the Chancellor that Britain
had no secret treaties with other countries but, in his opinion, if
France were to be aggressively attacked by Germany, Britain would
not sit on the sidelines. For his part, the Chancellor brought up
the sensitive question of a neutrality agreement, which he always
knew would be unacceptable to Britain. Haldane left the meeting
with the impression that Bethmann Hollweg was 'a high-minded
gentleman' who was as sincere about avoiding war as he himself.

He wrote in *Before the War*, 'I left the Chancellor with the sense I had been talking to an honest man struggling somewhat with adversity.'

Haldane met the less flexible individuals, in the form of the Kaiser and Admiral von Tirpitz, the next day for lunch. The atmosphere was not helped by news filtering through of a provocative speech made by Churchill back at home, characterising the German Navy as a 'luxury fleet'. Haldane was given a copy of the new Navy Law, which he put in his pocket. Speaking in German, he stressed the importance to Britain of secure sea-communications and the likelihood that the Royal Navy would lay down two keels for every one which Germany added to her programme. Although Haldane was well received, no real agreement on naval construction was reached and he came away with the feeling that both the Kaiser and his Chancellor were too weak to deal with Tirpitz. On 20 February there was a detailed discussion in Cabinet on the subject of the visit. The Admiralty had studied the new Navy Law, which detailed Germany's construction programme, and were alarmed. Large increases in the German fleet were contemplated, including a reserve squadron of battleships accompanied by more destroyers and submarines. Asquith and Lloyd George felt there was no point in continuing negotiations on the basis of the new Navy Law. Harcourt, Loreburn and the radicals unsurprisingly took a softer line, demanding that talks should immediately recommence on colonial matters in Africa and on the Baghdad Railway.

Hopes were raised again in March when Metternich, encouraged perhaps by Churchill's call for a 'naval holiday', informed Grey that the proposed Navy Law would be withdrawn if Britain agreed to a suitable political formula. It soon transpired that Berlin continued to insist the latter should contain a declaration of absolute neutrality by Britain in the event of Germany going to war with France. A divided Cabinet, much against Haldane's will, finally agreed on a non-aggression formula excluding the word 'neutrality':

England will make no unprovoked attack upon Germany and pursue no aggressive policy against her. Aggression upon Germany is not the subject, and forms no part of, any treaty, understanding or combination to which Britain is now a party, nor will she become a party to anything that has such an object.

Grey, backed by the Prime Minister, Nicolson and Crowe at the Foreign Office, absolutely refused to leave the French in the lurch. Without the inclusion of a 'neutrality agreement', any hope of a naval understanding vanished, and on 10 April Germany announced she would proceed with her new Navy Law. Germany's self-imposed 'encirclement' was now complete.

Grey had been unable to spend as much time at the Foreign Office as he would have liked during March because of his involvement in the miners' strike. It was Haldane who had assisted Nicolson with the drafting of the 'political formula', writing in his autobiography:

> I took a good deal of part in the German discussions and drafted certain difficult despatches in reply to some that came from Berlin. There it was evident that the Chancellor was not being left undisturbed, even in his own work when communicating with us. I also used at times to relieve Grey of the charge at the Foreign Office when he wanted a week of rest from his harassing labours. Morley and I used to sit at the Foreign Office when he was absent on these occasions, though holidays he did not often take.

The miners' strike began at the beginning of March over the question of a minimum wage. Low rates of unemployment and an enormous expansion of trade union membership in Britain had contributed to an intensive period of industrial unrest from 1911 onwards. In 1912 nearly 41 million working days were lost through strikes, compared with an annual average of 7 million over the preceding five years. The 'socialist' side of Grey was naturally sympathetic to the demands of organised labour and it was not

surprising to see him playing a leading role in the crisis. Along
with the Prime Minister, Lloyd George and Sydney Buxton, Grey
was a member of the Cabinet committee charged with securing a
settlement. When the mine owners turned down a minimum of
five shillings a shift as excessive, it was Grey who came up with a
solution. He suggested that if, after a year, the owners suffered a loss
then the government should indemnify them. The proposals were
accepted by an uneasy Cabinet and the miners went back to work.
Grey had spoken for the government in the second reading of the
Bill, Trevelyan writing in his biography, 'The quiet appeal to good
will and good sense, coming from him, helped the Bill to pass by
rather more than the usual Government majority.'

Lloyd George had supported Grey's foreign policy during
the Agadir crisis. Now Grey attached himself to the Chancellor
over labour relations on the domestic front. Charles Masterman
described this as 'a new alliance'. In Lord Riddell's diaries,
Masterman is quoted as saying, 'Lloyd George and Edward Grey
have now joined hands. That is a new alliance. It dates from the
Coal Strike. They are in sympathy regarding the Labour question
and foreign policy.' There is a further remark in the diaries for
13 July 1913 when Lloyd George says to Riddell, 'Grey is with
me. He is a kind fellow, the only man I would serve under except
Asquith. I would serve under Grey.'

Grey's views on labour relations a century ago were remarkably
far-sighted, almost clairvoyant. His many years on the Board of the
North Eastern Railway had helped him formulate his views. On
8 April he wrote to Katherine Lyttelton,

This Coal Strike is the beginning of a revolution. We shall, I suppose,
make it an orderly and gradual revolution, but labour intends to
have a larger share and has laid hold of power. Power has passed
from the King to the nobles, from the nobles to the middle classes
and through them to the House of Commons and now it is passing from the House of Commons to the Trade Unions. It will have
to be recognised that the millions of men employed in the great

industries have a stake in those industries and must share in control of them. The days when the owners said 'this industry is mine; I alone must control it and be master in my own house' are passing away. The owners still say that but it has ceased to be real because they cannot act upon it. The Unions may of course like blind Samson with his arms round the pillars, pull down the house on themselves and everything else, if they push things too far; or if the owners are too unyielding, there will be civil war. But I do think the good temper and spirit of compromise that is inherent in the English character will save us from catastrophe.

Even though Grey had played a central and fruitful role in settling the strike, he informed the Prime Minister that he would prefer to be excluded from any future Cabinet committees on labour relations. They proved too time-consuming and distracted him from his all-important foreign affairs brief.

Grey and Lloyd George were allies again when the third Irish Home Rule Bill was introduced to Parliament in April. With the passing of the Parliament Act the legislation would become law in 1914. Both men concluded that Irish Home Rule was the first step to federal Home Rule. In May, Grey spoke during the second reading of the Bill: 'There is an Irish national feeling and there is a national feeling in other parts of the United Kingdom. You cannot help it. The thing is there.' What he failed to foresee was the opposition of the Ulstermen. Organised resistance under the aegis of Sir Edward Carson was in place by year end. Grey continued in his speech, 'The animosity which may exist between different parts of Ireland today is no measure whatever and no guide to what the feeling will be when different parts of Ireland have for the first time a sense of joint responsibility.'

After the stress of the miners' strike it must have been a welcome relief for Grey to take his spring break on the Cassley in mid-April.

His eyesight was beginning to deteriorate, a condition which would progressively inhibit his dry-fly fishing although not his craving for exercise. On 8 April he wrote to Katherine Lyttelton,

It is so much better to bicycle than to drive. One gets in at midnight, warm and invigorated having had communion with the night. We should all be much happier if we could get nowhere except by the use of our own legs, though of course being used to trains and motors we should think we were miserable without them.

And again on 21 September, 'You might tell Neville that I got badly beaten by a youth of thirty-four at squash racquets the other day though I made him sweat awfully and found that I could last quite as well if not better than he could.'

Grey took his usual Whitsun holiday at the Hampshire cottage, catching thirty trout over the week. An entry in his fishing diary for 23 May reads, 'Fished Top Water, lost more fish than were landed', proof perhaps that his eyesight was on the wane. Grey adored being on the Itchen in May – it was, of course, his 'golden time'. The Whitsun weekend was 'Lilac Sunday' at The Cottage; the hawthorn, chestnut, laburnum, whin and broom were all in flower. Writing in *The Charm of Birds*, he rejoiced about his surroundings in the river valley:

In May we are overwhelmed. New green is spreading everywhere; flowering shrubs and trees and flowers of garden and field are too abundant for separate notice. All the birds are in full song. Neither eye nor ear, nor outward or inward sense of man is equal to it. Each of us can select for especial or particular enjoyment a few things: the tender green of young beech trees; the scent in a mass of whin; a glade of bluebells; a wide field of buttercups under the sun: but when we have done our best, we are yet oppressed by a feeling that we can but take in a small portion of the abundant beauty. There comes upon us also, not only a sense of abundance, but of haste; it is all passing; the leaves darken from day to day; luxuriance remains, but tenderness and delicacy are fleeting. It is only for a short time that the new beech leaves are so soft that the wind stirs them without a sound. In early spring we long to hurry the season; in May we would say to it, 'Stay! Thou art fair.' And it cannot be stayed: ''Twere all as well to bid a cloud to stand.'

While Grey was anticipating the joys of an English spring, ominous events were unfolding in the Balkans. He had seen the Italian occupation of Libya six months before as just the kind of irresponsible action that could set the Balkans alight. His worry was that Serbia and the other Balkan states might take advantage of Turkey's difficulties and view the situation as an opportune moment for a war of independence. His worst fears were justified on 13 March 1912 when, encouraged by N. V. Hartwig, the Russian representative in Belgrade, Serbia and Bulgaria signed an alliance. Shortly afterwards Greece and Montenegro joined the pact to form the 'Balkan League', with its main aim being the ejection of the Turks from Europe by way of the conquest and partition of Macedonia. Grey was embarrassed by Russia's encouragement of Slav nationalism. He dreaded European complications on account of Russia's Balkan ambitions. Austria-Hungary feared Slav nationalism as much as the Turks, viewing it as a major threat to their own empire. The last thing they wanted was further Ottoman decline. On 15 April Grey wrote the following Foreign Office minute:

> We shall have to keep out of this and what I fear is that Russia may resent our doing so; the fact that the trouble is all of her own making won't prevent her from expecting help if the trouble turned out more than she bargained for. On the other hand Russia would resent still more our attempting to restrain her now in a matter that she would at this stage say did not concern us.

On the western front, Haldane's visit to Berlin and the discussions over a neutrality formula had caused the French much anxiety. In the middle of April, Nicolson had a strained meeting with Cambon at the Foreign Office, as the French were convinced that the Germans were looking to create an incident that would lead to war. Although contrary to his personal wishes, Nicolson stated that the present moment was not the time to think of upgrading the Entente into an alliance. The Cabinet, let alone the Liberal back-benchers, would simply not agree to it. On 4 May, Cambon again met Nicolson at the Foreign Office. The ambassador suggested that prior naval discussions conducted by Jacky Fisher and Sir Arthur Wilson with the French naval attaché should be resurrected. The French were seeking a redistribution of their naval resources. They wished to concentrate their fleet on the Mediterranean and leave Britain to police their Channel and Atlantic coasts. This proposal suited Churchill, who was now the self-appointed leader of the Cabinet's 'Imperialist wing' and keen to initiate a full alliance with France. He wanted to move more battleships into the North Sea to meet the growing German menace. The move would also have the added advantage of helping to limit naval expenditure. Grey brought up the French request at a Cabinet on 16 May, which in turn initiated a whole series of discussions throughout the summer both in Cabinet and at the Committee of Imperial Defence.

In late July a draft agreement was forwarded to the French naval attaché by the Admiralty, outlining a plan for Anglo-French naval cooperation. Rumours were quick to circulate and there was an outcry in the press about the proposed naval cutbacks in the Mediterranean. There were general worries that if Britain gave up the policing of the Mediterranean to the French, the quid pro quo might necessitate a greater commitment to France on land, thereby plunging Britain into a deeper European complication. Churchill made an announcement in the House on 22 July to the effect that Britain would concentrate her battleships in the North Sea but would maintain a force of three *Invincible* battlecruisers and a cruiser squadron based on Malta. The latter was a compromise to keep the Foreign Office happy. Grey's officials were worried that Britain's interests in the Mediterranean would suffer if denuded of sufficient naval protection, as Austria, Italy and Turkey had all been participating in the recent naval build-up.

At a meeting of the CID on 11 July, Grey stated: 'I will sum up matters by saying that foreign policy and naval policy are now most intimately connected. The smaller our naval power the more difficult our foreign policy.' The French had decided to withdraw their battle fleet to the Mediterranean in order to protect their lines of communication with their north African colonies. It was to be stressed in the agreement that both dispositions were made on an independent basis and there was no legal obligation on the part of Britain to protect the Atlantic and Channel coasts of France. Churchill went on to reassure the House that British superiority over Germany in the North Sea would represent a margin of 60 per cent and that eight out of a total of forty-one battleships would be based at Gibraltar to guard the Mediterranean. Although Grey understood the importance of naval power, his lack of interest in all things military continued to infuriate General Wilson, who recorded in his diary after the July CID meeting at which five Canadian ministers were present: 'The outstanding feature of the meeting was the way in which Grey entirely and absolutely ignored the military problem.'

Grey was also on his feet in the House on 30 July explaining the agreement with France. He described the two main reasons, in his mind, for Britain's extravagant naval construction programme. Firstly, battleships were needed for Britain to have a sufficient margin of naval strength in home waters, and secondly, a presence was necessary in foreign waters to provide backbone for Britain's diplomacy. In the latter case he moved swiftly on to prepare his audience for the possibility of a naval alliance with France, the essence of his argument being that it was not necessary to maintain a powerful fleet in the Mediterranean to counter possible enemy fleets when a squadron could be moved in at a moment's notice from Gibraltar. The French moved eighteen battleships from their Atlantic stations to the Mediterranean and one German newspaper reported sardonically, 'The concentration of the French fleet in the Mediterranean should not be taken too tragically and probably has a tactical rather than an offensive purpose.' Others saw it as a joint movement by Britain and France to further hem in Germany, whereas the *Westminster Gazette* reminded their readers that as the dispositions of the French fleet were made entirely at their own initiative, it was a misfortune that such action should be interpreted in terms of British policy.

Although the French accepted the autonomous nature of the new naval dispositions, their foreign minister, Raymond Poincaré, admitted to Ambassador Bertie that the decision would not have been taken if it was thought that the British would not come to France's aid in the event of an attack on their Channel ports by Germany. This statement redefined the Entente and laid an even greater moral obligation on Britain to support France in the event of an invasion by Germany. As many people thought Britain's commitment in time of war would be purely naval, these discussions implied a stronger moral commitment to France than the military conversations of 1905. As late as 2 August 1914, Asquith himself saw the despatch of an Expeditionary Force to France as serving no purpose. Grey was walking the usual tightrope. On the one hand he knew that Britain's hands must be free so that Parliament could decide on a course of action at the crucial moment; on the other, if Britain decided to support France she must be in a position to act in a meaningful manner. This necessitated ongoing discussions between the respective naval and military staffs.

Grey realised all too well that the military conversations created a moral tie together with expectations on the French side, but the alternative was unthinkable: Continental Europe dominated by a militarist Germany. The new Navy Bill became law in the Reichstag on 14 June and Grey was now convinced that the continued arms escalation would end in disaster. Trevelyan writes in his biography of Grey:

> The new distribution of French and British ships drew the Entente closer than before. It rendered it yet more unthinkable that we should stand neutral while France was attacked since she would now plead that she had denuded her northern coasts relying upon our fleet to protect them. For this reason the fleet movements of 1912 committed us more than the Military Conversations of 1906. But in fact, as Grey realised better than many of his countrymen, we stood 'committed' not by this or that word or act, but by the brute need of self-preservation: if we permitted France to be destroyed as a Power, her loss of independence would speedily be followed by our own downfall.

After these extensive Anglo-French discussions, some clarification of the overall position was needed. The Cabinet radicals led by Harcourt, Morley and McKenna wanted an explicit statement as to the non-committal nature of the military and naval conversations. On the other hand, Paul Cambon the French ambassador was seeking some sort of consultative agreement whereby the two governments would agree to discuss the situation in the event of either of them being exposed to aggression by a third power. On 22 November Grey and Cambon finally exchanged letters recognising three important points: firstly, that conversations between military and naval experts had taken place; secondly, that these did not bind their governments to action in any way and finally that in the event of a threatening situation the respective governments would discuss the situation with one another. Amazingly, everyone ended up satisfied. The French were relieved that the whole British Cabinet now acknowledged the joint plans, the radicals accepted the proposals because Britain was 'not committed' and the Foreign Secretary was thankful to have his critics off his back.

✣

On 9 May Grey hosted a farewell dinner at the Foreign Office for the outgoing German ambassador, who had been made a scapegoat for the Agadir debacle and the failed naval discussions. Metternich had been a popular ambassador who had played a straightforward and honourable role in keeping the peace between the two countries. He was considered 'a good friend of Germany's in England and an equally good friend of England's in Germany'. Grey wrote in his autobiography, 'I regretted his departure, and the farewell dinner given to him at the Foreign Office was not a political gesture but a genuine expression of personal regard.' Metternich had been treated outrageously by his superiors in Berlin, who refused to listen to his advice. On countless occasions he had written to his superiors explaining the myth of 'encirclement' and how the great majority of Englishmen desired peace. Berlin had long since tired of his warnings that their naval programme would result in war with Britain no later than 1915. A footnote in Trevelyan's biography of Grey quotes from a letter written by the Kaiser on 28 February to the Foreign Minister, Kiderlen. Metternich had apparently upset the Kaiser during his search for a non-aggression pact with Germany. The Kaiser wrote of his ambassador, 'He must avoid all discussion of naval matters, supplementary bills etc. until England has submitted to me, for my information, the draft for a political agreement including a neutrality clause! Until then I refuse to negotiate further.'

Metternich's warnings to Berlin that Germany would not be able to reach a political agreement with Britain without genuine cuts in her shipbuilding programme always went unheeded. Although Metternich was rigid in upholding the views of his government like any faithful servant, Grey never doubted that his reports to Berlin put across the Foreign Office's views in the most favourable light. The German ambassador had the sympathetic ear of the Chancellor, who was keen for some sort of naval accommodation with Britain, but at this time Bethmann Hollweg was not the ruler in Germany. With the backing of the Kaiser, it was Tirpitz who was pulling the strings, even though the composition of the Reichstag had swung towards the Chancellor following the left's victory in the January elections. The left wing was now set against earmarking further funds for the Navy and furthermore, the right had been alienated by the introduction of an inheritance tax.

Metternich was succeeded by Baron Marschall von Bieberstein, who was a past Foreign Secretary and one of the ablest diplomats in Europe. As ambassador in Constantinople he had been most successful in furthering German interests in the Turkish Empire. His appointment demonstrated how serious Germany was at this time to improve her relations with Britain. After a short period in office, Bieberstein died of cancer and was replaced by Prince Lichnowsky. Grey met the new ambassador for the first time in mid-November. The Prince was in many ways a strange appointment. He was an enemy of Kiderlen and carried little weight at the German Foreign Office. He had spent the last thirteen years languishing on his estates in Silesia, but on the plus side he was the personal choice of the Kaiser and was keen to promote closer Anglo-German relations.

In late September the Foreign Secretary spent two rather testing days at Balmoral in the company of Sazonov, the Russian Foreign Minister. Perhaps with a wary eye on his critics, he took a tougher line on Persia but as ever he was not prepared to go so far as to threaten the Entente with Russia. Grey informed Sazonov that the continued presence of Russian troops in northern Persia was exposing him to invidious criticism in the House of Commons. He also told the Foreign Minister that Britain would not be willing to accept the return of the former Shah and made it quite clear that the Russian bombardment of Muslim shrines had greatly offended public opinion across the Empire. He would almost certainly also have touched on the situation in the Balkans, where there were rumours coming through that Bulgaria and Serbia were mobilising against Turkey. There was a feeling in the air that the break-up of the Ottoman Empire, postponed by the Young Turk revolution of 1908, was now at hand, and the Foreign Secretary was concerned about possible Austro-Russian antagonism, so narrowly avoided after the annexation of Bosnia and Herzegovina. When asked over cigars and brandy what Britain would do if Russia went to war with Germany, Grey gave his standard reply. It would depend how the war came about. No British government could enter hostilities unless backed by public opinion and the latter would not support an aggressive war. Back at the Foreign Office, the ardent Russophile Permanent Secretary Arthur Nicolson was so worried his chief would offend Sazonov that his doctor ordered him to take six weeks' rest.

Grey's relationship with Nicolson was never as close as that with Hardinge. There was no real working partnership between the two men; the once close relationship had all but disappeared by 1912. The Cabinet committee on foreign affairs set up after Agadir curtailed Nicolson's influence, and the following year Grey was preoccupied with domestic politics. Nicolson did not conceal his contempt for the anti-Russian Liberal radicals, and their views on Home Rule for Ireland was the last straw. He unfairly thought his chief too weak to stand up to both the radicals and his close pro-German political ally Haldane. In addition, he was strongly opposed to Haldane's mission to Berlin and the ensuing naval talks. When Grey decided to take a harder line with Russia over Persia, their association deteriorated further still. In the matter of standing up to Russia, Grey was encouraged by his private secretary, William Tyrrell, who was keen to promote closer Anglo-German relations. Tyrrell was immensely loyal to Grey and had replaced Hardinge as the trusted adviser. He was more sensitive to public opinion than Nicolson and desperately tried to protect his chief from the recent criticism over his foreign policy. As with the majority in the Foreign Office, he was loyal to the policy of ententes, believing Germany to be the main European threat, yet he was also convinced that Britain should extend the hand of friendship to the offending party.

❧

In early October the powder keg blew yet again in the Balkans. The smaller states had insisted on taking internal reforms into their own hands. They demanded that the European provinces of Turkey be given autonomy, with Christian governors and elected assemblies within six months. The Turks had excused themselves for not executing their wishes on account of the activities of armed revolutionary bands. Indirectly encouraged by Russia and taking advantage of Turkey's preoccupation with the Italian war, the Balkan League made its move. On 8 October Montenegro declared war on Turkey and a week later, Serbia, Greece and Bulgaria followed suit. Events moved so quickly that on this occasion Europe was spared a major catastrophe. Within a few weeks from the outbreak of war, the outnumbered Turks had collapsed and lost 90 per cent of their possessions in Europe. By mid-November they stood with their backs to Constantinople. There simply wasn't time for Austria or Russia to become involved. Even so, a measure of sabre-rattling ensued, with Austria calling up 200,000 reservists in Bosnia-Herzegovina and Russia ordering a partial temporary mobilisation in response. Grey was concerned that Austria might invade Serbia. The Austrians were fearful of further Serbian expansion and were determined to prevent Serbia acquiring a Mediterranean port. To this end, they insisted on the creation of an independent Albania.

Despite the breakdown in the naval discussions, Germany was willing to take certain steps to improve Anglo-German relations. She agreed to act together with Britain and did her best to rein in Austria in order to localise the Balkan crisis. Russia had played her part too. Relieved that Turkey had been beaten, she warned Serbia not to expect unreserved Russian support for further territorial gains. Russia would instead encourage Serbia to try and secure railway access to the Adriatic via a neutral free port. All the powers seemed reasonably satisfied with the outcome of the war. There was a general feeling in Europe that the departure of the Turks was for the good of civilisation. But in the meantime Austro-Hungarian interests would need to be secured. With Serbia having made significant territorial gains, Austria was concerned about her trade routes to the Mediterranean and Aegean.

Turkey finally appealed to the powers to halt the war. She would have to sacrifice Thrace and Macedonia to save Constantinople. On 4 December a general armistice was signed, Bulgaria having enacted a ceasefire some weeks earlier. Both Grey and the German Chancellor wished to act within the Concert of Europe and were determined that Russia and Austria should play a lead role in agreeing any territorial changes. In late November, when Grey suggested an ambassadorial conference in London to seek a peaceful solution to the crisis, he was enthusiastically backed by Germany. On 16 December Grey welcomed the Turkish and Balkan delegates to the peace conference, which was held at St James's Palace, and on the following day he formally opened the Conference of Ambassadors. The idea was for the latter to run alongside the former and the ambassadors to have informal discussions on the most controversial items on the agenda, such as Albania and Serbian access to the Adriatic.

Grey was seen as the hero of the hour, as demonstrated in an article written by the St Petersburg correspondent for *The Times*:

> On every hand I hear unreservedly cordial acknowledgement of the practical and businesslike statesmanship which Sir Edward Grey has shown in bringing the Powers together on more or less common ground. We may take the fact that London has been chosen for the Peace Conference as evidence of the trust which he inspires. Sir Edward has never claimed credit for any act of policy during his long administration or retorted with the slightest asperity upon his assailants and critics. For that reason it is well that his countrymen should realise the unique position which he has won for himself in Europe by his long service and his steadiness and uprightness in all emergencies.

Over the best part of a decade, Grey had elevated himself into a position where he was now viewed as the most trusted, respected and experienced statesman in Europe.

Throughout the autumn, Germany had successfully restrained her Austrian ally. The Kaiser did not feel a war with Russia at this stage could be justified over Serbia's access to the Adriatic. But Austria was Germany's only meaningful ally, hence she could not afford to sit back and watch as the Austro-Hungarian Empire disintegrated. On 2 December the Chancellor declared in the Reichstag that if Austria was attacked by a third party as part of the defence of her interests, such as in a war with Serbia, then Germany would stand beside her ally. Then on 5 December, the Triple Alliance between Germany, Austria and Italy was renewed. Haldane had recently informed the new German ambassador in London that Britain would in all probability support France if she was sucked into conflict with Germany as a result of an Austro-Russian war. The Kaiser was furious and on 8 December called a war council, bringing together his top naval and military advisers. This would prove a defining moment, as thereafter it was a generally accepted fact amongst both military and political circles that a future war was inevitable. The Kaiser promptly called for a propaganda campaign to prepare German public opinion for war.

Moltke, Chief of the General Staff, was still keen for a preventative war against Russia in much the same way as he had been during the Bosnian crisis of 1909. He was convinced of the coming struggle between Slav and Teuton. Tirpitz, on the other hand, pleaded for a delay until the completion of the widening of the Kaiser Wilhelm canal in July 1914. In fact, the Army was also not yet ready, as demonstrated by the new Army Law which called for the addition of three new army corps. The naval budget had grown by 134 per cent between 1904 and 1912 against an army increase of only 47 per cent. Naval expenditure now represented over half the total expenditure on the armed forces. With the prospect of a war on two fronts, the German Army now needed quantity as well as quality. Neither side really wanted a war at this stage, Russia needing another three years to recover from her defeat at the hands of the Japanese in 1905.

On 9 December Grey received a letter from the King, who
had invited Prince Henry of Prussia for a shooting weekend at
Sandringham. Prince Henry had been very forthright and asked
the King whether Britain would support Germany and Austria in
a war against France and Russia. The King replied that he thought
Britain would not allow her friends to be crippled in a war of
aggression by Germany. Grey in turn replied to the King,

> Sir Edward Grey thinks it would be dangerous and misleading to
> let the German Government be under the impression that under
> no circumstances would England come to the assistance of France
> and Russia, if Germany and Austria went to war with them, and he
> thinks it very fortunate that Your Majesty was able to give an answer
> to Prince Henry that will prevent him from giving that impression at
> Berlin. Your Majesty's Government is not committed in the event of
> war and the public opinion of this country is, so far as Sir Edward
> Grey can judge, very adverse to a war arising out of a quarrel about
> Serbia. But if Austria attacked Serbia aggressively, and Germany
> attacked Russia if she came to the assistance of Serbia, and France
> were then involved, it might become necessary for England to fight
> for the defence of her position in Europe and for the protection of
> her own future and security.

And this, of course, is exactly what did happen twenty months later.

Haldane had given much the same answer to the new German
ambassador, Prince Lichnowsky, at an official meeting in London
a few days before. Prince Henry promised to relay British feelings
to the Kaiser. Bearing in mind the history of military and naval
'cooperation' between France and Britain, it surely did not take a
genius to see where Liberal Britain stood on this matter. After all,
Metternich had been warning Berlin for years of the inevitable
consequences for British public opinion and foreign policy of the
German shipbuilding programme. Foreign Minister Kiderlen died

suddenly in Berlin on New Year's Eve, to be replaced by Herr von Jagow, formerly ambassador in Rome. Kiderlen was a strong man who had a profound dislike of war and of Tirpitz in particular. Ambassador Goschen warned the Foreign Office from Berlin that Jagow did not have the backbone of Kiderlen. He feared that should a sudden crisis occur, both Bethmann Hollweg and Jagow would be swept away by the militarists.

Christmas at Fallodon, surrounded by his sisters and their children, saw a relieved, positive and quietly confident Foreign Secretary strolling amongst his wildfowl. He found himself in the unlikely yet happy position of working with the Germans to secure a peace treaty in the Balkans. Set against this was the failure of the Haldane mission, which represented the last roll of the dice in the search for a naval agreement with Germany. Even the pro-German Haldane returned from Berlin with a sense of foreboding, writing later in *Before the War*, 'I thought from my study of the German General Staff that once the German war party had got into the saddle it would be war not merely for the overthrow of France or Russia but for the domination of the world.' The disappointing outcome justified Grey's decision not to go to Berlin in person. He knew in his heart of hearts that an agreement was next to impossible without selling out France, and if he had led the mission himself its failure would have been all the more telling.

German intransigence had placed Grey's critics on the back foot and taken the pressure off his foreign policy. It also paved the way for the naval agreement with France, which, although a verbal understanding, came within a hair's breadth of turning the Entente into an alliance, a situation which would not now have unduly worried the Foreign Secretary. With little possibility of an increase in the naval budget or an agreement with Germany, a naval understanding with France seemed to Grey to be the obvious alternative. It also dovetailed in nicely with the military conversations. In the summer of 1912, Britain had virtually agreed to safeguard France's Channel and Atlantic ports from German attack, thereby making her involvement in any future European war a near certainty.

Reputation at a Peak: A Balkan Peace and a Developing Friendship with America

The new year witnessed an assertive, successful and internationally respected Foreign Secretary at the height of his powers. Despite this, it is obvious from his correspondence his heart was not in the job. He wrote to Katherine Lyttelton early in January, 'I am in high revolt against Office and London. I should like just for once for a year or two in my life to live in places and do things I don't detest.' It didn't stop him soldiering on and in the previous month, the ambassadors of all the great powers had gathered in London under his chairmanship to achieve a peace in the Balkans. He was very much his own man at the Foreign Office, as evidenced by his pursuit of a détente with Germany and the cooling of his relationship with Nicolson. He had won his major battles in Cabinet and fought off the radical backbench critics of his foreign policy. The Entente with France had been greatly strengthened by the recent naval agreement and although Russia was proving a most uncomfortable bedfellow, Grey had managed the relationship with tact, sensitivity and an increasingly firm hand. He now saw it as his next duty to cement a close relationship with the world's most powerful nation through his personal friendship with America's two formidable ambassadors, Walter Page and Colonel House.

The most sensitive issue Grey had to face as chairman of the Balkan Peace Conference was that of Albania, which had been taken from Turkey in the war. Austria was determined that Albania should not fall into the hands of the victors, Serbia and Montenegro. Serbia herself was desperate for a port on the Adriatic for commercial reasons, but Austria was only willing to grant Serbia guaranteed access to a neutralised port. If Austria decided to intervene and Russia supported the Serbs then a European war was inevitable. Grey found the proceedings of the conference 'protracted and sometimes intolerably wearisome'. He writes in his autobiography,

> There were six of us: Lichnowsky, Mensdorff and Imperiali, the ambassadors respectively of Germany, Austria and Italy; Cambon and Beckendorff, the ambassadors of France and Russia; and myself for Britain. Such responsibility as there was of presiding fell to me but we made the proceedings as informal as a committee of friends, which in fact we were. We met in the afternoons, generally about four o'clock, and, with a short adjournment to an adjoining room for tea, we continued to six or seven o'clock.

Grey's handling of the meetings demonstrated his patient states-manship. He saw his main task as preventing a clash between Russia and Austria. The powers agreed that Albania should be autonomous and hold all the Adriatic ports between Greek and Austro-Hungarian territory. Although Russia applied pressure on Serbia and went along with this proposal, it was a further blow to her prestige. When it came to fixing the boundaries of the new state, Russia understandably tried to secure as much territory as possible for Serbia and Montenegro. Arguments over territory led to a resumption of fighting. Turkey refused to cede Adrianople to Bulgaria and the King of Montenegro laid siege to Scutari, a Catholic city on the northern boundary of Albania. Grey took a tough line on the latter issue, siding with Austria, who wished

Scutari to remain part of Albania. He agreed to British participation in a naval expedition against Montenegro, which needless to say the Russians refused to join. Scutari fell to the Montenegrins in April and Austria immediately demanded international action to force the victors to evacuate the city. If pressure was not applied, the Austrians threatened to act on their own with dire consequences for European peace. In the end, with the inducement of both naval stick and financial carrot, the King of Montenegro backed down. It is interesting to note that in this instance, as part of his policy of working more closely with Germany, Grey took a firmer line with Russia. He had persuaded Germany to rein in the Austrians in return for Britain preaching moderation in St Petersburg. A peace treaty was signed between Turkey and the Balkan states at the end of May. There was much euphoria in the press about the role of the Concert of Europe and Grey's chairmanship. People started to believe that the Concert was capable of decisive action and could be a force for good in Europe when it came to peacekeeping. Grey was showered with praise from every quarter. He was referred to as a 'bridge builder' and complimented on his fairness, strength of character and experience. It is hardly surprising that he turned yet again to 'conference diplomacy' when faced with an even greater crisis twelve months hence.

It wasn't long before the participants disagreed amongst themselves over boundaries. The Serbs and the Greeks fell out with Bulgaria over the division of Macedonia; then the Bulgarians declared war. Turkey and Romania immediately climbed onto the bandwagon, making territorial gains at the expense of Bulgaria. The Turks retook Adrianople and Bulgaria was forced into a humiliating peace in August at the Treaty of Bucharest. The Austrians were secretly pleased to see the Balkan bloc falling out amongst themselves. Along with France and Germany, Grey remained committed to a policy of non-intervention and saw it as his duty to keep the great powers from falling out. He was determined to restrain possible Russian intervention against the Turks at Constantinople. If this happened, the Ottoman Empire might disintegrate and chaos would spread from Europe to Asia. Ominously, the real winner was Serbia, who doubled her territory and increased her population from 2.9 million to 4.4 million, thereby reinforcing her claim to head a South Slav state. Trevelyan writes:

> And so the Balkan situation simmered on for another uneasy year. Bulgaria, sore and despoiled, inclined now to the German rather than the Russian side in order to wreak vengeance on Serbia; while Serbia, deprived of her window on the Adriatic at the orders of Vienna, waited eagerly for a general European war, for the chance to break up Austria-Hungary and attach all her Serb and Croat Provinces to a great Yugo-Slav Kingdom centred at Belgrade.

On the face of it, Anglo-German relations had improved markedly by the summer of 1913. There was essential cooperation between the two countries over the Balkan crisis, even though one could argue that Germany was not ready for a full European war at this stage. Negotiations over a possible future division of the Portuguese colonies were continuing with Berlin through the Foreign and Colonial Offices. A fiercely Anglophile German ambassador was now installed in London and on 24 May, the King attended the wedding of the Kaiser's daughter to the Duke of Brunswick in Berlin. Grey certainly thought relations were moving in the right direction, writing in his autobiography,

> Very important was the attitude of Germany. I believe that from the beginning Germany intended the Conference to succeed; otherwise she would not have agreed to it at all. She was not prepared to hustle Austria, and often she allowed things to drag. But Germany was determined that war was to be avoided and for this purpose she had a wholehearted representative and agent in Lichnowsky. He hated the notion of war and Russia having at the outset conceded fairly the principle of an independent Albania, Lichnowsky made it evident that he considered the details in dispute not worth a European war.

Yet all was not peace and harmony between the two countries; there was still a deathly silence from Berlin on the vital issue of a naval agreement. There was never likely to be a meeting of minds on the naval issue and when Lichnowsky came to London he specifically asked Grey not to bring the subject up. Above all, the new Navy symbolised the industrial and technological might of Germany. Not only was the Navy the Kaiser's pride and joy but it was also a unifying force, popular across all classes of society. R. T. B. Langhorne in his essay on 'Great Britain and Germany 1911–1914' writes:

> The Navy was a symbol for some Germans of one aspect of their struggle for world power status. It was at the very core of their belief that England stood in their way. For others, it was a more subtle means of pressure whereby England might be induced to abandon her opposition to German continental ambitions. The Navy was to be used to extract a pledge of neutrality from England since circumstances precluded the building-up of the fleet into a genuine threat. But England could not permit an attempt to divide her from her friends, so that she might be dealt with separately later, nor allow her food supplies to be menaced. No bargain was possible on the basis of a naval détente – even for one year's holiday – and a political agreement: there was no common ground between the two ideas.

The naval question did briefly rear its head once again in March, by which time the Anglo-German naval arms race was becoming less of an issue, primarily because more funds were being channelled towards the German Army. At the end of the month Churchill presented to the House his naval estimates for 1913/14, which had ballooned to £48 million. He returned to his concept of a 'naval holiday' to soften the blow. No new ships would be built for a year. If Germany were to cancel two Dreadnoughts, Britain would cancel four. His ideas for economy received a torrent of criticism both domestically and in Germany. The Commons was proving nervous about losing naval supremacy over Germany and in the process seemed to have completely forgotten about spending economies.

The Germans conveniently hid behind social issues, postulating that thousands of shipyard workers would lose their jobs if the 'naval holiday' went ahead. Churchill was responding to a more conciliatory Tirpitz, who had recently presented less threatening German estimates. Grey was not being taken in by this surprising generosity. He wrote to Goschen on 5 March that the reason for this benevolence was not 'the love of our beautiful eyes, but the extra 50 millions required for the German Army'. The Germans continued to preach in public that they awaited positive proposals from Britain yet in private they intimated, largely through Lichnowsky, that such proposals would be unwelcome.

Grey's international prestige hit new heights in the summer of 1913 at the conclusion of the Balkan peace. Valentine Chirol, former editor of *The Times*, wrote to Hardinge at the end of May, 'The only member of the Government whose prestige stands higher than ever is Grey.' The King sent a letter to Grey offering his congratulations and expressing 'absolute reliance in your management of our foreign policy'; he wrote, 'You have by your patience, tact and statesmanship secured peace and gained the confidence of all the European powers, while inspiring a similar confidence in the Parliamentary Opposition in this country.' Even his arch post-war critic Lloyd George wrote, 'Your brilliant achievement, for it is entirely yours, is the greatest triumph yet scored for the Government. I shudder to think what would have happened in Europe had you not taken the lead.' Grey's diplomacy had worked because none of the powers really wanted war at this particular point. It would have been very difficult for all concerned to justify a war to their subjects on the basis of a remote Balkan issue. The peace represented a last triumph for 'old diplomacy' and the Concert of Europe.

Although deeply immersed in foreign affairs, Grey continued to keep a hand in domestic matters. On the afternoon of 6 May he was principal speaker in a Private Member's Bill in favour of female suffrage. Unfortunately, he was up against Asquith. The division went against him by 268 votes to 221. In Grey's mind, two factors mitigated against female enfranchisement. The first was excessive militancy, law breaking and arson, which continued daily. The second was the massive presence of the Prime Minister, who occupied such a commanding position in the Commons. Asquith was in opposition on the matter to a majority of his Cabinet and the Parliamentary Liberal Party, whereas Balfour, who was in favour of votes for women, was in opposition to a majority of the Unionist party.

Time and again in the months before the outbreak of war, Lloyd George and Grey worked together in trying to push through radical domestic policies. In addition to female suffrage, Grey gave the Chancellor strong support over his campaign for land reform. On 19 June it can even be argued that Grey saved Lloyd George's political career. The Marconi scandal broke in the early summer when charges were brought against Lloyd George, the Attorney-General Rufus Isaacs, the Postmaster-General Herbert Samuel and the Chief Whip, the Master of Elibank, for making 'injudicious' share purchases in the American Marconi Company. Even though the charges were greatly exaggerated, there was an element of insider trading involved, as the sister company, the English Marconi Company, of which the Attorney-General's brother was a director, had won a large contract to build wireless stations across the Empire.

As ever, when a sensitive subject came up, the Prime Minister put Grey in the firing line. The Foreign Secretary had to reply to an opposition motion led by Bonar Law condemning the purchase of shares. He won the day and on 20 June Grey replied to Lloyd George's letter of thanks: 'There was a very true sentence in your speech about mistakes being often more heavily censured than misdeeds, which is very applicable. I have often thought in public affairs that one is always being over praised or over blamed.' He concluded by relishing the fact that personal relationships seemed to survive the pressures of political life: 'The personal relations of all of us have not only stood the long strain but have gained in attachment to an extent that must be very rare if not unprecedented in the history of Cabinets.' How strange, therefore, that Chapter 3 of Lloyd George's *War Memoirs* is devoted entirely to a vitriolic attack on the character, achievements and abilities of the pre-war Foreign Secretary. The Welshman insinuates Grey was a boring speaker who hid behind his charismatic good looks and a dignified, restrained manner, writing, 'He did not command the flaming phrase that illuminates but sometimes also scorches and leaves behind an irritating burn.' Grey for his part was only too happy to leave the flowery oratory and amateur dramatics to Churchill and Lloyd George.

Grey spent most weekends in May and June down at The Cottage fishing with his brother Charlie. His eyesight was rapidly deteriorating and as a result he was determined to make the most of his last years with a dry fly. On 22 May he caught eleven trout, including one of 2 lb 4 oz on a Grey Quill. He fished the Aquarium to the Top Water and his diary reads, 'Very good rise about noon, put back five fish between 1 lb and 1 lb 4 oz besides those killed.' On 26 July Grey wrote to Eddy Tennant informing him how he had just caught twenty-two small trout and an eel on a worm in the Fallodon burn which must have brought childhood memories rushing back. His correspondence with Eddy concentrates almost entirely on matters of country interest; interestingly, there is next to no political gossip. One day there is a new type of fishing rod to try out, on another he eulogises about his roses at The Cottage or his wildfowl collection at Fallodon, and then there is a description of two hedgehogs fighting amongst some dried leaves or a weasel stalking a rabbit.

When not at The Cottage or spending the occasional weekend at Fallodon, Grey enjoyed weekends at Wilsford with Pamela. Her granddaughter alludes to the fact that he was much in love with Pamela at the time, writing in her book of 'Edward Grey, who will stand for a time unseen at the door and regard her with helpless admiration', and of 'his eyes already soft at the sight of Pamela in the doorway.' He adored the location on the river Avon, especially the way the garden ran into the water meadows, home to a great variety of finches, warblers and waterfowl. In *The Charm of Birds* he writes:

> At Wilsford, where the water meadows adjoin the garden with no fence to separate them, the reed-bunting is a garden bird. In spite of his noble appearance the reed-bunting has rather a paltry song: it suggests to me the ascent of steps, the first two or three being mounted sedately and the last taken trippingly.

Here is yet another example of Grey's brilliant ability to use an image to anchor an individual song in the memory.

Grey loved to take Pamela for walks on the downs in search of birds. According to her granddaughter, Pamela's most bewitching walk was past Springbottom Farm and on up the old drove road that climbs the downs to Stonehenge. Pamela believed Stonehenge was best seen in winter 'when the stones loom suddenly near, black as iron in the slanting rain'. But she always thought the downs were at their loveliest in early summer when covered in daisies, cowslips and meadowsweet. One of Grey's favourite birds was the stone curlew and in her book, *Shepherd's Crowns*, Pamela writes, 'Close to these Down roads you may find the eggs of the stone curlew or set the little plover running all in fluff, and without a feather, while the parent birds wheel and cry beyond you, to draw attention from their young.'

Although any hope of a naval agreement had long since vanished, Grey was determined to improve relations with Germany and demonstrate the détente had substance. To this end, by the end of October a deal on the partitioning of the Portuguese colonies was initialled and ready for signature. The Foreign Secretary was not opposed to German colonialism as long as it did not clash with

Britain's own interests and he was quite happy to accept German ambitions in Central Africa, specifically Angola. As early as December 1911, Grey had written to Sir Edward Goschen: 'I am to meet Harcourt next month and study the map with him in a pro-German spirit; then the Cabinet will review the situation.' The initial discussions were undertaken by Harcourt at the Colonial Office. The Foreign Office was concerned that too much ground would be conceded to Germany and Nicolson was scandalised by the proceedings, describing the treaty as 'the most cynical business I have come across in my whole experience of diplomacy'.

The purpose of the treaty was to amend an earlier secret Anglo-German agreement made by Balfour in 1898 when he was under severe diplomatic pressure during the unpopular Boer War. Portugal had been in financial difficulties for some time and there was the possibility she might need to sell part of her poorly administered African Empire to satisfy outstanding loans. Britain and Germany had agreed the territory should be divided up in roughly equal shares. The 1898 treaty was complicated by the fact that, a year later, Lord Salisbury signed a secret treaty with the Portuguese guaranteeing all their territories. In return, Britain's oldest ally was to give assistance against the Boers and promise not to declare herself neutral. Under the eagle eye of Eyre Crowe, the Foreign Office insisted the new treaty be published and also that the Anglo-German and Anglo-Portuguese treaties of 1898 and 1899 be simultaneously made public. The Germans baulked at this disclosure and the treaty was not ratified.

A quietly relieved Foreign Secretary had at least achieved his goal of being seen to be building bridges with Berlin. He always thought it unrealistic for Britain to bring pressure on the Portuguese to sell their colonies when bound by an alliance to protect and preserve those same colonies. The German ambassador appreciated Grey's efforts, writing in *Heading for the Abyss*:

Sir Edward honestly tried to confirm this rapprochement and his intentions were most apparent on two questions – the Colonial Treaty and the Baghdad Railway Treaty. The object of the negotiations between us and England was to amend and improve our Agreement of 1898 as it had proved unsatisfactory on several points as regards geographical delimitation. Thanks to the accommodating attitude of the British Government, I succeeded in making the new agreement fully accord with our wishes and interests. Sir Edward Grey intended to demonstrate his goodwill towards us but he also wished to assist our colonial development as a whole as England hoped to divert the German development of strength from the North Sea and Western Europe to the Ocean and Africa.

In the summer of 1913 an eerie calm prevailed across Europe. The great powers had worked together to achieve a Balkan peace. Germany had held back Austria and appeared to be working in harmony with Britain now that the naval issue had been pushed under the carpet. Russia had even played her part in putting the brakes on Serbian expansionism in the Balkans. But beneath the surface, powerful negative forces were at play. In October, Germany set about reaffirming her relationship with Austria-Hungary after their differences of opinion in the Balkan wars. Serbia had occupied several towns in northern Albania in contravention of the peace treaty. The Austrians delivered Serbia an ultimatum backed by Germany and Serbia backed down. The Kaiser then made a state visit to Archduke Franz Ferdinand, the heir to the Austro-Hungarian throne, and assured him that Germany would back his Empire in any conflict with Serbia.

By the autumn, Russo-German relations were rapidly deteriorating. Commercial antagonism, caused by agricultural and industrial tariffs, had been rife for some time. On top of this the Russians were deeply suspicious of German influence in the Ottoman Empire, symbolised by the Baghdad Railway Project. Then in October, Liman von Sanders, a German General, was appointed to command an Ottoman army corps at Constantinople. Russian insecurity deepened as they foresaw Germany holding a key to the Straits. A Russo-German press war broke out and diplomatic tension intensified. Although Germany backed down with Sanders being appointed to the less provocative role of Inspector-General of the Turkish Army, the Russians went on the offensive. Sazonov was now more determined than ever to win control of the Straits. The General Staff decided to revoke the renunciation of war which had been Russian policy since 1905, and control of the Straits became a war aim. At the same time a frightened Sazonov turned to the Entente and pressed Britain for a defensive alliance. For obvious reasons Grey was cool on the proposal, maddening Nicolson, who wrote to Buchanan in St Petersburg:

> How much longer we shall be able to follow our present policy of dancing on a high rope and not be compelled to take up some defi-nite line or other. I am also haunted by the same fear as you – lest Russia become tired of us and strike a bargain with Germany.

If the Austrians received little diplomatic support from their Triple Alliance ally over the Balkan peace, the same can be said on the other side of the alliance fence during the von Sanders affair, with Britain and France keeping their heads well down and offering little in the way of assistance to the Russians. Once again, the powers decided that Balkan discord was not worth the risk of war, but in the next few months Russian insecurity would spawn efforts to tighten up the Triple Entente by way of naval negotiations with Britain.

But it was not only the Russians who were feeling insecure. The Germans now felt threatened on all sides. With the aid of French capital, Russia had both industrialised and constructed a network of strategic railways, allowing the process of mobilisation to be accelerated. In 1905 the Schlieffen Plan assumed six weeks for Russian mobilisation, but by the end of 1913 the first troops could be transported into the battle zone within fifteen days. The Russian Army had been reformed and greatly strengthened. In 1913, Russia introduced a plan to increase the number of her army divisions from 114 to 122. By 1917 the Russian Army on its own would be three times the size of Germany's. Across the water in Britain, Sir

A portrait of Sir Edward Grey by John Singer Sargent in 1913, when his international reputation was at an all-time high.

'The Spring Run'. Grey fished the Rosehall beat on the River Cassley in Sutherland with his brother Charlie for a fortnight in April every year from 1903 to 1926, with the exception of 1906–7, which he missed owing to the pressures of Foreign Office work.

Henry Herbert Asquith, Grey's closest political ally and one of the greatest peacetime Prime Ministers Britain has ever had. Churchill wrote, 'His mind opened and shut smoothly and exactly, like the breech of a gun.'

A gathering at Glen, the Tennant family home. Prime Minister Asquith is on the left, his son Raymond far right. The brilliant Raymond was killed in the war. His future wife, Katherine Horner, gazes up at him (centre). Margot Tennant (Asquith) sits on the left and her step-daughter, Violet Bonham Carter, sits at the back in a large hat.

Four of Grey's heavyweights at the Foreign Office. Tyrrell was the only official who was not passionately anti-German. Left to right clockwise: top left, Eyre Crowe: author of the celebrated paper on Anglo-German relations in 1907. Charles Hardinge: mentor and good friend to Grey during his early days as Foreign Secretary. William Tyrrell, who suffered a nervous breakdown early in the war on the death of his son. Arthur Nicolson, hero of Algeciras and the Russian Entente, yet fell out with Grey later on, due to the Foreign Secretary's supposed lack of commitment to France and Nicolson's anti-Home Rule views.

King Edward VII and the Kaiser in Berlin, February 1909. Uncle and nephew experienced an uneasy relationship throughout their lives. The King looks overweight and ill; he would be dead within eighteen months.

Admiral Tirpitz. Ambitious, energetic, aggressive, domineering and obsessive in his dream to build a fleet of German battleships to match the British. Norman Stone writes, 'The last thing that Germany needed was a problem with Great Britain and the greatest mistake of the twentieth century was made when Germany built a navy designed to attack her.'

Count von Bülow, German Chancellor 1900–1909 and Secretary of State for Foreign Affairs 1897–1900. Outwardly elegant, urbane, polished and a brilliant speaker but 'for twelve years German foreign policy lay in the hands of a man who lacked purpose, scruples, courage and a vision of his own'. Holstein said that Bülow had read more Machiavelli than he could digest.

TOP Theodore von Bethmann Hollweg. German Chancellor 1909–17. Unlike his clever, ambitious predecessor, Bethmann was regarded as a man unconcerned with advancement; his moves up the ladder were attributed to obedience to duty. Desperate for better relations with Britain, he initiated new naval negotiations which ultimately ended in failure.

MIDDLE Three grand Liberals exit a Cabinet meeting in 1910. Left to right: Sir Edward Grey, Winston Churchill and Lord Crewe.

BOTTOM King George V posing nervously with his Prussian regiment in Berlin during 1913. The Kaiser stands on his left in the uniform of a British Admiral. One of the few unconstitutional acts undertaken by Edward VII was to make the Czar an Admiral of the Fleet without informing his ministers; Grey was not amused.

The calm before the storm. Winston Churchill and his wife Clemmie on the beach at Sandwich Bay in July 1914. They were staying with Nancy Astor at her seaside home, Rest Harrow, where the author spent many a happy weekend with the Seymour family nearly a century later.

Top-level Prussian militarism. The Kaiser and his six sons marching in Berlin just before the outbreak of war.

Grey and Lord Kitchener in Paris shortly before 'the lamps went out'. In April 1914 Grey accompanied the King on a state visit to France, which represented his first overseas trip in eight years as Foreign Secretary.

ABOVE Many ministers, including Grey, had no concept of the horrors a modern, defensive war would involve; indeed, with the exception of Kitchener, most thought the troops would be home by Christmas. Grey naïvely told the Commons on 3 August 1914, 'If we are engaged in war, we shall suffer but little more than we shall suffer even if we stand aside.'

LEFT David Lloyd George, the elder statesman. He fell out irreconcilably with Grey after the war over the direction of the Liberal party. In July 1920, Grey wrote of Lloyd George, 'He had some great qualities without being a great man. He was constitutionally incapable of understanding that straightforwardness is essential, "cleverness" fatal, to success in the long run.'

TOP LEFT President Theodore Roosevelt, who became a trusted friend of Grey; this may have marked the beginning of the 'special relationship' with the USA. Grey wrote to a friend, 'He has a peculiar faculty with it all of implanting healthy courage and vigour. I have loved him.'

TOP RIGHT Colonel House, President Wilson's unofficial roving ambassador on foreign affairs. Grey's close friendship with House was central to the growing 'special relationship'. Grey wrote, 'I found combined in him in a rare degree the qualities of wisdom and sympathy. In the stress of war it was at once a relief, a delight, and an advantage to be able to talk with him freely.'

BOTTOM Walter Page, US Ambassador to London. A great Anglophile who adored Grey, Page wrote to his President, 'Sir Edward Grey would make a good American with the use of very little sandpaper.'

Grey as special ambassador to Washington in 1919, when nearly blind. He is flanked by the Marquess of Reading on the left side of the photograph and Lord Curzon on the right. The gentleman with a beard is Lord Bryce, who was Chief Secretary for Ireland before being sent to Washington by Grey as ambassador.

Grey the elder statesman, outside the newly rebuilt Fallodon Hall. In 1917 much of the house was destroyed by fire. Grey rebuilt it following the original style but in two storeys rather than three.

On 4 June 1922, Grey and Pamela Glenconner finally married after a close relationship that went back many years. Simon Blow, Pamela's great-grandson, wrote of their previous friendship, 'No love letters survive, though strong suggestions have been made it was more than platonic.'

Viscount Grey of Fallodon in old age, demonstrating a remarkable ability to tame wild creatures.

Henry Wilson had not been letting the grass grow under his feet. He had attended the autumn manoeuvres of General Joffre, conferred with the Russian General Staff and made regular visits to Foch's XXth Corps, positioned on the German frontier. In addition he had familiarised himself with all the new German strategic railways converging on Aachen and the Belgian border.

The arms race continued across the Continent, propelling Europe towards war. A new law had been passed in Germany adding 170,000 men to her peacetime army, while in retaliation the French introduced an extended three-year period of military service. Grey was well aware of the danger of the preventive war advocated by Moltke. He knew there were two factions in Berlin at this time and that the 'peace party' led by Bethmann Hollweg was rapidly losing ground. The German exchequer was feeling the strain of the armaments race: the economy was in recession and 5 per cent of the workforce was out of work. Germany was more dependent than ever on its one weak ally, Austria-Hungary. If there was another clash in the Balkans between Austria and Serbia, war would surely be inevitable. Sir Fairfax Cartwright, the British ambassador in Vienna, certainly thought so. He sent Nicolson a memo in November warning of Serbian agitation in Serb-inhabited regions of the Austro-Hungarian Empire under encouragement from Russia. He was convinced Serbia would spark a European war.

On the other side of the Atlantic, Britain's relations with America at this time were far from easy. In 1912 the outgoing Taft administration had passed a Bill exempting American ships from paying tolls for passage through the Panama Canal. The Panama Act represented a breach of the Hay-Pauncefote Treaty with Britain whereby it was agreed in 1901 that all non-American ships using the Canal would be treated as favourably as US ships. As ever, Grey was keen to accommodate the United States. Demonstrating an admirable degree of tact and patience, Grey and Ambassador

Bryce in Washington eventually persuaded the new Wilson administration to repeal the Panama Act. On 8 September 1912, Grey
had written to Bryce,

> In the long run if we can get no agreement with the United States
> Government, and if they adhere to Taft's view of the meaning of the
> Hay-Pauncefote Treaty, we must ask for arbitration. If they refuse
> arbitration on such a point, it will put back the cause of arbitration
> a hundred years. That is why I do not want to precipitate a request
> for arbitration yet. It is a very serious prospect.

Congress finally repealed the Act in the summer of 1914. Grey
learnt over the episode just how strong anti-British feelings were
in America. He was particularly enamoured by the President's
remark that he 'knew trouble would be encountered in the Senate,
especially in the form of Senator O'Gorman, who constantly
regards himself as an Irishman contending against England rather
than a United States senator upholding the dignity and welfare of
his country'.

Woodrow Wilson had done his best to promote Anglo-American
relations early in his administration, but not before Grey had come
to the aid of the President in his own backyard. Britain's extensive
commercial interests in revolutionary Mexico were under threat
from the chaos and disorder resulting from regime change. Britain,
with a hawk-like eye on her oil interests, had recognised the new
Huerta administration while America, desperate for his overthrow,
supported opposition groups. Although Grey thought Wilson's
policy idealistic and unwise, he adhered to the President's policy of
rejecting interference in Mexican affairs. Grey had recognised the
Monroe Doctrine (which claimed that any intervention by external
powers in the politics of the Americas amounted to a potentially
hostile act against the United States) and was determined at all
costs to promote friendly relations with America. He writes in his
autobiography, 'Our conversations about Mexico were not always
very sympathetic. I made it quite clear that we should look passively

on with acquiescence in whatever policy the United States thought
fit to pursue about Mexico but I could not be enthusiastic about
the prospect.' The new ambassador to Washington, Cecil Spring-
Rice, and Grey's private secretary, William Tyrrell, both played an
important role in fostering friendly relations with the Americans.
Owing to Spring-Rice's poor health, Tyrrell was sent to Washington
as Grey's private ambassador in November, where he became
involved in the diplomacy surrounding Mexico and the Panama
tolls. Tyrrell was now considered a real heavyweight in diplomatic
circles and his name was being mentioned for both the Berlin and
Paris ambassadorial posts.

On 3 July, Grey gave a small luncheon party at his London home,
33 Eccleston Square, for two Americans who would become his
close friends. Their friendship with the British Foreign Secretary
would play a central role in improving relations with the United
States. The lunch was organised by the new US ambassador, Walter
Page, with the specific intention of introducing Grey to President
Wilson's roving ambassador, Colonel House. House writes in
his diary,

> Our luncheon consisted of a course of lobster, afterwards mutton
> cutlets, green peas and potatoes, then ice cream with raspberry
> sauce, cheese, fruit and coffee. We were waited on by two maids,
> no butler being present. The house is a simple one but exceedingly
> comfortable and well arranged. He rents it from Winston Churchill.

According to House, while Lord Crewe and Page discussed the
eradication of hookworm in India, House and Grey not unnaturally
alighted on the topical subjects of Mexico and the Panama tolls.

Grey immediately warmed to House. He was a man with whom
he could do business. He found him a modest man whose ambition
was to accomplish good things, his primary aim being for America
to play a part in keeping the peace in Europe. He particularly liked
the informal nature of their conversations and the fact that House
had no sense of his own self-importance. He was content for others

to have the credit for anything he might achieve. In his autobiography, Grey writes,

> When House came to London after the outbreak of war our conversations almost at once became not only friendly but intimate. I found combined in him in a rare degree the qualities of wisdom and sympathy. In the stress of war it was at once a relief, a delight, and an advantage to be able to talk to him freely.

For his part, House trusted Grey from their first meeting and more than anything it was the close friendship between these two men that laid the foundation for the 'special relationship'.

House's role was unusual to say the least. He held no official post; he was the President's 'eyes and ears'. House had travelled from Texas, where he was involved in local politics, to New York in 1910 in order to find a candidate who could win the Presidency for the Democratic Party in 1912. He came up with Woodrow Wilson. House's role is best described by Ambassador Page when writing to Grey to fix their initial meeting:

> There is an American gentleman in London, the like of whom I do not know. Mr Edward House is his name. He is 'the silent partner of President Wilson' – that is to say he is the most trusted political advisor and the nearest friend of the President. He is a private citizen, a man without personal political ambition, a modest, quiet, even shy fellow. He helps to make Cabinets, to shape policies, to select judges and ambassadors and suchlike merely for the pleasure of seeing that these tasks are well done.

1913 was a defining year for Anglo-American relations. It was a year marked by reciprocity between the two English-speaking nations. With a European war brewing over the horizon, closer ties could not have come at a more opportune moment. Grey's sensitivity to President Wilson's views led to a cooling of Britain's support for the Huerta regime in Mexico. Without such a prop, Huerta fled the country in July 1914. A month before, Congress had repealed the Panama Act of 1912. For his part, the President realised the strong feeling prevailing in Britain that by breaking an existing treaty over the Canal tolls, America had acted dishonourably. He genuinely wanted to maintain the bond of trust between the two countries.

These diplomatic successes were made possible by the efforts of five men: Grey and Tyrrell on one side of the Atlantic, President Wilson and Colonel House on the other and the Anglophile Walter Page oiled the wheels in the middle from the American embassy in London. In her book *Colonel House and Sir Edward Grey*, Joyce Williams writes,

> The process of getting acquainted during 1913 operated on both sides. Charmed by Grey at his home in London, later flattered by Tyrrell who told him how grateful Grey was that House arranged a meeting with the President, House felt that Grey approached his ideal of a statesman. Acceptance of House as a diplomat on the same level as himself beguiled the Colonel. Grey's artlessness in discussion of state matters, and an evident desire to maintain a friendship with the United States, made other European diplomats appear gauche. On the eve of the war House, impressed by the treatment accorded him through the Foreign Office, unknowingly had pledged Grey his allegiance.

It is evident from a letter written by Wilson to Grey just after the outbreak of war that the President himself liked and admired the British Foreign Secretary. Grey had written to the President on the death of his wife and received back the following words: 'My hope is that you will regard me as your friend. I feel that we are bound together by common principle and purpose.'

Grey's close friendship with Walter Page was also a vital factor in furthering Anglo-American relations at this crucial time and he worked closely with the ambassador in solving the diplomatic problems over Mexico. Walter Page was a clever visionary who understood the close links between the two English-speaking peoples. Grey realised that America was the superpower of the future and that without access to her capital and industrial resources during the war, Britain would be finished. Perhaps Page was thinking about Grey when he wrote to the President:

> Praise God for the Atlantic Ocean. It is the geographical foundation of our liberties. A civilisation, especially an old civilisation isn't an easy nut to crack. But I notice that men of vision keep their thought on us. Our power, our adaptability, our potential wealth, they never forget. They will hold fast to our favour for reasons of prudence as well as kinship. And whenever we choose to assume the leadership of the world, they'll grant it, gradually and loyally. They cannot become French and they dislike the Germans. They must keep in our boat for safety as well as comfort.

In the same letter Page demonstrates his fondness for the British Foreign Secretary, writing, 'Sir Edward Grey would make a good American with the use of very little sandpaper.' Grey, for his part, wrote of the huge significance of Page's presence at the American embassy during the early years of war:

> The forces that made for dangerous trouble between Britain and the United States were often formidable in the first two years of war. Page was earnest and active, in advice to us and by all persuasion and influence that he could use at Washington, to counteract and foil these forces. The comfort, support, and encouragement that his presence was to the Secretary for Foreign Affairs in London may be imagined, but cannot be over-estimated.

Americans couldn't help warming to Grey; he was their ideal of an English gentleman. His straightforward, honest and dignified persona made diplomatic negotiations an unusually pleasant activity. Lord Robert Cecil, Grey's Under-Secretary during the war, was convinced that Grey's character at the beginning of the war, gained favourable consideration of the World for our account of the causes which led to the outbreak of hostilities. Europe and the other civilised countries were prima facie disposed to accept as true anything that Grey said. Where he was in controversy with other countries as to the facts, they preferred to believe him. They trusted his veracity and fairness, and even when, later in the war, our blockade operations seemed inconsistent with neutral rights, foreign countries were ready to believe that our proceedings were really essential for our defence and were not the outcome of arrogant navalism.

Cecil was not the only person to admire the Foreign Secretary. Charles Hobhouse, who had entered the Cabinet in October 1911 as Chancellor of the Duchy of Lancaster, when discussing his Cabinet colleagues, writes in his diary during the war,

> Grey, we all like, admire and respect, for his transparent sincerity and honesty as well as for his courage, skill and steadfastness. He is always open to argument (except on a point of principle when indeed he is apt to narrow his views from conviction to prejudice), most patient, courteous, and conciliatory with all, a nice sense of humour, a horror of self-advertisement and a loathing of politics.

In a similar fashion, Margot Asquith records in her autobiography, 'Sir Edward Grey is a very complete person and part and parcel of a golden mixture of character and judgement.' Once, while staying at Windsor with the King, she partnered Grey on the bridge table after dinner and wrote, 'I am always happy with Sir Edward Grey and have a deep affection for him. His reality, thoughtfulness, and freedom from pettiness give him true distinction. He is unchangeable and there is something lonely, lofty and even pathetic about him which I could not easily explain.' Grey was venerated in the highest quarters. Just after the outbreak of war, the Prime Minister wrote to Venetia Stanley, 'I must send you the enclosed despatch of

E. Grey. It shows the kind of almost school-boy simplicity both in mind and speech which is intertwined with great qualities.' In the Prime Minister's 'class list', ranking Cabinet colleagues in order of all-round abilities, Grey came second to Crewe, with Lloyd George and Churchill coming equal fourth.

After his Balkan successes Grey was immensely popular across the country, and especially so amongst the opposition benches of the Conservative Party. With the exception of a few diehard Radicals, one and all felt comfortable with his common-sense, practical approach to foreign affairs. On 12 August, Bonar Law paid the Foreign Secretary a warm tribute in the Commons, declaiming,

> This country has had a great advantage in its dealings with the Near East question that from the beginning its neighbours recognised it had no selfish intent to pursue, but it also had the further advantage of possessing a spokesman whose personal candour and straight-forwardness were unquestioned by the most suspicious.

For his part, on 6 November, while receiving the freedom of the City of Newcastle, Grey expressed his gratitude to the opposition for 'their public spirit in refraining from making party capital out of foreign politics'. In a nutshell, people felt safe in his hands. He told his audience, 'None of the powers could prevent the war in the Balkans occurring but they could prevent it from spreading.' And no doubt with Mexico in mind, he continued, 'When dealing with situations outside one's control, foreign policy requires not striking efforts and bold strikes but careful and attentive steering.'

If Grey had been preoccupied with the New World towards the end of the year, luckily for him things were relatively quiet in the Old. Relations with Berlin were better than at any time over Grey's tenure in office, prompting Nicolson to write a few months later, 'Since I have been at the Foreign Office, I have never seen such calm waters.' But all was not well at home, with the Home Rule Bill hitting the rocks in the Lords and the very real possibility of civil war breaking out in Ireland over the Ulster issue. Families and

friendships across Britain were being torn apart by politics, especially in Ireland. There was even a dramatic rift in the cosy world of
The Souls. The Asquiths and their daughter, Elizabeth, were barred
from the Curzon ball in the summer, all because the Prime Minister
had embraced Home Rule for Ireland. Margot Asquith and Curzon
were both leading Souls. In her book *Winston Churchill, As I Knew
Him*, Violet Asquith writes, 'We had become inured to excommu-
nication by Society and we took it in our stride with equanimity.
Sir Edward Grey despised it, Winston defied it, my father ignored
it.' This demonstrates how different Grey was from other successful
politicians; he displayed a complete lack of social ambitions.

By November, the Home Rule Bill had passed through the
Commons twice and been rejected twice by the Lords. In the middle
of the month the Cabinet met to discuss the Prime Minister's meetings with Bonar Law about Ulster. The Leader of the Opposition
had agreed to accept Home Rule with an Ulster exclusion, but
the Cabinet were against any sort of half measures. They felt the
Liberal rank and file were strongly opposed to compromise and in
any case they did not take the threat of civil war too seriously. As a
basis for discussion, Lloyd George proposed that Ulster should be
excluded only for a definitive term of six years with the provision
for automatic inclusion at the expiration of that time. This would
hopefully eradicate the likelihood of violence and give the British
people the chance to air their voice by way of two general elections. Grey played a full part in the Irish debate. On 27 October he
spoke in Berwick and suggested a concession of 'Home Rule within
Home Rule', whereby Ulster would receive a substantial degree of
autonomy under a united Irish Parliament. He told his constituents
that the Irish question was only one part of an overall problem. In
his opinion, devolution was needed for the whole United Kingdom.
He was on the platform again at Alnwick on 18 December, when he
repeated his former suggestion that the Ulster Unionists could be
protected by Home Rule within Home Rule. He then poured cold
water on the idea of launching into a cross-party conference on the
Irish question 'unless there is a real disposition to settle matters'.

At a Cabinet meeting on 25 November, Grey advised his colleagues that Bonar Law should be told that although permanent exclusion was a non-starter, the government would accept either of the above alternatives. Here is yet another example of Grey working closely in agreement with Lloyd George. Indeed, on 5 December the Chancellor wrote to Grey, 'I thought your treatment of Ulster last night was simply first rate.' Christmas saw deadlock, with all parties in complete disagreement. To make matters worse, the King was becoming increasingly nervous about the constitutional implications of the Ulster impasse and was suggesting an early general election, which was the last thing Asquith wanted. The King had no grudge against the Prime Minister and had no wish to see the back of the Liberals, he merely felt an election would clear the air on the issue. The downside of this was the possible departure of Grey from the Foreign Office, and that, he felt, would be a disaster for Europe.

Spring: Friendly Relations with Germany

Although Grey's star was firmly in the ascendant, the new year saw Cabinet morale at rock bottom, with the Irish problem, suffragette violence and the bad publicity caused by the Marconi affair. The last thing they needed was another row over the naval estimates. Needless to say, this is exactly what Winston Churchill delivered. The First Lord had presented his estimates to Cabinet before Christmas. They totalled almost £51 million, some £3 million up on the previous year. Shocked colleagues immediately demanded a cutback in the construction of capital ships from four to two, as the Admiralty was also committed to an expensive programme of converting many warships from coal to oil fuel. Lloyd George faced either a deficit or a tax increase, neither of which he relished in front of a 1915 election. He needed to conjure up a successful Budget.

On 1 January the Chancellor put the cat amongst the pigeons by giving an interview to the *Daily Chronicle* in which he censured 'the overwhelming extravagance in our expenditure on armaments' and called for 'a bold and independent step to reduce armaments'. The Chancellor was facing a deficit of £10 million, which led the *Chronicle* to castigate Churchill for having 'a ducal disregard for mundane considerations of money'. The Tory press screamed for blood. They referred to the radicals as 'The Suicide Club' and called for a two-keels-to-one policy as against the existing margin of a 60 per cent majority in Dreadnoughts over Germany alone. While most of the Liberal Party would have agreed with the Chancellor, it was considered poor form to go public on such a delicate issue when it was still being discussed in Cabinet. Grey was furious with Lloyd George, thinking it just another example of the Welshman's untrustworthy behaviour. He was also worried that the 'reckless utterance of the Chancellor' might upset the French, who had just introduced a three-year national service term in response to a change in policy by Germany. Grey was not the only Cabinet minister to become disillusioned. Charles Hobhouse referred to Lloyd George in his diary as 'fickle, ungrateful and untruthful'. Luckily, the interview produced the opposite effect to that intended. Cabinet colleagues rallied around Churchill. No one wanted resignations and a possible dissolution before the Home Rule Bill was on the statute book.

In this instance, Grey was probably reasonably relaxed about a possible cutback in the estimates. He recognised that the German government, who were presently anxious to be on good terms with Britain, were in an uncharacteristically peaceful mood and in the back of his mind he was well aware that excessive spending on defence was holding back plans for social reform. Churchill, of course, won the day and on 11 February the Cabinet agreed to the naval estimates. Lloyd George accepted the situation as he wanted concessions made to Ulster and badly needed the First Lord's support. But in the end Churchill admitted his achievement was 'largely due to the unswerving patience of the Prime Minister and to his solid, silent support'. The Cabinet had been split 40–60 against any rise in the naval estimates. Grey, Haldane, Seely, Harcourt and Birrell supported Churchill while McKenna, Runciman, Simon, Pease, Hobhouse, McKinnon Wood and Herbert Samuel sided with Lloyd George. The Prime Minister, Crewe, Burns, Morley, Beauchamp and Buxton remained neutral and would eventually tip the scales in favour of the Admiralty.

Grey made a speech to the Manchester Chamber of Commerce on 3 February insisting there was no split in Cabinet and hinting that the naval estimates vote would be settled 'in favour of those who upheld national and imperial security'. The *Pall Mall Gazette* (which had recently returned to its Conservative leanings after a period of Liberalism) reported on his speech:

> Sir Edward Grey is one of those who belong to their country rather than their party. It is with him as with the Pitts, Canning and Palmerston; no one thinks of him belonging to this party or that but as British Foreign Secretary, the cool adroit statesman, in whose hands through difficult years have resorted the issues of peace and war for his country and, more than once, for the world.

The First Lord finally presented his naval estimates to the House in a two-and-a-half-hour speech on 17 March. Grey would doubtless have agreed with his words on that occasion: 'Our diplomacy depends in great part for its effectiveness upon our naval position, and our naval strength is the one great balancing force which we can contribute to our own safety and to the peace of the world.'

Progress over Ireland was proving much less successful. At a meeting between Asquith and the Irish Nationalist leader John Redmond, on 2 February, the Prime Minister suggested that Ulster might have special powers of veto in the Irish Parliament. Three days later Redmond turned down the proposal and Asquith immediately updated the King at Windsor. The King for his part warned his Prime Minister that if no common ground was forthcoming, many army officers might resign their commissions rather than fight against the Ulstermen. On 2 March Asquith had another meeting with Redmond, who initially agreed to the concession of a three-year exclusion for Ulster and then reluctantly moved to six. On 9 March, during the second reading of the Home Rule Bill, the Prime Minister announced the concession agreed with Redmond. Unfortunately, the Unionist leader Sir Edward Carson then produced a characteristically memorable parliamentary performance, declaring, 'we do not want a sentence of death with a stay of execution for six years', and brought proceedings to a halt.

At Westminster there was concern that Carson's Ulster Volunteers, who were already thought to outnumber the regular troops in Ireland, might move against arms depots in the province. There was also much criticism in Parliament of the government's military preparations for Ulster. It was decided to send in troop reinforcements and Churchill provocatively ordered the 3rd Battle Squadron to the Ulster coastline without the Prime Minister's knowledge. On 20 March, the King's worst fears were realised. Sixty officers at the Curragh cavalry barracks with Anglo-Irish connections refused to accept orders in the event of having to move against the Ulster Volunteers. Most of the blame must be attributed to General Sir Arthur Paget, the Commander-in-Chief in Ireland, who was too alarmist. Having been briefed by the War Office in London, he returned to Dublin and spoke to his officers of the whole country 'being ablaze in twenty-four hours'. Jack Seely, the Secretary of State for War, and Sir John French, the Adjutant General, both blundered by giving their officers a written assurance that troops would not be used to enforce Home Rule on Ulster. Both subsequently resigned. The government had to have the right to use the Army to coerce Ulster if it so required.

Grey was absolutely furious at the way a section of junior officers had played politics. To his way of thinking, they had been used by the opposition to influence the government. He wrote to Katherine Lyttelton on 3 April,

> I am inwardly boiling with indignation at this stupid prejudiced attempt to dictate policy to us and break us, for that is what it is really; and if it goes on I shall be for taking the hottest election, upon who is to govern the country, that has ever been in our time.

On 31 March Grey deputised for the Prime Minister in an impassioned debate on the Irish issue, when the government offered to drop all charges against members of the Army in 'an individual or collective capacity'. On the last day of the debate, 6 April, the Whips were caused great embarrassment as no senior member of the government was in the Commons. There was a chorus of cries of 'Where's Grey?' followed up by shouts of 'Gone fishing'.

Sure enough, the Foreign Secretary was not going to miss his annual spring salmon fishing holiday, this time on the Spey, where he was on the lookout for ospreys and crested tits. On 12 April he wrote again to Katherine:

> I am staying in a farmhouse with Eddy Glenconner and Jack Tennant and fish all day waist deep in the Spey. I hope you are having pleasant days too – as far as it is possible for a woman to have pleasant days – and that in your next Incarnation you will be born a man and like salmon fishing.

Six days later he was back at Fallodon and wrote, 'I return to London tomorrow night and then alas! to Paris.' He was obviously dreading the impending royal visit to France.

The government won the vote with a diminished majority of eighty. Meanwhile, the political temperature in Ireland continued to rise as 26,000 rifles together with ammunition were illegally shipped into Larne on 24 April and distributed to the Ulster Volunteers. At the same time the National Volunteers were becoming stronger by the day and by the end of June they would outnumber Carson's force. It was imperative that procedural progress in the Commons should be made as soon as possible. On 5 May Asquith met Bonar Law and Carson at Edwin Montagu's house in Queen Anne's Gate. It was decided that any changes to the Home Rule Bill should be contained in an Amending Bill, although there was still no agreement as to its content. The Home Rule Bill itself was finally pushed through the Commons by Whitsun.

In mid-April Grey accompanied the King to Paris. The tenth anniversary of the Entente Cordiale was suitably chosen to mark the King's first state visit and the Foreign Secretary's first trip abroad. Even though Grey disliked the idea of formal overseas engagements, the two men would have been at ease in each other's company. Harold Nicolson in his biography of George V describes the King's relations with Grey as being 'of unclouded mutual confidence'. Although Henry Newbolt found the King most uncharismatic – 'such a queer, shy, abrupt moving and small headed person' – Grey was always impressed by King George's modesty, patriotism and sense of public duty. If the King had a favourite minister, it was undoubtedly Edward Grey. He found it easy to relate to Grey. The Foreign Secretary was from the landed classes and a true countryman who was as accomplished a fisherman as the King was a shot. Unlike Churchill, Lloyd George and those shrill radicals, Grey was calm, reliable, dignified and unambitious. A few months before the visit, Lord Esher made a diary entry to the effect that the King dreaded the prospect of losing the Liberal government as a result of a general election caused by Home Rule. While he would have regretted the departure of Asquith, he was even more reluctant to see Grey leave the Foreign Office, regarding him as 'the most respected figure in the European diplomatic world and impossible to replace'.

One can imagine the mirth and merriment at the Foreign Office when this most English of Englishmen finally made his first official overseas journey. Tyrrell accompanied Grey and told his chief that when he was overheard greeting President Poincaré at lunch, Paul Cambon remarked, 'The Holy Ghost has descended on Sir Edward Grey and he now talks French.' The pair were warmly received and the visit must have been something of a personal triumph for the Foreign Secretary, who had spent the last decade strengthening the Entente. Grey certainly seemed to enjoy himself, writing in his autobiography, 'It was bright without being hot, the glorious brightness of summer combined with the freshness of spring. The horse-chestnuts in Paris were in flower; the foliage was a tender green ... All the people seemed happy and at ease ... The reception was most friendly.'

There is a moving passage in Grey's autobiography covering the state procession at Vincennes. He was seated next to the Premier, M. Doumergue, in a coach behind the King and President Poincaré. He could not help noticing the cavalry escort: two troopers, one thickset and swarthy, probably a countryman, and the other slender, frail and sensitive, possibly an artist or a poet. They were two very different human beings. Each of these young men were at an age when life should have been developing in different ways but they had found themselves trained to kill or be killed in defence of their country. He writes, 'It brought home to me as I have never felt it before, what conscription meant. I thought of what it was in the affairs of mankind that made conscription necessary; how unnatural it was that all this should be accepted and taken as a matter of course.' His observations demonstrate the anathema of conscription to a Liberal government, although it was generally accepted on the Continent. On his 'day off' Grey arranged a sightseeing tour of the City. The King's private secretary, Ponsonby, wrote to Bertie, 'The Foreign Secretary has not the slightest intention of going to the Races, as in the first place Racing bores him stiff, and in the second, he is anxious to see the sights of Paris.'

On his last morning Grey and Bertie attended a meeting at the French Foreign Office. The Prime Minister was present and paid a tribute 'to the eminent qualities of Sir Edward Grey, a statesman as remarkable for his great lucidity of thought and his knowledge of affairs as for his high conception of right and justice'. Cambon confirmed that relations between the two countries were excellent but there was one special request. Would Britain consider military conversations with France's ally Russia? They could take a form similar to those with France and would have the benefit of making Russia feel more involved. Relations with Russia were very strained at the time owing to their forward policy in Persia and there were worries at the Foreign Office that the Anglo-Russian Convention would have to be renegotiated. The Russians themselves were looking at ways of strengthening the Triple Entente and with the encouragement of Nicolson sought some sort of firm alliance with Britain.

Sazonov knew Parliament would never consent to an alliance, so he decided to pursue the idea of a naval agreement. At the outset Grey thought it wise to inform the Russians of the structure of Britain's military conversations with the French and on 19 May the Russian ambassador Benckendorff, together with Cambon, met Grey at the Foreign Office where, having obtained Cabinet consent in advance, the Foreign Secretary agreed to the initiation of naval conversations between Britain and Russia. There was absolutely no obligation on the part of Britain to side with Russia in a European war and, in Grey's words, 'the whole transaction was kept strictly within the limits laid down in the Cambon–Grey letters of November 1912'. As Grey saw it, the talks would have little strategic significance but, importantly, they would please the French. On the negative side there would be heated questions raised in Parliament when the news leaked out and, even worse, Germany's insecurity would intensify.

Should Grey have agreed to the naval conversations with Russia? His biographer, Trevelyan, thinks probably not. They caused more trouble for him in Berlin and Westminster than they were worth. Their reason was purely political, so shouldn't Grey have informed Parliament? As he found out to his cost after Agadir, the military conversations with France contained a subtle political element. They were certainly of vital strategic importance in the event of war but they also played a significant role in strengthening the Entente. Count Max Montgelas, the German historian, gives the whole issue as yet another example of Grey deceiving Parliament. On 11 June Grey answered a question in the House on the subject of a naval agreement with Russia. He neither admitted nor denied that naval conversations had taken place, he merely reiterated that there were no binding agreements with Russia. Although he never concerned himself with strategic detail, he always felt such information should not be made public, writing in his autobiography, 'So long as Governments are compelled to contemplate the possibility of war, they are under a necessity to take precautionary measures, the object of which would be defeated if they were made public.' All this aside, surely Germany would view the naval proceedings with Russia as an affirmation of the Triple Entente and a further pointer to the fact that Britain was unlikely to remain neutral in a European war?

On his return from France at the end of April, Grey spent a weekend at Fallodon when he walked over to Doxford, the country home of his Cabinet colleague Walter Runciman. The Agriculture and Fisheries Secretary had just stocked his new lake with trout. He was away on holiday in Greece and Grey wrote to him,

> On Friday I went to your lake, partly to fish it, partly to eat my lunch there and partly to see how Doxford looked in your absence. I ate my lunch on the seat of the embankment of the lake. The breeze and ripple came towards me and an April sun soon made all the ripple sparkle: the air was rich with thrush and blackbird songs and several willow-wrens were singing in the young wood. They only arrive this month and I heard them on Friday for the first time this year. Do you know their song? It has a sort of pleading cadence and made me get very fond of it. But the bird is badly named, being neither a wren nor a frequenter of willows in general. Some swallows skimmed the water and I heard a pair of sandpipers. There was a sort of bright spring happiness that makes me feel not only the prospect of summer but the possibility of heaven in some other planet not so very unlike the earth but with no cities and no influenza and where the foxes are not carnivorous (for my collection of waterfowl that I began thirty years ago is being destroyed and broken up by a fox). In about an hour I landed nineteen trout. I returned all but five because I did not want to deplete your stock.

Grey spent his usual Whitsun holiday alone at The Cottage, enjoying the blossom and birdsong of the 'golden time'. He was having
more and more trouble in tying his flies and had recently experienced difficulties in seeing the ball when playing squash. After his
holiday he consulted two Harley Street specialists who diagnosed
severe degeneration of the retina in both eyes. He was informed
there was no cure and unless he took a complete rest from work
he would be all but blind within a few years. He, of course, continued with his work and his consultant, Sir William Lister, wrote to
Trevelyan after the war, 'The condition he had would invariably
have got worse but he voluntarily gave up the chance of imped-
ing the deterioration and in this way I feel he gave his sight in the
service of his country.' Grey was wearing strong magnifying glasses
when at work and had even given up smoking. He wrote to Mrs
Creighton in February, 'There have been very few days when I have
not had a strong smoke after every meal and now for nearly five
weeks I have not had a whiff.' His smoking aside, the irony was
that he was only fifty-two and had kept himself in good shape over
nearly ten gruelling years at the Foreign Office. He gave up his real
tennis soon after taking office but continued to play squash. He
fished and bicycled at The Cottage and walked a good deal when
at Fallodon.

In London he was lucky enough to have St James's Park within a
few minutes' walk from the Foreign Office. The Foreign Secretary
needed no encouragement to cross the road. Not only did he have
a wildfowl collection at Fallodon but he also had a similar facility
within a few hundred yards of his office. Many times during tedious
ambassadorial meetings in the summer months his thoughts must
have been transported back to the Itchen by the loud whinnying
trills of the dabchick from the park lake. He writes in *The Charm
of Birds*,

One pretty way the dabchick has with its young was shown to me on
the water in St James's Park. When I was first in Office and kept in
London from 1892–95, I made the acquaintance with the man who

then looked after the waterfowl and who lived across the isthmus that is opposite the windows of the Foreign Office. At his cottage I used to call in the season to hear news of the breeding waterfowl, and he would show me various nests. One morning as he was taking me round the island he pointed out a dabchick's nest attached to some willow branches that hung into the water. When we came near he exclaimed that the eggs must have hatched since he had seen the nest earlier in the morning, for the nest was now empty. We heard a curious little noise on the water and looking out beyond the branches saw the parent dabchick and her lately-hatched young ones. Being suspicious of us, she had warned the young and now presented her body to them as they sat in the water. Instinct told them what was required: each bird got onto the back of the old one and was there covered by her folded wings. When all the young were mounted, the parent swam away with her whole family, compact, concealed and safe.

After the hiccup of the Russian naval conversations, relations with Berlin quickly settled down with the signing of the Baghdad Railway Treaty in late May. In fact, Trevelyan writes that Jagow told Goschen he was well satisfied with Grey's speech in the Commons about the Russian talks. The German Foreign Minister stated that 'he had so much confidence in Grey's loyalty and straightforward- ness that his mind was now completely at rest'. Agreement over the Baghdad Railway brought to a close ten years of prevaricating. It was a most satisfactory conclusion as both sides secured equal advantages. Britain agreed not to oppose the project on the condi- tion that her important commercial rights in the Persian Gulf were not threatened. Germany accepted that the terminus would be at Basra and Britain would have control over the Mesopotamian rivers. In addition, the Germans agreed not to build any port or railway terminus on the Gulf without Britain's approval. Largely thanks to the Foreign Secretary, in the months before the outbreak of war, relations between Germany and Britain were better than they had been at any time over the last decade.

On 1 June Colonel House and the US ambassador, James Gerard, lunched with the Kaiser at the Imperial Palace in Potsdam. Dressed in their tailcoats and surrounded by the Emperor and his military entourage, they looked, according to the Kaiser, 'like two black crows against a colourful background'. President Wilson had given his close friend House a free hand in European foreign affairs. In his own rather straightforward way the Colonel was determined to bring Britain and Germany together to pledge non-aggression and restrict armaments. He believed that the two countries were unnecessarily frightened of each other and, with the United States acting as mediator, the waters could be smoothed. In his quest, he had two willing collaborators in Walter Page and Grey's private secretary, William Tyrrell. Tyrrell asked House to explain to the Kaiser that in light of the growing Anglo-American friendship it would be sensible for Germany both to cease expanding her Navy and to curtail militarism. Page was dreaming of a narrower English-speaking entente between the US, Britain and her colonies but House was determined to bring Germany and France into the net. The Colonel would soon be frustrated in his mission both by the war party in Berlin and by the assassinations in Sarajevo.

House arrived in Britain towards the end of the first week in June having spent a few days in Paris on the way, where he found no one wanted to talk about foreign affairs. The nation was obsessed with the Caillaux trial. Joseph Caillaux was a left-wing ex-Prime Minister of France who had recently attacked the government's decision to extend the period of military national service from two years to three. He then became the object of a smear campaign by France's most powerful journalist, Gaston Calmette, who was threatening to publish some of Caillaux's love letters to his former mistress, Henrietta. The lady in question, who had by now become Caillaux's second wife, walked into Calmette's office and shot him six times. The country became riveted by the trial and as a result was completely unaware of the imminent crisis developing in Europe. It

then took House the best part of a week before he could meet the
Foreign Secretary in London. It appeared that Britain had distrac-
tions of her own what with a looming civil war in Ireland, suffragette
violence ... and Ascot week. Finally, on 17 June, Tyrrell and Grey
hosted a lunch at the Foreign Office where House debriefed his
English friends on his visit to Germany. The Colonel was genuinely
worried about the general atmosphere in Berlin. He described it as
'militarism run stark mad', writing to President Wilson that 'unless
someone acting for you can bring about a different understanding,
there is some day going to be an awful cataclysm'. He was sure no
one in Europe could perform such a role: 'There was just too much
hatred and too many jealousies.'

House told Grey that, aside from the Kaiser, Tirpitz was the most
forceful man in Germany and he harboured a dislike of the British
that bordered on hatred. Tirpitz had great respect for the Royal
Navy but disliked the patronising attitude many Britons displayed
towards the German Navy. As a young officer visiting Gibraltar,
he overheard an English woman say of his ship's crew, 'Don't they
look just like sailors?' When Tirpitz asked her how they should look,
she replied, 'But you are not a sea-going nation.' When arms limitation was discussed, Tirpitz vigorously defended 'the necessity
of Germany maintaining the highest possible order of naval and
military organisation'. He found the suggestion of arms limitation
distasteful and suggested that the best way to maintain peace was
to put fear into the hearts of one's enemies. Tirpitz spoke of the
anti-German feeling in the USA, telling House he thought that
Admiral Mahon's articles on naval matters always contained a pro-
British leaning. For his part, the Colonel replied that Britain would
not tolerate indefinitely Germany's ever-increasing naval strength
as well as her vast well-trained army. He thought the Kaiser was
a totally different character from the Admiral. The Emperor was
well-mannered, charming and a good listener. He was less prejudiced and belligerent than Tirpitz. He spoke kindly of Britain and
described the Americans, Germans and British as kindred peoples
who should draw closer together. This gave House cause for

optimism, but was the Kaiser actually in the saddle in Berlin? The old chestnuts of the Navy and the Triple Entente were raised. The Kaiser declared that 'the folly of Britain lay in forming an alliance with the Latins and the Slavs' and complained of 'encircle-ment': 'the bayonets of Europe are directed at us'. House stated that the key to an understanding with Britain was a slowdown in naval construction. The Kaiser replied that Germany needed a large Navy to protect her commerce and also to confront the combined fleets of Russia and France. The old impasse remained stubbornly in place.

House informed the Foreign Secretary that his brief stay in Paris was a non-event. He was delighted to say he did not find the war spirit dominant as it was in Berlin and was convinced that French statesmen no longer dreamt of revenge and the recovery of Alsace-Lorraine. The French were only too well aware that the German population exceeded theirs by 50 per cent; all they wanted was to be left unmolested by threats of German militarism. As lunch progressed, the Americans began to speculate on possible reasons why Britain should go to war with Germany. The great Anglophile, Walter Page, stated that German militarism was *the* crime of the last fifty years and that Germany had been working towards a major European confrontation for a generation. He said prophetically to Grey, 'In my opinion you will be dragged into war by your treaty obligations to Belgium.' House then interjected,

> I have no doubt in my mind that the real purpose of Britain's entry into such a war will be quite different. The stress of the European situation has compelled her to side with France and Russia against the Central Powers. You will fight because Germany insists on having a dominant army and a dominant Navy, something that Britain cannot tolerate in safety to herself.

Both men were correct. It was in Britain's national interests to fight, yet the German invasion of Belgium provided the unifying reason for war.

House decided that the next round of discussions should take place at Kiel between the Kaiser, Grey and himself as mediator. Grey had misgivings and certainly did not want to upset France and Russia, but he did promise to discuss the idea with the Prime Minister. The Kaiser was also sceptical, remarking to House in Berlin that as Grey had never travelled to Germany, and only once to the Continent, he was not in a position to understand the Germans. As it was, the news from Sarajevo would postpone the unlikely event indefinitely. Cecil Spring-Rice puts forward the interesting theory that House's peace mission to Germany might actually have stimulated war by alarming the war party in Berlin and Vienna. He wrote to House,

They probably knew why you were in Berlin, and what you said to the Kaiser. They also knew why you went to England and they undoubtedly knew the contents of your letter to the Kaiser. That, together with Sir Edward Grey's conversations with the German Ambassador in London, alarmed the war party and they took advantage of the Archduke's murder and the Kaiser's absence to precipitate matters ... believing it was now or never.

The July Crisis

On 28 June the Archduke Franz Ferdinand, the heir to the Austro-Hungarian throne, and his wife were assassinated in Sarajevo by a group of amateur Young Bosnian terrorists. Although there was no proven direct link to Serbia, the Young Bosnians believed in a Greater Serbia and received encouragement, logistical assistance and in all likelihood their weapons from 'the mother country'. Austria-Hungary's powerful Chief of General Staff, Conrad von Hötzendorf, backed by a weak foreign minister, Leopold Berchtold, vowed revenge. The former was a fatalist and had for some time thought it would be necessary for Austria-Hungary to fight a preventive war against Serbia to preserve its status as a great power. The assassinations provided an excellent excuse for taking action. So began 'the July crisis', which led to war during the first few days of August.

These highly charged few weeks represented the climax of Sir Edward Grey's political career. For a full week after the Austrian ultimatum to Serbia he was the only statesman in Europe who strove for peace. In the course of the month, as events overwhelmed him, he surrendered to the inevitable and concentrated on preparing the Cabinet for war. Grey was not alone in his feeling of helplessness. There was a general resignation throughout Europe that things were out of control. Austria was set on crushing Serbia, the Russians, at third time of asking, were determined to give the Serbs total support, and a militarist Germany was bent on a preventive war against Russia.

Few people were expecting problems to emanate from the assassinations. On 29 June Grey reviewed his foreign policy in a debate in the House. He paid a tribute to Archduke Ferdinand and told the House that the political consequences of the crime could not yet be fully foreseen. Perhaps with his developing relationship with America in mind, he then gave President Wilson full credit for the Panama Tolls Bill. The *Pall Mall Gazette* summarised the Foreign Secretary's long tenure in office: 'Sir Edward Grey is handling our foreign affairs as well as any living statesman could handle them. Any other might do very much worse.' Praise indeed from a Conservative newspaper on the eve of the war.

Everything seemed calm on the Continent. The British press were more interested in the death of Joseph Chamberlain on 2 July than that of the Archduke. It is interesting to note that on 6 July Nicolson wrote to the British ambassador in Vienna stating that, apart from Albania, 'We have no very urgent and pressing question to preoccupy us in the rest of Europe.' However, Monday 6 July became a significant date in the countdown to war. It was the day that Austria received her 'blank cheque' from Germany granting her permission to send to Serbia whatever kind of ultimatum she desired. On 2 July Emperor Franz Joseph had written to the Kaiser asking for Germany's support over the coming confrontation with Serbia. Any action against Serbia had to be managed in a way that didn't provoke Russia, in order to prevent an international crisis. The Austrians believed that Russia could be deterred from intervening if at the outset they had received a promise of German support.

Conrad von Hötzendorf and the young Foreign Office hawks in Vienna knew that a South Slav unification was inevitable. Hew Strachan in his book *The First World War* states, 'To avoid diplomatic humiliation a showdown with Serbia could not be avoided. As it turned out it was the Austrian General Staff, not the German, for whom war was a strategic necessity.' The Foreign Minister's hawkish envoy, Count Alexander Hoyos, delivered the message to the Austrian ambassador in Berlin and on 5 July the German Crown

Council met to consider its contents. It was quickly decided to encourage Austria-Hungary in its policy of constructing a Balkan League, consisting of Bulgaria, Turkey and Romania, to counter the Serbs. Most significantly Germany agreed to provide her support in the event of any Russian intervention if the Austrians decided to invade Serbia. The next day the Kaiser presented his 'blank cheque' to Hoyos, who immediately returned to Vienna. The Kaiser then boarded the royal yacht, the *Hohenzollern*, for a three-week cruise off the Norwegian coast.

Also on 6 July, a worried Lichnowsky called on Grey at the Foreign Office in London and warned him of sinister events taking place in Vienna and Berlin. The Germans at this stage may well not have realised the seriousness of their actions and probably calculated that even if the Austrians did invade Serbia, the conflict could be localised with a halt at Belgrade. Grey, meanwhile, fresh from his success in the Balkan wars, was hoping to work with Berlin to urge caution on the Austrians. Lichnowsky pleaded with him to do the same with the Russians. It appears that at this time the Foreign Secretary was working on his own. He kept the Prime Minister, Churchill and Haldane informed of events but strangely did not allow Nicolson into his confidence; a chasm had opened up between the two men as a result of Nicolson's rigid pro-Ulster views.

On 7 July the Austro-Hungarian Council of Ministers met to consider their next step. It was decided to present Serbia with a set of stiff demands which, if not satisfied, would justify military action. Crowe and Nicolson soon realised that a major crisis was brewing. Both wanted an open declaration of support for the Entente partners. Nicolson particularly wanted to tie Britain closer to Russia, whereas Crowe argued that without British support the French would be defeated. Crowe was also convinced that if Germany took control of the Channel ports it would only be a matter of time before she turned on Britain. Grey refused to be drawn and on 9 July gave Lichnowsky his usual line: Britain wished to preserve an absolutely free hand, so that in the event of Continental complications she might be able to act according to her own judgement. He did however reassure the German ambassador how, both directly and indirectly, through Cambon, he had done his best to persuade the Russians to take a calm and considered view of any Austrian action with Serbia over the assassinations. Public sympathy in London at this time lay on the side of Austria-Hungary.

At 6 p.m. on 23 July, Vienna broke her self-imposed silence and delivered the ultimatum to Serbia. There were two good reasons for the delay, the most important being that most of the Army was on leave to assist with the harvest and they would not be able to return before the 22nd. Secondly, Berchtold had cunningly delayed the ultimatum to coincide with the departure of the French President from St Petersburg. Poincaré and his Prime Minister, Vivani, had been conducting a state visit to Russia and were not expected to be back in Paris until the 29th. Berchtold decided to wait until the French statesmen were at sea before delivering the ultimatum. He calculated, wrongly as it turned out, that if the allies were unable to consult each other, French support for Russia in the event of a Balkan confrontation might not be forthcoming. In the background, German leaders repeated their backing for Austria and urged swift action; they were convinced they had to support their ally if she was to survive as a great power. Ironically, a few hours before the ultimatum was delivered, Lloyd George had risen in the House of Commons to urge economy on naval spending as relations with Germany were better than they had been for years.

When the Amending Bill on Home Rule was introduced to Parliament at the end of June, it was, not unexpectedly, butchered by the Lords. The extreme Unionist demands were incorporated. All nine counties of Ulster were to be excluded and without a time limit. At the suggestion of the King, it was then agreed to hold an all-party conference on the Irish problem at Buckingham Palace. The conference met on 21 July and ended three days later in complete failure. There was no agreement on the geographical boundaries. In Churchill's memorable words, 'It lost itself in the muddy by-ways of Fermanagh and Tyrone.' The Cabinet was briefed on 24 July. Just as proceedings were about to terminate, Grey made a statement on the recently announced Austrian ultimatum to Serbia. Ministers were aghast. There was a deathly silence in the Cabinet room.

The Foreign Secretary told his colleagues that in his opinion the Austrian proposals represented 'the most formidable document ever addressed by one state to another that was independent' while the *Westminster Gazette* described the ultimatum as 'so urgent and severe that compliance with its demands is extremely difficult to an independent state which though relatively small has a high opinion of its own importance'. The ultimatum demanded, quite reasonably, that the Serbian government condemn anti-Austrian propaganda in addition to bringing those Serbian citizens involved in the plot to justice. What was much more difficult for the Serbs to swallow was the Austro-Hungarian insistence that their own representatives were to be involved in the 'clean-up' operation on Serbian soil. To cap it all, the Serbs were given only forty-eight hours to agree to all the points. It was obvious that the Austrians were trying to force the issue.

Everybody at this stage, except perhaps Bethmann Hollweg and the Kaiser, knew that a war between Austria-Hungary and Serbia could not be localised. Grey had relayed his strong feelings on this to Lichnowsky on the 24th. The next day the ambassador wrote to Jagow in Berlin, 'As for the "localisation of the conflict", you will surely admit that such a thing, if it should come to a passage of arms with Serbia, belongs in the category of pious wishes.' After receiving Grey's briefing at the Cabinet meeting Asquith wrote to Venetia Stanley,

> This means, almost inevitably, that Russia will come on the scene in defence of Serbia and in defiance of Austria; and if so, it is difficult both for Germany and France to refrain from lending a hand to one side or the other. So that we are within measurable, or imaginable, distance of a real Armageddon.

No one in the Triple Entente saw Austria-Hungary as an independent player. Ever since Algeciras, Austria-Hungary had been tarred

with the same aggressive brush as Germany. Russia was convinced
Germany was seeking a preventive war and saw the Austrian ultimatum as linked to that goal.

While the British Cabinet was being briefed by Grey on the ultimatum, a nervous Czar called a meeting of his Council of Ministers
in St Petersburg. The Council took the same line as Grey in asking
Vienna to postpone its deadline by forty-eight hours. At the same
time they pleaded with Belgrade to be conciliatory. Of much
greater significance, they then ordered the four military districts of
Kiev, Odessa, Moscow and Kazan to prepare for mobilisation. The
key military district of Warsaw, part of Russia's western defences
against Germany, was left dormant. The decision to call for partial
mobilisation preceded Serbia's reply to the Austrian ultimatum,
thus presenting the Serbs with a blank cheque of their own. By now
it was clear to all that those in Berlin and Vienna who thought that
vigorous action by Austria supported by Germany would deter the
Russians were seriously mistaken. The Russian decision accelerated
the process of mobilisation across Europe. Russia had to mobilise
fast if it was to aid Serbia but Germany had to mobilise faster still.
Germany's whole war strategy was based on taking advantage of
Russia's sluggish mobilisation procedures to knock out France in
the first few weeks and then to let loose the full weight of their
armies on the eastern front.

Grey first fully realised the seriousness of the situation on the 23rd
when the Austrian ambassador, Count Mensdorff, gave him some
idea of the Austrian demands and the tight 48-hour deadline in
which Serbia had to reply. He had known at once that Russia could
not allow Serbia to be crushed. As a result he spent most of the next
two days working on the feasibility of some sort of joint mediation
similar to that successfully executed during the Balkan crisis. He
also urged Austria to extend her two-day time limit over the ultimatum. Events moved on rapidly over the weekend of 25–26 July.
On the Saturday, Churchill gave orders to keep the First Fleet
together at Portland following exercises, as a warning to the central
powers. Vessels of the Second Fleet were to remain at their home

ports in proximity to their reserve crews. Having already lost half his precious weekend, Grey decided to set out for the Hampshire cottage on Saturday evening, leaving Nicolson in charge at the Foreign Office on the Sunday. Robbins writes in his biography, 'With unflappable sang-froid, or culpable disregard of duty, Sir Edward disappeared to his fishing cottage to think on things.'

He must have arrived late as there is no entry in his fishing diary for the weekend. Grey never fished on a Sunday. His last comment before the outbreak of war and indeed the final one for the year was on 18 July: 'Caught three fish and put back six between ¾ lb and 1 lb.' On Sunday afternoon the Foreign Secretary was summoned back to London. The Austrians had decided that the Serb reply to the ultimatum was inadequate. The Serbs had cleverly accepted all the terms except the one emasculating their sovereignty, thereby appearing to be the injured party and winning widespread sympathy. Grey and Nicolson, encouraged by their success in the Balkan wars, gave a last throw of the dice and sent out formal invitations for a conference of the four disinterested powers. All the major players, after all, were still at their desks in London. On the Saturday Lichnowsky had sent a telegram to Jagow at the German Foreign Office:

> I should like to call your attention once more to the importance of Grey's proposal of a mediation by the Four Powers between Austria and Russia. I see in this proposal the only possibility of avoiding a World War ... If we decline, Grey, too, will make no further move ... I do not think that England could possibly remain disinterested should France be drawn in. Once more urgently advise the acceptance of the English proposal and that this be announced in Vienna and St Petersburg.

It was met with a deafening silence.

On Monday 27 July, with the morning papers proclaiming that 'Sir Edward Grey has acted wisely and promptly in proposing the renewal of the Conference of London', Germany turned down

Grey's suggestion, insisting that the dispute concerned only Russia and Austria and should be settled by them alone. It had become clear by now that Berlin was paying little attention to the pleadings of her ambassador in London. France and Italy had promptly agreed to a conference. Russia, initially sceptical, also fell into line, having quickly realised that direct talks with Vienna were going nowhere. Needless to say, confusing signals were coming from the Germans. That same morning, Lichnowsky had assured Grey that his government accepted 'in principle' the idea of a conference to mediate between Russia and Austria. Later in the day, Sir Edward Goschen, Britain's ambassador in Berlin, telegraphed the Foreign Secretary:

> Secretary of State says that the conference you suggest would practically amount to court of arbitration and could not, in his opinion, be called together except at the request of Austria and Russia. He could not, therefore, fall in with your suggestion, desirous though he was to cooperate for the maintenance of peace.

Grey had done his best, as recognised by the *Pall Mall Gazette*:

> The courage, promptitude and clear sight of Sir Edward Grey in proposing the Four Power Conference has unmistakably eased the situation in Europe. The Foreign Secretary realised at once the exceptional position in which this country stands for offering good offices and was prompt to take occasion by the hand. He has deserved and must receive the support of all parties.

At a Cabinet meeting in the afternoon, Grey raised for the first time the question of Britain's possible entry into war if France was attacked by Germany. Not unexpectedly there was fierce opposition to any British involvement, although Churchill's decision to keep the fleet together was approved by Cabinet. In the background the Tory press were crying out for the government to make a public statement in support of France, stating that honour, loyalty and national interest alike demanded that Britain should assist the French against German aggression. The press insisted that two factors were essential to Britain's safety: the preservation of the independence of France and the Low Countries, and no one nation being in a position to dominate Continental Europe. Both were essential to Britain's control of the Channel, on which depended her national life.

Before Grey left the Foreign Office that evening, he asked the German ambassador to pass on to Berlin an urgent request for Germany to persuade the Austrian government to accept the Serbian reply. The Kaiser arrived back in Potsdam from his cruise on the same day (Monday 27 July) and, according to Asquith, on hearing of Grey's suggestion of a conference, wrote, 'This is superfluous, as Austria has already made matters clear to Russia, and Grey can propose nothing else. I am not intervening – only if Austria expressly asks me to, which is not probable. One does not consult others in matters of honour and vital questions.' Lichnowsky sent three detailed cables to his Foreign Office in Berlin on the 27th. He reiterated two important points. Firstly, that everybody in Britain was convinced that Berlin was the key to peace. Grey had willingly complied with German requests to recommend moderation at St Petersburg. It was now up to Berlin to restrain Vienna. Secondly, the ambassador informed his superiors in Berlin that Britain felt that the current crisis was rapidly developing into a trial of strength between the Triple Alliance and the Triple Entente. If Austria did use the present crisis as an opportunity to crush Serbia, he felt that Britain would ally herself unconditionally to France and Russia. It appeared that no one in Berlin was listening to the German ambassador in London.

The Kaiser, having read Serbia's accommodating reply to the ultimatum, had second thoughts and urged the Austrians to halt their advance in Belgrade and so hopefully localise the war. The Kaiser's sudden caution conflicted with the aggressive demands of Moltke, who wanted instant Austrian mobilisation. This begs the question, who was actually in charge in Berlin at this time? One of the problems that Grey faced in his long term in office was putting his finger on who exactly controlled Germany's foreign policy. There never seemed to be any continuity. Was it the Kaiser, the Foreign Secretary, the Chancellor or the military? Before hostilities began between Austria and Serbia on the 28th, it was Bethmann Hollweg. After this date, when events spiralled out of control with Russian mobilisation, it was Moltke and the military. Hew Strachan writes in *The First World War*:

> The lack of either continuity or clarity in German policy was in itself a reflection of the absence of a guiding authority. Supreme command was in name vested in the Kaiser but by 1914 Wilhelm no longer commanded the respect that his titles demanded: the monarchy was venerated as an institution rather than in the personality of its incumbent. Technically, the reconciliation of the views of the Chancellor and the Chief of General Staff in late July was Wilhelm's responsibility. In practice the management of the crisis reflected the dominance of first one personality, Bethmann-Hollweg, and then another, Moltke. Bethmann had guided events up to 28 July by acting in isolation: he had encouraged the Kaiser to put to sea and Moltke to continue his cure. When the Kaiser returned, the belligerence he had expressed to Hoyos on 5 July had softened. Wilhelm, however, was caught in his own self-image, that of steely warrior, and thus his reluctance to fight was compromised by his relationship with his military entourage and, above all, with Moltke.

On Tuesday 28 July, when Austria began to shell Belgrade, she declined direct discussions with St Petersburg to end the conflict, stating her quarrel with Serbia was 'purely an Austrian concern'. The following day Russia formally ordered the mobilisation of her four southern districts. By now events were running out of control. There was no effort by Germany to check their ally. Lichnowsky wrote, 'It needed but a hint from Berlin to induce Count Berchtold to be satisfied with a diplomatic success. But the hint was not given. On the contrary, the war was hurried on.' Grey then cabled Berlin to say he was ready to accept any form of mediation that they suggested: 'The whole idea of mediation or mediating influence was ready to be put into operation by any method that Germany could suggest, if mine was not acceptable'.

Bethmann Hollweg continued to blame Grey for not curbing St Petersburg, so the Foreign Secretary's drive for peace came to nothing. Grey's proposals for mediation had been passed on to Vienna but without German endorsement. This suited Berchtold, who by now was well and truly on the warpath. Bethmann had passed on the Kaiser's request to 'halt in Belgrade' but Berchtold had postponed replying. Grey still refused to accept defeat. He welcomed the possibility that a 'halt in Belgrade' might provide enough time for further negotiation between Austria and Russia. In reality, by the afternoon of Wednesday 29 July, Grey's hopes for a diplomatic solution had all but vanished. Although the Germans had passed on to the Austrians Grey's view that Serbia's reply was sufficiently conciliatory to serve as a basis for negotiation, the Foreign Secretary was told uncompromisingly that events had now moved on too rapidly for further discussions. He also during that day had to turn his attention to his Cabinet colleagues at home.

Discussions in Cabinet had proved as frustrating for Grey as those with the Triple Alliance. The Cabinet was split down the middle, so it was impossible for Grey to secure a promise of support for France, let alone Russia. The 'peace party' consisted of ten members, of which Lloyd George was the most influential. Others included Morley, Burns, Simon, Harcourt, Beauchamp, Samuel and Runciman. To a man they were determined not to be drawn into a war over a Balkan question. Even the Conservative Party was not united in favour of war at this stage. Bonar Law did, however, inform Grey on the morning of Wednesday 29 July that a German invasion of Belgium would swing the party unanimously in favour of intervention. Meeting that morning, the Cabinet did take some positive action. It decided to initiate a 'precautionary period' whereby all naval, military and colonial stations were put on a state of readiness. In addition, Churchill received the

necessary authority to move the battle fleet from Portland to Scapa
Flow. Owing to his Cabinet straitjacket, a frustrated Grey was
simply not in a position to give the Entente partners the support
they required. He told Cambon that public opinion would not
allow Britain to go to war over a Balkan issue. He then used his
standard reply: It was a case that we would have to consider ... We
were free from engagements and we should have to decide what
British interests required us to do. Maybe he was quite relieved. In
the back of his mind he always worried that a firm British commitment might encourage France and Russia to take an unnecessarily
aggressive stance towards Germany.

Even as late as 29 July, elements of the press were still hopeful that
the Austro-Hungarian war with Serbia could be localised. They felt
that diplomacy could win the day and that Russian fears should be
allayed if the Austrians agreed not to annex any Serbian territory
or threaten her sovereignty. The British Foreign Secretary was seen
as the one man who could best deliver peace, the *Westminster Gazette*
leader column stating,

> It is an advantage to us and it has at other times been an advantage
> to all Europe that we have at the Foreign Office a man of long expe-
> rience who inspires confidence in all camps by his disinterestedness
> and straight dealing. Let us, if we can, reap the full benefit of that
> circumstance in the crisis.

The following day, as rumours of Russian mobilisation filtered
through, the same newspaper still clung to the faint hope that Grey
could localise the quarrel through negotiation or by conference:

> We are confident that Sir Edward Grey will exhaust every conceiv-
> able opportunity of keeping the peace by these means and in the
> meantime we strongly deprecate any attempt to tie his hands and
> commit him in advance to a particular course of action. His one
> chance of helping Europe in this emergency is to stand uncompro-
> mised as a mediator between the camps.

Grey must have been hoping that the French ambassador had read the morning papers.

When Grey returned to the Foreign Office from Downing Street, a highly excited Lichnowsky was waiting for yet another interview. He had been meticulously conveying Grey's concerns to Berlin and working hard for mediation between the powers. Grey liked the ambassador and respected his efforts for peace. He did, however, feel it necessary to warn him that he should not be misled by the friendly tone of their discussions into believing that Britain would stand aside if Germany and France went to war. Although Grey had consistently refused to turn the Entente with France into an alliance, he had on many occasions warned the Germans that in all likelihood Britain would side with the French if the latter were attacked from across the Rhine. The Foreign Secretary's views had been reiterated to Berlin by no lesser beings than Haldane and the King. Hew Strachan writes in his book,

> Over the previous decade the German General Staff had entertained little doubt that, in the event of war in the west, the British would stand by the French. Clear statements to that effect had been made to Germany by Haldane in 1911 and by Grey in 1912: the implications were there in the Anglo-French staff talks and in Lloyd George's Mansion House speech. Bethmann had not shared the Anglophobia of Tirpitz but the British naval talks with the Russians had convinced him of the rightness of the assumption that Britain would not be neutral in the event of a European War.

As if his day had not been fraught enough, just before close of business the Foreign Secretary received from Germany a bid for British neutrality in the event of war with France. Bethmann Hollweg promised to maintain French territorial integrity in the event of a German victory but made no mention of the French colonies. Grey was overcome with a feeling of despair and disgust. It meant that the German Chancellor now thought that war was imminent. This desperate bid by Germany was an affront to Grey's dignity, in Douglas Hurd's words, 'as an Englishman, a Member of Parliament, an educated gentleman, a Liberal and a Grey'. The Foreign Secretary declined the German request by return, despatching the following telegram to Goschen in Berlin:

> It would be a disgrace to us to make this bargain with Germany at the expense of France – a disgrace from which the good name of this country would never recover. The Chancellor also, in effect, asks us to bargain away whatever obligation or interest we have as regards the neutrality of Belgium. We could not entertain that bargain either.

He wrote later in his autobiography, 'Did Bethmann Hollweg not understand, could he not see he was making an offer that would dishonour us if we agreed to it? What sort of man was it that could not see that? Or did he think so badly of us that he thought we should not see it?' Grey was not the only member of the Foreign Office disgusted by Bethmann Hollweg's request. Eyre Crowe wrote in a minute,

> The only comment that need be made on these astounding propos-als is that they reflect discredit on the statesman who makes them …
> It is clear that Germany is practically determined to go to war and that the one restraining influence so far has been the fear of England joining in the defence of France and Belgium.

Yet much to the annoyance of France, Russia and his Foreign Office officials, Grey refused to commit himself. His Entente partners were convinced that if Britain came out in the open with her support, there would be no war.

One other issue was discussed by a divided Cabinet on Wednesday 29 July, and that was Britain's obligations to Belgium. The vital interests of Britain and France touched each other in Belgium. The flat countryside provided an invading army with a direct route to Paris, and Antwerp was famously described by Napoleon as 'a pistol pointed at the heart of England'. Belgium was a subject of massive significance, as in a few days' time the German ultimatum and the Belgian reply would enable Grey to carry the Cabinet with him into a European war. Keith Robbins wrote of this same Cabinet meeting, 'There was a great deal of hesitation about Britain's duty and some were still of the opinion that it would be possible to consider the defence of France quite separately from an Austro-Russian war.' It was indeed not a Cabinet at peace with itself. Britain, France and Germany had guaranteed Belgium's independence by a treaty of 1839. The 'peace party' in the Cabinet wondered whether a single guaranteeing state had to take action under the treaty if other signatories refused to comply with their obligations. The Cabinet tamely agreed that if the matter arose it should be treated as a decision 'of policy rather than legal obligation'.

The Cabinet's deliberations several days before the outbreak of war make a mockery of Lloyd George's criticisms of Grey in his *War Memoirs*:

> Had Grey warned Germany in time of the point at which Britain would declare war – and wage it with her whole strength – the issue would have been different. I know it has been said he was hampered by divisions in Cabinet. On one question, however, there was no difference of opinion – the invasion of Belgium. He could at any stage of the negotiations have secured substantial unanimity amongst his colleagues on that point.

Would half the Cabinet have agreed to such a warning being given to Germany at the 24 July Cabinet meeting following Austria's ultimatum to Serbia? Churchill certainly did not think so. Douglas Hurd also disagrees with Lloyd George's claim that the Germans would not have invaded Belgium if they knew Britain would enter the war, writing in *Choose Your Weapons*, 'We now know that the German General Staff accepted that the Schlieffen Plan might lead to war with Britain, but judged that the arrival in France of a small British Expeditionary Force would not alter the fundamental military calculation.' Lord Crewe, the only Cabinet minister whom Asquith ranked higher than Grey, wrote to Trevelyan in May 1936, having had much time to reflect on events:

I have never been one of those who are able to believe for a
moment that the German attitude would have been modified by
knowledge that we should resist the invasion of Belgium. Surely
those who think so are confusing their knowledge of the power which
we and the whole Empire were able to exert in the four years of
war with the actual resources which everybody, including ourselves,
knew to be available in August 1914.

On Thursday 30 July, the Foreign Secretary, against overwhelming odds, was still working for peace. There appeared to be a brief
window of détente as Germany encouraged Austria back to the
negotiating table with Russia. Had Lichnowsky's warnings to Berlin
that Britain might well not stand aside struck a chord? It was more
likely that Germany was concerned to shift any blame for starting a war onto Russia's shoulders. Germany had to be seen to be
doing her bit for peace. Sazonov suggested Russia might halt all
military preparations if Austria agreed to ditch any points that
violated Serbian sovereignty in the ultimatum. Grey immediately
put forward a variation on the Russian proposal. He suggested that
if the Austrian advance halted in Belgrade then the powers would
explore ways in which Serbia could satisfy Austria without impairing Serbian independence.

It was all to no avail, as the following day Russia and Austria
mobilised against each other. It was probably at this time that the
military party in Berlin gained the ascendancy over an unstable
Kaiser and his Chancellor, neither of whom, now faced with the
immediate prospect of war, wanted it. The military was most
anxious that full mobilisation should be enacted immediately
otherwise Germany would lose her advantage. Speed was of the
essence in a two-front war. Grey has been criticised for failing to
prevent Russian mobilisation but after Germany had turned down
his proposal for a conference it was very difficult for him to put
pressure on Russia. Everyone knew that Russia was less prepared
for war than Germany and she would then have asked for British
support in the event of war, which Grey would have been unable

to give. The French also played their part on 30 July, urging the Russians to proceed with caution and not to give the Germans a pretext for mobilisation. The French leaders had only arrived back from Russia the day before so had been unable to participate in the peace process to a meaningful extent. They didn't, however, waste much time in reminding Britain of the exchange of letters between Grey and Cambon in 1912 in which it was agreed that if war threatened the two countries would discuss joint preparations.

At Westminster there was good news. The Ulster crisis had been averted and all eyes could now focus on Europe. Both sides in Ireland, anxious to prove their patriotism, had suggested to the Prime Minister that the Amending Bill be postponed until the European crisis was over. It was unanimously agreed that the Home Rule Bill itself should become law but that its operation would be suspended until a new Amending Bill was passed. This magnanimous gesture by Redmond would lead Grey to famously tell the House, 'Ireland becomes the one bright spot in this dark scene' and in the words of Asquith, 'Britain would now be able to speak and to act with the authority of an undivided nation.'

On Friday 31 July, news of Russian mobilisation and German *Kriegsgefahr* (imminence of war) effectively put an end to any kind of continental diplomacy. There were rumours that Germany had been secretly mobilising for the past week. Across the Continent there was a struggle taking place between ministers who were keen to continue with diplomatic initiatives and General Staffs who were desperate for full mobilisation; the latter were winning. In Britain the Prime Minister had stated the country had no interests of its own directly at stake and the press called for Grey to continue in his role as a moderating influence, but events were running out of control. Although Grey had warned Lichnowsky in the morning that Britain would probably be drawn into war on the side of France, the Foreign Secretary still refused to give any commitment to Cambon. Grey's hands were tied by a split Cabinet. Meanwhile at the Foreign Office, Grey's officials were becoming increasingly concerned, Crowe noting, 'The theory that England cannot engage in a big war means her abdication as an independent state.' If there was fear in the Foreign Office that Britain would not stand by France, it was worse in the City, where it was thought that war was inevitable. The Bank of England doubled its discount rate to 8 per cent and the Stock Exchange closed its doors.

While the drama unfolded, the direct conversations initiated by Grey between Vienna and St Petersburg continued in a gentlemanly fashion. There also appeared to be a ray of hope for peace as the Czar and the Kaiser exchanged telegrams of cousinly goodwill. Then suddenly the German government sent an ultimatum to Russia stating that unless mobilisation was halted within twelve hours, she herself would declare a general mobilisation. The German Chancellor followed up with a telegram of remarkable effrontery to Paris, enquiring if French neutrality would be observed in a war with Russia. Grey was not surprised; he had been there before. At the end of an exhausting day the Foreign Secretary took himself to dine at Downing Street with the Prime Minister, Margot writing in her diary, 'I watched Grey's handsome face and felt the healing freshness of his simple and convinced personality. He is a man who "thinks to scale" as Lord Moulton once said to me about Rufus Reading, and obliges one to reconstruct the meaning of the word Genius.'

The Cabinet meeting on 31 July continued to emphasise Britain's freedom of action, yet it was increasingly clear that Belgium was becoming the paramount issue. It was imperative that Asquith kept the Cabinet together. During the Agadir crisis the 'peace party' was weakened by the defection of Churchill and Lloyd George. By the summer of 1914 the influential Chancellor of the Exchequer was firmly back in the anti-war camp. The Prime Minister knew that Lloyd George held the key to a united Cabinet and everything would pivot on Belgian neutrality. After the Cabinet meeting, Grey telegraphed the French and German governments asking them for assurances that they would respect the neutrality of Belgium. France replied positively by return while Berlin maintained its silence. An increasingly hysterical Lichnowsky was quite obviously disgusted by Berlin's lack of action and cabled his Foreign Office yet another warning:

> The reply of the German Government with regard to the neutral-ity of Belgium is a matter of profound regret, as Belgian neutrality affects feeling in this country. If Germany could see her way to give the same positive reply as that which has been given by France, it would materially contribute to relieve anxiety and tension here, while on the other hand if there were a violation of the neutral-ity of Belgium by one combatant while the other respected it, it would be extremely difficult to restrain public feeling in this country.

On Saturday 1 August, Belgium announced she would 'defend her neutrality'. The following day Germany would go one better than she did with France and Britain in seeking Belgium's neutrality. She presented Belgium with an ultimatum offering friendly neutrality as long as the German armies could have free passage through Belgian territory en route to the French border.

This ham-fisted action by the German government is what swung Lloyd George and the majority of the waverers into Grey's camp. After many hours of debate the Cabinet finally agreed that any violation of Belgian neutrality by Germany would be regarded as a *casus belli*. As late as Saturday 1 August, Asquith was writing to Venetia Stanley that the bulk of the party were for staying out of war. He described the position of some of his key colleagues:

> Morley and Simon are on what may be called the *Manchester Guardian* tack, that we should declare now and at once that in no circumstances will we take a hand. Lloyd George – all for peace – is more sensible and statesmanlike, for keeping the position open. Grey, of course, that if an out and out uncompromising policy of non-intervention at all costs is adopted, he will go. Winston very bellicose and demanding immediate mobilisation. Haldane diffuse ... and nebulous.

He concludes by saying, 'Of course, if Grey should go I should go and the whole thing would break up.'

As Germany declared war on Russia, France ordered general mobilisation on Saturday 1 August yet Grey still doggedly refused to admit that Britain had an obligation to help the French. A fraught Nicolson shouted at his chief, 'You will render us a byword amongst nations.' At least the Foreign Secretary was consistent. He stated to Lichnowsky that Saturday morning: 'Our hands are still free. Our attitude will be determined largely – I will not say entirely – by the question of Belgium which appeals very strongly to public opinion here.' However, the Cabinet were slowly becoming more bellicose and at the Sunday afternoon meeting – by which time the Germans had invaded Luxembourg – a compromise was reached with the 'peace party' whereby the German fleet would not be allowed into the Channel to attack the French northern and western coasts. Grey gave the French ambassador the following statement:

> I am authorised to give an assurance that if the German Fleet comes into the Channel or through the North Sea to undertake hostile operations against the French coasts or shipping, the British Fleet will give all the protection in its power. This assurance is, of course, subject to the policy of His Majesty's Government receiving the support of Parliament, and must not be taken as binding His Majesty's Government to take any action until the above contingency of action by the German Fleet takes place.

Asquith had secured the agreement of all his colleagues on this decision with the exception of Burns and Morley. The radicals had reluctantly fallen into line because they viewed any intervention as a limited naval affair rather than a full continental commitment.

At this late stage, very few were willing to send the Expeditionary Force to France. Even the *Westminster Gazette*, the only Liberal newspaper that was not non-interventionist, heralded on 3 August, 'We cannot throw this army into the seething cauldron of the European struggle.' The newspaper felt the Army should be held back for home defence and commitments to the Empire whereas the Navy should be used to full effect against Germany. The *Westminster Gazette* did, however, like Kitchener, have the vision to recognise that the war would be a long one. Russia with her vast territories and peasant population could postpone peace for an indefinite period. As the newspaper was being printed, hundreds of trains were moving German troops to their battle stations along the Belgian border. The invasion began in earnest the next day. The German General Staff had won the day against an ineffectual Kaiser and his lame Chancellor. A last-ditch effort had been made by the Kaiser to turn his armies eastwards and thereby secure Britain's neutrality. But it was too late – the momentum of mobilisation was too great and the General Staff's strategy was set in stone. The German legions would wheel through central Belgium, outflank the French, take Paris within forty days and then turn eastwards against Russia.

In London, the Cabinet met at 11 a.m. on Monday 3 August. During the night, King George had received an appeal from King Albert imploring Britain to uphold her treaty obligations and defend Belgium's sovereignty. The Cabinet agreed to mobilisation of the British Fleet and Army, but no decision was taken to send the Expeditionary Force to France, which would have to wait on the outcome of Grey's speech to the Commons that same afternoon. Grey had started work on his speech the night before and at Cabinet he reviewed the main points with his colleagues. He returned to the Foreign Office at lunchtime to polish his notes, only to be confronted by a distraught German ambassador desperate to know the contents of his speech. Although pressed for time, Grey felt it was his duty to see him. Nobody had worked harder to avert war than Lichnowsky. The ambassador pleaded with Grey not to make Belgian neutrality a condition of war. Grey replied that in an hour's time the whole world would be privy to Britain's stance but he could say nothing in advance of his Commons statement. This would be the last time the two statesmen met at the Foreign Office.

The Great War

The British Expeditionary Force, considered by many to be 'the best-trained, best organised and best-equipped British Army that ever went forth to war', began its well-practised embarkation on 9 August. Transports departed from Southampton and Portsmouth at intervals of ten minutes to receive a hero's welcome on arrival at Rouen, Boulogne and Le Havre. The Navy had successfully blocked off the Channel and not a single ship was lost. There were, however, ominous signs of disagreement to come on the War Council. The stubborn side of the new Secretary of State for War, Lord Kitchener, quickly came to the fore, as he insisted two divisions be held back for defence of the homeland, meaning that only four divisions and the cavalry were sent at the outset. He also wanted his forces to concentrate seventy miles further back, at Amiens rather than at Maubeuge where he expected they would bear the full force of the invading German armies. He was afraid that his small army would be annihilated, leaving no hardcore of professional soldiers to train the seventy or so divisions that he foresaw as necessary to fight a long war.

In 1914 the size of the German Army was formidable. It totalled over 4 million trained and well-armed men with superior artillery and machine guns. The process of mobilisation was well practised and the necessity for swift rail access to the Belgian and French frontiers had been foreseen. Germany's military superiority was to an extent balanced by Britain's naval supremacy, which at this time allowed it to have control of the seas and later to deny the shipment of food and supplies to Germany. In the early stages, however, the success or failure of the land forces was to be all-important.

On the outbreak of war, the German advance into Belgium started well enough but it was quickly obvious that the Schlieffen Plan was not turning out as expected. On 7 August the Germans took the strategic railway city of Liège and then moved on across the Belgian plains towards Paris at the impressive rate of twenty miles a day. On 23 August the right wing of the German Army, von Kluck's First, met the British Expeditionary Force, which was dug in along the Mons-Conde canal. The Germans thought they were facing machine guns but in reality the deadly firepower came from highly trained British infantrymen firing fifteen rounds a minute from their Lee Enfield rifles. Hugely outnumbered, the British started a long orderly retreat parallel to the French Fifth Army. The German advance soon became stretched. Two-thirds of their lorries broke down, the 84,000 horses needed to transport the artillery and supplies lacked the necessary fodder to keep going, the Belgians had sabotaged the railways, the troops suffered from exhaustion in the August heat and poor communications meant that the German Generals had little idea of the whereabouts of their neighbouring armies. On top of this, the right flank was weakened by the removal of troops to other arenas: two army corps to deal with Belgian resistance, particularly around Antwerp, and two more to keep the Russians at bay in East Prussia. Schlieffen had always insisted his plan would only work if the right number of troops were used in the first place.

The French Fifth Army checked the Germans again at Guise and on 26 August the British put up some stiff resistance at Le Cateau. On 3 September, von Kluck abandoned the idea of enveloping Paris and moved his army to the east of the city to keep in touch with Bülow's army to his left. The Battle of the Marne, one of the decisive actions of the war, began on 5 September when the German armies were finally checked and Paris saved. Joffre decided to move fresh troops in by railway and attack von Kluck's flank. In addition, reinforcements were famously rushed in from the capital by a fleet of taxis with their meters running. Low on ammunition, Moltke ordered his armies to retreat. Between 9–14 September, the Germans retreated from the Marne and took up secure positions along a chalk ridge above the river Aisne. The scene was now set for a four-year stalemate.

Denied Paris, the German Army surprisingly failed to move to take the Channel ports. If it had done so, access to France from England and the ability to send reinforcements and supplies would have been greatly impeded and the conduct of the war danger-ously changed. The Germans' later attempts to reach Boulogne and Calais were successfully defended by the British and they penetrated no further than Ypres.

Military strategy might not have been Grey's strong point but he had played his part to the full in August 1914. His speech to the House of Commons on 3 August was the zenith of a long, unbro-ken period in office and arguably one that no one else could have accomplished. It had carried a united country into war and solved the ministerial crisis. Simon and Beauchamp decided to remain in the Cabinet, with only Morley and Burns tendering their resig-nations. On his death *The Times* obituary columnist referred to Grey as 'the diplomatist thanks to whom the pure and honourable character of our motives for the most momentous decision for one hundred years was made generally manifest'. Most people looked on the speech as a personal triumph but Margot Asquith saw it very differently, describing it as 'the culminating point of a personal tragedy', for Grey as Foreign Secretary had 'one supreme purpose – to keep the peace of Europe – and he had failed'. The following afternoon, Grey was visited by Walter Page, the American ambas-sador, and with tears in his eyes said to his good friend, 'If Germany fails to reverse its assault on Belgium's neutrality we will be at war at midnight. The efforts of a lifetime go for nothing. I feel like a man who has wasted his life.'

After the outbreak of war, Grey was a changed character,
perhaps even a broken man. He was a man of peace and, although
no one blamed him at the time, his policy had failed. He became
irritable and melancholic with his officials. Asquith wrote to
Venetia Stanley in October of Grey in Cabinet: 'E. Grey (as usual)
was most dolorous and despondent.' His confidence had been
drained and his eyesight was deteriorating by the day. It would
perhaps have been better if he had resigned after the outbreak of
war and retired on a high. He remained in office primarily out
of loyalty to Asquith, although he could not be blamed if in the
back of his mind was the worry that resignation would be seen
as an open declaration of personal failure. He was simply not a
Foreign Secretary for a wartime environment. He had no interest
in military matters, as witnessed by his lack of interest in the military conversations, and if there was little opportunity for European
diplomacy he was not ruthless enough for cloak-and-dagger
Balkan diplomacy.

Grey had worked himself into the ground in his quest for peace
and when the Blue Book was published on 5 August, presenting
the correspondence between the Foreign Secretary and his ambassador in Berlin, the Liberal and Tory press alike felt his actions
had been vindicated. Referring to the German bid for British
neutrality on 29 July when the Germans promised to respect the
territorial integrity of France in the event of the latter's defeat,
with no mention, of course, of her colonies, the Conservative *Pall
Mall Gazette* commented, 'Sir Edward Grey added to his own fair
reputation and to the honour of his country by the high-minded
attitude which he took towards the sinister and subtle proposals
which reached him from Berlin.'

The war was not slow to visit Grey at a personal level. On 4
September he wrote to Katherine Lyttelton:

I have just heard that my nephew is reported missing and we may
never know what has happened to him. He may have been wounded
and left in the field when our force was retiring before those fearful

odds at Mons. It is terrible for my sister. I have just telephoned and written to her.

And then again on 17 September, 'I have just heard that my brother Charlie has been wounded fighting Germans in East Africa. He is doing well in hospital but they have amputated his left arm above the elbow.' Things looked up in early October, however, when he learnt that Cecil Graves was a prisoner of war. Charlie made a quick recovery and Grey wrote to Katherine with his usual sense of humour, 'My brother takes his remaining arm back to his regiment soon in East Africa.'

Grey's relationship with Pamela, in particular, would have provided him with great solace at this stressful time. The fact that the Glenconners' London house was only a few minutes' walk from the Foreign Office would have allowed him to unwind after long hours at his desk. Emma Tennant writes in *Strangers*,

> Pamela stands as silent as her daughter and away from her, so she can look down the street and see Edward Grey come up from Birdcage Walk. An hour without the cares of the Foreign Office … He has troubles enough, in this war which has taken seven young men from Eddy's family and as many again from Pamela's own; she sees him, as he walks elegantly along, in the guise of a figure painted in brush-strokes on a Cretan vase: the Minotaur of War lurks in the labyrinth as he weaves his way through cab horses and motor cars to the woman he loves.

There is ample evidence at this time that their long-standing love affair was known in the highest circles. On 29 September Asquith wrote to Venetia Stanley, 'Edward Grey came to see me today to talk over the military situation. He is in better spirits than he was and Margot elicited from him at tea time that our Pamela was arriving to take part in his weekly rest cure!' Again on 9 October he wrote, 'Edward Grey and Winston dined here last night; it is impossible to imagine a greater contrast. Pamela Glenconner who sat next to me kept a watchful eye on Grey', and on 29 November, 'Meanwhile Edward Grey is taking Sunday off, he left on Friday, I need not say for Wilsford and Haldane is in charge for a couple of days at the Foreign Office.'

❦

The role of the Foreign Office was greatly diminished in the early years of the war, during which it played a secondary role to the considerations of the military. Eyre Crowe and George Clark presided over a new War Department at the Foreign Office which resulted from a merger of the old Western and Eastern Departments. Although the Cabinet met almost daily at the beginning of the war, Kitchener and Churchill led on matters of war, with the Committee of Imperial Defence no longer of importance. Asquith set up a Council of War in the autumn consisting of Kitchener, Churchill, Lloyd George, Grey and Balfour, its primary role being to review military strategy. After the formation of the coalition government in May 1915, the Council of War became the Dardanelles Committee, which contained a majority of Unionist members. Grey himself was still responsible for any major diplomatic initiatives at the beginning of the war, his efforts being dominated by an unsuc-cessful search for allies in Constantinople and the Balkan states. However, his major concern remained the continuation of good relations with Washington, which were immediately compromised by the economic blockade of Germany.

At this fraught time all was not well at the Foreign Office. A weak chief obviously undermined the ministry but there were also prob-lems with some of the key personnel. In the autumn of 1914 there was a clash between Grey and Crowe that put a halt to the latter's mete-oric career. Crowe understood the strength of Germany's civilian and military populations. He felt the government were not ener-getic enough in their prosecution of the war. Like Lloyd George, he was concerned that Grey worried too much about the formalities of diplomacy and international law. To complicate matters further,

Crowe, with his German connections, would in 1915 become a victim of the anti-German press campaign in a similar fashion to Haldane. Worse was still to come. Tyrrell, Grey's right-hand man, would have a complete breakdown in the spring of 1915 following the death of his son on the Western Front. There were problems at the top, too. Nicolson protested about Grey's fruitless Balkan diplomacy, particularly disapproving of his chief's efforts to bring Bulgaria into the war. He argued that only a substantial military victory would win them over. Finally, the return of Hardinge from India in the summer of 1916, to take over from Nicolson, hardly steadied the ship. He was too old-school for the wartime Foreign Office and, like Tyrrell, had suffered a personal loss at the front.

By the end of 1914 there was widespread discontent with the Asquith government's conduct of the war. There was no immediate victory on the battlefield and there were continued rumblings about Grey's unsuccessful Balkan diplomacy once he had failed to secure the neutrality of Turkey. The Foreign Secretary became increasingly depressed as the war dragged out; like many others he had wrongly thought it would be over in a matter of months. The impasse on the Western Front led to pressure for a diversion elsewhere and the War Council settled on a second front at the Dardanelles. The main objective was to secure a new supply route to Russia. The campaign was launched in February 1915 as a purely naval one, with a heavy bombardment by a large number of old but available battleships and a token armed force for land occupation. The naval action failed and a military action was hastily planned and executed in April. The disorganised campaign lasted eight months and also failed, with 220,000 casualties.

As usual Asquith and Grey had concurred with the views of the Generals. Kitchener had supported the venture, as it took the pressure off the Russians, and Churchill was desperate for naval glory. Fisher had remained unconvinced. Grey always accepted that he was not blameless for the venture, writing in *Twenty-Five Years*, 'There were diplomatic objections to the attempt to force the Dardanelles. I must take the responsibility for not having urged them beforehand as a reason for not undertaking the affair at all.' During the naval operation, a rift quickly developed at the Admiralty which in May 1915 resulted in Fisher's resignation and the fall of the Liberal government. The government's plight was not helped by a severe shell shortage on the Western Front which became evident at the Battle of Neuve Chapelle in early March.

Asquith's pragmatic loyalty to his colleagues was vividly demonstrated at this trying time. There were whispers abroad that Churchill was plotting to have Grey removed from the Foreign Office and replaced by Balfour. These rumours were quickly quashed by the Prime Minister, who had great respect for Grey's integrity and common sense. The Foreign Secretary was held in high esteem across the country and his resignation would have had a negative effect on public morale. Ironically, at this juncture a section of the Liberal Party was keen to see Grey take over from Asquith as Prime Minister. In reality, the Foreign Secretary's energy levels were no higher than those of his chief and what is more his eyesight was deteriorating daily. Asquith, however, was not to show anything like the same level of loyalty to his oldest political ally, Richard Burdon Haldane.

On 19 May, Bonar Law agreed to Asquith's reluctant proposal of a coalition government, the two main Liberal casualties being Churchill, who shouldered the blame for the Dardanelles, and Haldane. The Conservatives, backed by Lord Northcliffe's string of newspapers, had waged an iniquitous campaign against Haldane's supposed pro-German leanings. It was pure prejudice. No man had played a greater part in preparing Britain's military for war. Grey was disgusted and tried to intervene on his friend's behalf, but to no avail. He was determined to resign but Asquith yet again exerted moral blackmail on his Foreign Secretary, reminding him that the two of them were more responsible than anybody for taking Britain into war. They had to see it through together. Asquith was finished without Grey's support, so the Foreign Secretary yet again stayed out of loyalty to his old chief. The final make-up of the Cabinet consisted of twelve posts to Liberals, eight to Conservatives, one to Henderson of the Labour Party and one to Kitchener. Asquith pushed up those who he liked or trusted amongst the Unionists, such as Balfour, who was given the Admiralty and Curzon, who was made Lord Privy Seal. Lloyd George's energy was rewarded with Munitions while Bonar Law had to be content with an unsatisfactory post at the Colonial Office as Asquith gave McKenna the Exchequer. The Prime Minister was much more generous to Carson, who became Attorney-General.

On 25 May 1915 Grey aired his disgust at the hounding out of his oldest political ally in a letter to Asquith, referring to Haldane as 'one of the most patriotic, public spirited and devoted Ministers and most loyal colleagues who have ever sat in Cabinet'. He wrote angrily to the Prime Minister:

I think it should be known how extraordinarily unjust are the attacks that have been made on Haldane in certain quarters. I understand that he has been accused of intriguing with Germany behind the back of his colleagues; of weakening the Army, more particularly reducing the artillery; and of opposing or obstructing the sending of an Expeditionary Force to France. The true facts are that he has had no dealings with German authorities that were not undertaken either at the request or with the full knowledge and consent of his colleagues including particularly myself. It was due to the work done by him in the War Office that there was an Expeditionary Force of a certain strength and with a full equipment of artillery to be sent abroad ... and the Territorials and their organisation which has proved such an invaluable strength in this emergency, were created by him.

Asquith must have hated himself for the dismissal of Haldane and admitted to his daughter Violet that 'it was a shameful sacrifice' but one that had to be made as the Conservative opposition insisted on it. He thought of resigning himself but that would have meant a complete break-up of government, which would have sent out all the wrong messages at a most difficult stage in the war. He told his daughter, 'I have had the utmost difficulty in persuading Edward Grey to stay. He is, rightly, outraged.'

Grey must have also felt a sense of remorse about the removal of Churchill from the Admiralty; after all, he himself had meekly agreed to the Dardanelles venture. The two men had grown close since Churchill had been appointed First Lord and Grey was now a godfather to his son. If it was difficult for Grey to stay in office after the expulsion of two of his closest friends from Cabinet, then it must have been a nightmare for him to live with the guilt of taking his country into war as the casualty lists rolled in, especially as they included the names of many of his friends' sons. One can only assume he rationalised his predicament on the basis that war was inevitable and he had worked so hard for peace in the decade before its outbreak. In December 1916 Grey wrote to his old friend Rosebery about his long tenure as Foreign Secretary:

> They have been years of almost continuous storm and trouble at home and abroad, ending in the greatest war the world has ever known. As I look back and reflect, I cannot but think that tremendous forces have been at work in the world and that individuals have been helpless to arrest them. We could take an honourable part but we could not control the whirlwind.

Just because Grey could write poetically about the spring song of the curlew and was a disciple of Wordsworth, it did not follow that he was weak. He was made of sterner stuff than many give him credit for. A lonely childhood with responsibility thrust upon him at an early age, coupled with the experience of tragedy throughout his life, had moulded a tenacious character with an impressive ability to suppress the emotions, the latter proving a great asset in his distinguished parliamentary career. Violet Asquith writes a revealing piece in her book on Churchill, explaining how her father only came to realise how different his colleagues were in terms of character and temperament when the chips were down on the eve of war. The Prime Minister wrote in his diary:

> Winston who has a pictorial mind brimming with ideas is in tearing spirits at the prospect of war, which to me shows a lack of imagination. Crewe is wise and keeps an even keel; no one can force Grey's hand, he and I see eye to eye on the whole situation; Lloyd George is nervous; Haldane, Samuel and McKenna very sensible and loyal.

One can see why Asquith was happy to give Grey an almost free hand in running Britain's foreign policy. He had complete confidence in his Foreign Secretary's judgement and trusted him implicitly.

It was a stormy autumn for the new coalition government. Against a background of military setbacks both at the Dardanelles in the east and the three-week Battle of Loos on the Western Front, where the objectives were not attained and the casualties amounted to 50,000, the Prime Minister was faced with a compulsory service crisis and a spate of resignations. Throughout history, military conscription has been controversial because of conscientious objection to national service or because of political objection to service for an unpopular government or because it violates individual rights. Most Liberals believed that participation in war was a matter for the individual conscience and amongst the Non-Conformists, who mostly voted for the Liberals, the Quakers in particular harboured a historic rejection of war. The Military Service Act of 1916 did provide for exemption on conscientious grounds. Tribunals were set up by local authorities to deal with applications on a case-by-case basis, which often meant inequitable treatment.

The Conservatives, backed by Lloyd George, were calling for immediate conscription, which was to cause an irreparable split in the Liberal Party. Grey, along with McKenna and Runciman, thought its introduction would have adverse effects on domestic industry. On 19 October the Attorney-General Sir Edward Carson put a spanner in the works by resigning over his general dissatisfaction with the course of the war and his determination to influence the immediate introduction of conscription. Lloyd George was threatening resignation if Kitchener was not replaced at the War Office and for some time there had been constant briefings against Sir John French, commander of the Expeditionary Force, who was eventually replaced by Sir William Robertson in late November. The one crumb of comfort was the evacuation of the Gallipoli peninsula. It took place without loss just before Christmas, evoking the success of Sir John Moore's retreat to Corunna a century earlier.

As if this wasn't enough, Grey and three of his colleagues, Simon, McKenna and Runciman, were considering their positions over conscription. However, it wasn't just out of loyalty to Asquith and his Cabinet colleagues that Grey decided to remain in the coalition government. He had been Foreign Secretary for the best part of a decade and represented stability and continuity in British foreign policy. Britain's Entente partners would be shocked if he departed. Charles Hobhouse writes in a diary entry for 14 October 1915,

I went down for two weekends to Nuneham to shoot partridges, who were not shot last year and had really got too numerous. Our guns, varying from day to day, were J. Pease, Tennant, the Speaker, Fritz Ponsonby, the Duke of Marlborough, E. Grey and Edwin Montagu – we got 1,828 in four days. I then went to Blenheim where we shot 425 in one day with four other guns. E. Grey's position is that he loathes conscription only a little less than he does the Coalition but he fears the effect of a break-up on the Entente. His own withdrawal, the special hatred of Germany for him considered, would have a damaging result. Russia in particular would find it hard to get over. But for that consideration, he would resign tomorrow, as he told me himself, and set off on a walking tour from Land's End to John O'Groats, a six weeks' job which would be long enough for him to forget the war. One eye has a third of the vision, the other eye a half, obscured – and he is indescribably weary of it all.

Two things come immediately to mind. Firstly, one would have thought the other guns would not relish being drawn next to the Foreign Secretary with such poor eyesight, especially in a partridge drive, and secondly, how physically fit he must have been to have contemplated such a journey!

As witnessed by his shooting invitations, Grey did manage to enjoy a certain amount of leisure time during his war years in office. He was a senior citizen in the government and everyone knew his eyes were in a seriously poor condition. The oculist had told him his eyesight might be saved if he took time off work and wore dark glasses for eighteen months. Needless to say, he continued to push himself to the limit, but in 1915 did manage to spend three weeks at Fallodon in June, writing to Katherine Lyttelton, 'Having not seen Fallodon in June for fourteen years several things which we planted twenty or thirty years ago I have now seen for the first time in flower.' And again on 16 September he wrote, 'I had a few beautiful days at Glen which was all that I expected to be able to get and then came back in time for the worst Zeppelin raid which was hellish but not near me.' In August the following year he was back at Glen to shoot grouse, returning via Cloan to stay with Haldane.

There was a further blow awaiting Grey in the autumn. The Prime Minister had been keen to keep Churchill in the Cabinet following his removal from the Admiralty so had offered him the Duchy of Lancaster. Churchill accepted this appointment, as he felt that with a seat on the War Committee he still had a role to play in the direction of the war. When it was decided that this body was too large and he would have to go, Churchill decided to resign from the government and leave for the front. There was some respite for Grey on 30 November, when he attended the wedding of Violet Asquith to the Prime Minister's personal secretary, Maurice Bonham-Carter, at St Margaret's Westminster. Along with Balfour, Haldane and Kitchener, Grey was one of the signatories at the register. Although he didn't socialise with the Asquith family, this showed how close to them he really was. The bride described Grey at this time as her father's 'closest and most deeply valued friend and colleague'.

Matters came to a head in Cabinet at the end of December, when the conscription issue reached its uneasy climax. Asquith knew that the introduction of some form of conscription could not now be avoided. With the aid of Grey, a compromise was reached limiting conscription to single men, which had the effect of holding the Cabinet together, and the Military Service Bill passed safely through the House of Commons. At the same time, plans for a major offensive by the British and French armies were agreed between General Joffre and the British with the objective of achieving a decisive penetration of the German front on the river Somme. The preparations were hindered by a German attack on the French positions at Verdun on the river Meuse, but the offensive commenced on 1 July 1916 with the British taking a leading role. On the first day the British suffered 60,000 casualties. The battle, which lasted over four months, was generally indecisive and failed to achieve its objectives. The total British casualties numbered over 400,000.

Lloyd George spearheaded the post-war critics of Grey's wartime diplomacy. He claimed that the Foreign Secretary was an unimaginative conservative who stuck to old-fashioned methods of diplomacy. He suggested that roving ambassadors be sent into the field invested with full powers and thereby able to make independent decisions. He writes in his *War Memoirs*,

> Grey failed to keep Turkey, and afterwards Bulgaria, out of the war. His stiff and formal beckoning to them to cross over to our side could only provoke ridicule. There were many obvious expedients – including the sending of a special envoy to Turkey and Bulgaria who would be empowered to promise financial support – that he might

have employed to keep both or either out of the war. He resorted to none of them. These last two failures, which a more strenuous or resourceful Foreign Minister would have converted into success, prolonged the war by years and very nearly caused defeat of the Allies. His advice to Greece in 1914 not to join forces with the Allies was a calamity which cost us the Gallipoli Peninsula and conducted the overthrow of Serbia. He hesitated and fumbled in his negotiations to bring Italy into the war.

A few of Grey's Cabinet colleagues, led by Lloyd George and Churchill, wished to see the formation of a Balkan Federation, consisting of Bulgaria, Serbia, Greece and Romania, which would drive a wedge into Central Europe from the south-east. Bulgaria proved to be the stumbling block. Following the Balkan Wars she had lost territory to Serbia and Greece. Now she demanded concessions which her neighbours refused to concede, namely a port on the Aegean and claims in Macedonia. Bulgaria's decision to join the central powers in October 1915, together with her attack on Serbia, was a serious blow to Grey's wartime diplomacy and resulted in a barrage of criticism of his foreign policy in the House of Commons. Grey's long experience of the Balkan mentality led him to take a pessimistic view of such a grouping, but perhaps more importantly he was afraid of upsetting the Russians, who regarded Britain as trespassers in a region that was rightfully theirs. When the attack on the Dardanelles was being planned, so great was the Foreign Secretary's concern over Russian sensitivities in connection with control of the Straits that in March 1915 a secret treaty was signed granting Russia post-war possession of Constantinople. In return, the Persian 'neutral zone' was to fall under the British sphere of interest.

The promise of Constantinople no doubt perked up Russian spirits during a series of disastrous military defeats in 1915. It was these reverses, coupled with the British fiasco in the Dardanelles, which explain why Bulgaria attacked Serbia and entered the war on Germany's side in the autumn of 1915. The concept behind

a breakthrough to Constantinople was not just to relieve pressure
from the stalemate on the Western Front but also to induce Italy
and the Balkan States to join the Allies. Lord Robert Cecil wrote
to Trevelyan,

> We failed to prevent Bulgaria from joining our enemies and it is
> possible to criticise some aspects of British diplomacy in this connec-
> tion. But it is quite certain that the determining factor in Bulgarian
> action was the course of the war which was altogether outside the
> sphere of the Foreign Office. Bulgaria waited to see what would
> happen at Gallipoli and when we were defeated there she joined the
> Central Powers.

Grey can certainly be blamed for his negative approach to the value
of diplomacy during the war, yet military success was essential if
the Foreign Secretary was to make any progress in the Balkans. In
Twenty-Five Years, Grey writes,

> As far as Europe was concerned diplomacy in war counted for little.
> When it appeared to fail most, it was when the Allies were having
> military reverses; when it appeared to succeed, it was because the
> Allies were having military success or because the military achieve-
> ments of Germany were falling short of the expectations that had
> been formed of her invincibility.

As noted earlier, Lloyd George criticised Grey for failing to keep
Turkey out of the war. This is surely a harsh judgement, as in
the early months of the war Grey, to no avail, repeatedly offered
Turkey a formal guarantee of her territorial integrity. Grey was well
aware that Russia was anxious to avoid war with Turkey and consequently he ensured that both France and Russia participated in that
guarantee. His ambassador on the ground, Louis Mallet, worked
desperately to keep the Turkish government onside while all too
aware that the Allies were contemplating the eventual collapse and
break-up of the Turkish Empire. It was only going to be a matter

of time before Turkey joined the central powers. They had already signed a secret treaty with Germany – of which the Foreign Office professed ignorance – and there was a substantial German military mission in Constantinople together with a vocal pro-German element in the Turkish Cabinet. The Turks had earlier been pushed closer still to Germany by the Admiralty's insistence in July 1914 on seizing two Turkish Dreadnoughts being built in British yards. The Turks then refused to intern or repatriate the crews of the German warships, *Goeben* and *Breslau*, that had taken refuge in Constantinople. On 29 October Turkey showed her true colours. The two German ships, together with elements of the Turkish fleet, sailed out and bombarded Russian Black Sea ports; war was imminent. Up to this point Grey's policy had been to delay Turkey's entry into the war until all Indian troops were safely through the Suez Canal on their way to France, and to make it clear that if war materialised it came by the unprovoked aggression of Turkey. In both these objectives he was successful.

Lloyd George should have saved his criticism of the Foreign Secretary for the period after the outbreak of hostilities, when Grey was too slow to join 'the scramble for Turkey'. Grey always felt that Britain controlled as much territory worldwide as she could hold and advocated putting off distasteful decisions over partition until the war was won. With France panting for Syria and Russia for Constantinople, this attitude irritated his more forceful colleagues both at the Admiralty, who had their eyes firmly fixed on oil-rich Mesopotamia, and in the India Office, who were ever mindful of protecting Britain's position in the Persian Gulf. The post-war problems associated with Arab independence can all too easily be traced back to Grey's watch. He failed to exercise enough direct control over Middle Eastern policy, leaving vital decisions to Mark Sykes who was on Kitchener's staff, and the British High Commissioner in Cairo, Sir Henry McMahon. As a result, embarrassing 'grey areas' materialised in connection with British promises and intentions in Arabia. Marian Kent, in an essay on 'Asiatic Turkey 1914–1916', writes:

The wartime conduct of Britain's foreign policy towards Asiatic Turkey provides a sad epitaph for a man imbued with the highest personal ideals and probity. But it also shows that this man, Grey, in this area at least, was not the right man for the job. His policy was traditional, cautious, and short-sighted, producing a lack of incisiveness, of understanding and of effectiveness. War ended Grey's world and the man who could pursue traditional policy reasonably successfully in pre-war Asiatic Turkey presented a very different picture by the end of 1916.

Once again, it was Grey's sensitivities to the wishes of his Russian allies that led him to decline Greece's offer of military assistance to the Allied cause in August 1914. As we have seen, Lloyd George viewed the decision as 'a calamity which cost us the Gallipoli Peninsula'. In Grey's defence, there was a strong likelihood that Greece's attachment to the Allied cause would bring both Turkey and Bulgaria in on the side of the central powers and Sazonov was 'not going to allow Greece to drag Russia into a war with Turkey'. The Russians knew all too well that Greece had long since dreamt of taking Constantinople and consequently they vetoed any Greek military involvement over the Dardanelles campaign.

For the first six months of the war Grey was reasonably relaxed about Italy's stance on participation. Italy had been vacillating and arrogantly proposing her terms for entry on the Allied side. She was worried about the state of her military, the practicalities of fighting in the winter and the possibility of social unrest on the streets. In his very English way, Grey was adamant that Italy must first come to a firm decision and only then discuss terms. The Russians did not set much store by the Italian war machine. Italian intervention was, however, yet again valued for its effects on the Balkan states, particularly as Greek involvement had been vetoed by the Russians. The Dardanelles adventure brought a more urgent face to Italian participation and by 15 March the Cabinet had agreed to Italy's demands for a large section of the Dalmatian coast at Slav expense as the price for their participation. To give

effect to this, the parties signed the Treaty of London at the end
of April.

One area in which Grey's 'old-fashioned' style of diplomacy proved
invaluable to his country during the war years was that of the
blockade and its ramifications with the United States. The Royal
Navy had been stopping American and other neutral ships carrying contraband to countries such as Holland and Sweden from
where it could be channelled on into Germany. A serious disagreement broke out between America and Britain over the export of
cotton from the southern States to Europe, where it was used in the
munitions industry. Grey pointed out to the Americans that their
exports to neutral countries adjacent to Germany had increased
hugely since the beginning of the war and that these countries were
becoming bases of supply for the enemy. He saw little difference
between the British blockade of Germany and that of the Union's
blockade of the Confederate ports in the American Civil War.

Grey believed that the preservation of Anglo-American relations was his special domain. He fully comprehended the enormous
importance of the relationship. Aside from the necessity of nurturing American intervention, he well understood the pressure building
in America for a ban on the export of arms to the Allied countries.
While the central powers were self-sufficient in armament and munitions production, Britain had to rely on imports from across the
Atlantic. Another dispute arose at the height of the German submarine offensive when the Americans called for the disarming of British
merchantmen. Grey's tact, patience and conciliatory manner, coupled
with a sensitivity to American economic interests, invariably resulted
in a satisfactory compromise which shored up the budding relationship between the two countries. Grey writes in his autobiography:

In all this discussion of contraband with the United States we were
like men who had to steer a ship through an uncharted sea, perilous

with shoals and rocks and treacherous currents. We kept on our course and came safely through, but we had to feel our way and often to go slow.

The Germans took a different course and ended up on the rocks. Their unrestricted campaign of submarine warfare, introduced in the autumn of 1916, brought the United States into the war which in turn contributed to their defeat.

In July 1915 a weight was taken off Grey's shoulders when Lord Robert Cecil took over responsibility for the blockade. Cecil found it easier to take a more aggressive line with the Americans. In the autumn Grey magnanimously agreed to create a new department responsible for the blockade with its own Cabinet seat under the auspices of the Foreign Office. Cecil's appointment not unnaturally led to a further diminution of Grey's power. After the war Cecil wrote to Trevelyan as follows:

> During the war, by almost an accident, I became Grey's Under-Secretary and, until his resignation, worked very closely with him. He was a most generous chief, always ready to make the best of any work done for him. From the outset I was concerned with the so-called blockade – really the organisation of economic pressure of all kinds on the enemy. At the first, other Departments, like the Board of Trade and the Treasury and, of course, the Admiralty, had their say on different aspects of it, and I represented to Grey that it would be better to have a Cabinet Minister in charge. Accordingly, several people were asked to undertake it, including, if I remember rightly, Lord Curzon and Lord Milner. They refused, and Grey then went to the Prime Minister and asked that I should, as Under-Secretary, be put in the Cabinet, which was done. It was characteristic of him that the possibility of difficulty arising from two Cabinet ministers in the same office – which to lesser men has seemed very formidable – never gave him any anxiety.

Anglo-American relations in the first two years of the war caused Grey much anguish. Not only did he have to deal with the question of blockade but also to juggle with President Wilson's proposed peace negotiations. Colonel House arrived in London in early February 1915 for a series of meetings with the Foreign Secretary before taking soundings in Paris and Berlin. Grey was in an unenviable position. He always felt that America was the key to ending the conflict, either by way of a negotiated peace or direct military intervention. He had to consider the views of the Allies, take account of domestic public opinion and convince Germany that a reasonable offer would be considered. A peace settlement was becoming more complicated with the necessity of satisfying the demands of other countries such as Italy and Romania. It was not just a question of independence for Belgium and the return of Alsace-Lorraine to France. The Allies were beginning to talk about splitting up German and Austrian possessions. Grey did not want to offend the Americans but he knew that the basis for a settlement did not exist in early 1916. The war was not going well for the Allies and public opinion in Britain and France would not countenance any deal except on the most favourable terms. France and Russia were angered by the fact that they were shouldering proportionately too great a burden of the war effort. As a result, Grey felt that Britain could never play the lead role in recommending peace to the Allies.

House was sensitive to his friend's difficulties. He would meet Grey informally at Eccleston Square and talk far into the night. House writes in his diary,

> Grey answered questions with the utmost candour telling me the whole story as he would to a member of his own Government. It was an extraordinary conversation and I feel complimented beyond measure that he has such confidence in my discretion and integrity … We talked of nature, solitude, Wordsworth … We sat by the fire in the library facing each other, discussing every phase of the situation with a single mind and purpose.

An idea that came out of these fireside chats, and one that House relayed to his chief, was Grey's interest in post-war international security through a League of Nations. The Foreign Secretary viewed the idea of a League as a substitute for the old Concert of Europe.

In February 1916 the two men drafted a memorandum setting out the peace terms that President Wilson would be willing to put forward if the right situation arose. The President would propose a conference attended by all the belligerents. If the Allies accepted the proposal and should Germany refuse it, the United States would probably enter the war against Germany. As it happened the memorandum became redundant. House, like Ambassador Page, was a devout Anglophile. He believed that a German victory would not be in the best interests of America and mediation should not take place until Germany was sufficiently beaten to consent to proposed peace terms. In any case soundings taken by House in Berlin and Paris convinced the Americans that it would be next to impossible to bring any parties to the table. Grey wrote in *Twenty-Five Years* that 'The German manner of countering his mediation policy must surely have turned President Wilson's thoughts in the direction of war, but in the end it was the unrestricted submarine campaign that precipitated American entry.'

The summer of 1916 proved a miserable period for the Foreign Secretary. Against a background of Kitchener's drowning at sea and the Royal Navy's disappointing engagement against the German High Seas Fleet at Jutland, Grey's eyesight grew steadily worse, leaving him in a part-time capacity at the Foreign Office. In May he wrote to his old friend Sydney Buxton,

> The oculist assures me that if I could give up work for a year or more I might keep my sight for the rest of my life, but unless I can limit the use of my eyes I may lose the power of reading for good. I compromise by getting Crewe to come into the Foreign Office and taking some ten days leave once in every two months or six weeks, but it is a poor compromise.

On top of these misfortunes, the slaughter on the Somme which dragged on throughout the summer was made all the more poignant by the death in September of Pamela's eldest son, Edward 'Bim' Tennant, and of Raymond Asquith. Pamela was utterly devastated and turned to spiritualism. As if all this was not enough, a stream of vitriol emanated from the Northcliffe press, attacking the Prime Minister for his lacklustre direction of the war. There was some respite in late August when Romania joined the Allied cause. This cheered the Foreign Secretary, with Henry Newbolt reporting on 13 September, 'He was sunny, humorous, interested in everything, talkative, indiscreet and very friendly.' In July a relieved Grey accepted a peerage, thereby lightening his political responsibilities even further; in any event he had been determined to leave politics at the next general election. He was introduced to the Lords by his close friends Haldane and Bryce as Viscount Grey of Fallodon.

The autumn saw the coalition government on its last legs. Lloyd George had his eye firmly set on the main chance and although not trusted by any of his Unionist colleagues, he was determined to oust Asquith. In September Lloyd George had infuriated the Foreign Secretary by speaking out of court on foreign affairs. He told an American journalist that Britain 'would fight to the end', thereby pouring cold water on any peace initiatives contemplated by President Wilson. The President had been under pressure for some time from local Irish and German opinion to make a peace move. As demonstrated by the Lansdowne memorandum circulated in November, there was also a groundswell of opinion in Britain favouring the possibility of a settlement as a result of the stalemate on the Western Front and the increasing effectiveness of the German submarine campaign. Grey wrote to Lloyd George on 29 September, 'It has always been my view that until the Allies were sure of victory the door should be kept open for Wilson's mediation. It is now closed for ever as far as we are concerned.' After the Lansdowne memorandum became public, the Northcliffe press campaign reached new heights of intensity, blaming Asquith and Grey for a fainthearted and defeatist attitude.

Lloyd George, Bonar Law and Carson saw their opportunity and called for the establishment of a reconstituted War Committee. It was to be a much smaller body, independent of the Cabinet and its chairman would not be the Prime Minister. Asquith refused to contemplate such a radical change to his personal position with regards to the running of the war. Balfour and other Unionist colleagues moved over to Lloyd George's side and the government disintegrated in early December. Grey had little involvement in the embittered machinations, recording in his autobiography:

> Lloyd George forced a crisis by resigning; the Liberal members of the Government held a separate meeting with Asquith to decide what course should be taken. The opinion in favour of resignation was unanimous. Whether we were all of the same opinion for the same reason, I cannot say. My own view was clear; the present position was very unsatisfactory; people were not working well together, and the Government was not receiving from the country the confidence and support that were essential to make it efficient. The only thing to be done was for the Government to clear up the situation by resigning.

Grey gave up the seals of office on Monday 11 December, eleven years to the day after he received them that foggy morning at Buckingham Palace.

Was Grey a great Foreign Secretary? No one will ever bracket him with the brilliance of a Salisbury or Palmerston, yet he was operating in a much more dangerous and volatile world than his Victorian counterparts. Britain had been overtaken as an industrial power by Germany and America. Across the world she was confronted for the first time by serious imperial and naval competition. In the words of Arthur Murray, Grey's policy was 'to enlarge the field of British friendship but not at the expense of existing friendships'. In this goal he was immensely successful. He cemented the Entente with France, signed a new Entente with Russia, rolled-over the treaty with Japan and laid the foundation of the 'special relationship' with the United States. In addition to this, Grey initiated the military conversations with France which ensured Britain had a sensible strategy at the outbreak of war. He encouraged Haldane's army reforms and consistently supported the 'big Navy' group. Over his nine pre-war years in office he prepared his country for the inevitable, and for this achievement alone he must rank as a first-class Foreign Secretary. Although it is true his performance declined during his wartime tenure, he was still worth his weight in gold for so skilfully steering Britain's diplomatic relations with the United States through the economic blockade of Germany.

Grey has been criticised by some historians, and particularly Niall Ferguson, for committing Britain to the side of France and Russia in spite of the fact that Britain did not have the land forces to honour such a commitment in 1914. In reality, there was no way a Liberal government could have promised the enormous related expenditure, let alone introduced conscription, in the years leading up to the Great War while at the same time carrying through its hallowed social reforms and staying ahead of Germany in terms of naval construction. As it was, the small yet highly trained Expeditionary Force served its purpose and prevented von Kluck's armies from outflanking the French in the early days of the war. If Britain had committed only her naval resources to the Allied cause, Paris would have almost certainly fallen by early September 1914. Grey was convinced that if France lost her independence it would only be a matter of time before Britain would be in mortal danger from German aggression.

Grey's success as a Foreign Secretary was greatly assisted by his sound character and attractive personality. These qualities encouraged trust not only in the insecure Chancelleries of Europe but also across the globe, particularly in the United States. (The Germans, of course, had a completely different view of Grey. In the same way as they regarded King Edward VII as 'Satan' – the man who wanted to encircle Germany – so they viewed Grey as Mephistopheles, the crafty, sardonic statesman who was determined to bring on Armageddon.) But despite his generally accepted fine attributes, it would be a great mistake to view Grey merely as 'a nice Northumbrian' or 'the perfect example of an English country gentleman' who loved nature and fly fishing. There was an inner steel to him, coupled with a stubborn side that constantly threatened resignation. He survived eleven years in office over one of the most turbulent periods in Britain's domestic and international history. He concealed the military conversations from the majority of his Cabinet colleagues, fought off the radical critics of his foreign policy after Agadir and told the Balkan delegates of the 1913 Peace Conference 'to sign or go home'.

Could Grey have done more to prevent the outbreak of war? Probably not. There were too many tectonic plates rubbing up against each other in Europe at the time. The Alliance system, the arms race, German insecurity over 'encirclement', Prussian militarism, Austro-Russian antagonism and the spark of local nationalism in the Balkans made war inevitable.

A number of factors over the previous decade contributed to the outbreak of war in 1914 and it is remarkable that conflict was avoided during the previous crises of 1906, 1908, 1911 and 1913. Grey's obituary in *The Times* commented, 'It has been argued that a greater statesman might have averted the catastrophe but most students of Prusso-German ambitions are satisfied no statesman could have done more than postpone it.'

The tragedy is that none of the great powers, with the possible exception of Austria-Hungary, wanted a European War in 1914 and even the Austrians only wanted a restricted conflict with Serbia. The Austro-Hungarians were finally determined to crush the Serbs, who presented a very real threat to their decaying Empire. Russia, having failed to back up Serbia in the past, was not to be found wanting a third time and Germany, who was seeking a preventive war against Russia, believed it was her duty to support her only reliable ally, Austria. Austria's unforgivable sin lay in the fact she knew in her heart of hearts that this time Russia would support Serbia but she demonstrated an irresponsible lack of concern as she had Germany's unconditional support. The German military must also shoulder a large share of the blame as, with Russia's strength growing daily, they were well aware a conflict was needed sooner rather than later. A Balkan conflagration was unavoidable. France would then back her Russian ally in a war of revenge on account of Alsace-Lorraine, taken by Germany in the Franco-Prussian war of 1870, and Britain would fight for the independence of France. Within a blink a localised struggle had become a European war. By 1917 the U-boat would have transformed the most horrific conflict in history into a world war, with the participation of the United States.

One man alone could perhaps have prevented war and that was a statesman of the stature of Bismarck in Germany. The Iron Chancellor would never have made Caprivi's mistake of failing to roll over the Secret Insurance Treaty with Russia, thereby propelling a formidable neighbour into the arms of France. Likewise he would never have allowed Tirpitz to build a fleet against Britain. Successive German Chancellors blundered at every turn, whether upsetting Britain with an aggressive naval policy, France over Morocco or Russia by courting Turkey. If Britain had not entered the war in August 1914 and Paris had fallen, would a militaristic Germany under the control of Moltke and Tirpitz have brought the troops home as Bismarck did in 1870? Surely, with their new weapons of war, the submarine and the mine, they would have developed naval bases on the French coasts to counter the economic blockade of the powerful British Navy. The chances are, then, that Britain would have entered the war at a later date in much more disadvantageous circumstances. In August 1914 it was simply not in British interests to see France and Belgium lose their independence, with Germany gaining access to the Channel ports.

It has been said by some, particularly David Lloyd George, that Grey should have warned Germany at an earlier date of British intervention if the frontiers of France and Belgium were violated.

In the decade before the war the Foreign Secretary had on many occasions hinted to his German and French counterparts that in his opinion Britain would fight for the independence of France. Haldane had made the same point on an official visit to Berlin and the King had warned his German cousin of such danger over a shooting weekend at Sandringham in December 1912. It was impossible for Grey to upgrade the Entente to a full alliance – even if he had wanted to – because Parliament would simply not agree to it. In the last days of peace Grey was desperate to keep the Cabinet and Liberal Party united. In a speech to the Lords in 1928 he recounted those fateful days:

> It is well known that in the early days of the last week in July 1914, the Government were so deeply divided that the division was apparently irreconcilable. The House of Commons was divided. The country was divided. It is my opinion that if there had been a precipitate attempt to force a decision it would not have helped these divisions of opinion, it would have brought them out and made them irreparable.

And who was leading the non-interventionists? David Lloyd George, of course. In his book *Master and Brother*, Arthur Murray recalls a statement from Walter Runciman:

> When the crisis came it found Lloyd George vacillating. Right up to tea-time on Sunday August 2nd, he told us that he was doubtful of the action he would take. In the course of conversations with about one half of our ministerial colleagues in Number 11 on the afternoon of that day, he told us that he would not oppose the war, but he would take no part in it and would retire for the time being to Criccieth.

How could Grey have possibly committed Britain to defend the frontiers of Belgium and France at an earlier stage if the leader of the 'anti-war' party was 'vacillating' to within a few hours of the outbreak of war? Time and again the student of Edward Grey is confronted by contradictions between the text of Lloyd George's *War Memoirs* and historical fact. Murray is convinced that Lloyd George's disingenuous opinions of Grey's capabilities as Foreign Secretary were coloured by post-war events, writing,

> Grey had criticised severely the chameleonic attitude adopted by Lloyd George towards the General Strike in 1926 when the bulk of the British nation was fighting hotly to retain its constitutional liberties, and that he did not hesitate to express publicly a few years later not only his strong disapproval of the use for political purposes of the Lloyd George personal fund, but also his complete lack of confidence in Lloyd George as leader of the Party. Perhaps Lloyd George, when writing his *Memoirs*, remembered these critical remarks about himself by Grey.

But what of the stance of the Belgian government? They had issued no declaration by the end of July. Britain therefore had no clear idea whether they would resist a German invasion. Indeed, two days before the outbreak of war, Grey was informed by the Belgian government that 'they had no reason whatever to suspect Germany of an intention to violate their neutrality' and that 'they had not considered the idea of appeal to other guarantee powers, nor of intervention should a violation occur'. How could Grey have issued an ultimatum to Germany when Belgium insisted she wished to be left alone? It is worth mentioning that at no point did Lloyd George raise the question of sending an early ultimatum to Germany in Cabinet, no doubt because he was busy rallying the non-interventionists. Surely the Chancellor would have led a revolt in Cabinet if Grey had acted prematurely, thereby splitting the country down the middle.

Churchill took the opposing side to Lloyd George, 'watching with admiration Grey's activities at the Foreign Office and his cool skill in Council'. He writes in his *World Crisis*:

> Suppose again, that now after the Austrian ultimatum to Serbia, the Foreign Secretary had proposed to the Cabinet that if matters were

so handled that Germany attacked France or violated Belgian territory, Great Britain would declare war on her. Would the Cabinet
have assented to such a communication? I cannot believe it.

He tells us that 'the more I reflect on the situation the more
convinced I am that we took the only practical course that was open
to us or any British Cabinet.'

The contrast between the man who entered the Foreign Office
as Foreign Secretary aged forty-three and the one who left it eleven
years later could not have been more distinct. Grey was a changed
man after the outbreak of war, both emotionally and physically.
He was exhausted and depressed by the July crisis in addition to
being tormented by the possibility that he could have done more
to prevent war. A year later, when *The Times* newspaper conducted
a vicious campaign against the Asquith government, their leader
writer referred to the Foreign Secretary as 'thoroughly tired and
stale'. Unlike Churchill, he hated war and was horrified by the
slaughter. When Winston was sacked in 1915, Grey wrote sympa-
thetically, 'It adds to my hatred of war – I shall look upon it if I
survive it, as a time of horrible memory. I hated it beforehand and
I hate it now, though I do not see how it could have been avoided.'
Grey's style of old-fashioned gentlemanly diplomacy was not suited
to a wartime situation, when a more unconventional and unilateral
approach was needed. No doubt there is some credence in Lloyd
George's unflattering remark that Grey at times mistook 'correcti-
tude for rectitude'. Ronald Munro Ferguson understood his close
friend's predicament only too well when he wrote to a colleague,
'E. G. was never intended for the service of Mars.'

Elder Statesman

The fall of the Asquith coalition came as a welcome release for Grey. He had been desperate to retire for several years. Only his deep sense of public duty and loyalty to Asquith kept him in office. His health had deteriorated dangerously and a gastric haemorrhage caused uncomfortable stomach pains. He had been living on 'spoonfulls of bread and milk' since the summer. He would miss certain aspects of constituency life and his many friends accumulated over thirty years, but he was heartened by the continuity at the Foreign Office. He spent Christmas at Fallodon, writing to Professor Gilbert Murray on 23 December,

> The best chance of saving my eyesight is to stay at home and be in the open as much as I can. I didn't intend to seek the chance till after the war but now it has come I can't help taking it. It is a great relief and an abiding satisfaction to me that Balfour and Cecil are at the Foreign Office and that Eric Drummond continues as private secretary. With all this and with Hardinge still there all that the Foreign Office can do to keep things right with America will be done.

Within months of his retirement America had entered the war and a decade's work at the Foreign Office had been vindicated.

It was typical of Grey that he demonstrated no bitterness when Lloyd George took over the reins. Grey was well aware of the new Prime Minister's strengths, though still venting his criticism on the press. He wrote to Buxton on 29 May 1917,

I have no knowledge but I have a feeling we are winning the war. If so, Lloyd George deserves great credit. I was told in London the other day that he really did push a lot of things through and get them done and that the effect of his spending two days in the Admiralty was very great in speeding up the machine. There were certainly very many unpleasant circumstances in the way the Asquith Government was displaced and many of us including myself had shamefully unfair things said about us; but then, so far as I am concerned I was at one time very much over praised and I was really always miserable and out of place in public life. So long as I am left alone in private life I have a feeling that it is sort of quits.

In March 1917 Grey was on the Brora River in Sutherland, writing to Haldane,

It is the most beautiful and remote place and I should be very happy if it were not for anxiety about the course of the war. I have for the time gone into the world that suits me. London and politics have always been really alien to me and unless it seems I am really wanted I shall not return to public life at all.

He continued to fish with his brother Charlie, both on the Itchen until 1923 and on the Cassley until 1926. By 1919 his impaired eyesight made dry-fly fishing all but impossible, yet he continued to fish for salmon and with a wet fly for trout. He was such an accomplished fisherman that he still managed to hook a trout on a dry fly without seeing the rise. He writes in *Fly Fishing*,

By 1918 I had ceased to be able to see a small fly floating on the water. It was, however, possible to judge distance more accurately and to present a dry fly effectively to a rising trout more frequently than I should have supposed to be possible under such disadvantage. Nevertheless it happened more than once in this season that I struck to the sound of a rise without seeing it and found that I had hooked the trout for which I was trying. It had taken my fly on the

surface and I had failed to see the rise, even though my eyes had
been directed to the place where I knew the fish to be. It was evident
for me the end of the dry fly fishing was very near.

Salmon fishing he found easier, although that too had lost much of
its former enjoyment. In 1930 he wrote an additional chapter for a
new edition of *Fly Fishing*, recollecting,

> It is twelve years since I have been able to see my fly fall on the water
> or to watch the line. These things were a matter of course in salmon
> fishing: not till I lost sight of them did I realise what an integral part
> of salmon fishing they were. The salmon angler watches the fall of
> his fly at each cast and his eyes are ever on the draw of the stream
> on his line. To be deprived of the latter is an even greater loss than
> it is to be able to see the fly fall on water.

In his later years, as his eyesight failed completely, he would learn
to read books in Braille at St Dunstan's, being the only non-military
person to be taught there.

Tragedy stalked Edward Grey. Everything he loved was plucked
from him. In May 1917 Fallodon was burnt down. A few of his
possessions on the ground floor were all that could be saved. He
rebuilt the house after the war in two storeys rather than three
and lived in the kitchen wing in the intervening period. Dorothy
had stamped her personality on the house and in a letter to
Eleanor Paul, Grey demonstrates how much he missed his
late wife:

> I kept everything in the house in the place where Dorothy put it and
> now I shall never see the familiar rooms again. And of course my
> nursery and the room where I learnt the alphabet and memories
> like that are swept away. It makes me feel that affections should be
> set in the open air and the seasons and the stars and things that are
> less perishable. But after all how gladly I would have had the house
> burnt if only Dorothy might have lived.

Following the 1918 election when so many of his friends who formed the Independent Liberal Party lost their seats, Grey wrote pathetically to Pamela from his club, Brooks's:

> The destruction of the Liberal Party in which I spent public life is sad and the exclusion of so many old friends is very painful. Public life has great and ruthless catastrophes. But the destruction of my house, the loss of my sight and the separation from what I love most makes political woes seem small by comparison in personal feeling. I feel we are on the eve of great events. If only I had eyes with which to follow events and to enjoy country things in independence I should feel quite brave but loss of sight is partial death in life.

But it wasn't just his eyesight; his general health was deteriorating as well. On 31 August 1920 he wrote to Eddy Tennant,

> Even the common pleasures of eating and drinking are to be denied to me for I must live on the simplest food to have a chance and even so not a certainty of avoiding these attacks of acidity. Nevertheless I shall enjoy taking you on one of my old walks in the New Forest. Its beauty is greatest in the autumn and winter and we could do it from Wilsford.

Sadly their plan was never enacted as Eddy died on 21 November.

There was perhaps only one issue that could pull Grey back into public life: the League of Nations. He believed passionately in the League as a future conduit for world peace. In November 1918 he accepted the Presidency of the League of Nations Union formed as a result of a merger between the League of Nations Society and the League of Free Nations Association. Grey took no part in the peace negotiations at Versailles and had become increasingly disenchanted by developments. He had always hoped that the terms would be negotiated and not dictated, thus resulting in a lasting settlement. Although he was disappointed by the harsh treatment Germany suffered at the hands of the Allies, exemplified by the extent of reparations and the annexation of their colonies, he was delighted by the creation of the League of Nations. His one major concern was that the League might be destroyed by the Senate in the United States. Public opinion in Britain was strongly in favour of the League and Grey's close political ally Lord Robert Cecil had been appointed by Lloyd George to coordinate all related activities. Trevelyan relates how Grey wrote to a friend in February 1917,

> Without the United States a League would be at best but a revived concert of the Great Powers of Europe, liable at any time to split into rival groups. With the United States it would have a stability and be on a high plane that has never been attained by anything of the kind before.

It was this deep concern about the United States' attitude that led Grey to accept a request from the government to go to Washington as a temporary ambassador in September 1919. Just before he sailed across the Atlantic Grey spent a few days at Balmoral, an invitation that showed the esteem in which he was held by the King. He wrote to Eddy Tennant telling him how the fishing on the Dee was bringing back many old memories and that he very much hoped the Tennant family, including Christopher, would join him in America that winter. Lloyd George and Curzon were well aware of Grey's high standing in the eyes of the American President. Grey would lead a special mission to smooth the waters for America's entry into the League and discuss, amongst other thorny issues, the subject of Irish independence. Unfortunately the issue of America's entry into the League had become a question of party politics between the President and the Senate. A group of Republicans headed by Senator Cabot Lodge led the opposition and President Wilson was showing little signs of compromise. It was therefore unlikely the treaty would pass through the Senate with the required two-thirds majority. With the help of his good friend Colonel House, Grey hoped to persuade the President to make the necessary concessions.

The mission never really got off the ground. As Grey and Tyrrell steamed into New York Harbour they were handed a note by US Customs to the effect that the President had been taken seriously ill in Washington. In the five months Grey remained in America he never managed to see the President, his predicament not being helped by the fact that Colonel House's influence was now on the wane. In his diary entry for 1 July 1943, Chips Channon suggests there were other reasons for this lack of contact. According to Brendan Bracken, a famous story circulated in Washington that one of Grey's subordinates had made indiscreet remarks about the President and Mrs Wilson's early relations which were repeated at the White House. Apparently Mrs Wilson had declared, 'When Woodrow proposed to me I was so surprised I nearly fell out of bed.' Grey was convinced that the issue of Irish Home Rule was blocking his way, writing to Curzon in late September, 'I am constantly coming upon instances in which Americans are behaving badly and twisting things against us. There is an Irishman everywhere and Irish antagonism is at the bottom of all our troubles.' The frustration of failure aside, he greatly enjoyed his brief stay in the United States, writing to Ella Pease in November,

> I love the Americans. They seem to me more easy to get on with than English people but they are very civilised and wear white waist-coats and have not as a rule got any passion for country life; and I, being at bottom primitive and uncivilised, would have to go and live in the backwoods if I stayed in the country. Nevertheless life in Washington, if I was an Ambassador, would be far more tolerable than life in London.

While in America Grey gave the first of a series of lectures which in 1927 were published under the title of *The Fallodon Papers*, becoming a bestseller. In December 1919 he travelled north to give an address at the Harvard Union on the subject of 'Recreation'. He was particularly delighted to accept the invitation as Harvard was Theodore Roosevelt's alma mater. The ex-President had died a few months previously and Grey decided to present his address as a memorial to his close friend. He would tell his audience of 1,000 students not only of his own love of books, poetry, nature, sport and gardening but also of his bird walk in the New Forest with Roosevelt and how a shared love of nature brought them together. A nearly blind Grey explained to his audience how nature provided a welcome refuge from the stresses of public life, particularly during the Great War:

> In England every village was stricken, there was grief in almost every house. The thought of suffering, the anxiety for the future, destroyed all pleasure. It came even between oneself and the page of the book one tried to read. In those dark days I found some support in the steady progress unchanged of the beauty of the seasons. Every year, as spring came back unfailing and unfaltering, the leaves came out with the same tender green, the birds sang, the flowers came up and opened and I felt that a great power of Nature for beauty was not affected by the war.

The only attempt to bring Grey back into political life after the war ended in failure. Following his return from America, Arthur Murray and Lord Robert Cecil tried desperately to persuade Grey to lead a new Centre Party. The idea was for Cecil to bring over some of the more liberal-minded Conservatives who found the coalition repugnant, while there was also a chance that a few 'moderate' Labour members might join the cause. Murray was backed by Liberal grandees such as Cowdray, Gladstone, Spender, Runciman and Crewe. These non-coalition Liberals were desperate for a leader who would galvanise a dispirited and divided party. In the spring of 1921, Cowdray wrote to Murray, 'Our destinies as a nation are dependent on Grey coming back and taking the reins.' But it was not to be. Although he returned to the fray for a short time in the autumn, being in the process fiercely critical of the Lloyd George government, his heart was not really in the venture. His eyesight had all but failed and he felt tired. Besides, he was far too loyal a party man to replace Asquith without the latter's wholehearted consent, which was not forthcoming.

Grey was exasperated by Lloyd George's meddling in foreign affairs. He disapproved of Britain's involvement in Russian politics, which, he believed, encouraged Bolshevism. He was also deeply critical of the government's Irish policy, which had resulted in so much bloodshed. He was convinced Britain had lost the peace at Versailles and blamed Lloyd George, writing to Spender in July 1920, 'He had some great qualities without being a great man. He was constitutionally incapable of understanding that straightforward-ness is essential and "cleverness" fatal to success in the long run.' Asquith took exactly the same line as Grey. While acknowledging Lloyd George's many brilliant qualities, Asquith was adamant he would not serve under the Welshman on account of his character defects. In the Asquith Papers (held in the Bodleian Library) for 28 May 1917, he writes,

I had learned by long and close association to mistrust him profoundly. I knew him to be incapable of loyalty or lasting gratitude. I had always acknowledged, and did still, to the full, his many brilliant and useful faculties, but he needed to have someone over him. In my judgement he had incurable defects, both of intellect and character, which totally unfitted him to be at the head.

Grey fully realised that, unlike him, Lloyd George was a modern-day politician 'well-suited to an age of telephones, moving pictures and modern journalism', but he hated his modus operandi. Nothing was more repugnant to Grey than the sale of peerages which Lloyd George initiated in order to fund his breakaway wing of the Liberal Party. In 1929 Grey wrote to Stanley Baldwin, 'The iron entered into my soul when Lloyd George's Government, after the war, let down and corrupted public life at home and destroyed our credit abroad.'

Asquith and Grey simply refused to forgive Lloyd George for his general behaviour. Grey felt Lloyd George had been intensely disloyal to a leader to whom he should have felt profoundly indebted. As early as 1910 Lloyd George had promoted a scheme for coalition government. Four years later he was encouraging his Conservative opponents to scheme against the Asquith government. His energy and vision were vital to the war effort but at the back of his mind was always his own political advancement. Trevor Wilson in *The Downfall of the Liberal Party* writes,

Lloyd George's great abilities in war, far from helping the Liberal Government, contributed to its fall. He was so detached from most of his colleagues that his achievements did not rebound to their credit but rather highlighted their short-comings, thus enhancing the case for a new government in which his talents would be better supported.

As soon as the Asquith coalition government was formed in May 1915, Lloyd George was briefing against his colleagues in the press over industrial and military conscription. In December he shocked Parliament by censuring the coalition in which he was a key member for general incompetence and for being 'too late' in all its deliberations. It was widely thought he was plotting to overthrow the coalition and appropriate the premiership for himself. Even his Conservative colleagues were exasperated by his behaviour, Trevor Wilson writing,

Bonar Law, in June 1916, berated him to his face for his ambition and self-seeking, and Austen Chamberlain, just after Lloyd George had become Prime Minister, remarked that he took 'no pleasure in a change which gives me a chief whom I profoundly distrust – no doubt a man of great energy but quite untrustworthy.

In September 1916 it seemed Lloyd George's arrogance knew no bounds. Without consulting Grey, he assumed the Foreign Secretary's responsibilities by giving an interview to an American journalist suggesting that any proposed peace talks put forward by the US government would be viewed as 'pro-German'.

Nowhere was Lloyd George's scheming more in evidence than during the run-up to the November 1918 general election, which he called twenty-four hours after the termination of hostilities. On 12 November he addressed a prestigious Liberal gathering at Downing Street, where he pronounced his devotion to the party's cause. He called for a just peace and outlined a programme of social reform. He told his audience, 'I was reared in Liberalism ... I am too old to change now ... I am too old to change. I cannot leave Liberalism. I would quit this place tomorrow if I could not obtain the support of the Liberals.' Within days, Lloyd George was singing from a totally different hymn-sheet. Grey had always hoped the Allies would not extract excessive retribution from Germany at the Peace Conference but at a speech in Bristol on 13 December Lloyd George demanded that Germany should 'pay for the whole cost of the war', declaring 'We shall search their pockets for it.'

Lloyd George went even further in his attitude to the Liberal Party. At a speech in London on 16 November, he viciously attacked Asquith for not having supported his coalition government. Furthermore, having espoused the cause of Liberalism at the beginning of the week, by the end of it he had broken away from the Liberals and thrown in his lot with the Conservatives. Asquith dubbed the 1918 election 'the Coupon Election' because Lloyd George stitched up the constituencies by drawing up lists of 'official government candidates' to stand, in many cases, at the expense of Asquith's followers. The coupon placed a ban on all other candidates in a particular constituency. Lloyd George drove a nail into the coffin of the Liberal Party by agreeing with Bonar Law that only 159 Liberals would receive the coupon as opposed to 364 Conservatives. Grey writes in *Twenty-Five Years*:

After the Peace, more especially in the last two years of the Lloyd
George Government, its proceedings and conduct of affairs stirred
me with indignation and despair such as I have never felt about any
other British Government; but this has no bearing on either the recol-
lections or judgement of what passed when we were in office together.

Grey's words are another example of what makes Lloyd George's
scathing post-war attack on Grey's tenure as Foreign Secretary in
his *War Memoirs* so surprising. The two statesmen worked in successful harmony together during their time in office before the war on
both international and domestic issues.

In 1921 Grey's growing distrust of the coalition government
forced him back into the open and he worked with Asquith for its
overthrow. When the coalition fell to the Conservatives the following year, Grey accepted the role of Leader of the House of Lords
to help Asquith, but because of past bad blood with Lloyd George
there was no Liberal reunion. At the general election in November
1922 the Liberals lost ground to Labour, with their seats split
equally between Asquith's supporters and Lloyd George's supporters. Robert Cecil continued to rue the day that failed to produce
a Centre Party led by Grey, writing to Spender after the election,
'What a chance the Liberals did miss in not taking our advice about
Grey, as things have turned out I verily believe they would have
swept the country with Grey as their alternative Prime Minister.'
Following a Liberal reunion Grey participated in the 1923 campaign
in an unrewarding effort to defeat the Tories and then continued as
Liberal Leader in the House of Lords until the following autumn,
when he resigned on grounds of non-attendance.

On 20 January 1925 Asquith accepted a peerage and took over
the Liberal leadership in the Lords. Grey did, however, keep a toe
in the political water when, in December 1926, he became the
first President of the Liberal Council, a post held until his death
seven years later. The Council consisted of a number of anti-Lloyd
George colleagues whose main object, according to Trevelyan,
'was to enable Liberals who desire to uphold the independence of

the Party to remain within it for the furtherance of the aims of
Liberalism'. During 1929 Grey grew more and more anxious about
the levels of public spending under the Labour government and
felt that their policies would lead to national ruin. In January 1931
he led a national call for economy and 'sound finance' at a large
meeting in the City which he then repeated at the Eighty Club and
the Liberal Council. Finally at the October election he gave valuable support to the national government, but when a Conservative-
dominated Cabinet decided on a policy of full-scale tariffs he
strongly approved of the Liberal resignations. Grey was a Liberal
free trader to his dying day.

After his retirement from politics Grey took up from where he left
off in the winter of 1905. He based himself at Fallodon and rejoined
the Board of the North Eastern Railway. Board meetings were held
once a month at York and occupied both Thursday and Friday. He
was often away at weekends, as he joined the Trustees of the British
Museum, who met in London on a Saturday morning. In addition he had become a Fellow of his old school, Winchester College,
where they also convened on a Saturday. Grey would stay Friday
night at the Warden's lodgings before spending the balance of the
weekend at The Cottage or at Wilsford with the Glenconners.
The following letter, written to his friend Captain Barton in October
1917, explains why Grey spent a good deal of time at Fallodon in the
latter stages of his life:

> The remarkable thing here at present is a great outbreak of tameness
> towards me personally; whether it is due to some improvement in
> my aura or to the approach of the Millennium (isn't the Millennium
> to follow Armageddon?) or to what I cannot say. In the first place
> the retriever dog, the relict of a keeper who left two years ago, has
> become absurdly attached to me; though I don't even feed it myself.
> A wild teal arrived in August and will now feed within a yard of my

boots and is so tame that I never see it on the wing. Three waterhens also have become perfectly tame, which is not unprecedented but unusual … The really happy life is to hit on one pleasant way of spending a day and to be able to repeat it day after day after day. These country pleasures never pall, and the sun never fails to rise and set, though it does with variety.

The letter also shows what an important role Grey's wildfowl collection played in his life, giving him an immense sense of enjoyment on a daily basis. Although his life was scarred by tragedy, his simple country interests provided him with a constant source of happiness. Every day at sunset, Grey would participate in the 'duck dinner'. When he was not at home, Mr Henderson, the gardener, was delegated to chair the proceedings. Grey would feed his ducks bread and grain by hand from his favourite bench under the big larch tree. He had an amazing ability to tame birds and animals, demonstrating the same sense of trust and patience that had stood him so well at the Foreign Office. In his letter he tells Barton about the wild teal that had arrived at his pond late one summer. The teal is the most difficult of all wild duck to tame, as evidenced by Grey informing the reader in *The Charm of Birds* that 'only twice in forty-three years have pinioned teal [which have their wings clipped and are unable to fly] nested at Fallodon'. Grey believed his wildfowl epitomised the romance of birds. He relished the beauty of their plumage, gained enormous satisfaction from those that nested each spring and above all thrilled to the arrival of wild duck on his reserve. When he started his collection most birds were pinioned, but as time went by he delighted in free-flying birds. He received a tremendous feeling of elation when an un-pinioned bird returned to the fold in the autumn after nesting in the far north.

In October 1921 he gave an address to the Berwickshire Naturalists' Club in which he stated,

I have got a lot of birds still, mostly bred on the place, but I have not the same number of species that I had; and now, partly because my sight is so much impaired, I find most interest in having as many as I can un-pinioned, as tame as possible and yet at perfect liberty. There is a sort of romance in having naturally shy birds, perfectly free and un-pinioned, coming, as some of my widgeon and pintail do, to feed with perfect confidence out of my hand, while I know all the time that any day they may join the wild ones to go south in the winter or far north in the spring.

Sadly he had to take the ups with the downs, when his joy would often be countered by intense disappointment. A brood of duck-lings being reared under a bantam would often be destroyed by rats, or in the winter months a fox might penetrate the wire fence defences and slaughter the pinioned birds in the enclosure.

On 4 June 1922 Grey married his long-time lover Pamela, which delighted their close group of friends. Captain Barton wrote,

> The announcement in Tuesday's *Times* gave me a thrill of quiet joy, the same or similar sense of joy that the song of a blackbird in a wide wood gives me, being as it were cheerful testimony to the fact that all is right with the Old World still despite limelight and machines.

On 8 November 1921 Grey had written to his old friend Louise Creighton, intimating marriage was likely:

> For some years as I supposed people knew I have had a very delight-ful and intimate friendship with Pamela Glenconner. It did not impair my close relationship with her husband and I was equally in the confidence of both of them. What would probably be best is that people should understand we are attached to each other but that nothing is likely to happen soon.

After the wedding, Grey wrote to Eddy's younger brother Jack Tennant, from Wilsford, informing him of the happy event:

Pamela and I were married in the church here by the vicar this morning. We wanted to have it quietly. Christopher is here; and my sister, who lives about twenty miles off, came over in her car but no one else except our two selves and the vicar were in the church. It is a great happiness to me that we have been able to marry as we had intended early in the summer. It will make a great and happy differ-ence in my life and I like to think it will be Pamela's happiness too, and will not make the home a less happy one for her sons. We shall each continue to keep up our own homes as we have been doing. We have each a memory in the past to cherish.

It is interesting that only Christopher and one of Grey's sisters attended the ceremony. Another pointer perhaps that Christopher was Grey's son?

Pamela had a strong and beneficial creative influence over the later years of Grey's life, when she encouraged him to write. After he resigned the Liberal leadership of the Lords in 1924, for the next few years his activities were literary rather than political. Her influence can be detected throughout *The Charm of Birds*, which was published in 1927. When writing this bestseller he drew on a huge bank of happy memories, many of them stored in *The Cottage Book*. Grey's brilliant impressions of the songs of the goldcrest, corn bunting and blackcap can be traced directly to Pamela's book, *Shepherd's Crowns*, published four years earlier. Above all else Grey loved birdsong. It cannot be overstated that his overriding success with *The Charm of Birds* lay in his ability to use an image to stamp an individual song in form and sound in the memory. Hence with the nightjar he writes, 'It is that class of stationary, sooth-ing, continuous sounds such as the hum of a threshing machine, or the noise of the waves on the shore heard at a distance which dispose us to sit still and listen indefinitely.' Both Grey and Pamela read and were influenced by the same verse. In *The Cottage Book* for 27 June 1899 he describes sleeping out at night by the banks of the Itchen and waking at first light: 'I got the little breeze that says "the dawn – the dawn", and dies away.' The final three lines

of Pamela's poem, 'Dawn', in *Windlestraw*, published in 1910, are
composed as follows:

> As if the leaves upon each slender spray
> Were listening, waiting for the little breeze
> That says, 'the dawn – the dawn', and dies away.

One cannot help feeling it was a team effort.

He fully recognised the debt due to Pamela, particularly during
the years when he was nearly blind. In 1925 Grey published *Twenty-
Five Years*, the first record by a Foreign Secretary of his period in
office. It was not only a justification of his own actions but also
an important historical account of the road to war. Mrs Belloc
Lowndes quotes from one of his letters to Pamela:

> It becomes very clear to me that but for you *Twenty-Five Years*
> would never have been written. It is due to things and influences
> you brought, much rarer even than your material help, and which
> could have come from no one else … Your part was much more
> than material, it came from the subtle and pervading influence, the
> stimulating and quickening that a woman has upon a man's mind if
> he loves her and if she loves in return. Also if there be between them
> that particular sympathy that there is between your mind and mine.
> It eludes words because it is so intimate.

In one way Grey and Pamela were well matched. Like Dorothy,
she shared many of his interests, notably poetry, birds, a passion
for the changing seasons and a rural way of life. She wrote her own
poetry and in 1912 published a personal anthology titled *The White
Wallet*. Grey was a great admirer of her written work, quoting a
description of the dawn chorus in *The Charm of Birds* as the best
he knew:

> It is worthwhile to wake early during these days, because of the dawn
> chorus. It opens with a few muted notes of the song thrush. This

sets the tits waking; they have no half tones. There are the sawing notes, the bell notes, the teasing notes, and the festoon of small utterance that belongs especially to the Blue. But you can hardly pick out the individual songs before the whole garden is ringing. There is the loud beauty of the thrushes. Seemingly further away, and in remoter beauty, comes floating the blackbird's voice. The notes are warm, and light as amber, among the sharper flood of song. The dawn chorus is like a tapestry translated into sound. The mistle thrush, with merle and mavis, perhaps the rounded note of an owl, these stand out chief figures in the design. All the others make the dense background of massed stitches; except the wren; he, with resounding scatter of notes, dominates the throng. Then as suddenly as it arose, 'this palace of sound that was reared' begins to subside. One or two thrushes persist. The greenfinch goes on with his two modes of single utterance. Perhaps a linnet continues his husky song. He can be heard now. Then the sun rising flushes the water-meadows and the snipe start drumming. The grass is all bent and straggled with its weight of cold dew.

In another way they were very different characters, each coming from contrasting backgrounds. Pamela was sprung from a great aristocratic dynasty while Grey enjoyed the upbringing of a country squire. Their personalities did, however, complement each other. According to her granddaughter, Emma Tennant, the beautiful Pamela was a handful: spoilt, narcissistic, self-satisfied, expensive to run, bad-tempered and prone to jealousy. She spoilt her children and dressed her young boys as girls. According to his biographer, Max Egremont, Siegfried Sassoon (lover of Pamela's son Stephen) found Pamela 'a slightly chilling woman' and he 'brooded on unflattering stories about Lady Grey: her ordering that all the cockerels in the village should be killed because their morning crowing woke her, her snubbing of the local gentry'. She was also a deeply jealous person and her granddaughter relates how she failed to cope when Grey, on his brief mission to Washington, fell for the charms of writer Opal Whiteley. By contrast Grey was modest, thrifty, calm, patient, unflappable, soothing and diplomatic, 'benign, watchful as the herons he loves to see on the silver stretch of Avon between Great Durnford and Amesbury'. Sadly there were no children from their marriage. Pamela was over fifty years old and not surprisingly experienced a miscarriage, leaving Grey distraught, as he was desperate for an heir to enjoy his beloved Fallodon.

Pamela made sure that Grey did not turn in on himself in old age. She actually persuaded him to travel. They toured California together before Grey returned from America in 1920, they visited Stephen at his clinic in Switzerland in 1923 and the following year made a pilgrimage to Kwambo Bay in Tanganyka to stay with his brother Charlie. In January 1925 they visited Paris together. Grey was determined not to be beaten by illness and his deteriorating eyesight. In the late summer of 1920 he had returned to his beloved Hebrides, writing to Eddy Tennant of his stay on South Uist,

> Grogarry is a very fine sporting place both with rod and gun and the Bensons are really worthy of it. Greylag geese breed there, Barnacle geese and many sorts of duck come in the autumn and one large loch is said to be white with wild swans in the winter. Many pairs of Mute swans breed there and as is the habit of their kind they are quite tame but they are often on the wing and the sound of their magnificent pinions have become quite familiar to me. There are two first rate sea trout lochs ... For those who like wild sport the place is most attractive. I would very much like to go there again when free from pain and discomfort. This last illness has taken a lot out of me and I'm afraid I couldn't get Christopher a reel and line before I left for the Hebrides. Guy Benson spoke of Christopher spontaneously with most warm commendation.

If the destruction of Fallodon wasn't enough, The Cottage was burnt to the ground in 1923, closing out the happiest chapter of his life. It was not to be rebuilt; Grey would live with his memories. He received a melancholy letter from his caretaker: 'My Lord. What can I say to you? I am sore vexed but your pretty cottage is burnt to the ground. What will you say my Lord?' Furthermore, his nephew Adrian Graves had been killed at the front in March 1918, Grey writing to Katherine Lyttelton, 'My nephew died splendidly. He held the Germans off a hill with his machine guns for a whole day, he was wounded twice and unable to walk was carried away by a sergeant when he was shot through the head and killed instantly.' There was some consolation in that Cecil Graves returned from his prison camp after the war to inherit Fallodon.

To his great sadness Pamela, aged fifty-seven, predeceased Grey in 1928. She died alone at Wilsford and he was unable to be by her side. Grey was at Fallodon and as soon as he heard that Pamela was seriously ill he ordered a special night train to take him south. Christopher met him at King's Cross in the early morning to break the news of her death. Lady Tweedsmuir famously referred to Pamela in her memoirs as 'an Olympian character who because of her aloofness from mundane things floated to and fro between Wilsford and Glen appreciating their different beauties and was so well buttressed by wealth that she never had to catch a bus or think about the price of fish'. A great Edwardian Lady had passed away. Confidante and lover of Grey for over thirty years, political hostess, fabulously wealthy aristocrat, countrywoman, poet and over-indulgent mother; Britain would not see her like again. That same year Grey's brother and fishing companion, Charlie, was killed by a buffalo when big-game hunting in Africa, while his third brother, Alexander, also died following an unsuccessful operation in Trinidad. Grey was deeply affected by the suffering of his many friends who lost children in the war. When his godson Edward Pember was killed in the Royal Flying Corps he wrote to Frank Pember, then Warden of All Souls,

I know very well that there is no escape from the suffering of grief. We cannot love much without suffering much, and the very pain of the suffering is an evidence of the strength of our love, so that we cannot even wish grief to be less than it is and must be.

Grey was fastidious when it came to his stepfatherly duties, which were to prove challenging at the best of times. It is obvious from the Sassoon diaries that the Tennant children were fond of their stepfather and they kept in touch after Pamela's death even though Grey found it increasingly difficult to leave Fallodon because of his poor health and eyesight. In 1926 when Clare left her second husband Lionel Tennyson, she began seeing an American named James Beck. Both Pamela and Grey were desperate she didn't marry again so soon after two failed marriages. Diana Cooper writes of Clare at the time, 'She is a worried poor little creature – Lionel has the detectives on her all the time, and Edward Grey is continually giving her lectures down the telephone.' Grey had been very supportive of David when he opened the Gargoyle Club in Soho in 1924 and his 'benign patronage' had given the club a well-needed air of respectability. The membership was an eclectic mixture of 'Society', artists, poets and stars of screen and stage. Stephen must have been a constant source of concern to Grey, particularly after his relationship with Siegfried Sassoon had ended. Stephen was part of the rowdy, party-going and largely homosexual set known as the 'Bright Young Things' and was quite capable of causing his family the utmost public embarrassment. At one stage, with the help of Sassoon, the Greys thought it necessary to rush Stephen out of the country because of suspected illegal activities with 'rent boys'. It didn't stop Stephen visiting Grey at Fallodon, and Grey visited Christopher at Wilsford. On 14 April 1930 Grey wrote to his sister-in-law, Mary Wemyss, following the death of her lover Arthur James Balfour, 'The only weekend when I shall be in the south is 17 May and that I am to spend with Christopher at Wilsford. I have not been there for a year and I often long for it.' Apparently Lord Riddell had written an article on Balfour's thoughts on various men in public life and the ex-Prime Minister had been full of high praise for Grey. Grey had wanted to thank Balfour but it was now too late. Christmas 1930 was spent quietly at Fallodon with his youngest sister, Constance Curtis, and her family.

In 1928 Grey received perhaps his greatest honour when he

was elected Chancellor of Oxford University. He must have been amused by the irony of the appointment, as forty-four years earlier he had been sent down from Balliol 'for incorrigible idleness', returning only to take a Third in Jurisprudence. Henry Newbolt tells an amusing story as to how shocked Haldane professed to be when Grey was elected Chancellor. Haldane opined that intellectual ability was required for such an appointment and that Grey had never read a book. Archbishop Lang then stuck up for Grey, saying he had indeed read Wordsworth, whereupon Haldane replied that Wordsworth was not a book. Another friend thought Haldane wrong and that Grey did enjoy intellectual interests. To which Haldane replied, 'Yes, but amongst the birds and fishes.'

A cursory glance at Grey's correspondence with friends suggests Haldane had a wicked sense of humour. Grey mentions his favoured reading list in a letter to Katherine Lyttelton:

> I go on with the *Adventures of Philip*. It is very early Victorian, and oh! the difference between Thackeray's women and Meredith's. You cannot think of any of Meredith's women in a crinoline, nor any of Thackeray's out of one … I also continue with Gibbon. He has a naughtiness which amuses me, as when he speaks of 'the pious obstinacy' of the early Christians when persecuted. But he has a respect for Athanasius, which I hadn't before but I have now. I leave these books here, Gibbon and Thackeray, when I go to London. And when I come back, I find Gibbon with my mark in it and Thackeray open where I left off on the reading stand by the bed. That is homey.

In May 1924 Grey had given an address to the Royal Society of Literature in which he told his audience that, next to poetry, he most enjoyed reading the classic novels, what Tennyson referred to as 'these large still books'. Jane Austen was a particular favourite, as demonstrated in some of Grey's correspondence with Pamela when he refers to her as Emma and she to him as Mr Knightley. Haldane was an intellectual heavyweight, so there was probably a degree of jealousy involved in Grey's appointment – or perhaps Haldane still harboured a grudge over his exclusion from the Asquith coalition in 1915.

Dr Cyril Bailey wrote to Trevelyan of Grey's installation in the Sheldonian:

> He asked me to write his Latin speech for him, giving me in English what he wanted to say. He was by that time very blind and it would be impossible for him to read it. So he suggested first that I should read it for him. A little later he wrote to me 'I have been looking at your speech and the roll of a Latin sentence is coming back to me. I might learn it by heart.' I shall never forget the magnificent dignity of his walk up the floor of the Sheldonian to his seat. When it came to the speech he delivered it just as if he were Cicero making it up as he went along, and there was never the faintest need for a prompt. When we met in the evening at the Balliol Gaudy he said to me, 'I hear I used some words that were different from what you printed and Pember said that mine were better', and then went off into one of his glorious chuckles.

Today Grey has his own memorial at Oxford, the Edward Grey Institute, which was founded in his memory and is now the most important organisation for scientific field ornithology in Western Europe.

One of Grey's last public appearances was at his seventieth birthday lunch, given for him by his friend Sir James Barrie, the creator of Peter Pan. On 20 May 1932 Arthur Murray, Grey's former Parliamentary Private Secretary, received a letter from Colonel House expressing his sorrow that he could not attend the lunch:

> I wish I might have been present for there is no man in the world for whom I have a higher regard or admiration. He is 'the salt of the earth and the fullness thereof' and if men like him were guiding the destinies of the great nations today, a different story might be told. Every day I wish there were men like Grey in public life. He is one of the few I have ever met that I trusted from start to finish. Please give him my love and tell him I think of him constantly.

House, being President Wilson's closest friend and adviser, played a vital role in Anglo-American cooperation during the war. Bearing in mind the closeness of the relationship between the two men and the high esteem in which House held Grey, how fortunate it was for Britain that Grey was running the Foreign Office in those difficult early years of blockade.

Grey was a born Victorian who openly admitted he had some difficulties in coping with the adjustments imposed by a more modern world. In the 1930 edition of *Fly Fishing*, Grey looked back on the days he and Dorothy composed *The Cottage Book* and considered the changes that had taken place in the Itchen valley. Perhaps it was for the best that The Cottage burnt down in his later life. He wasn't happy with the new ribbon development in the village or the telephone lines in his precious water meadows and, after all, he was well practised at living with his memories:

> The Cottage that I put up on the Itchen in the 1890s was intended only as a fishing cottage; a place in which to get food, sleep, and shelter when I was not fishing. It became a sanctuary. The peace and beauty of the spot made it a sacred place. Great changes, however, had been taking place that were inseparable from a new epoch. For the first fifteen years there was little change and had been little change for many years before this time. I had seen the old mill at the village not far away replaced by a new building, and the dull, monotonous sound of a turbine had replaced the lively splashing of the waterwheel; but otherwise things remained as they were. The Cottage was invisible from any road; it was approached by an old lime avenue, long disused, and the track down this was not suited for any wheels but those of a farm cart. There was a little wayside station on a single railway line close by; but the quickest route from London was to go by a fast train to Winchester and thence drive a distance between four and five miles to the nearest point to the

cottage that was accessible by wheels. This was a drive of at least half an hour in a one-horse fly. Presently taxi-cabs took the place of the horse conveyance and reduced the time of the drive to a quarter of an hour. Was this an advantage? On balance it was not. For escape from London meant that hurry, noise and bustle had been left behind: I had entered unto leisure, where saving of time was no object, and often I would walk from Winchester to enjoy the country. There was a footpath way on each side of the river. By one of these one entered the cottage without, except for the momentary crossing of one road and of three secluded lanes, having had touch or sight of a road. There were thirty-three stiles on this path. There was much charm in this midnight walk. Traffic had ceased, cottage lights had been put out, the inmates were all at rest or asleep. Now and then one heard the passing song of a nightingale or a sedge warbler but in the main there was silence. It was pleasant after the hardness of the London streets and pavements to feel the soft dust about my feet. On a still summer night there were sweet and delicate scents in the air, breathed forth from leaves and herbs and grass, and from the earth itself. It was as if one's own very being was soothed and in some way refined by the stillness, the gentleness and the sweetness of it all.

Then came the age of motors and tarred roads. Few people, I imagine, seek the smell of tar for its own sake. To me there is nothing unclean or nauseous in it, but it is a coarse rough smell. The sweet and delicate scents of the night were obliterated by it, as if, over-powered and repelled, they had sunk back into the leaves and earth from which they had ventured into air. The strong smell of the tar seemed to disturb even the stillness of the night: the soft dust was no more, and the road was as hard as a paved street. Not all, but much of the charm of the night walk was gone. There were other changes too; small houses of the villa type were built along the road that was nearest to the cottage: doubtless there are more of them now, for the cottage was accidentally destroyed by fire in January 1923 and I have not seen the place for some years. The sense of change was in the air. It may be that change is for the good:

The old order changeth, yielding place to the new,
And God fulfils himself in many ways,
Lest one good custom should corrupt the world.

It is not for us, who cannot foresee the future, who perhaps cannot rightly understand the present, to chide or repine too much. Only it is impossible for us, who in our youth gave our affections to things that are passed or passing away, to transfer our affections to new things in which a new generation finds delight.

The beauty, however, of chalk-stream valleys still remains wonderful. The river still waters meadows that are unspoilt and unchanged, and its clear purity is guarded and protected.

Still glides the stream and shall for ever glide,
The form remains, the function never dies.

Although Grey possessed many laudable Edwardian values and a prose style that might now seem old-fashioned, in many ways he was a surprisingly modern and far-sighted politician. Over his long career he had fought for land reform, workers' rights, women's suffrage, Home Rule and reform of the House of Lords. He was also a pioneer conservationist who cared passionately for the preservation of the beauty of the countryside and in 1924 he was created Vice-President of the National Trust. His last speech in the Lords was on 14 February 1933. It took the form of a visionary plea for controlling the oil spillage from ships. Not only was he concerned about the effects on seabirds – no doubt in the forefront of his mind were the auk populations around his native Farne Islands – but also the general devastation caused by oil pollution on the local seashore.

My Lords: I do not wish for a moment to minimise the terrible effect of oil pollution on bird life which has been so forcibly put before your lordships. But there is one other aspect of the matter I would like to bring forward. One of the most famous tributes in our literature to our sea is that it performs its work of preventing the pollution of our shores.

He went on to quote one of his favourite Romantic poets, Keats:

> The moving waters at their priest-like task
> Of pure ablution round the earth's human shores.

Grey died on 7 September 1933, the day on which the reviews of Lloyd George's *War Memoirs* appeared in the newspapers. At least he was spared the pain of reading them. Grey had been suffering from stomach and kidney problems for some time. Thankfully he was not long confined to his bed. He presided over the 'duck dinner' and walked the lanes of Northumberland to his dying day. His ashes were placed beside Dorothy in a young plantation behind his duck ponds at Fallodon. The funeral service was held at Embleton Church and his friend Mr Dawson gave the address:

> He meant far more to us than we can ever say, and to try to put into words what he was to us here is as impossible a task as it would be to a man to define the ties that bind him to his own stretch of countryside, its woodlands, its burns and its hills. This was his home. Here he was amongst his own people. We felt we understood him and he understood us. As one of our fishermen said to me lately, as together we discussed the bulletin on the gate, 'He belongs to us here.' For us who knew him and lived beside him and encountered him on our daily walks, he had the unmistakable qualities of greatness that a man, when he sees them, immediately recognises and reveres.

As Grey was descended from one of the oldest landed families in England it was no small irony that by taking his country into war and supporting the radical policies of his Cabinet colleague David Lloyd George, he was more responsible than most for breaking the aristocracy's centuries-old hold on the governance of Britain. Grey played a central role in terminating the golden era of Edwardian England. He was a much more effective and successful Foreign Secretary than Lloyd George and history have given him credit for. He held the Seals of Office for a longer consecutive period than Palmerston, Granville or Castlereagh. During the decade before the outbreak of war he prepared his country for what many saw as the inevitable conflict and, although exhausted and half blind, he was the only European statesman who fought hard for peace during the July crisis. As a character, Grey was the antithesis of so many modern politicians, being an unambitious, reluctant states-man who possessed old-fashioned values such as honour, duty and loyalty. Happily for Grey, and unlike many of his more aspiring colleagues, he possessed a hinterland – a pastoral one – and as a result he has left behind as a lasting legacy two of the finest books ever written on the British countryside.

Because of the trust he engendered, coupled with his endear-ing personality, Grey always seemed to have public opinion on his side as well as invariably enjoying strong cross-party support in the Commons. The socialists and radicals on his own benches couldn't help admiring him as captured by his obituarist in *The Times*:

> The simplicity and straightforwardness of character, the unques-tionable absence of self-seeking in any form, the admirable combi-nation in him of good family, the sportsman, the naturalist, the lover of literature, the patriot, the loyal colleague and hard worker conquered the respect and almost the affection of even those who were most opposed to the policy for which he stood.

Tributes poured in from across the world, no more so than from France, where the press devoted leading articles to his memory: 'He was a statesman who never changed and, once having given his word, displayed the utmost consistency in keeping it.'

Immediately after his death J. H. Whitley, an ex-Speaker of the House of Commons, gave a broadcast tribute to Grey, speaking of him in Chaucerian terms:

In our boyhood we learned the tales of chivalry: the story of the very perfect English knight, without fear and without reproach, of Bayard and of Galahad. Never is it given to us in our time to find a man who is the complete embodiment of our youthful heroes. Yet who comes nearer to it than Sir Edward Grey?

His memorial service was held at Westminster Abbey and was well attended by the great and the good. But perhaps it was his first biographer and fellow Northumbrian, George Trevelyan, who best captured what Grey meant to the nation:

It was not amiss to say, as many did say upon his death, that 'a great Englishman' was gone. For many troubled years and at one terrible crisis, he had represented England at her best – her reasonableness, her justice, her desire for peace and friendship between all, and with that her determination not to be frightened into a submission or dazed into a tardiness that would allow one power to enslave the world.

Acknowledgements

I would like to thank my wife Lucinda for introducing me to Sir Edward Grey by way of a copy of *The Capital of Happiness* some twenty-five years ago.

I would also like to thank Mr and Mrs Peter Bridgeman of Fallodon Hall for their kindness and hospitality over a number of years while working on my Grey books, and Mrs Pat Brockway, a Grey devotee, for the loving attention she continues to lavish on the Cottage site at Itchen Abbas. In addition I would like to thank the Graves family, particularly Sir Edward's great-nephew, the late Christopher Graves, for offering me their encouragement in my endeavours.

Two people in particular deserve my deepest gratitude. Jeremy Norman, one of my oldest and closest friends from my Cambridge days, dreamt up the title *Edwardian Requiem*. David Lawman, who served alongside my father in the Guards Armoured Division in Normandy in 1944, supplied me with invaluable creative and editorial advice over most of the project.

Other good friends who have provided continual and much-valued encouragement and assistance over the four years it took to write the book are Tom Sackville, Humphrey Wakefield, Andrew Duncan, Clare Shenkman, Sarah Fraser, Ian Beith and Brian Fitzpatrick.

Two friends on the Isle of Wight warrant a special mention: Martin Sanders, an IT genius and long-suffering Southampton supporter, showed enormous patience and tact in keeping my computer functioning, and Chris Longley, a railway historian, furnished me with a wealth of fascinating information on the North Eastern Railway, of which Sir Edward was Chairman and a long-serving director.

EUROPE IN 1914

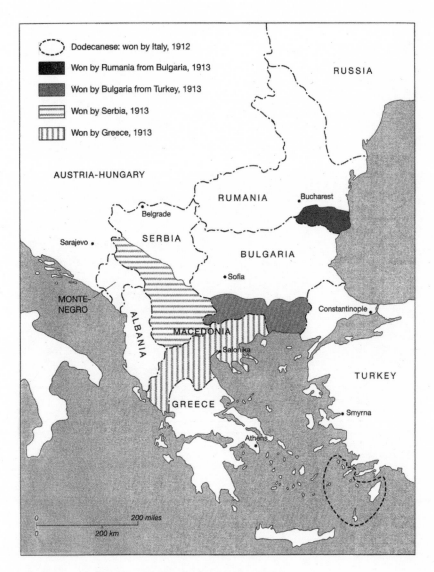

Dodecanese: won by Italy, 1912

Won by Rumania from Bulgaria, 1913

Won by Bulgaria from Turkey, 1913

Won by Serbia, 1913

Won by Greece, 1913

RUSSIA

AUSTRIA-HUNGARY

RUMANIA

Bucharest

Belgrade

Sarajevo

SERBIA

BULGARIA

MONTE-
NEGRO

Sofia

ALBANIA

Constantinople

MACEDONIA

Salonika

TURKEY

GREECE

Smyrna

Athens

0   200 miles

0   200 km

THE BALKANS AND THE EFFECTS OF THE BALKAN WARS

Select Bibliography

Asquith, H. H., *The Genesis of War* (London: Cassell & Co., 1923)

Asquith, H. H., *Letters to Venetia Stanley* (Oxford: Oxford University Press, 1985)

Asquith, Margot, *An Autobiography* (London: Methuen, 1985)

Blow, Simon, *Broken Blood* (London: Faber, 1987)

Bonham Carter, Violet, *Lantern Slides* (London: Phoenix Giant, 1997)

Bonham Carter, Violet, *Winston Churchill: As I Knew Him* (London: Weidenfeld & Nicolson, 1995)

Buxton, Earl, *A Liberal Life* (Hassocks: Newtimber, 1999)

Cecil, Algernon, *British Foreign Secretaries 1807–1916* (London: G. Bell & Sons, 1927)

Chance, Cecilia, *The Widdrington Women* (Andover: Phillimore & Co Ltd, 2010)

Charmley, John, *Splendid Isolation* (London: Hodder & Stoughton, 1999)

Churchill, Randolph, *Young Statesman* (London: Minerva, 1991)

Churchill, Winston, *The World Crisis, 1911–1014* (London: Thornton Butterworth, 1923)

Clay, Catherine, *King, Kaiser, Tsar* (London: John Murray, 2006)

Creighton, Louise, *Dorothy Grey* (London: Spottiswoode & Co., 1907)

Dangerfield, G., *The Strange Death of Liberal England* (London: Constable & Co., 1936)

Egremont, Max, *Siegfried Sassoon: A Biography* (London: Picador, 2005)

Ferguson, Niall, *Empire* (London: Penguin, 2004)

Ferguson, Niall, *The Pity of War* (London: Allen Lane, 1998)

Fromkin, David, *Europe's Last Summer* (London: Vintage, 2004)

Grey, Edward, *The Charm of Birds* (London: Weidenfeld & Nicolson, 2001)

Grey, Edward, *The Cottage Book* (London: Weidenfeld & Nicolson, 2001)

Grey, Edward, *The Fallodon Papers* (London: Constable & Co., 1928)

Grey, Edward, *Fly Fishing* (London: Deutsch, 1984)

Grey, Edward, *A Rural Land* (1892)

Grey, Edward, *Speeches on Foreign Affairs 1904–1914* (London: Allen & Unwin, 1931)

Grey, Edward, *Twenty-Five Years* (London: Hodder & Stoughton, 1925)

Grey, Pamela, *Shepherd's Crowns* (Blackwell, 1923)

Grigg, John, *Lloyd George: From Peace to War, 1912–1916* (London: Methuen, 1985)

Haldane, Richard Burdon, *An Autobiography* (London: Hodder & Stoughton, 1929)

Haldane, Richard Burdon, *Before the War* (Cassell, 1920)

Hardinge of Penshurst, Lord, *Old Diplomacy* (London: John Murray, 1947)

Hattersley, Roy, *The Edwardian* (London: Little, Brown, 2004)

Hinsley, F. H., *British Foreign Policy under Sir Edward Grey* (Cambridge: Cambridge University Press, 1977)

Hobhouse, Charles, *Inside Asquith's Cabinet* (London: J. Murray, 1977)

House, Edward Mandell, *The Intimate Papers of Colonel House* (Boston; New York: Houghton Mifflin Co., 1926)

Hudson, W. H., *Hampshire Days* (Oxford: Oxford University Press, 1980)

Hurd, Douglas, *Choose Your Weapons* (London: Weidenfeld & Nicolson, 2010)

Jenkins, Roy, *Asquith* (London: Collins, 1964)

Jenkins, Roy, *Churchill* (London: Macmillan, 2001)

Jenkins, Roy, *A Gallery of 20th Century Portraits* (Newton Abbot: David & Charles, 1988)

Joll, James, *The Origins of the First World War* (London: Longman, 1992)

Keegan, John, *The First World War* (London: Hutchinson, 1998)

Lambert, Angela, *Unquiet Souls* (London: Macmillan, 1985)

Lichnowsky, Prince, *Heading for the Abyss* (London: Constable & Co., 1928)

Lloyd George, David, *War Memoirs* (Little, Brown & Co.: Boston, 1937)

Lowndes, Mrs Belloc, *A Passing World* (London: Macmillan & Co., 1948)

McKinstry, Leo, *Rosebery* (London: John Murray, 2005)

Magnus, Philip, *King Edward VII* (Harmondsworth: Penguin, 1967)

Massie, Robert, *Dreadnought* (London: Cape, 1992)

Matthew, H. C. G., *The Liberal Imperialists* (London: Oxford University Press, 1973)

Maurois, André, *King Edward and his Times* (London: Cassell & Co., 1949)

Monger, George, *The End of Isolation* (London: Thomas Nelson & Sons, 1963)

Montgelas, Count Max, *British Foreign Policy under Sir Edward Grey* (New York: A. A. Knopf, 1928)

Morgan, Ted, *Churchill, 1874–1915* (London: Cape, 1983)

Murray, A. C., *Master and Brother: Murrays of Elibank* (London: John Murray, 1945)

Murray, Gilbert, *The Foreign Policy of Edward Grey* (Oxford: Clarendon Press, 1915)

Nicolson, Harold, *Diaries and Letters, 1930–1939* (London: Collins, 1971)

Nicolson, Harold, *Lord Carnock* (London: Constable, 1950)

Politicus, *Grey of Fallodon* (London: Methuen, 1935)

Robbins, Keith, *Lord Grey of Fallodon* (London: Cassell, 1971)

Rose, Kenneth, *King George V* (London: Macmillan, 1984)

Shannon, Richard, *The Crisis of Imperialism, 1865–1915* (St Albans: Paladin, 1976)

Sheffield, Gary, *Forgotten Victory* (London: Review, 2002)

Spender, J. A., *Life, Journalism and Politics* (London: Cassell & Co., 1927)

Spender, J. A., *The Life of Sir Henry Campbell-Bannerman* (London: Hodder & Stoughton, 1923)

Steinberg, Jonathan, *Tirpitz and the Birth of the German Battle Fleet* (Aldershot: Gregg Revivals, c1992)

Steiner, Zara, *The Foreign Office and Foreign Policy 1898–1914* (Cambridge: University Press, 1969)

Stevenson, David, *The History of the First World War* (London: Penguin, 2005)

Stone, Norman, *A Short History of World War One* (London: Allen Lane, 2007)

Strachan, Hew, *The First World War* (Oxford: Oxford University Press, 2001)

Tennant, Emma, *Strangers* (Leicester: Charnwood, 1999)

Tomlinson, William Weaver, *The North Eastern Railway* (Newton Abbot: David & Charles, 1987)

Trevelyan, George, *Grey of Fallodon* (London: Longmans, Green & Co, 1937)

Tuchman, Barbara, *The Guns of August* (London: Robinson, 2000)

Tuchman, Barbara, *The Proud Tower* (London: Macmillan, 1980)

Williams, Joyce, *Colonel House and Sir Edward Grey: A Study in Anglo-American Diplomacy* (Lanham: University Press of America, c1984)

Wilson, Trevor, *The Downfall of the Liberal Party* (London: Collins, 1968)

Index

POLITICOS.co.uk
THE ONLINE POLITICAL BOOKSTORE

WE'RE BACK

BREAKDOWNS OF THE
BEST POLITICAL
LITERATURE ON
THE HORIZON

BE REWARDED FOR YOUR LOYALTY
WITH OUR POINTS SCHEME

AN ONLINE COMMUNITY OF
POLITICAL BOOK LOVERS

THE POLITICOS.CO.UK
TEAM ON HAND TO
OFFER YOU GUIDANCE
AND BESPOKE
BOOK SUGGESTIONS

TAILORED BESTSELLERS
LISTS FROM RECESS
READING TO POLITICAL
RESEARCH MATERIALS

WEEKLY POLITICAL
BOOK PODCASTS

SPECIALIST, CONSTANTLY UPDATED,
POLITICAL CONTENT

Politicos.co.uk is owned and managed by Biteback Publishing. @Politicos_co_uk